# Haggai, Zechariah, Malachi

## John L Mackay

**Christian Focus Publications**

© 1994John L Mackay
ISBN 1-85792-067-8

Published by
Christian Focus Publications Ltd
Geanies House, Fearn, Ross-shire,
IV20 1TW, Scotland, Great Britain.

Printed and bound in Great Britain by
The Guernsey Press Co. Ltd, Guernsey, Channel Islands

Cover design by Donna Macleod

Scripture quotations are from the New International Version, published by
Hodder and Stoughton.

# CONTENTS

THE SECOND BURDEN:
ON THAT DAY (Zech. 12:1–14:21)

# MALACHI

*Study Questions*
These study questions are designed to assist individual reflection on the significance of each section for today. They may also provide useful starting points for those leading discussion groups. The Biblical references indicate passages of relevance to each topic, but we may not always have a complete or final answer to what is asked.

## Significant Dates

| | |
|---:|---|
| July 586 B.C | Jerusalem falls to the Babylonians |
| October 539 B.C. | Babylon captured by the Persians |
| 538 B.C. | Cyrus' decree permitting the Jews to return |
| April 536 B.C. | First attempt to rebuild the Temple |
| December 520 B.C. | Foundation laid in the Temple |
| March 515 B.C. | Temple completed |
| 458 B.C. | Ezra returns to Jerusalem |
| 445 B.C. | Nehemiah returns to Jerusalem |
| 332 B.C. | Alexander invades Palestine |

# INTRODUCTION

On October 29th, 539 B.C., there was a great victory parade in Babylon. Seventeen days before, forces loyal to Cyrus, king of the Medes and Persians, had entered the city unopposed and had captured it. Now Cyrus had arrived to celebrate his latest acquisition in a series of conquests. Over the previous fifteen years he had extended his empire from his original kingdom of Anshan, north of the Persian Gulf, both eastwards to India and westwards through Asia Minor to the Mediterranean Sea. Babylon was the latest and grandest prize to fall into his hands.

But it was not just the occupying army that was rejoicing in Babylon that day. The Babylonians were too. They had become very dissatisfied with their previous rulers, Nabonidus and his son Belshazzar, whom Nabonidus had left in control in Babylon. The Persians in fact offered a welcome change from their own rulers. Under Cyrus they had adopted tolerant policies. The powers that had previously been dominant in the Middle East, the Assyrians and after them the Babylonians themselves, had ruled their empires with a ruthless cruelty. But the Persians tried to win the loyalty of their subject peoples by taking local opinions and customs into consideration. They had captured Babylon with very little bloodshed, and there was no disruption of ordinary life. The Persians respected the gods of the local people and reinstated their worship — something which had been allowed to lapse in Babylon while Nabonidus ruled. So the people of Babylon and the surrounding towns were happy to welcome Cyrus as their liberator.

Such anticipation of better things to come extended to others in Babylon as well. As part of their repressive policies, the Assyrians and Babylonians had been responsible for transporting many peoples from their homelands to Mesopotamia. Uprooted and dispossessed peoples were less likely to mount successful rebellions, and they also provided a ready supply of labour for state building projects. Among those to be found in and around Babylon were the Jews. Their exile from their native land had been divine punishment for their idolatry and refusal to obey the LORD. Their intransigence, even when repeatedly warned, had led to their land being devastated by the Babylonians. But their prophets had long foretold of one called Cyrus whom the LORD would raise up and who would rebuild

4

Jerusalem and set the exiles free (Isa. 45:13). Now they too were looking for an end to their seventy years of exile, and the opportunity to return home.

In line with his enlightened policy of returning deported peoples to their homelands, Cyrus issued a decree in 538 B.C. authorising the Jews to return to Jerusalem. In Ezra 1:1-4 we have a Hebrew copy of this proclamation, and later on in Ezra 6:3-5 there is a memorandum regarding the same event in Aramaic, the language of government and international diplomacy. The people were permitted to return, authorised to rebuild the Temple and given state support for the project.

Thus through the providential control of God, the Jews were restored to their land. But that in itself did not mean an end to their problems. God had again shown them mercy, but God's restored people had now to learn how to live out a proper response to that mercy. The record of their struggles with this task is found in five books of Scripture, the three prophetic books that we are going to study here—Haggai, Zechariah and Malachi—and also in the two historical books of Ezra and Nehemiah.

What is recorded there makes it clear that the trauma of the Exile had purged the community of the tendency to relapse into gross idolatry. Worshipping other gods and engaging in the practices of heathen religion had been a recurrent national problem in earlier centuries, and had culminated in judgment, in the Exile. The restored people, however, shunned such acts of disloyalty to the LORD. There is no doubt about where their basic loyalty lay. This can be seen in the way they rejected offers of help from the mixed community of peoples who had been settled in the former northern kingdom by the Assyrians. They professed to worship the LORD, but their religion was in fact a corrupt amalgam (2 Kgs. 17:24-41). Quite apart from the terms of Cyrus' edict, which they used as a polite excuse, they did not want any collaboration with paganism, such as had destroyed their forefathers.

But faith must be obedient faith, and the restored community had to grapple with more insidious pressures to compromise their single-hearted commitment to God. No doubt those that returned—many did not—were fired with enthusiasm that all the LORD'S promises of a glorious future for his people would now be fulfilled. They had to learn that their timetable and God's did not coincide. The record of the next hundred years is of a struggle to live true to God despite recurrent dejection.

Their problems began almost immediately. Writing a century later, Ezra tells us that on the first day of the seventh month of their first year back, the exiles built an altar on the ruins of the old one and celebrated the first Feast of Tabernacles since the Exile (Ezr. 3:1-6). In the second month of the following year, 536 B.C., they laid the foundations of the temple (Ezr. 3:8-11). However, when the book of Haggai begins in 520 B.C., we find that the Temple is still a ruin. The people had lost heart, but through the ministry of Haggai, the LORD stirred them from their inertia. Haggai was soon joined by Zechariah, and together these prophets were used to stimulate the people to new endeavour. It was a time of revival— and the Temple was completed five years later in March 515 B.C.

But restoring the Temple was never an end in itself. The Temple symbolised God's presence with his people, and for all the blessings associated with that to be realised, the people had to obey and please God. They had to learn to be patient and trust God. Many of them had been expecting a period of great prosperity and success once the Temple was completed. When it did not come, they again became disillusioned and spiritually careless. Zechariah's later ministry was directed at giving them a vision of the future purposes of God to sustain them when their spirits were at a low ebb.

We are given further insight into their situation in the record of the prophet Malachi, who ministered about ninety years after the return from the Exile. He had to deal with people who had become cynical, and so used to the second-best in their devotion to the LORD that they could see nothing wrong with it. They were prepared to defend themselves against criticism of their ways. Malachi's ministry challenged the formality of their worship and urged them in view of the impending judgment of God to repent and amend their ways.

The record of the ministry of these three prophets, Haggai, Zechariah and Malachi, is a record of how God deals with the people he has restored as they try to translate their basic loyalty to him into practical action. Whatever mistakes they made in their understanding of how God wanted them to live, and however forgetful they became of the need to give his requirements priority in their living, their problem was different from that of their ancestors before the Exile. They did not stray into idolatry. But they had to learn how to live out consistently their covenant profession as the people of the LORD. It is the same challenge that faces us today.

# HAGGAI

## OVERVIEW

Haggai is a very brief book of two chapters and thirty eight verses, and the events that are narrated cover a period of only four months at the end of the year 520 B.C. It was not a remarkable year in terms of the secular history of the time, but it was a spiritual watershed in the history of God's people and the unfolding of the divine plan of redemption. God sent the prophet to stir up the community in Jerusalem to new obedience, and his ministry was blessed with revival. The record of those months is a memorial to God's grace and a challenge to the obedience of subsequent generations.

Haggai's first message (1:1-11) exposed the double standards that prevailed in the community. The people were prepared to exert themselves for their own comfort, but were quite happy to delay work on the Temple—and then they wondered why God was not blessing them in the way they expected! Haggai called on them to give careful thought to their ways (1:5, 7).

The second message of the book (1:12-15) tells how the people responded to this call for repentance. There was a united recognition that the delay had been wrong, and they resolved to resume the long postponed work.

But this did not mean that all problems immediately vanished. The people had to contend with their own memories of how splendid the first Temple had been, and how lacking in splendour a replacement would be. In 2:1-9 Haggai challenged them to be strong in what they were doing. The LORD promised that he was with them, and that he would bless their endeavours.

The prophecy concludes with two messages delivered on the day the foundation of the Temple was laid. The first message (2:10-19) encouraged the people with the prospect of divine blessing on obedience, and the second (2:20-23), addressed to their governor, Zerubbabel, showed that the LORD's intention to raise up the Messiah from the house of David was still operative. The blessing to be anticipated extended beyond better harvests to the inauguration of his kingdom.

**Haggai 1:1-11: The Half-Committed Community**

Things had not been going well for the restored community in Jerusalem. They had returned from the Exile in Babylon full of great hopes. But now they were unhappy. There had been a series of poor harvests. They were frustrated by the opposition they had encountered, and the Temple was still a ruin. Sixteen years before its foundations had been relaid (Ezr. 3:8-11), but since then nothing had happened. The great vision and grand resolutions had faded. The people were discouraged and apathetic.

But the LORD was not prepared to leave his restored people in that state. He sent his prophet Haggai to stir up their leaders, and through them, the people, so that they all applied themselves once more to the tasks before them. Haggai had the blessing of seeing his prophetic ministry of remonstrance being effective in recalling the people to obedience. The response of the people who heard him presents a challenge to succeeding generations to renewed endeavour in the LORD's cause. When what we have to do seems to be beyond our resources, and when the difficulties facing us seem to increase all the time, we are not to flag but rather to follow Haggai's injunction and rethink our attitudes.

*The Dispirited Community (1:1-2).* **In the second year of King Darius (1:1)** is in itself a sad indication of the changed circumstances of the LORD's people. They were back in the land of promise, but were still far from regaining their independence. Formerly the books of their prophets had been dated by the reigns of their own kings (see, for example, Isa. 1:1, or Amos 1:1). But now they are part of the Persian Empire, and it is a foreigner, Darius II (522-486 B.C.), who rules over them. He is not lauded with the profusion of extravagant titles commonly accorded to rulers by heathen writers, but the stark mention of 'the king' shows there was no escaping the political realities of the day.

Darius' reign had begun with a period of considerable internal confusion in the Persian Empire, but after two years he had established a fair measure of security throughout the Empire. Of the domains that Cambyses (530-522 B.C.), the previous Emperor, had ruled, only Egypt remained unsubmissive–and Darius would deal with it in the following year (519 B.C.). It was a time when it could be said the whole world was at rest and in peace (Zech. 1:11).

**On the first day of the sixth month** is the first of five dates given in this short prophecy (the others are at 1:15; 2:1, 10, 20). The period covered is just under four months. We are also able with a fair degree of certainty to correlate this date with modern chronology as 29th August 520 B.C. During the Exile the Jews adopted a spring start to the year, which was the Babylonian custom, in place of the autumn start that had previously been more common.

It was the first of the month, the feast of the New Moon (Num. 10:10; 28:11; 1 Sam. 20:5; Ps. 81:3). We know that before the Exile, meetings were held at the sanctuary at that time (Isa. 1:13; 2 Kgs. 4:23; Hos. 2:11), and there would certainly have been additional services at the restored altar in the Temple ruins. It might well have been a public holiday. The larger than normal attendance at the Temple site would have made it a suitable time to bring up the matters the prophet had to speak about.

**The word of the LORD came.** We have no record of any prophetic voice in the promised land since the time of Jeremiah. Daniel and Ezekiel had been prophets in Babylon, but now the long silence is broken and the restored community hears the LORD's voice again. It is the traditional formula for the reception of the prophetic message that is used. We do not know by what inner processes a prophet received his message, but this phrase certainly tells us that it was not just something that he thought up for himself. It was not some superior insight into the conditions of the day that the prophet had. Rather the LORD conveyed his message to the prophet's consciousness in a way of which few details are given. It was communicated perfectly, in that the LORD condescended to express his word precisely in a way that matched the vocabulary and mode of expression natural to the prophet who received it. The prophet had then in turn to pass the message on to the covenant people. Those who had come back to Jerusalem were privileged to be addressed by the LORD in this way. He was not silent about their situation.

**Through the prophet Haggai.** The name Haggai means 'festal', or 'my feast', and may have been given to him because he was born on a feast day. Although he is mentioned in Ezra (5:1; 6:14) in company with Zechariah, we know remarkably little about him. It is often supposed that he was one of those who had returned from the Exile, and that, already an old man, he died soon after the completion of the Temple. His silence over the previous years may be accounted for by assuming that his call to the prophetic ministry was of relatively recent date. But these are just suppositions. It is the message, not the messenger, we are to focus on.

It is surprising that here at the start of his prophecy we are given no genealogical details about him. What mattered was that he was 'the prophet'. Unlike others (Zerubbabel and Joshua) he did not gain his standing by his descent, but by the LORD's direct appointment. 'Through' (literally it is 'by the hand of') rather than 'to' is unusual in the introduction to a prophecy (elsewhere only at Mal. 1:1), though it is used frequently of Moses, and also in 1 Kings 14:18 and 2 Kings 14:25 of other prophets. The phrase emphasises that the prophet is the channel through which the message from the LORD is transmitted. He is an intermediary in the process of communication.

**To Zerubbabel son of Shealtiel.** The exact identity of Zerubbabel has been a cause of much perplexity (see on 2:21), but it was because he was a prince of the house of David that the Persians had selected him to lead the restored community. As civil ruler, he is mentioned first, and his status must have been equal to that of the high priest, if indeed it was not greater. He is said to be **governor of Judah**. We are not certain of the precise status that Judah held in the Persian Empire at this time. It may have been a sub-province under the general jurisdiction of the governor of Trans-Euphrates (Ezr. 5:3). So Zerubbabel held a position of real authority granted by the Persian authorities, but the area under his control was limited.

**Joshua son of Jehozadak, the high priest** was the religious leader of the community. His grandfather Seraiah had been high priest when Jerusalem fell to the Babylonians in 586 B.C., and he had been executed at Riblah along with other notable citizens (2 Kgs. 25:18-21; Jer. 52:24-27). However, his son, Jehozadak, had been spared and taken to Babylon (1 Chr. 6:15). Now his son, Joshua, is high priest in the restored community. He is called Jeshua in Ezra 2:2, where he is listed among those returning from Babylon, and also in Ezra 3:2, 8, 9. Like Zerubbabel he had gained his position in the community through his links with the past.

In this verse we have the three offices of the theocracy—prophet, priest and king—brought together again. What is more, the roles they play also resemble those of the past. The prophetic word does not come first of all to the people. That had become common in the later pre-exilic prophets because the rulers had rejected the LORD's message to them, and the prophets were sent directly to the people. In addressing the civil and religious rulers of the people, Haggai is not only acknowledging their role, he is also conceding that they were genuine in their allegiance to the LORD though falling short in their conduct. It is a reversion to the situation that prevailed in the earlier monarchy, when the prophets had directly addressed the king and so sought to shape the destiny of the covenant people (see, for example, 2 Sam. 24:11; 2 Chr. 16:7). It was a time of restoration of the old order which had been found in spiritually healthier days.

The formula **This is what the LORD Almighty says (1:2)** marks out Haggai's claim to be faithfully relaying the message already committed to him as the LORD's prophet. 'The LORD Almighty', the LORD of hosts, presents the LORD as the one who has control over all powers that exist. It is a title Haggai uses 14 times, perhaps to emphasise the power and resources of God to people who were very conscious of their own weakness. (For further discussion of the name, see on Zech. 1:3.)

The message Haggai has for the two leaders of the community consists of a summary of the prevailing opinion of the day. This is not what Haggai thought it was, but what the LORD himself summed it up as being. **These people say** is significant for the degree of alienation indicated by the phrase 'these people' rather than 'my people' or 'the Lord's people'. Their attitude had created a barrier between them and the LORD (Isa. 6:9, 10; Hos. 1:9). The message as a whole accuses the people of neglect.

**The time has not yet come for the LORD's house to be built.** There are a number of translation difficulties in these words, perhaps because they reflect colloquial speech. The Hebrew text is probably to be understood as saying, 'Not yet time for coming, time of the house of the LORD to be built.' The NIV smoothes them out by adopting the understanding of the early Greek translation of the Old Testament, the Septuagint.

Obviously the reference is to the rebuilding of the Temple, which the Babylonians had set on fire a month after they captured the city (Jer. 52:13). 'House' is the ordinary word for a building occupied by a family (Deut. 19:1), but it was also commonly applied throughout the east to shrines and temples of deities, who were considered to dwell there ('Dagon's temple', literally 'house of Dagon', 1 Sam. 5:2; similarly, 'the temple of the Ashtoreths', 1 Sam. 31:10). From earliest times, long before there was a temple in Jerusalem, Israel used this idiom to refer to the sanctuary of the LORD (Ex. 23:19; 34:26; Deut. 23:18). It expresses the truth that the sanctuary was God's dwelling-place among his people (Ex. 25:8). This stimulated the desire on their part to dwell with the LORD (Ps. 23:6; 27:4).

The respect accorded the physical structure was an index of the spiritual vitality of the people. That they had abandoned their earlier attempts to restore it showed a faltering faith.

What had gone wrong? Mention might be made of many factors.

*(1)* Hostility of neighbouring peoples: though Cyrus had ordered the work to be carried out (Ezr. 1:2-4), from the very start neighbouring peoples were hostile (Ezr. 3:3). When the offers of help from the Samaritans and other groups were refused, they successfully obstructed the work (Ezr. 4:4-5). The reaction that did occur when rebuilding eventually resumed shows that this hostility had not decreased with the passage of time (Ezr. 5:3).

*(2)* The unsettled international situation: Cyrus' son, Cambyses, added Egypt to the Persian empire. This meant that foreign troops were passing through Palestine in the intervening years, with all the disruption consequent upon that. Indeed, it was while returning from Egypt that Cambyses committed suicide near Mount Carmel, an event that led to an unsettled period throughout the empire before Darius consolidated his position. Zechariah 8:10 describes some of the tensions and difficulties of the period.

*(3)* The poor economic conditions: the land to which they returned was still suffering from the devastation of war, and required considerable effort for reconstruction. This was compounded by poor harvests and inflation (1:6)—though the people did not recognise the true reason for their occurrence. They probably argued that though the Temple ought to be completed, the economy ought to be put on a sounder footing before engaging in such a major project.

*(4)* The gap between their expectations and reality: although some of those who returned might have had a less than total commitment to the project from the start, many were fired by the promises that had been given by the prophets (Isa. 60-66; Ezk. 40-48). When these did not immediately come true, their faith faltered. Other priorities began to rule in their lives.

To excuse their disinclination to exert themselves, they were not saying, 'No', but 'Not yet.' But there is never a right time for engaging in the LORD's work, if we are waiting for a time without problems. It is always possible to point to those who will hinder and oppose, and to the difficulties that will arise from lack of resources.

*Challenged Priorities (1:3-4).* By repeating the formula already used, **Then the word of the LORD came through the prophet Haggai** *(1:3)*, the prophet emphasises the contrast between the attitude and saying of the people and the question of the LORD. Haggai speaks through the two leaders to the community gathered round them. It is a rhetorical question that is being asked, not to gain information, but to stir up the people to consider their situation. **Is it a time for you yourselves to be living in your panelled houses, while this house remains a ruin?** *(1:4)*. 'You, yourselves' emphasises the contrast that existed between the state of the Temple, the house of the LORD, and their own houses. The word 'panelled' comes from a root that indicates a covering. It may be of a roof over a house (1 Kgs. 6:15), or of wooden panels on the walls (1 Kgs. 7:7). While there could be a contrast between their own houses that had been roofed over and the Temple ruins without a roof, it is more probable that the contrast is even more extreme—between the finely decorated houses they were living in, and the desolation they were prepared to worship in.

The only problem with this interpretation is whether the later descriptions of the economic situation of the land make it probable that the people had in fact been able to afford such housing. Panelling was a sign of luxury and comfort (Jer. 22:14; 1 Kgs. 7:7), and it has been suggested that perhaps only the dwellings of the governor and high priest had been so decorated. But the people had not been slow as regards their own housing (1:9). Also the community that had returned had initially been quite wealthy. They had a high proportion of slaves (one to every six freemen: Ezr. 2:65), perhaps a sign of the guilty consciences of the Jews who stayed behind. Notice also the size of the gifts they were able to afford (Ezr. 2:68-69; see also Neh. 7:66-72). Their homes may well have been fitted out to the highest contemporary standards.

But whatever the extent of the work, the fact that it had been done cut off the excuses they might have brought forward, such as the harshness of their economic circumstances and the opposition they had encountered. Unlike David, they did not have the building of the LORD's house on their hearts (2 Sam. 7:2; Ps. 132:2-5). They had allowed the opposition and hostility to change the priorities of their living. When they had decided to come back from Babylon, they had originally shown quite different priorities from the majority of the Jews who remained there in comfort. Now they were putting their own material well-being first (Mt. 6:33; Mt.

13:22; Luke 8:14). Though secondary matters are quite proper in their own place, they should not have allowed them to control their living. They had forgotten to assign paramount importance to what God required of them, because he was no longer central to their thinking.

'Ruin' is associated with words that had been used to refer to the downfall of Jerusalem ('desolate waste' in Jer. 33:10; 'desolate' in Jer. 33:12; ruins in Ezk. 36:35 and Neh. 2:3). Ezra 3:6-13 implies that some work had been done at the Temple site 16 years before. Money had been gathered for expenses, and they had sent to Tyre and Sidon for cedar wood. But whatever work had been done did not amount to much, and they may have had to start all over again.

*Frustrated Endeavours (1:5-6).* **Now this is what the LORD Almighty says** *(1:5).* Arising out of the analysis of the situation that has been presented, Haggai challenges them with the LORD's message that their present economic situation has its roots in their attitude towards the Temple. **Give careful thought to your ways.** This is a favourite phrase of Haggai (occurring also in 1:7; 2:15, 18). Literally, it is 'set your heart on your ways'. (For 'ways', see on Mal. 2:8.) It required careful consideration in the first instance of what had already happened to them. Perhaps it is ironic in that the emphasis is on what they had not done. But the first steps to renewed obedience require a realistic assessment and appraisal of what has gone wrong. Self-analysis can be indulged in to the point where it is a substitute for action, but if it does not occur, our lives are likely to be misdirected. The covenant between the LORD and the people was always based on the history of what had happened to them, so that they could see their relationship with him in a right perspective (Deut. 1-3; Josh. 24:2-15). Haggai is in fact calling on the people to renew their covenant engagement with the LORD.

**You have planted much, but have harvested little** *(1:6).* They had not understood what had been happening to them. They had to interpret their situation in the light of Scripture. As far back as the days of Moses, it had been made clear that disobedience to what the LORD required in the covenant would bring upon his people the frustration of having their hopes and ambitions thwarted. 'You will sow much seed in the field but you will harvest little, because locusts will devour it. You will plant vineyards and cultivate them but you will not drink the wine or gather the grapes, because worms will eat them. You will have olive trees throughout your country but you will not use the oil, because the olives will drop off' (Deut. 28:38-40). Now the LORD uses these threats of the broken covenant to interpret for his people their own experience. The recent poor harvest would still be in their minds. Though they had put much effort into their farming, the yield had not matched their expectation. There was enough to survive, but only just.

**You eat, but never have enough.** A similar threat is found in Leviticus 26:26. Perhaps it relates to a time of scarcity as a result of the poor harvests, or it may reflect disease in the community which left them perpetually unsatisfied (Mic. 6:14). **You drink, but never have your fill.** This too arises out of a similar sort of situation, where their desires are continually frustrated (Ps. 107:33-34). **You put on clothes, but are not warm.** The expression used suggests that this is the experience of each individual. Was there insufficient material to replace old threadbare garments? Or is this a testimony to the insatiable desire for more that arises from a materialistic attitude to life? **You earn wages, only to put them in a purse with holes in it.** Although coins were becoming more widely used in the Persian empire, it is unlikely that they would be used to pay labourers in Palestine at this time. Wedges and discs of silver or brass were weighed on scales, and used as a means of exchange. They would often have rough edges which could wear holes in the pieces of cloth they were wrapped up in. But this refers to more than the misfortune of losing hard-earned money. They were experiencing the ravages of inflation, where the earnings they thought would be enough to buy them much did not stretch half as far as anticipated.

The situation that is described was one of considerable hardship and economic distress. But had they stopped to ask why these things were happening? That was the challenge being issued to them: to see their unfortunate circumstances as God's fatherly chastisement to recall them to himself. He was afflicting them out of a genuine concern for their well-being, which required them to live in a right relationship with him.

This process is also set out in Amos 4:6-11, where five sets of temporal misfortune are described, each ending with the comment, ' "Yet you have not returned to me," declares the LORD.' The examples of the past were more than sufficient for the people in Haggai's day to have worked out what was really happening. Their occupation of the land was part of their covenant inheritance. To enjoy it fully, they had to live in accordance with the terms set out by the landowner who had given them the right of occupancy. Ignoring his requirements had very serious consequences.

*Call to Action (1:7-8).* **This is what the LORD Almighty says** (*1:7*) repeats substantially the formula of 1:2. The whole verse is the same as 1:5 without 'now'. Here, however, **give careful thought to your ways** looks forwards rather than backwards, for the LORD goes on to indicate how they should act to remedy the situation. It is not a call just for inner change but also for the works of repentance (Mt. 3:8-9; 21:28-32). If they act as indicated, that would prove they had considered their ways and genuinely turned towards the LORD and what he required (Ps. 119:59).

**Go up into the mountains and bring down timber and build the house (*1:8*).** Presumably the stones that were left in the burned remains of Solomon's Temple could be reused, and so timber is mentioned as the main material required to permit the reconstruction work to proceed. Timber was used as a course between layers of stones to provide resilience in earthquakes (Ezr. 5:8; 6:4). Solomon had sent to Phoenicia for wood, particularly cedar from Lebanon (1 Kgs. 5:1-11; 2 Chr. 2:8-10), and when the Jews had originally returned from Babylon they had acted on the royal permission given them to use the same source of supply (Ezr. 3:7). We do not know if the timber had ever been delivered, or if it had been used for some other purpose. Perhaps it was still available, but only in sufficient quantities for the main beams. The people are therefore urged to gather locally the other timber needed for the project. During the years of the Exile, the land had been left untended and many trees would have reached maturity. Furthermore, in the straitened economic circumstances of the people, it is unlikely that they could afford to pay for further supplies from Tyre and Sidon.

**So that I may take pleasure in it** refers to more than a mere building. It was not the physical, but the spiritual, reconstruction of Jerusalem that was the LORD's target. Completion of the rebuilding project would say much about how the people were faring in that respect. The Temple was where the LORD's presence was particularly focused among them. This had been visibly indicated at the inauguration of Solomon's Temple when the cloud of the LORD's presence filled the Temple with his glory (1 Kgs. 8:10-11; see on 2:9 and Zech. 2:5). Restoring the Temple would show that the people recognised their strength and well-being derived from the LORD's presence with them. Such an attitude of dependence and expression of covenant fealty would render what they did acceptable to God. 'Take pleasure' is often used as a technical expression for the divine acceptance of worship and gifts brought to him (Mic. 6:7; Amos 5:22; Mal. 1:10, 13; Ps. 51:17; Jer. 14:10, 12).

**And be honoured** may be understood reflexively, 'permit myself to be honoured'. That is, the rebuilding of the Temple and the worship that would be offered there would be acceptable homage to the LORD. But the word may also be rendered 'glorified', and so look forward to the glory that would be associated with it in time to come (2:7, 9).

The people had been all too ready to act for their own seeming advantage. Here they are challenged to express their loyalty to the LORD and give his service top priority in their living (Jn. 15:8; Phil. 1:11). Pleasing him, and considering his interests and desires, have to be paramount. And **says the LORD** reinforces the point that it is God himself, their covenant ruler, who is addressing them directly, and making known his mind to them.

'Be honoured' is in Hebrew spelled without its expected final letter. As this letter could also stand for the number five, later Jewish rabbinic exegesis took its omission to indicate five things that would be missing from the rebuilt Temple: the ark, with its cover and cherubim; the holy fire; the Shekinah, or glory-cloud, indicating the LORD's presence; the spirit of prophecy; and the Urim and Thummim. While that approach reads too much into an early spelling mistake, the list itself is interesting in that it brings out the partial nature of the restoration at that time. No doubt the absence of these items was designed to wean the people off the merely physical aspects of their religion and intensify their desire for the spiritual reality the types and symbols represented. The loss of the ark and the tables of the covenant pointed forward to the new covenant where the law would be written within them (Jer. 31:33). But it can easily be seen how the absence of such things might disappoint the less spiritually perceptive.

*The Reason for the Blight (1:9-11).* The LORD again reminds them of their frustrated hopes. **You expected much, but see, it turned out to be little (1:9).** The verb indicates that it was not just once, but repeatedly over the years, that this had occurred. 'Much' and 'little' resume the contrasts between expectation and reality found in 1:6, but the first expression here goes beyond agricultural yields. When the people had come back, they would have been encouraged by the messages previously proclaimed by the prophets, such as 'O afflicted city, lashed by storms and not comforted, I will build you with stones of turquoise, your foundations with sapphires. I will make your battlements of rubies, your gates of sparkling jewels, and all your walls of precious stones' (Isa. 54:11-12), or the picture of a superabundant harvest in Amos 9:11-15. From the very first the reality had not matched their expectations. The going had been slow and hard—but they had not seen why.

**What you brought home, I blew away.** 'Brought' is the same word as 'have harvested' (1:6), and perhaps this refers specifically to the poor harvests they had been experiencing. When ears of corn were winnowed to extract the grain, it was the unwanted chaff that was blown away by the wind. But the harvests had been so poor, and the grain so thin, that it too was blown away. The expression may be used metaphorically of the poor return from all their enterprises. All the fruit of their labours dwindled away because it did not enjoy the LORD's blessing. He did not permit them to prosper so that they would be forced to analyse their living at a deeper level.

**"Why?" declares the LORD Almighty.** The facts of what has been happening to the community are not in dispute. It is rather the reason for them that has to be established. It is not to be traced to the prevailing economic or political situation. At most, these were secondary factors in the situation. Of primary importance was the community's attitude towards the LORD and his commands (Josh. 7:10-12; 2 Sam. 21:1). **Because of my house** (coming first for emphasis) **which remains a ruin, while each of you is busy with his own house.** 'Is busy with his own house' is literally 'runs with respect to his house'. If there was anything that was needed for their own property, they were quick to get it (a similar use of 'runs' is found in Prov. 1:16), but they had not given due thought to the situation of the LORD's house (Mt. 10:37-39; Lk. 8:14; Rev. 2:4). There was prevailing apathy in spiritual matters, but zeal in selfish pursuits, as everyone looked out for his own interests, not those of Jesus Christ (Phil. 2:21).

**Therefore** (*1:10*) points out clearly the causal link between their behaviour and their situation. It is therefore difficult to decide between the equally valid translations **because of you** and 'above you'. **The heavens have withheld their dew and the earth its crops**. The inanimate heavens are under the control of God, and do his bidding (Ps. 135:6). So the curse of the broken covenant has come on them from above. 'The sky over your head will be bronze, the ground beneath you iron. The LORD will turn the rain of your country into dust and powder; it will come down from the skies until you are destroyed' (Deut. 28:23-24; Lev. 26:19-20; Deut. 11:17). Their attitude towards the things of God had resulted in hardship and scarcity coming upon them. 'Dew' played an important part in the agriculture of Palestine. During the summer no rain fell, but instead there would be heavy dew from moist winds coming in at night off the Mediterranean. This would provide the crops with sufficient moisture to prevent them from wilting and being scorched before they matured. If the dew failed, then the harvest would be meagre indeed (1 Kgs. 8:35).

What had been expressed indirectly, is now expressed as a direct consequence of divine action. **I called for a drought on the fields and the mountains, on the grain, the new wine, the oil and whatever the ground produces, on men and cattle, and on the labour of your hands (1:11).** God called for famine and shortage as instruments of his wrath (2 Kgs. 8:1; Ps. 105:16). It was not an arbitrary judgment. The logic of what had come upon them is made clear by a word play between 'drought' *(horeb)* and 'ruin' *(hareb)* in 1:9. The one was the just consequence of the other: the ruins of the Temple brought on the drought on the land.

The effects of the drought extended throughout the land—no aspect of living was unaffected. Grain, wine and olive oil were the three staple crops of Palestine (Deut. 7:13; 11:14; Jer. 31:12; Hos. 2:8). 'New wine' refers to the juice of grapes just harvested and pressed. 'The labour of your hands' includes every other activity they engaged in. All were blighted by the presence of the drought, and the whole situation could be traced back to their unwillingness to act to restore the Temple. The whole of the created realm was involved in the consequences of the sin of man.

God does not promise the believer a life that is free of problems. On the contrary, 'in this world you will have trouble' (Jn. 16:33). This is to test and strengthen faith. Knowing the reality of God and having confidence in his power engenders the attitude of David—'With your help I can advance against a troop; with my God I can scale a wall' (Ps. 18:29)—or Paul—'I can do everything through him who gives me strength' (Phil. 4:13). It was never going to be an easy option to return to a land that still obviously bore the ravages of war and to re-establish a viable community there. But a faith, conscious of God and dependent on him, would persevere.

The restored community wanted to be loyal to the LORD but they had failed to implement what he wanted in all aspects of their lives. Partial obedience (which, of course, inevitably involves partial disobedience) had distorted their commitment to God. On his part, the LORD had been warning them that matters were not right through the poor harvests and other difficulties they had experienced. The people had, however, failed to interpret these providential signs correctly. Haggai now openly presents them with their failure to give God's demands priority in their living, and the consequences of this. He challenges them to change their ways. Only if they whole-heartedly live for God, will their situation come right. 'But seek first his kingdom and his righteousness, and all these things will be given to you as well' (Mt. 6:33).

Each generation has to learn how to live out its commitment to God. Our economic and political environments often distort our thinking and cause us to look for easy options. But compromise with worldly attitudes and aspirations undermines our individual spiritual health and the testimony of the church to those around it. What is good politics may not bring the results envisaged, and may well be contrary to sound religion.

*Study Questions*

**1:3**  Compare the people's attitude of discouragement and complaint to those described in Num. 13:31; Prov. 26:13-16; 29:25. What should we learn from this? Lk. 3:14; Phil. 4:11; 1 Tim. 6:6-8; Heb. 13:5.

**1:4**  How important is it to get our priorities right? Mt. 6:33; Phil. 2:21. What tasks are there that we should face up to? Are our reasons for delay adequate?

**1:6** What role does thinking about our past play in spiritual renewal? Lam. 3:40; Lk. 15:17-20; 2 Cor. 13:5; Gal. 6:4.

**1:11** Is it right nowadays to relate physical well-being to loyalty to God? Jn. 9:1-3; 1 Cor. 11:30.

**Haggai 1:12-15: 'I Am With You'**

There is no greater earthly privilege for a servant of God than to see the word of God he has presented take root and bear fruit in hearts and lives. This was what happened to Haggai. His message did not fall on deaf ears. In this brief section he tells how his proclamation evoked a positive response from the community. There seems to have been three stages: an immediate response on August 29th when he first spoke (1:12); a further strengthening of their resolve at an unspecified later date (1:13-14a); and the actual commencement of the work three weeks later on 21st September (1:14b-15). Throughout it is emphasised that this change of attitude did not occur apart from the transforming work of God within them.

*Aroused Consciences (1:12).* **Then Zerubbabel son of Shealtiel, Joshua son of Jehozadak, the high priest, and the whole remnant of the people** *(1:12).* 'Remnant' does not just refer to the rest of the people other than Zerubbabel and Joshua. It had become a standard way for the prophets to refer to the faithful nucleus who were left after the judgment of the LORD on his unfaithful people (Isa. 10:20-22; 37:32; Jer. 23:3; Mic. 4:7; Zech. 8:6). It is not quite the same as those who returned from Babylon. There were others who had never left the land. The remnant are the survivors from the community before God's judgment fell on them, and it is to them that the restored blessing comes. Here they prove their spiritual identity by their obedience.

Unlike 1:1 where only the governor and high priest are mentioned, here the rest of the community are acknowledged as equally involved. It is a picture of harmony and unison. The leaders did not have to coerce a reluctant populace, nor did the people have to convince their leaders what to do. All were agreed on it.

Their response is twofold. *(1)* They **obeyed the voice of the LORD their God.** This is a frequent expression in the Old Testament for acknowledging the demands of the LORD, the covenant king, and acting in accordance with them. 'We will do everything the LORD has said,' was the commitment Israel gave at Sinai when the LORD required, 'Obey me (literally, my voice) fully' (Ex. 19:5, 8). Unfortunately their subsequent history is often a sad record of how they failed to live up to that pledge. 'I warned you when you felt secure, but you said, "I will not listen!" This has been your way from your youth; you have not obeyed me (literally, my voice)' (Jer. 22:21). The response of the restored community here shows how much the situation had changed from that before the Exile (2 Kgs. 17:14; Jer. 42:21). It is like a return to the devotion of their youth (Jer. 2:2). Although they did not immediately begin to work on the Temple, their inner recognition and resolve that they should do so are credited to them for obedience. They would carry out the obligations imposed on them by their covenant king.

How had the voice of the LORD come to the people? They recognised that it was indeed the LORD who had commissioned Haggai. **And the message of the prophet Haggai, because the LORD their God had sent him.** 'And' here might well be rendered 'even' or 'that is'. It does not add another source of information, but clarifies how the LORD's voice had come to the people. Haggai's proclamation had produced in them a deep conviction of their own failure, and left them in no doubt about the genuineness of his credentials as a prophet of the LORD. Sometimes God's word makes us uncomfortable: it reproves us (2 Tim. 3:16). But they did not become angry: rather they acknowledged that what Haggai was saying was right. This shows their hearts to be genuinely inclined towards the LORD.

*(2)* There was a second reaction. **And the people feared the LORD.** 'Fear' is often used to refer to that attitude of reverence and awe that should characterise us before God. For instance, in Proverbs 1:7 the fear of the LORD which is the beginning of knowledge refers to a true and saving response to God (see also on Mal. 3:16). But the expression here is not the usual one, but rather 'feared before the LORD' which indicates consternation and fright. It is used to express the people's fear of the fire of God at Sinai (Deut. 5:5) and later of their fear of the king of Babylon (Jer. 42:11; see also Ex. 9:30; 1 Kgs. 3:28). On this occasion it might have arisen from their consciences being smitten by awareness of their former lapses. They had not carried out all the plans they had made. They had failed to do what God required. The solemn reality came home to them of how dreadful a thing it is to fall into the hands of the living God (Heb. 10:31). How different this was from the way their forefathers had resented and spurned the messages brought by the former prophets.

*Divine Encouragement (1:13-14a).* **Then Haggai, the LORD's messenger, gave this message of the LORD to the people** *(1:13).* We are not told how Haggai felt when he saw this change come over the people, but rather that he continued to fulfil the function divinely assigned him. 'Messenger' is the same word as 'angel' (see on Mal. 3:1). The prophets as God's messengers (2 Chr. 36:15, 16; Isa. 44:26; Mal. 3:1; 2 Cor. 5:20) do not say something they have thought up themselves, but relay what the LORD has entrusted to them. That is the emphasis here. It was God who took the initiative. He saw how the people had responded, and lest their grief over their past sin and failure paralyse them, he replaces his message of rebuke with one of encouragement. By acting to allay their fears, he permitted something positive to emerge from the situation.

"I am with you," declares the LORD. This succinct formula says much. It does not refer to divine omnipresence whereby God fills heaven and earth (Jer. 23:24; Ps. 139:1-13; Heb. 4:13). Rather it indicates the resumption of the relationship between God and mankind, severed by the fall and restored in the covenant of grace. 'I am with you,' is a message addressed to those who are within the bond of faith, assuring them of God's favour and the reality of divine reconciliation. The God who is *with* them is also the God who is *for* them, and so they may find courage. 'If God is for us, who can be against us?' (Rom. 8:31; Ps. 23:4). Reminders of God's presence with his people are often accompanied by a 'Fear not' (2 Chr. 20:17; Isa. 41:10; Acts 18:9-10).

The reality of God's reconciled and restored presence was signified by the Tabernacle and Temple. When the people had come out of Egypt, they were called upon to build the dwelling-place of the LORD (Ex. 26:1-37; 35:4-29). When it was constructed (Ex. 40:33), the LORD descended into it, and his glory filled it (Ex. 40:34-37). It was a perpetual reminder that the LORD was with his people. Having redeemed them, he would lead them and prosper them. When Solomon built the permanent replacement of the portable tabernacle, the glory cloud again filled the structure (1 Kgs. 8:10; 2 Chr. 5:13). The LORD's presence was the pledge of the fulfilment of his covenant promises. (See further on 2:4.)

'I am with you' had often functioned as a source of consolation and encouragement in times of difficulty and danger. When Jacob was fleeing to Paddan Aram, the LORD had said to him, 'I am with you and will watch over you wherever you go, and I will bring you back to this land. I will not leave you until I have done what I have promised you' (Gen. 28:15). This assurance of the divine presence and assistance extends to the most difficult circumstances of life. 'When you pass through the waters, I will be with you' (Isa. 43:2). It therefore forms the chorus of praise of those who have known the ever-present help of God in trouble. 'The LORD Almighty is with us; the God of Jacob is our fortress' (Ps. 46:7, 11).

God repeatedly uses the promise of his presence to encourage those whom he has called to particular tasks where they will feel pressure and be exposed to danger. This was the message he brought to Moses at the burning bush (Ex. 3:12), to Joshua when he succeeded Moses as the leader of Israel (Josh. 1:5), to Jeremiah when he called him to be a prophet in hard times (Jer. 1:8, 19). It is with the same message that Jesus ends the Great Commission, 'And surely I am with you always, to the very end of the age' (Mt. 28:20). Grasping this promise and all that it involves gives the confidence needed for the tasks that lie ahead of us, as much as it did for the Jews of Haggai's generation when they acted with renewed obedience and faced up to rebuilding the Temple. Notice that this promise comes to encourage them after they had inwardly returned to the LORD and resolved to act. 'The LORD is with you when you are with him' (2 Chr. 15:2) always acts as a condition for the enjoyment of this blessing.

So the LORD **stirred up the spirit** (*1:14*) indicates what took place as Haggai spoke. The LORD made the word effective by working within the people to change their attitude. The 'spirit' of an individual refers to his inner being (Ps. 32:2), the animating principle of his rational and immortal life. It therefore refers to reason, will and conscience, which come together to shape our life and conduct. 'Stir up' is literally 'wake up' (it is the word used in Zech. 4:1). The people had become lethargic—with respect to divine things, at any rate. God makes them willing and glad to carry out what is required (Ps. 110:3; 2 Cor. 8:16).

But this was only part of the whole story. Twenty years before, the LORD had intervened in the life of Cyrus, the king of Persia. He had moved Cyrus' heart (the same two words are used, 'stirred the spirit') to permit the exiles to return (Ezr. 1:1). At the same time the LORD had moved the heart of the group of exiles who had volunteered to return from Babylon (Ezr. 1:5). He was not going to permit his purposes to be frustrated, and again he acts to enthuse and energise his people. It is only by the action of the Spirit of God that the project will be completed (Zech. 4:6).

All were involved. **Zerubbabel son of Shealtiel, governor of Judah.** His official title and precedence show him as being the leading figure in the community. **The spirit of Joshua son of Jehozadak, the high priest, and the spirit of the whole remnant of the people.** They had been unable to keep themselves going in their own strength. But God had not abandoned his work, and provides what is required. He is the God 'who works in you to will and to act according to his good purpose' (Phil. 2:13; 1 Cor. 15:10; Jn. 15:5).

*The Work Started (1:14b-15).* **They came and began work on the house of the LORD Almighty, their God.** There would first have been need to plan what was to happen. This does not refer to laying the foundations, which did not take place until the 24th day of the ninth month (2:18). There would, however, have been need for preparatory work in clearing the site, and bringing supplies to it. 'Began work' is literally 'performed work' and recalls the construction of the Tabernacle which involved 'every skilled person to whom the LORD had given ability and who was willing to come and do the work' (Ex. 36:2; see also Ex. 35:29). Note that this is then different from the construction of Solomon's Temple, which involved heavy taxation and forced labour (1 Kgs. 5:13-14; 9:15; 10:14). All was now being done voluntarily.

**On the twenty-fourth day of the sixth month in the second year of King Darius** *(1:15)* marks the end of the first section of the book. What had begun with Haggai's remonstrance on 29th August was brought to realisation on 21st September with the actual resumption of the work in the Temple. It would be wrong to talk of a three-week delay. The sixth month was the time of harvest, and there would have been much work to complete on their farms while plans were formulated. It is the speed of the response that is noteworthy. Three weeks from conception to beginning work on the site is remarkable whether by ancient or modern standards!

While we rejoice at the change that took place in the restored community, we are clearly shown that it would never have happened without divine intervention. In the work of God's kingdom there is need for a spirit of unanimity between leaders and people. When there is a united grasp of the reality of God's presence with his people, great things are accomplished in his cause.

*Study Questions*

**1:12** How does God's word operate powerfully? Isa. 55:11; 1 Thess. 1:5-6.

How does a right attitude of fear towards God shape our response to him? Ps. 112:1; Eccl. 12:13; Acts 9:31; Heb. 12:28.

**1:13** What tasks have we to undertake that particularly need increased confidence to face?

**1:14** In what ways can we be stirred up when we are spiritually lethargic? 2 Cor. 8:16; 2 Tim. 1:6; Heb. 3:12-13.

### Haggai 2:1-9: Looking Backwards and Forwards

Once before the people had started to restore the Temple (Ezr. 3:8-13), but the work had ground to a halt in the face of external opposition and their own lack of faith. Again despondency threatens their endeavour, and Haggai is sent to challenge them to keep going. Faith has to learn how to act so as to overcome difficulties, and to persevere in doing what is right once the excitement of the initial commitment has faded. This involves a realistic appraisal of the past (2:1-5) and also a grasp of what is promised for the future (2:6-9). In this the people are again called to trust in the LORD they are serving. His presence and blessing will ensure the success of the project.

*Looking Backwards (2:1-5).* **On the twenty-first day of the seventh month, the word of the LORD came through the prophet Haggai (*2:1*).** See on 1:1 for the language used. The date corresponds to 17th October 520 B.C., not quite a month since the restoration programme had restarted. It is unlikely any great progress had been made. Although there had been some work done sixteen years previously, the site would have had to be cleared again, an assessment made of what stone still remained and could be used, tests conducted as to what parts of the structure could be allowed to stand and what would have to be demolished, and all the other preparatory work undertaken, such as organising teams of workmen and getting supplies.

Furthermore, the intervening month had been one with many religious festivals on which no work was allowed. The first day of the seventh month was the Feast of Trumpets (Num. 29:1), and the tenth day the Day of Atonement (Lev. 23:26-32). On the fifteenth day of the month the Feast of Tabernacles, or Booths, began. This lasted for a week during which everyone lived in temporary shelters in memory of the time the nation had spent in the wilderness. It was also designated as a time of rejoicing in the harvest (Lev. 23:33-36, 39-44; Deut. 16:13-15). Given that the yield of the crops had recently been so poor (1:10-11; 2:16-17), thinking about the harvest might well have engendered a spirit of dissatisfaction and complaint.

It was on the last ordinary day of the Feast of Booths that Haggai spoke again. The next day, the twenty-second day of the month, was a solemn rest-day (Lev. 23:39). **"Speak to Zerubbabel son of Shealtiel, governor of Judah, to Joshua son of Jehozadak, the high priest, and to the remnant of the people"** (*2:2*). The leaders of the community are again addressed, and along with them the ordinary people (see on 1:12), as the prophet carries out his task of relaying the LORD's message.

Many of the people lived outside Jerusalem. When they attended the festival, they would again be confronted by the destruction wrought in 586 B.C. While they had no doubt heard much about the new plans to restore the Temple, they would quickly have seen how little work had in fact taken place. As they worshipped in charred and ruined buildings in a devastated city, the magnitude of the task before them would have been all too obvious.

Furthermore, the fact that it was Tabernacles would have reminded them of the grand occasion at a former Feast of Tabernacles when Solomon had dedicated his Temple (1 Kgs. 8:2). Comparisons with the past caused much negative thinking, and Haggai is ordered to expose and challenge this with three questions. **Ask them, 'Who of you is left who saw this house in its former glory?'** (*2:3*). This is directed towards bringing out into the open the sentiments that were discouraging the people. We know how at the re-laying of the foundation stone of the Temple in 536 B.C. the shouts of joy were mingled with the tears of the older people who remembered what the Temple of Solomon had been like (Ezr. 3:8-13). Even then the youngest of those who remembered would have been about 55 years old. Now they would be well over 70, and remembering what their childhood impressions had been. Quite possibly their memories of what things had actually been like in the years before 586 were coloured by the accounts of the wealth Solomon had been in a position to lavish on the Temple's original construction. Over the years there had been various depredations, not least those of Nebuchadnezzar in 597 B.C. (2 Kgs. 24:12-13; see also 1 Kgs. 14:25-26; 2 Kgs. 12:17-18; 16:17-18; 18:13-16).

Nonetheless the building had been one of grandeur. The reference to its 'former glory' is to its stateliness as a building, and not to the indwelling presence of the LORD. By saying 'former' Haggai is implicitly recognising that an unfavourable comparison might well be made. But notice that he also says 'this house' (see on 1:2), showing both that they were gathered at it, and that there was essentially only one Temple. Though then in ruins, it was to be rebuilt. It was not a matter of providing a substitute, because the Temple pointed to God's presence with his people, and that remained the same.

**How does it look to you now? Does it not seem to you like nothing?** Haggai articulates what this group of older people were thinking, and perhaps also saying to others (Zech. 4:10). Their renewed zeal for the work in hand led them to being discouraged that they could not make things as they had once been, and as how they felt things ought to be. Such an approach might quickly plunge them back into their previous hopelessness and lack of endeavour. By exposing their thinking, Haggai alerts them to its potentially damaging consequences.

The comparison was not a matter of mere size. The dimensions mentioned in Cyrus' decree—ninety feet high and wide (Ezr. 6:3)—compare favourably with those of Solomon's Temple — ninety feet long, thirty feet wide and forty-five feet high (1 Kgs. 6:2). Rather they were thinking that they could never make it like it was before in terms of its grandeur and magnificence. All the stonework had been covered with cedar panelling, and there had been gold everywhere—even on the floors (1 Kgs. 6:30). There was no way they could do that now!

The implicit defeatism and demoralisation caused by the unfavourable comparison are countered by a threefold exhortation to take courage, addressed in turn to each of the three parties named in verse 2. **'But now be strong, O Zerubbabel,' declares the LORD. 'Be strong, O Joshua son of Jehozadak, the high priest. Be strong, all you people of the land,' declares the LORD (2:4).** They are exhorted to adopt a positive frame of mind so that they could effectively and joyfully pursue the project through to completion (Zech. 8:9). In this they would be aided by the example of the past. The command to be strong was one frequently addressed to

Joshua (Deut. 31:7, 23; Josh. 1:6, 7, 9, 18) and to Israel (Deut. 31:6; Josh. 10:25) as they came into the promised land. These passages had no doubt figured in the Scripture readings over the days of the Feast of Tabernacles when that period was remembered. Joshua in particular had to cope with the problem of potentially unfavourable comparisons with the past. Could he ever be an effective successor to the great Moses? 'All you people of the land' is a reference to the rest of the populace, and not to the enemies of the restored community as in Ezra 4:4 or Nehemiah 10:28.

The command to take courage was addressed to each in turn, and it is followed by the injunction **and work**, addressed to them conjointly. It was not merely an inner attitude that was being enjoined, but also the practical obedience that should follow from it (Jas. 2:14-18).

A similar command to take courage is found in Mark 6:50, where Jesus said to his terrified disciples, 'Take courage! It is I. Don't be afraid.' There too it is linked with the recognition of his presence. If we know he is with us, then we have the spiritual stamina to undertake what he requires of us. **'For I am with you,' declares the LORD Almighty.** (See on 1:13.) This is what distinguishes the advice of the world, 'Be strong. I know you've got it in you' from the counsel of Scripture which recognises that we have not got it in us, but that God's presence with us will make all the difference. The Jews had taken their eyes off God, and their relationship with him, and because they were assessing their situation just in terms of human resources, they were stumbling. When memories of Solomon's Temple were on their minds, they should have recalled the assurance that David had given Solomon. 'Be strong and courageous, and do the work. Do not be afraid or discouraged, for the LORD God, my God, is with you. He will not fail you or forsake you until all the work for the service of the temple of the LORD is finished' (1 Chr. 28:20).

**This is what I covenanted with you when you came out of Egypt (2:5).** These words are sometimes thought to be a scribe's marginal comment that has become incorporated in the text. They are not found in the Septuagint, the early Greek translation, and so are omitted in some modern translations. The Hebrew expression is, '<according to> the word which I cut with you when you came out of Egypt'. Though it is unusual (and perhaps omitted by the Septuagint because of that), it is not impossible. 'To cut a covenant' is the standard Hebrew expression for making one, derived from the ceremony associated with it (Gen. 15:10-21; Jer.

34:18-20). Here it is transferred to the 'word' which gave expression to the covenant bond (Ps. 105:8). Also, the reminder regarding what the LORD had said and done at Sinai fits in with the Feast of Tabernacles setting (Ex. 29:45, 46). The LORD had promised to be with his people.

**And my Spirit remains among you.** In the days of Moses God had set his Holy Spirit among them to protect and guide them (Isa. 63:11). He had given them his good Spirit to instruct them (Neh. 9:20). Over the intervening years, it was by the Spirit that God admonished the people through the prophets (Neh. 9:30). So God's presence, as evidenced by his Spirit working powerfully to instruct and protect them, will continue. Therefore they are urged, **Do not fear.** The LORD's faithfulness in the past and the present is the basis for future encouragement. It is not the appearance of the building, but the presence of his enabling Spirit that will make the crucial difference.

*Looking Forwards (2:6-9).* The LORD then goes on to display the ultimate background against which they should view their situation. They can leave the status and grandeur of the Temple as a matter for him to deal with. The surety of God's promise and the fact of his ever-present Spirit should be enough to calm their fears, but, beginning 'for', he adds an additional reason why they should not fear. **This is what the LORD Almighty says: 'In a little while I will once more shake'** *(2:6).* The phrase, which literally is 'still, one, <it is> a little while and I <will be> shaking', is difficult to interpret. It is, however, the only part of Haggai's prophecy to be quoted in the New Testament. At first that quotation seems to increase the difficulty of understanding these words, but in fact it provides the decisive key for doing so. The quotation occurs in Hebrews where the writer is encouraging his correspondents to godly behaviour, and he points to the difference between their situation and that of the Jews at Sinai. They 'have come to Mount Zion, to the heavenly Jerusalem, the city of the living God' (Heb. 12:22). Notice how these Old Testament descriptions are transferred to the New Testament age. If those with lesser privileges were punished for disobeying God's commands, how much more will those who refuse to acknowledge the full revelation be punished. Referring to Sinai, the writer continued, 'At that time his voice shook the earth, but now he has promised, "Once more I will shake not only the earth but also the heavens." The words "once more" indicate the removing of what can be shaken—that is, created things—so that what cannot be shaken may remain. Therefore, since we are receiving a kingdom that cannot be shaken, let us be thankful, and so worship God acceptably with reverence and awe, for our "God is a consuming fire" ' (Heb. 12:26-29).

The first shaking is therefore that connected with Sinai. 'The whole mountain trembled violently' (Ex. 19:18) when the LORD descended on Sinai (Ps. 68:8; 114:4). All nature was moved by the decisive coming of God. It marked the start of a new epoch in the LORD's dealings with his people (Judg. 5:4-5; Ps. 68:8; Hab. 3:6). What Haggai is presenting to the people is the prospect of a new era, just as markedly different as that instituted by the giving of the law at Sinai. The rebuilding of the Temple formed part of the necessary preparations for the great change that was coming.

When the LORD says that he will shake **the heavens and the earth, the sea and the dry land,** this indicates how far-reaching the changes that are going to take place will be. But will these changes be physical? Descriptions of what had happened at Sinai had been employed figuratively for God's presence in judgment. Often natural forces were used as instruments of divine judgment (Ps. 60:2), sometimes with overtones of the flood (Isa. 24:18b-20). At other times such language is used of divine intervention to deliver (Ps. 18:7-15). It is employed of the overthrow of Babylon (Isa. 13:9-13). This shaking indicates a sudden intervention of God in judgment (Isa. 24:18-20; 29:6).

The focus is not primarily on physical destruction, but on the impact on the nations, as the next verse and 2:21-22 make clear. **I will shake all nations** *(2:7)* envisages an upsetting of the political and social structures that the nations had put in place by their own power and wisdom, and which they thought would last. When they have served their God-ordained purpose, it will be an easy matter for him to thrust them aside, and to reverse the flow of history. The Jews were hesitant about what the future held. Perhaps they would incur the wrath of the Persians, but they are encouraged to view earthly governments in the perspective of the power of divine intervention.

While this prophecy might to some extent be taken as realised in the political upheavals that would shortly affect the Persian empire, and ultimately lead to its overthrow in 333 B.C., that is far from exhausting it. The citation in Hebrews shows that these earlier shakings presage the great shaking to come at the final judgment, when what is created will be removed, so that what pertains to the eternal kingdom of God, which cannot be shaken, may remain. In the same way here the Jews are being warned to assess matters in the light of eternity. The presence of God with them is an asset that will stand the test of shaking. They should not be taken up with the lack of gold or elaborate ornamentation of the Temple (Prov. 11:4).

**The desired of all nations will come.** There is an old interpretation of these words, stretching back to the Rabbis and the Vulgate (the early Latin translation of Jerome), that 'the desired of all nations' is a reference to the Messiah. The immediate problem with this is that 'the desired' is a singular noun and 'will come' is a plural verb in Hebrew. There is therefore now a consensus in favour of taking 'the desired' as a collective noun, equivalent to 'the desired things', with which the verb agrees in sense. The reference is then to what the nations consider precious and desirable. The noun is also used in the phrases 'articles of value' (2 Chr. 36:10) and 'all kinds of valuables' (2 Chr. 32:27), and in 'costly gifts' (Dan. 11:38) and 'riches' (Dan. 11:43). Those who wish to argue for a directly Messianic rendering have to change the vowels of the word 'desired' into those of a related plural form (to agree with the verb) and have also to note that the plural is used of Daniel in the sense 'highly esteemed' (Dan. 9:23; 10:11, 19). While this procedure may be acceptable in that it does not involve any alteration of the consonants of the Hebrew text, it still fails to meet a basic theological problem, that elsewhere it is stated that the Messiah is one not desired, but rejected when looked on with natural eyes (Isa. 53:2-3; Jn. 1:11).

Although the coming of the Messiah is not here directly foretold, prophecies of the wealth of the nations being brought to Jerusalem are found elsewhere (Isa. 60:5-7; 61:6; Mic. 4:13; Zech. 14:14), and so this prophecy is indirectly Messianic, that is, it describes features of his reign rather than of his person or work. Here it is clear that the gifts are donated by the nations for sacred purposes. In part this was fulfilled when state revenues were made available for the Temple project by Cyrus and Darius (Ezr. 6:4, 8-9). There were also the gifts sent by the Jews of the dispersion (Zech. 6:10). The dedication of the wealth of the world to the cause of God is also indicated in the gold, incense and myrrh brought by the Magi to the infant Jesus (Mt. 2:11). But these are pale shadows of what will ultimately occur when the glory and honour of the nations are brought into the new Jerusalem (Rev. 21:26).

It is doubtful if the refurbishment of the Temple, begun in 20 B.C. by Herod the Great, should be included in the list of the desired things that the nations bring. Herod undertook a massive and costly improvement of Zerubbabel's Temple, so that it was almost entirely rebuilt. When it was completed, the pinnacle of the Temple was covered with gold. These were not the actions of reverence, but political expediency. Herod desired to impress and win over the Jews. He did not succeed in mitigating their hatred of him, but he certainly did impress them. The disciples were not alone in expressing their wonder—and pride ?— in the Temple. 'Look, Teacher! What massive stones! What magnificent buildings!' (Mk. 13:1). This was the opposite of what the LORD intended. The second Temple ought not to have been as outwardly splendid as the first, because the Jews were being weaned off types and symbols and being taught to focus on the realities signified by them. Jesus' teaching about the relative importance the Jews attached to the gold of the Temple and the Temple that makes the gold sacred (Mt. 23:16-17) shows that Herod's Temple had effectively diverted their attention from the God whose presence was symbolised by the Temple to mere outward adornment.

If the 'desire of all nations' is not directly Messianic, the same cannot be said of **I will fill this house with glory.** 'Glory' is used of the splendour and beauty of the building as in 2:3. But God's purpose at this time was not focused on how physically impressive the structure might be made. 'Glory' also signifies the presence of God, and it is with that glory as revealed in Christ that the Father will adorn this Temple. 'The Word became flesh and made his dwelling among us. We have seen his glory, the glory of the One and Only, who came from the Father, full of grace and truth' (Jn. 1:14).

In the days of Solomon the land had been very wealthy. Now there were not the resources to adorn the Temple as Solomon had done. The LORD, however, asserts that is not because of any frustration of his purposes or power. He is the ultimate owner of all earth's treasures (Job 41:11; Ps. 24:1; 50:10-11), not the Persians. **'The silver is mine and the gold is mine,' declares the LORD Almighty** *(2:8).* If he felt that external adornment was needed, then he had the right and power to call upon the resources required. But God's estimate of things is very different from ours. Man looks only on the outward appearance, while God's way of working proceeds on a different basis (1 Sam. 16:7; 1 Cor. 1:27-28).

**The glory of this present house will be greater than the glory of the former house** *(2:9)*. This could be translated 'the latter glory of this house will be greater than the former <glory>', which would be in keeping with the previous emphasis that the house is one throughout. It is also the case that here the emphasis on glory is clearly on that associated with the presence of God, which perhaps is never quite absent from references to the glory of the Temple. 'Glory' is used by Ezekiel to refer to the presence of the LORD in his opening vision (Ezk. 1:28). Later he saw the glory departing from the Temple (10:3-4, 18). It was the presence of the LORD as represented by the glory-cloud that gave the dwelling of the LORD its basic, real and enduring glory. (Note also Ex. 40:35; 2 Chr. 5:14). The Second Temple never had the glory-cloud. But the LORD of the Temple came (Mt. 12:6), and by his presence provided more than the cloud could ever have done (Jn. 1:14; 2 Cor. 3:9-10). Indeed, through Jesus' coming the Temple, representing the presence of God with his people, was superseded (Jn. 2:13-22). That reality is now achieved through the indwelling of the Spirit (1 Cor. 3:16; 6:19). All that is involved in it is finally realised in the New Jerusalem (Rev. 21:22-27).

**And in this place I will grant peace.** 'Place' can be used to describe a sacred site (Deut. 12:5, 14; 14:23; Neh. 1:9; Jer. 17:12; Ezk. 43:7). Here it probably refers to both the Temple and the city, with a play on the name 'Jerusalem' which may mean 'city of peace'. 'Peace' *(shalom)* sums up all the blessings of the Messianic age. It begins with the removal of all difficulties in the way of approach to God, and encompasses the blessings that attend a new relationship with him (Ps. 85:8, 10; Isa. 9:6-7; 53:5; Zech. 6:13; Mal. 2:5). It can only be achieved through him who is his people's peace (Jn. 14:27; Eph. 2:14).

It is still very easy in building the kingdom of God, the Temple of New Testament times, to be overcome by pessimism, seeing only the problems and not the possibilities. What has the church managed to achieve since it was given its commission by Christ? But unless we start, unless we try, what can come but failure? The way forward is to act in faith.

It also requires that we act with values determined by God's perspective. It is not a matter of grand structures or visible splendour. The church is not assessed in this way. It is a matter of lives dedicated to him.

This can be achieved by the presence of the Spirit. Paul may plant the seed and Apollos water it, but the growth is from God alone (1 Cor. 3:6). Let us not discount our greatest asset.

*Study Questions*

**2:4** What sources are there for spiritual strength? 1 Cor. 16:13; Eph. 6:10-18; 2 Tim. 2:1.

**2:5** God's Spirit is still present with his people. How should we respond to him? Isa. 63:10; Mt. 12:31-32; Jn. 16:13-15; Acts 5:3; Rom. 8:5; 1 Cor. 3:16; Eph. 4:29-32.

**2:6** Do we place too much emphasis on outward material aspects of living and worship, and not enough on what really matters? Prov. 23:5; Mt. 6:19-21; Lk. 12:21; 1 Tim. 6:9-10; Heb. 13:5; Jas. 5:1-3.

**Haggai 2:10-19: 'I Will Bless You'**
It was three months to the day since the people had resumed work on the Temple site with new resolve (1:15). Now the project had advanced sufficiently for there to be a solemn service when the Temple foundation was relaid (2:18). On the day this formal recommitment was made, the prophet Haggai received two messages, which both focused on important parties who were present on the occasion: in 2:10-19 use is made of the priests to illustrate the divine message, and in 2:20-23, it is the governor, Zerubbabel, who is the centre of attention. The messages are linked by the common theme of the LORD's blessing.

Since the people had responded by obeying the LORD's message, Haggai shows that their obedience will be rewarded. The community will have such a successful harvest compared to those of the previous sixteen years that it will be evident that God has blessed them. On this basis they should move forward with confidence.

**On the twenty-fourth day of the ninth month, in the second year of Darius, the word of the LORD came to the prophet Haggai** (*2:10*). The significance of the new date, which corresponds to 18th December 520 B.C., is brought out in verse 18. Zechariah had begun his ministry a few weeks earlier (Zech. 1:1) with a message which implied that the community had still some way to go in the matter of repentance. Haggai's message here too fits in with the people struggling to achieve a whole-hearted response.

The early rains would have begun in the middle of October, and shortly after that there would be a period of intense agricultural activity. Seed would be scattered over the newly moistened soil, and then ploughed in. The winter months of December to February were much colder, and little farming could be done. That left people with more time for other things, such as the Temple rebuilding project.

*The First Question (2:11-12).* The people had gathered at the Temple site for the foundation laying ceremony, and Haggai was to take advantage of this to ask the priests publicly for instruction. The authority of the priests in such a matter is being recognised. There is no suggestion that they are being criticised for their teaching. **This is what the LORD Almighty says: 'Ask the priests what the law says'** *(2:11).* The priests had a duty not only to instruct the people in what the law of God required, but also to answer any questions they might have about how it applied to their particular situation (see discussion of Mal. 2:7). It was therefore not uncommon for them to be asked to give an official ruling in this way. However, the questions that Haggai asked were ones to which the answers were obvious and already well-known to everyone. By posing these questions, common ground was secured from which a more telling application to the current situation could be made.

The questions that are asked establish the fact that ritual purity cannot be indefinitely passed on by physical contact, but that ritual defilement can. It is the non-transmission of purity that is questioned first. **If a person carries consecrated meat in the fold of his garment, and that fold touches some bread or stew, some wine, oil or other food, does it become consecrated?** *(2:12).* 'Consecrated meat' (Jer. 11:15) refers to the flesh of sacrificed animals. Apart from the burnt offering where everything was burned, in the other offerings portions were allotted to the priests (Lev. 6:26; 7:6-7, 31-34). In the fellowship, or peace, offering much of the animal was returned to the offerer to take away and eat at a festive meal (Lev. 7:15; Deut. 12:7, 17). Particularly with the Temple precincts being in ruins, the priests would often have had to carry away portions of the sacred meat. Using a fold in their long robes was a common way of carrying things (2 Kgs. 4:39; Ezk. 5:3).

The circumstance is then envisaged of that fold of the garment touching some other food. Those mentioned include many of the staple foodstuffs of Palestine: wheat (bread), wine and olive oil (see on 1:11). The stew was probably some form of vegetable broth (Gen. 25:34; 2 Kgs. 4:38-40). The question that was asked was whether that other food then became holy.

The thinking behind this question arose from the warning of Leviticus 6:27, 'Whatever touches any of the flesh will become holy, and if any of the blood is spattered on a garment, you must wash it in a holy place.' Ezekiel 44:19 presents the possibility of other people becoming consecrated through coming into contact with the priests' official robes. But the precise circumstances presented here are not dealt with elsewhere in Scripture, and so the priests answer on the basis of the traditional understanding of such matters that had developed in Israel. Even if part of the garment that had been in direct contact with the consecrated meat subsequently came in contact with other food, there was no secondary transmission of holiness. That was the point Haggai was making: the transmission of holiness stops. So when **the priests answered, "No"**, it was just as Haggai expected they would. The narrative here is compressed. It is not actually said that the prophet carried out the LORD's instructions. That is assumed.

What was the point of the question? Israel had originally been set apart by the LORD as holy (Ex. 19:6), but that did not mean that all they did was on that account sacred and acceptable to God. Holy status required holy obedience. Even though God's covenant relationship with them was renewed in their return to the land, that recognition of their 'holy' status did not convey automatic approval of all that they did—or hadn't done in the case of the Temple. As for the future, there might be an implicit warning that though they had now started to rebuild the Temple, it still did not follow that there was blanket approval for all that they did. They were not to fall into the ways of the past when the mere presence of the Temple in Jerusalem was wrongly interpreted to imply that divine favour rested on the land come what may (Jer. 7:4). The Temple was not a good-luck charm that automatically transmitted holiness. Each activity had to be assessed on the basis of the LORD's covenant standards for his people. Only in that way could his approval be assured.

*The Second Question (2:13-14).* Haggai then puts a different case to the priests. He is undoubtedly doing this on the instructions of the LORD, though again the details are not fully spelled out. **Then Haggai said, "If a person defiled by contact with a dead body touches one of these things, does it become defiled?"** (*2:13*). The dead body is human, and any individual touching a corpse became unclean (Num. 19:11). This was viewed as a most serious defilement, requiring the individual to be put out of the camp (Num. 5:2), to be excluded from the normal celebration of the Passover (Num. 9:6-12), and to be ritually sprinkled with water of cleansing over a period of a week (Num. 19:11-21). The priests in particular were to avoid such pollution (Lev. 21:1-4, 11; 22:6). This defilement was contagious (Num. 19:22), and would spread to the items mentioned in the preceding verse. **"Yes," the priests replied, "it becomes defiled."**

Haggai then presents the LORD's application of this principle. **'So it is with this people and this nation in my sight,' declares the LORD. 'Whatever they do and whatever they offer there is defiled'** (*2:14*). As before (1:2), 'this people' shows the LORD as distancing himself from them. By their disobedience the people had become defiled, and so everything they touched, including their offerings, became unclean. It might even be that the ruined Temple in their midst was being likened to a corpse that was defiling the whole nation and its worship. The only remedy was that by God's grace the people should repent, and give proof of that not just by working on the Temple, but in the attitude that they took towards what they were doing. A good work is soured if it is done in a reluctant spirit. All must be brought into alignment with the covenant. 'If anyone turns a deaf ear to the law, even his prayers are detestable' (Prov. 28:9; Isa. 1:11-14). To know the fulness of God's blessing they must ensure that there is no sinful corruption spreading its contagion throughout all their efforts. Whoever would stand in the holy place must ensure that he has clean hands and a pure heart (Ps. 24:3-4).

*The Change to be Expected (2:15-19).* **Now** (*2:15*) may be used as in English as equivalent to 'at this time' or 'in these circumstances'. Both fit this context, but perhaps the preference is to be given here to indicating the consequences of the previous argument. **Give careful thought** uses the same phrase that is found at 1:5, 7. **To this** is a translator's supplement to bring out one way of understanding the words that follow. The phrase rendered **from this day on**, literally 'from this day and upwards', may apply backwards 'to the days past' (as in NIV footnote) or forwards, and either may be fitted into the context. But it is much more likely that they are being commanded to mark closely the change that is going to occur and assess its true significance (Hos. 14:9).

**Consider how things were before one stone was laid on another in the LORD's temple.** In Ezra 3:10-13 it is recounted how in 536 B.C. the foundation stone of the Temple was relaid (see on 2:18). But it is improbable that is the reference here, for if it were, Haggai would be looking back to the time of the Exile. What they are being urged to consider is how they had fared in the period before the relaying of the foundation that took place in 520 B.C.

It is here that Haggai refers for the first time to the structure that was being rebuilt as 'temple' rather than 'house' (see on 1:2). The words are often used interchangeably, but 'temple' may be used of any large building, and can be applied to a palace, for example, that of Ahab (1 Kgs. 21:1) or of the king of Babylon (2 Kgs. 20:18). The temple of a god was often considered his dwelling-place, and this was true of the LORD's presence in the Temple. In the accounts of the construction of Solomon's Temple (1 Kgs. 6-7; 2 Chr. 3-4), 'temple' refers to the inner holy area, while 'house' is used for the structure as a whole.

The first word of the Hebrew text of verse 16, which means 'since they were', does not make sense as it stands. The NIV translators take it with the previous verse, and understand it to mean 'how things were' with 'consider' as a supplement. Other translations deal with it differently.

Two examples are given of the poor agricultural returns that had caused the economic crisis in the preceding years. **When anyone came to a heap of twenty measures, there were only ten (2:16).** The heap is presumably of harvested grain. Approaching it, the size of the heap was such as to lead to an expectation of there being a return of twenty measures of usable grain. The word 'measure' is a general one. The emphasis is not on the absolute amount involved, but rather on the extent to which the yield was less than their expectation. So poor was the quality of their harvest, that once the crop was winnowed, the grain that was separated from the chaff was only half the amount expected.

It was the same with the grape harvest. **When anyone went to a wine vat to draw fifty measures, there were only twenty.** 'Wine vat' is strictly speaking 'wine press'—often a pit in rock where grapes were crushed by foot after they had lain in the sun for some days. The juice that was squeezed from them would run off through a channel into the vat. The situation envisaged seems to be that after the harvest the grapes lying in the sun had led to the expectation of a yield of fifty measures (again the word is not specific). But when one went to the vat where the juice was gathered, it was well under half of what he expected was there. This is a description of the earlier period that has already been referred to (1:6, 9-11). It was quite the opposite picture from what could be expected for those who were using their resources in the LORD's cause (Prov. 3:9-10).

The explanation is given as to why the returns from their farms had been so poor. **I struck all the work of your hands with blight, mildew and hail (2:17).** Literally it is 'I struck you <with respect to> all the work of your hands.' The emphasis on 'you' is important. The LORD's covenantal dealings are personal and direct. These three disasters were part of the curse of the covenant for those who did not carefully keep all that the LORD of the covenant required of them (Deut. 28:22). They had also been referred to by the prophet Amos regarding the way the LORD had dealt with the northern kingdom of Israel in the years before its fall in 721 B.C. ' "Many times I struck your gardens and vineyards, I struck them with blight and mildew. Locusts devoured your fig and olive trees, yet you have not returned to me," declares the LORD' (Amos 4:9). The LORD's action in sending unfavourable circumstances to them was one of fatherly chastisement to recall them to himself. It had not worked with Israel, and it had not worked to date with the restored community.

'Blight' refers to the scorching effect of the east wind coming in from the desert, drying up plants and shrivelling the grain, so that the yield dropped dramatically (Gen. 41:6). 'Mildew' might well have been associated with the more moist winds coming in from the Mediterranean. These would have led to damp conditions in which the fungus could thrive, preventing plants from ripening properly (1 Kgs. 8:37; 2 Chr. 6:28). 'Hail' was associated with severe storms and wind, which would leave plants flattened, and possibly cause injury to people and animals. It too was associated with the LORD's judgment (Ex. 9:25-35; Josh. 10:11; Isa. 28:2). Whatever they tried to grow, their disobedience ensured that the LORD frustrated their endeavours.

**'Yet you did not turn to me,' declares the LORD.** Literally, it reads 'not you to me.' 'Turn' is a translator's supplement to bring out the fact that all this constituted a divine appeal to them to repent (see on Zech. 1:4). What the LORD had been doing was designed to make them think about their situation, to ask 'Why?' and so to alert them to the error of their ways. But the series of poor harvests had not achieved its purpose.

Having looked at what happened in the past, Haggai then urges the people to give careful thought (2:15) to what was going to happen from then on. **From this day on, from this twenty-fourth day of the ninth month, give careful thought to the day when the foundation of the LORD's temple was laid (*2:18*).** It is not just to what happened on that day that they were to turn their attention. It was to the fact that that day would mark a turning-point in their relationship with the LORD. If they came to their senses, and acted as the LORD desired them to, then they would know the blessings of a renewed relationship with him (Lk. 15:17-24).

There is no necessary conflict between this verse and what is recorded in Ezra 3:10-13, where another foundation laying ceremony took place, probably in 536 B.C. It does not seem that the foundations below ground of Solomon's Temple had been destroyed. The new work was on top of them. In the intervening period they had surveyed the site, cleared away debris, and gathered supplies, particularly of wood, so that they could begin the actual work of restoration. They had got thus far before, but the work had come to nothing because of the opposition they faced. On both occasions the start of the work was marked by an official ceremony. Furthermore 'foundation' may not be a technical term, but may be simply equivalent to restoration (2 Chr. 24:27). There is also the possibility that more than one ceremony was carried out at various initial stages of the work.

**Give careful thought: Is there yet any seed left in the barn? (*2:18-19*).** It was December and the time for sowing (October-November) when the early rain softened the ground had passed. As a result there would be no seed left. They were waiting through the winter months of December to February for the latter rains of March and April to see what the harvest would be like. There was no surplus brought forward from the past. When the next harvest was substantially better—and at the time of year when Haggai prophesied there was no way that any of them could have humanly known what the next harvest was going to be like—they would know to attribute it to the LORD. **Until now, the vine and the fig-tree, the pomegranate and the olive tree have not borne fruit.** This looks back to the poor yield of the fruit trees in the past decade. But this was going to change. Or, it may indicate that at that time of year the new growth of the fruit trees was not yet evident. When it came, the yield would not reflect the poor results of the past.

**From this day I will bless you.** By the time this message came to Haggai, the sowing would have been over, and the community would be waiting to see if their hard work would be accompanied by a more fruitful harvest than these past years. The blessing God promises obviously includes this, but it extends beyond agricultural yields. God's blessing is total and affects every aspect of life.

The examples from the ceremonial law make this section seem remote from our situation today, but it still contains both a needed warning and a promise. The tendency to rest satisfied with an outward connection with God's cause is still prevalent. Just as the Jews of Haggai's day might have considered all to be right between them and God because a start had been made on rebuilding the Temple, so there are many who think well of themselves because they attend church services, give to the LORD's cause and to charities, and engage in various good works. But however commendable such actions may be in themselves, they do not transmit holiness to those who perform them. True holiness requires first the renewing work of the Spirit and an inner commitment to the LORD, of which good works are an outward expression. If there is not a renewed heart within the individual, then acts of devotion in themselves are just a charade.

There is also here the promise that those who have given God his proper place in their thinking will find that he blesses them. Those who have no time to devote to God's interests will find that he has no time to devote to theirs. But those who seek him will find that his blessings, even in prospect, far outweigh any temporal disadvantages. 'For our light and momentary troubles are achieving for us an eternal glory that far outweighs them all' (2 Cor. 4:17).

*Study Questions*

**2:17** How should we respond to God's fatherly chastisement? Amos 4:6-12; Jn. 15:2; 1 Cor. 11:32; Heb. 12:5-13; Rev. 2:21; 3:19.

**2:18-19** What relationship does Scripture demonstrate between obedience and blessing? Mt. 6:33; Mk. 6:4; Acts 3:19.

**Haggai 2:20-23:   The LORD's Signet Ring**

On the day that the foundation of the Temple was relaid (2:18), Haggai received two messages from the LORD. The second of them focused on Zerubbabel, the civil leader of the restored community. It was prophesied that the LORD was going to act on behalf of Zerubbabel in the same powerful way that he had acted on behalf of his people in the past. This message had significance for the whole community because Zerubbabel was of the line of David, and so was a precursor of the Messiah. This was the ultimate and grandest blessing that the LORD would bestow on his covenant people—to send them his anointed king to rule over them and provide for all their needs. The LORD was going to act through the remnant, and from among them he would raise up the Messiah. This vision of his future victory was given to them to spur them on to renewed endeavour in the LORD's cause in their own day. **The word of the LORD came to Haggai a second time on the twenty-fourth day of the month (2:20).** This introduction parallels that of 2:10, both messages being given on 18th December 520 B.C., the day when there was a formal ceremony in the Temple ruins to mark the resumption of the restoration work

*Zerubbabel (2:21a).* Although Haggai's message is of significance for all the people, he is ordered in the first instance to **tell Zerubbabel (2:21).** There are many aspects of Zerubbabel's ancestry and history that are obscure. We have already been told that he was the son of Shealtiel (1:1, 12, 14; 2:2). The significance of this can be found in 1 Chronicles where Shealtiel is listed as the eldest son of the exiled king Jehoiachin, also known as Jeconiah (1 Chr. 3:17). In 597 B.C. Jehoiachin had been taken prisoner to Babylon after a short reign of three months and ten days (2 Kgs. 24:15; 2 Chr. 36:9-10). Zerubbabel was therefore of the line of David, and as such he appears in the genealogies of Christ (Mt. 1:12; Lk. 3:27).

But this overlooks two other pieces of information. In the same genealogy in 1 Chronicles, Zerubbabel is listed as being one of the sons of Pedaiah, who was another son of Jehoiachin (1 Chr. 3:19). Since Shealtiel is not listed there as having any offspring, it is often supposed that he died young and that Pedaiah married his widow in terms of the levirate marriage law (Deut. 25:5-10; Mt. 22:24-28). Another explanation that has been advanced is that it was Pedaiah who died, and that Zerubbabel was adopted by his uncle Shealtiel.

In its genealogy of Christ, Luke 3:27 lists 'Zerubbabel, the son of Shealtiel, the son of Neri' and traces the line back through Nathan, one of David's sons. It may be that the clue to unravelling this is to be found in the prophecy of Jeremiah: 'This is what the LORD says: "Record this man as if childless, a man who will not prosper in his lifetime, for none of his offspring will prosper, none will sit on the throne of David or rule any more in Judah" ' (Jer. 22:30). Jehoiachin's own sons were taken to Babylon, and if they were there made eunuchs (Isa. 39:7), then he may have adopted the sons of Neri, Shealtiel among them, as his official heirs, so that the line of David would not die out.

A further problem is that of the connection between Zerubbabel and Sheshbazzar, who is mentioned in Ezra 1:8, 11; 5:14, 16. In this last verse Sheshbazzar is said to have laid the foundations of the house of God in Jerusalem in 536 B.C., whereas the same action is attributed to Zerubbabel in Ezra 3:8-11. Some have supposed that while Zerubbabel actually laid the foundation, he was doing so under the direction of Sheshbazzar. As Sheshbazzar was the one who was known to the Persian authorities, it is his name that is mentioned in Ezra 5:16. Others argue that Sheshbazzar died soon after the return of the Jews to Jerusalem, and Zerubbabel took his place. Since, however, Sheshbazzar is not mentioned in the list of those who returned (Ezr. 2:1-61) and since the name Sheshbazzar is found in official contexts dealing with the Persians, there is still strong support for the older theory that both names refer to the one person. Just as Daniel had a Babylonian name Belteshazzar (Dan. 1:7), so Zerubbabel (which means 'one born in Babylon') had a Babylonian name, Sheshbazzar, which was used in official business. Sheshbazzar may be a Hebrew version of a Babylonian name, meaning 'Sin (the moon god) protect the father.'

Zerubbabel was **the governor**, having been recognised by the Persian authorities as the leader of the group (Ezr. 1:8, assuming his identity with Sheshbazzar). This would have fitted in with Cyrus' approach of recognising local rulers and working through them. According to 2 Kings 25:27-30 Jehoiachin had been released from prison by the newly-crowned king of Babylon, Evil-Merodach (562-560 B.C.), and given the privilege of eating at the king's table—a fact also attested by tablets found at the Ishtar Gate in Babylon, listing the provisions allotted him. The Judean royal house had therefore been in good standing in Babylon even before the Persians captured the city.

It is not certain how the provinces of the Persian empire were organised at this time. It is unlikely that Zerubbabel's authority extended outside Judea. He was probably answerable to Tattenai, governor of Trans-Euphrates (Ezr. 5:3; 6:13).

Although responsible for the work starting in 520 B.C., Zerubbabel is not mentioned in connection with the completion of the Temple (Ezr. 6:13-22). But too much may not be made of this. Joshua, the high priest, is not listed either, and there is no suggestion that he was not in office. The prophecy of Zechariah 4:9 requires that Zerubbabel be still governor at that date. We do not know what happened to him subsequently. He may have died and not been replaced. Some have suggested that Messianic claims for him were misunderstood by the Persians, and he was removed from office. He does not seem to have had an immediate Jewish successor, the governor mentioned in Malachi 1:8 presumably being a Persian official. It was the high priest who became leader in the Jewish community.

*Zerubbabel's Messianic Significance (2:21b-23)* The divine message that is brought to Zerubbabel is **I will shake the heavens and the earth.** The language of shaking looks back to 2:6-7. It is the language of theophany, where the LORD's presence causes the earth to shake. Here the scope is cosmic. 'Heaven and earth' is a Hebrew idiom for the whole created realm (Gen. 1:1). But the shaking is more than a physical response to the LORD's intervention. What is referred to is the action of the LORD upsetting not so much the physical framework of the universe, but those political and social structures that seemed so oppressive to the Jews. All was under his control, and he would act to ensure that the domination exerted against them would come to an end. It is the LORD who acts on a universal scale for the sake of the house of David and for the good of his people.

**I will overthrow royal thrones (2:22).** 'Overthrow' is a word very much associated with the destruction of Sodom and Gomorrah (Deut. 29:23; Isa. 13:19; Jer. 20:16; Amos 4:11). It is the LORD's prerogative and power to cause kingdoms to fall (Ps. 46:6; Dan. 4:34-35; 5:26). The LORD will also **shatter the power of the foreign kingdoms.** Literally, it is 'kingdoms of the nations'. They will be devastated (Isa. 14:23) and unable to operate against God's cause and people. This shows quite clearly what lies behind the general language of the previous verse. As the political head of the restored community, it was appropriate that the message about the political scene was addressed to Zerubbabel.

**I will overthrow chariots and their drivers; horses and their riders will fall.** Chariots were a major part of the Persian army. The picture is reminiscent of the scene at the time of the Exodus (Ex. 14:17, 28; 15:1,4-5). **Each by the sword of his brother** adds another layer of reminiscence, that of the victory given by the LORD to Gideon (Judg. 7:22; see also Ezk. 38:21; Zech. 14:13). This picture of internecine warfare among those who seem united as a formidable foe confronting the LORD's people is one that clearly reveals their powerlessness (2 Chr. 20:23; Isa. 9:19; 19:2).

**'On that day,' declares the LORD Almighty, 'I will take you'** *(2:23)* refers to what the LORD will do for his own people against the background of universal turmoil and disaster. 'On that day' may have eschatological overtones (see on Mal. 4:1). 'Take' is used in a special sense of selecting for God's own purposes ('brought' in Gen. 24:7; 'take' in Ex. 6:7; Deut. 4:20; Josh. 24:3; 2 Sam. 7:8; Amos 7:15). **My servant Zerubbabel** gives him the title that is appropriate in the light of God's purpose, rather than the one given him by the Persian overlords. 'Servant' and 'chosen' are found together in Isaiah 40–55 (Isa. 41:8; 42:1; 44:1). **Son of Shealtiel** reminds us of who Zerubbabel was in relation to his descent. He was the heir of Jehoiachin who had ruled Judah. Zerubbabel is therefore mentioned here not so much for what he was personally as for what he represented as a ruler from the house of David. Not only had the LORD restored the nation, but there was still the line of David, through whom the Messiah would come. The repeated **declares the LORD** gives solemn assurance that this, the grandest of all promises, is not forgotten.

**I will make you like my signet ring.** It was through Jeremiah, just over a decade before Jerusalem fell to Nebuchadnezzar, that the LORD announced, 'Even if you, Jehoiachin son of Jehoiakim king of Judah, were a signet ring on my right hand, I would still pull you off' (Jer. 22:24). The signet ring would have an identifying device or name on it, and was used to impress a clay tablet, or a wax or clay seal affixed to a document. It attested ownership and was closely guarded, generally being worn on the person (Song 8:6). The LORD had told Jehoiachin that even though he had been as precious and important as such a signet ring, he would still be handed over to Nebuchadnezzar, and die in exile. Now, in a reversal of that divine rejection, the LORD reveals to Zerubbabel that he is reinstated in favour, and that he (and the line of promise that he represented) would be looked after with divine care. As the signet ring symbolised the authority of the owner, so Zerubbabel was authorised to act in the LORD's name. In this way God was going to use him to authenticate his blessing to the people, as shown in the completion of the Temple project (Zech. 4:9).

Zerubbabel's part in the work to hand would be brought to a successful conclusion because he was the one sovereignly chosen by God. **"For I have chosen you," declares the LORD Almighty.** This choice is not an arbitrary act of God, but a selection determined by his good pleasure as one that will further his purposes. Divine choice of an individual implies not only status but also responsibility. 'I have chosen David to rule my people Israel' (1 Kgs. 8:16; see also Deut. 18:5; 1 Sam. 10:24; 1 Chr. 28:5-6, 10). It was divine choice that had selected Israel as his people. 'Out of all the peoples on the face of the earth, the LORD has chosen you to be his treasured possession' (Deut. 14:2). But here this choice shows that the history of the line of David had not come to an end. Zerubbabel's presence and rule pointed the people forward to the realisation of the promise, 'My servant David will be king over them' (Ezk. 37:24). He supremely is the chosen servant (Mt. 12:18; 1 Pet. 2:4). 'On him God the Father has placed his seal of approval' (Jn. 6:27).

The provision made for God's people is never fully understood until it is seen in the light of the one who has won that blessing for them. It is the Messiah who is the sole basis of our hope. If we see him as divinely appointed and divinely accepted, then no matter what convulsions wrack the world around us, we will be in a position to stand secure.

*Study Question*

**2:21** The day is coming when nations and powers will be shaken: how should this affect our conduct now? Mt. 23:4-8, 29-30; Heb. 12:28; 1 Pet. 1:3-6.

# ZECHARIAH

# OVERVIEW

Zechariah is generally assumed to have been a younger man than Haggai, and his prophetic activity seems to have continued for much longer. Initially his ministry complemented that of Haggai to the restored community in Jerusalem. His first message (1:1-6) is dated during the course of Haggai's ministry, and urged the people to pay attention to his message in the light of the experience of their forefathers, who had rejected the warnings of the earlier prophets until it was too late. They should now repent and return to God.

*Zechariah 1:7-8:23.* During the years 519-518 B.C., while the Temple was being restored, Zechariah's ministry took various forms. He was granted eight visions (1:7-6:8) which were designed to counter the feelings of weakness and hopelessness that sapped the effectiveness of the covenant community. The visions showed that the LORD had not forgotten his people, and that he would protect them, overthrow their enemies and provide for all the needs of his own people. Although the promises of God start from where the people were then, it is revealed that they reach forward to, and are centred on, the Messiah. This is particularly brought out in the prophetic enactment (6:9-15) in which Zechariah crowned the high priest in symbolic anticipation of the combined priestly and royal role that would be fulfilled by the Messiah.

The third aspect of Zechariah's ministry at this time is to be found in the prophetic discourse of chapters 7 and 8. In response to an inquiry from some Jews who were wondering how they should act in the changed circumstances of restoration to the land, Zechariah sets out the need for covenant obedience in every aspect of their living and the blessings that would follow from it. No mention is made of the completion of the Temple in 515 B.C., and this suggests that chapters 1-8 were written before that, no doubt by Zechariah himself.

*Zechariah 9-14.* Although there are problems in interpreting some of the details of Zechariah's visions, it is the second part of his prophecy (9-14) which has given it the reputation of being a difficult book. Jerome, the Biblical scholar noted for his translation of the Scriptures into Latin, began his comments on the second part of

50

Zechariah with the words: 'We pass from the obscure to the more obscure, and with Moses we enter cloud and darkness. Deep calls to deep in the voice of the floods of God, and the Spirit goes curling round in coils, and turns back on his own paths; we endure Labyrinthine wanderings, and we direct our blind footsteps by the thread of Christ.' Martin Luther wrote two commentaries on Zechariah. In the first of them, chapter 14 is passed over without a mention. In the second, he said, 'In this chapter I surrender, for I am not certain of what the prophet treats.'

Even so, subsequent writers have not shirked the challenge of Zechariah. Many modern scholars argue that chapters 9-14 were not written by Zechariah. Indeed it is common to consider chapters 9-11 and 12-14 as separate works that were only later added to Zechariah's prophecy. The differences in style and subject matter are, however, better understood in terms of the traditional hypothesis that they come from a subsequent stage of his ministry (perhaps over twenty years later) and deliberately adopt another style suited to the task of presenting the future of the people of God. This was done to encourage the faithful of his own day to continued loyalty to the LORD.

These chapters undoubtedly present many difficulties for the interpreter. But there are two features which are helpful.

*(1)* Though we do not know the precise details of when these messages were given, they were intended for the people of Zechariah's day. They must have made sense to them—though they may not have understood them completely. An interpretation which is based on factors inaccessible to Zechariah is therefore improbable.

*(2)* There is Jerome's 'thread of Christ'. A significant number of passages are referred to in the New Testament in connection with the life of Christ, and they provide fixed reference points which help elucidate others.

## Zechariah 1:1-6:  The Basis for Blessing

There was no escaping from the past in the Jerusalem of Zechariah's day. Everywhere one went or looked there were the charred ruins of the once grand city. They constituted a perpetual reminder of what had happened because of the past sins of the nation. But in the introductory message to this prophecy, the past is used as a warning for the present. 'Do not repeat the mistakes of your forefathers.' When Zechariah first spoke, the people had already begun the work of Temple restoration, but their motive for acting was as important as their actions themselves. The LORD wanted them to return to him with whole-hearted obedience.

**In the eighth month of the second year of Darius (***1:1***)** shows that Zechariah began his ministry two months after Haggai. The specific day of the month is not given, presumably because the message was not tied down to one specific occasion in the way that Haggai's messages seem to have been related to feast days or times when the people were gathered in Jerusalem. The eighth month began on 27th October, and so it is reasonable to think of this message as being delivered, probably on a number of occasions, in early November 520 B.C. As before (Hag. 1:1) the identification of the year in terms of the Persian king's reign shows the political subjugation of the LORD's people at this time. They had indeed returned to their land, but they had not regained their former independence. The children were still having to live with the consequences of the rebellion of former generations.

**The word of the LORD came** is a phrase characteristic of the prophets, especially Jeremiah and Ezekiel, and so it embodies the claim that Zechariah followed in their footsteps. He is described as **the prophet Zechariah son of Berekiah, the son of Iddo.** This genealogy contrasts with the rather anonymous introduction to Haggai. In Ezra 5:1 and 6:14 he is described as 'a descendant of Iddo,' literally 'son of Iddo,' where the Hebrew word 'son' is used to indicate a relationship spanning more than one generation. In Nehemiah 12 there is a list given of the priests and Levites who returned with Zerubbabel, and it is then stated that in the next generation the head of the priestly family of Iddo was Zechariah (Neh. 12:16). Now, though Zechariah was a popular name, it is likely that this refers to the same person as the prophet. In that case Zechariah was also a priest. Ezekiel had been one too (Ezk. 1:3), and Jeremiah also was of priestly descent (Jer. 1:1), though in his case it is unlikely that he ever functioned as one.

In Ezra and Nehemiah, no mention is made of Berekiah (or Berechiah, as his name is usually transliterated). Some have suggested that his name has been inserted here due to scribal confusion with the earlier Zechariah, son of Jeberekiah in Isaiah 8:2. But it is more probable that in Ezra only his better known grandfather is mentioned. Perhaps his father died relatively young and never attained the leading position in his clan.

Mention should also be made of the problem raised by our LORD's reference when he spoke to the Jews about 'the blood of Zechariah son of Berakiah, whom you murdered between the temple and the altar' (Mt. 23:35). If this indeed points to this prophet, it would give us otherwise unrecorded information abut his later life. But it is generally considered that the reference is to another Zechariah whose death is described in 2 Chronicles 24:20-22, even though he is there clearly identified as being the son of Jehoiada, the high priest, rather than of Berakiah, which might have been another name for the same person.

Zechariah's message begins abruptly. There is no formal indication of who is being addressed, but it is clearly the case that the prophet is speaking to the people of Jerusalem. **The LORD was very angry with your forefathers (1:2).** This was the inescapable fact that had shaped their national destiny over the previous century, and whose implications had still not been totally worked out. Because of the sin of his people and their unwillingness to mend their ways, the LORD had been angry with previous generations, culminating in the catastrophic events of 586 B.C. 'Your' should not be taken to imply a distancing of the prophet from those he addresses. Rather the phrase emphasises the people's links with the past. Unlike Haggai who urged them to rethink their position in the light of their own recent experience (Hag. 1:5-11; 2:15-17), Zechariah looks to their national history and the rebellious attitudes that had been repeatedly displayed (Jer. 7:25-26). The danger was that the current generation too would slip into wrong ways of thinking and acting, and so incur the same wrath. Later post-exilic generations acknowledged the accuracy of such a summary of the nation's past (Ezr. 9:7, 13; Neh. 9:26-27).

It is against the background of the attitude of past generations that Zechariah is commanded, **Therefore tell the people (1:3).** Literally, it is 'And say to them', which again is abrupt, but the intention is obvious. The people are being urged not to repeat the errors of the past. **This is what the LORD Almighty says.** The title the LORD Almighty, or the LORD of hosts, stresses the power of God and the vastness of his dominion. Its origin is no longer certain. It is not found in the earliest books of the Old Testament, but becomes common from the time of Samuel onwards, being used first by Hannah in her vow (1 Sam. 1:11). In 1 Samuel 17:45 reference is made to 'the LORD of hosts, the God of the armies of Israel', which supports the idea that the 'hosts' are the 'armies' of the LORD's people, and he is being presented as the one who leads them into battle and grants them success. He is 'the Lord, the LORD of hosts, the Mighty One of Israel' (Isa. 1:24) who himself fights his and their enemies. Even if that is the origin of the title, 'hosts' was readily extended to include much more than Israel's armies. Drawing on the occurrence of the term 'host' ('vast array' NIV) in Genesis 2:1—itself another possible origin of this name of God—it was used to emphasise the supreme control of the LORD over the realm he had created. He is the true king of the universe, before whom the seraphs continually call out, 'Holy, holy, holy is the LORD of hosts; the whole earth is full of his glory' (Isa. 6:3, 5). The NIV translation 'Almighty' is based on this understanding and reflects one of the ways the Septuagint, the early Greek version of the Old Testament, rendered the term. God has all the created realm under his control, and therefore a message relayed from him should be accorded the greatest respect. Three times this title is used of the LORD in this one verse to emphasise the extent and power of his dominion and therefore how ready the people should be to give careful consideration to the warning he gives them.

The message itself is very brief. **'Return to me,' declares the LORD Almighty, 'and I will return to you,' says the LORD Almighty.** This is the essence of the prophetic word of warning and of the promise attached to renewed obedience. The spiritual process involved had often been spelled out at key points in the nation's history, from their earliest days (Deut. 4:27-31; 30:2-10), at the inauguration of the Temple (1 Kgs. 8:47-48), and by the prophets (Jer. 3:11, 22; 4:1; Ezk. 33:11). It will be taken up later by the prophet Malachi (Mal. 3:7). It is a promise based on the mercy of the forgiving God who receives graciously and loves freely (Hos. 14:2, 4). For those seeking the thrill of some prophetic disclosure of future events, it must have been a great disappointment. It was not a new message, but the truth required repetition.

'Return' has many shades of meaning in Hebrew. It is primarily a verb of physical motion, and so could here be construed of a return to the land of promise. In doing so the people had in one sense returned to the LORD. But their physical return to the land of the LORD's inheritance had to be matched by a spiritual return in obedience to him. It was all very well that they had made such great sacrifices in leaving Babylon—sacrifices many of their contemporaries had been unwilling to make—but now they must ensure that they had learned the spiritual lessons from the past. When they come in repentance to the LORD, giving him first place in their lives, then they will know the closeness of his presence. The message emphasises the personal nature of the bond that existed between the covenant LORD and his people. It does not imply they had had second thoughts about their decision to proceed with the work on the Temple. Rather it indicates that their attitudes were not yet wholly right, and there was no scope for spiritual slothfulness.

**Do not be like your forefathers (*1:4*).** There is always a strong influence from one generation to the next. But the bad example of their forefathers was such that they had to make a conscious effort to distance themselves from the attitudes of the past, especially with regard to the LORD and his messengers. Their forefathers had been the ones **to whom the earlier prophets proclaimed: This is what the LORD Almighty says: 'Turn from your evil ways and your evil practices.'** The use of the phrase 'the earlier prophets' (cf. 7:7, 12) shows that there was now no doubt about the status of prophets like Isaiah, Jeremiah and Ezekiel. Their message had already become normative and canonical for the community. Their warnings about the impending catastrophic judgment of God had come true, and there was no doubt left that they were divinely sent messengers and their message authentic. That they are called 'earlier' or 'former' indicates the searing impact that the Exile had made on the thinking of the community. A line was drawn under what had gone before. But there is the obvious claim that Zechariah is continuing in the line of former prophets, though in a different situation. The message given to previous generations was that of the need for repentance and abandonment of their evil ways and practices. Insofar as 'ways' (Mal. 2:8) and 'practices' can be distinguished, the former would refer to a general outlook on life and style of conduct, whereas 'practices' is more specific particular actions. There are many passages in the earlier prophets where such messages can be found (Jer. 18:11; 25:5; 35:15; Ezk. 33:11), but there is no need to identify any one of them as forming the basis for Zechariah's citation. It is the essence of the prophetic warning delivered on many occasions that is being mentioned here.

The sad fact was that the repeated warnings given to the people before the Exile had not been heeded. **But they would not listen or pay attention to me, declares the LORD.** The people had been so hardened in their attitudes that they were unresponsive to the warnings that were given to them.

The questions in the next verse are difficult to interpret. **Where are your forefathers now?** (*1:5*). This is obviously a rhetorical question, asked not to solicit new information but to reinforce a point. But what point is being made, and why? One way of understanding it is that the first question is asked by the prophet to underscore the fact that past generations suffered the due reward of their intransigence. Their forefathers had been killed or taken into captivity. That's what happens to those who continually neglect the word of God. The words, **And the prophets, do they live for ever?** might then be a retort by the people, in effect saying, 'What is so significant about the death of our forefathers? The prophets have died too.' This would be to suggest that they were trying to escape the thrust of the prophet's challenge. However, this understanding seems at variance with the spiritual outlook of the people at the time.

It is more probable that both questions are addressed to the people, and point to the transitory nature of human life. Both the past generations—no matter what their sin—and the prophets—no matter how faithfully they had delivered the LORD's message—had passed away. None could deny that. The point is not the similar fate endured by bad and good alike. Rather the thrust of the questions is to bring home the fact that there is no immunity from the march of time. The people are being urged to recognise their need to respond *now*, while the opportunity is afforded to them. 'Your forefathers passed away, and the prophets who brought them the message of warning have passed away too. No matter who we are, the time will come when the place that knows us now will know us no more for ever. Make sure then that you do not neglect the warnings that God's current messengers are bringing to you, for rest assured the divine message does not pass away.' When considering the lessons of the past, there is always the need not to dwell there, but to address ourselves to what we should be doing now, because our life here is finite (Eccl. 9:10; Jn. 9:4; Eph. 5:16).

**But did not my words and my decrees, which I commanded my servants the prophets, overtake your forefathers? (*1:6*).** The answer is, of course, 'Yes'. There was no disputing the fact that the warnings of the LORD did come true. Previous generations had not passed away unaffected by his sentence against them. Because they had broken the requirements of the covenant, the curse of the broken covenant had come upon them. If that had come true in the case of their forefathers, then the people of Zechariah's day could be sure that it would in their case also, if they neglected the LORD's requirements and warnings.

'Overtake' pictures a pursuer capturing someone who is fleeing, a hunter catching his game, or a wild animal grasping its prey (Gen. 31:25; Ex. 14:9; 15:9). So their forefathers were pursued and caught by the inescapable curse of God. This metaphor is also found in Deuteronomy 28:15, 45, which provides a probable background for this passage. 'Words and decrees' would then refer to the curses of the covenant found in Deuteronomy 28:15-68. For 'decrees', see Malachi 3:7. They formed the basis of the warnings conveyed by the prophets.

**"Then they repented and said, 'The LORD Almighty has done to us what our ways and practices deserve, just as he determined**

to do.'" The problem is that of determining who 'they' are: is it a reference to the forefathers, or to the current generation? It seems more likely to refer to previous generations, as the NIV punctuation indicates. (The quotation marks and the new paragraph are a translators' device to bring out what they consider to be the meaning of the passage. They do not correspond here to anything in the original text.) When the punishment of the LORD had come upon them, they were brought to recognise its justice, and the folly of the way they had been behaving. 'The LORD is righteous, yet I rebelled against his command' (Lam. 1:18).

But it is not a picture of impending doom that is presented. It is rather a challenge to faithfulness. Zechariah points to the fact that it had taken the trauma of the destruction of Jerusalem and the Exile to bring the previous generation to their spiritual senses (Lam. 2:17; Dan. 9:4-14). They had been forced to recognise that the LORD's warnings were not idle, and that their own expectations and conduct had been blameworthy. But that recognition had come too late as far as they were concerned, because the calamity had already engulfed them. However, it was not too late for the generation that had been restored to Jerusalem, if only they were prepared to learn the lessons of the past. They must ensure that they were living close to God, or all their enterprises would also be liable to be swept away. They are being challenged to live obediently, without God having to chasten them to bring them to their senses.

Zechariah begins by showing that although the work on the Temple has resumed—and that is good—it needs to be accompanied by a total inner commitment to God. Obedience and faithfulness are to be practised not just in one but in every respect. Thus the people who had begun well are being urged to continue, and not to presume that rebuilding the Temple makes their lives totally right with God. There is the need for ongoing repentance and a close walk with him.

Cynics often argue that the only lesson we learn from history is that we don't learn lessons from history. Certainly the pace of change which has drastically increased the rate of technical obsolescence in our modern world—even at the level of the gadgetry that is to be found in our homes—reinforces the attitude that the knowledge of yesterday is outmoded and irrelevant. But whatever may be true in the realms of science and technology, what has happened in the past still provides valuable spiritual lessons. Our environment may have changed; our nature has not. We delude ourselves if we think we are morally or spiritually superior to the past. Just as there were lessons for Zechariah's generation to learn from the past, so too there are for ours. As Paul said in discussing the significance of Israel's history, 'Now these things occurred as examples to keep us from setting our hearts on evil things as they did ... These things happened to them as examples and were written down as warnings for us, on whom the fulfilment of the ages has come' (1 Cor. 10:6, 11). Nowhere is this need greater than in the lesson Zechariah was teaching of the need to turn away from our evil practices and come in repentance to God.

*Study Questions*

**1:3** What does the New Testament have to say about God's attitude towards those who return to him with repentance? (Lk. 15; Jas. 4:8-10).

**1:5** What are we to learn from the brevity of life? (Job 14:10-12; Ps. 90:10) How should it affect our present conduct? Is it morbid and unhealthy to remind people that they are going to die one day?

## VISIONS OF JERUSALEM'S FUTURE (Zech. 1:7–6:15)

The second division of Zechariah's prophecy (1:7-6:15) consists principally of eight visions which were divinely granted to him. The LORD had said he would reveal himself to those who were his prophets in visions and in dreams (Num. 12:6). It is not entirely clear what constituted the difference between them, except that in a vision it would appear that the prophet was able to interact with what was presented to him whereas in a dream he was a passive viewer of what was revealed. Visions were not confined to the night-time. Zechariah's occurred at night, but he may not have been asleep in the ordinary sense of the term when he received them. Notice the careful use of language in 4:1, 'wakened me, *as* a man is wakened from his sleep'. But he was certainly no longer aware of his ordinary surroundings. In the Old Testament, visions were particularly associated with Ezekiel, Daniel and Zechariah. It is the apostle John in the book of Revelation who is the principal New Testament recipient (Rev. 9:17), but note also Peter and Paul (Acts 10:17; 16:9). Paul had such a vivid awareness of what was being revealed to him in one vision, that he could not tell whether he had been bodily transported to the third heaven or not (2 Cor. 12:1).

In Zechariah's visions there are a number of common features, in that the scene is described and the interpreting angel is often present both to quiz the prophet as to his understanding of what he was seeing and to answer his questions about what he did not understand. The visions are never left as conundrums, but are explained.

Not only are there features that are found throughout the visions, there is also a thematic connection between the visions. Vision 1 (1:7-11) presents the message of the LORD's concern for Zion, which is elaborated on in vision 2 (1:18-21) in terms of the overthrow of her enemies, and in vision 3 (2:1-13) in terms of the protection and prosperity of the restored community. The two central visions that follow form a pair, focusing on the two leaders of the community— Joshua, the high priest, and Zerubbabel, the governor. Through the reinstatement of the high priest, vision 4 (3:1-10) shows how the community can be accepted before God. Vision 5 (4:1-14) focuses principally on the governor, and reveals the source of the community's strength in serving the LORD. Visions 6 (5:1-4) and 7 (5:5-11) deal with the need for purity within the community. The last vision (6:1-8) features, as did the first, horses and angelic messengers, showing the universal scope of the LORD's dominion.

A number of times in the reports of the visions, what is being said is connected with the person and work of the Messiah (2:6-13; 3:8-9; 4:14). This 'thread of Christ' culminates in the final section of this division of the book where Zechariah symbolically crowns the high priest to portray the coming unity of priest and king (6:9-15). This would be realised in the Messiah, and provides the key to the fulfilment of all the visions. It is only in Christ that the blessing and security of the people of God will be achieved.

The visions are not intended to be merely personal experiences for the prophet. They convey to him truth that he is to pass on to the people of Jerusalem. Their purpose is to encourage them to abandon the survive-for-the-moment mentality that persisted among them and to persevere in the work they are undertaking, by setting before them the glorious promises of God concerning their future as the people of God. This was a ministry of consolation to the struggling remnant in the land. They could locate themselves in terms of the LORD's future prospects which extended to include the Messiah and the advance of his cause in New Testament times.

## Zechariah 1:7-17: Vision 1: Among the Myrtle Trees

The people of Zechariah's day were unsettled and uncertain. They were not sure what was happening to them and how God was working in their lives and in the lives of the nations around them. Their perplexity was undermining their confidence, and so God sent Zechariah to show them that he had not abandoned his people. By means of the symbolic representations of the visions, God revealed to them the spiritual dimension to the events of their day. In this first vision it is emphasised that all human life is under God's supervision, and the situation of his people is near to his heart.

**On the twenty-fourth day of the eleventh month, the month of Shebat, in the second year of Darius** (*1:7*) again places the revelation that was given against the background of the foreign control over the life of the people. Previously they had been able to date events in terms of their own ruling kings, but now their lives were controlled by foreigners. This verse corresponds to 1:1 except for the change of date, which is equivalent to 15th February 519 B.C. in our calendar. It is therefore some three months after Zechariah's first recorded address (1:1), and five months after work had begun on rebuilding the Temple (Hag. 1:15). Shebat, the Babylonian name for the month, is used (see also 7:1). The existence of this second introductory title may indicate that the visions were recorded separately before being incorporated into the prophecy as we now have it.

**The word of the LORD came to the prophet Zechariah son of Berekiah, the son of Iddo.** The passage ends with the word 'saying' (not translated in the NIV), which in Hebrew usually introduces direct speech. But on this occasion the message from the LORD takes the form of a vision. Note the use of 'word', although the passage goes on to describe a vision. These are usually thought to be two different modes of revelation, but perhaps Scripture does not make as decided a break as we might.

*The Vision (1:8-11).* **During the night** (*1:8*) relates specifically to the night mentioned in the introduction of verse 7. There is no reason to suppose that these visions were not given to Zechariah on the one night. **I had a vision** renders what is simply 'I saw', but there can be no doubt that it was a vision Zechariah had. He deliberately avoids the word 'I dreamed' to indicate that he was conscious and able to participate in what he saw. That this happened at night may well reflect that it was a time when he was less likely to be disturbed.

**There before me was a man riding a red horse!** The focus is on this individual, to the extent that it is never explicitly said that the other horses had riders on them. His identity is further clarified in 1:10-11 where he is called the Angel of the LORD. He was mounted on horseback, though as Zechariah saw him **he was standing**, or stationary, in that the horse was drawn to a halt.

In interpreting the visions we have to decide what significance is to be attached to the details given; for instance, the fact that it was a *red* horse. One approach is to treat them as merely incidental. Red, or whatever other colour is mentioned, is only a way of distinguishing one horse from another. It shows that it was a real horse that Zechariah saw, and not one of the extraordinary figures he was later to encounter, such as the women with wings (5:9). But the fact of its being specifically *red* has, in this view, no separate significance.

On the other hand, it is noticeable that the amount of detail given by Zechariah as he relates the visions is sparse, and that what he does say may on that account be presumed to be significant. Red is the colour of blood, and so is associated with judgment and vengeance (Isa. 63:1-2). In Revelation 6 mention is made of four horses—white, fiery red, black and pale. Though it is not possible to equate them with either group of horses in Zechariah (1:8; 6:2-3), yet the role assigned to the riders of the horses can shed light here. The rider of the red horse 'was given power to take peace from the earth and to make men slay each other' (Rev. 6:4). Here the rider is on a red horse to indicate his attitude of hostility towards the nations (1:15). He has the authority and power to punish those who have offended God.

It is unlikely that we are to pass over the further details added that the man and the horse were **among the myrtle trees in a ravine.** It is possible that Zechariah's visions were seen against a background that was familiar to him. Since the Hebrew is literally 'in the ravine', if any definite location is sought, nothing more specific may be intended than a reference to the lower part of the valley of Kidron outside Jerusalem, where there was a deep gorge with many myrtle trees. We would then have a picture of the Angel of the LORD outside the city indicating that they did not yet fully enjoy the blessings of the LORD's presence with them, but at the same time he was not far from the city, and was watching over it protectively. Indeed, the Angel was receiving the reports of the horsemen because he was going to order the affairs of the world to suit his plans for his people.

There may perhaps be even more indicated by this description. Myrtles are shrubs that are common in Palestine. (There is nothing in the Hebrew text to correspond to 'tree'.) They grow on hillsides, and reach a height of 2-3 metres, though perhaps higher in a less exposed location such as the valley mentioned here. They have fragrant dark-green leaves and scented white flowers. They are referred to as replacing the brier in the wilderness when the LORD restores the fortunes of his people (Isa. 41:19; 55:13), and may be an apt symbol of the restored community. They were not yet enjoying the full favour of God, and so the myrtles are represented as being in a valley, symbolising their lowly condition, indeed their distress (Ps. 88:6). But the Angel of the LORD who cares for them is in their midst, and it is with reference to them that he receives the reports of the horsemen.

**Behind him were red, brown and white horses.** Obviously we must assume that these horses had angelic riders, who later report to the Angel of the LORD (1:11). Horses are used to indicate the speed and thoroughness with which these angelic beings carried out the mission assigned them by their leader. The colours of the horses are of significance, representing the variety of God's dealings with the nations. Red, as we have seen, symbolises bloodshed, war and judgment. White, as well as being associated with purity, is the colour of triumph, victory, peace and joy (Rev. 2:17; 6:2; 19:11). The third colour, here rendered 'brown', has perplexed translators since earliest times. It may well represent a colour between red and white, that is, brown, bay or sorrel, or else a dappled appearance. In either case it symbolises a mixed state of affairs, neither peace nor war, neither victory nor defeat.

Zechariah is at first unable to work out what it all means. **I asked, "What are these, my lord?"** (*1:9*). 'Lord' is merely a title of respect, and does not indicate that Zechariah was according divine status to the angel when he asked about the assembled horsemen. **The angel who was talking with me answered, "I will show you what they are."** Notice that the angel who was talking with him (often known as the interpreting angel) is not the same person as the man on the red horse in 1:8. (For angels in general, see on Mal. 3:1). He was a divine messenger, for that is what the word 'angel' signifies in Hebrew—commissioned by God to explain to the prophet what he was seeing, similar to the angel who attended John in Revelation (Rev. 17:1, 7; 19:9; 21:9, 15; 22:1, 6, 8-9).

But it is not the angel with whom Zechariah was speaking who answers. Perhaps we are to picture him as being on the point of replying when the other figure, who presumably was close to them, speaks. **Then the man standing among the myrtle trees explained, "They are the ones the LORD has sent to go throughout the earth"** (*1:10*). He had heard Zechariah's inquiry, and responded to it directly. The picture being used seems to be derived from the practice of the Persian emperors. They maintained a very efficient system of messengers to keep them informed of all events in their realms. It was also the case that the Persian emperor sent inspectors to each of the satrapies every year to report on what was happening there, so as to be in a position to rectify any administrative blunders and also forestall any possible trouble. Here it is the LORD of all the earth who has sent his messengers out to carry out a similar mission, going throughout his domains to make a careful assessment of the state of affairs. Perhaps the response involved him pointing to the other angels. He does not include himself among those who are so described. He is their commanding officer.

**And they reported to the angel of the LORD, who was standing among the myrtle trees (*1:11*).** The Angel was 'standing' as in 1:8. As he had looked and gestured in their direction, the horsemen take it that they are to report on their recent commission. The angels are those who do God's commands, and now report on what they had done, having been sent out to reconnoitre.

The description of verse 11 clearly identifies the man mentioned in verses 8 and 10 as standing among the myrtle trees with the Angel of the LORD. This title is used elsewhere in Scripture for a somewhat enigmatic figure, who sometimes is portrayed as angelic and at other times as one with the rights and prerogatives of deity. He can speak in the first person as God (Gen. 16:10; 31:11-13; Ex. 3:2-6; Judg. 6:12-14), and he received worship (Ex. 3:5; Josh. 5:14). When Manoah and his wife saw him, he thought they were doomed to die because he had seen God (Judg. 13:22). He should be identified as the one who appeared to Abraham in the plains of Mamre, and with whom Abraham pleaded for the cities of the plain (Gen. 18). He came to Jacob before his meeting with Esau and wrestled with him (Gen. 32:22-32). He appeared to Moses at the burning bush (Ex. 3:1-14) and to Joshua at Jericho where he had a drawn sword in his hand and explained that he had come as the captain of the LORD's armies (Josh. 5:13-15). He is found again at Zechariah 3:1, and probably is present at 2:3 and 6:7 also. He is generally understood to be a pre-incarnate appearance of the Second Person of the Trinity in angelic form. His presence on this occasion assures the people that God's care of them is the same as that shown in earlier periods of their history. That care is further seen in the petition of the following verses where the Angel expresses his watchful and compassionate concern for them.

The angelic messengers reported diligence in carrying out their mission, **We have gone throughout the earth and found the whole world at peace and rest.** There is no real reason to doubt the accuracy of this stage in Darius' reign. In his first few years he had to wage war on many fronts to secure his position, but by this stage in 519 B.C. he had effective control of the empire, and the period of unsettledness had quietened down. Questions may well be asked about the precise significance of the words rendered 'at rest and peace'. 'Rest' indicates sitting down relaxed (Isa. 13:20; Jer. 17:6,

25; Ezk. 26:20), and 'peace' is not the usual word *shalom* (see on Hag. 2:9), but another expression related to 'had rest' (Josh.11:23; 14:15). It may not refer to a contented peace, but simply to an absence of strife. It is, however, a description of a situation that contrasted with the current condition of the LORD's people, who might understandably have been perplexed by it. How could God have allowed the unbelieving world to settle down even to a measure of prosperity while his own people were still enduring great difficulties? It is never easy to read God's providence, but faith always grasps that even behind what is unfathomable 'in all things God works for the good of those who love him' (Rom. 8:28). That is the truth the vision is designed to emphasise.

*The Angel's Plea (1:12-13).* The contrast between the rest of the world and the situation of the LORD's people impels the Angel of the LORD to intercede on their behalf. This is the same ministry that the risen LORD still conducts on behalf of his church. He is 'the one who speaks to the Father in our defence' (1 Jn. 2:1) and who 'always lives to intercede' for those who come to God through him (Heb. 7:25). Since he is 'the Lamb that was slain from the creation of the world' (Rev. 13:8), the basis of his intercession is always the same—the efficacy of his own shed blood (Heb. 9:12).

The next two verses are the focus of the vision, containing its central message. **Then the angel of the LORD said, "LORD Almighty, how long will you withhold mercy from Jerusalem and from the towns of Judah, which you have been angry with these seventy years?"** (*1:12*). The divine designation, 'LORD Almighty', or LORD of hosts, suits this situation; it views God as the covenant God who is in command of all the created realm. What is happening here is his concern, and he has the right and power to intervene. 'How long?' recalls the plea uttered in many psalms when there was a tension between the reality the psalmist perceived around him and the promises given to faith (Ps. 6:3; 13:1-2; 80:4; 90:13; 94:3). The question proceeds on the basis that the covenant is still in some sense operative. There was no doubt that the LORD had been justifiably angry with the people because of their sin, but it had been prophesied that their exile would last for only seventy years (Jer. 25:11; 29:10).

That time has now elapsed, the time for the restoration of Zion has come (Ps. 102:13; Dan. 9:2), and the Angel of the LORD voices the question of how much longer the delay is going to be. Such intercession is appropriate to the one who 'always lives to intercede', imploring divine compassion and interposition on behalf of the covenant people.

There are problems over the calculation of the seventy years. One approach is to start with the first encroachment of Babylon into Judah in 605 B.C. and to count forward to the time when the exiles returned from Babylon around 537 B.C. which gives a period of roughly seventy years. It seems to be this period that is in mind in certain passages of Scripture, such as Daniel 9:2. It is also possible to arrive at seventy years by starting with the destruction of Jerusalem and the Temple in 586 B.C. and counting through to the completion of the rebuilding of the Temple in 515 B.C. Insofar as the Angel's words imply that the period of the LORD's anger has not yet come to an end, it would seem that the latter calculation is in mind here.

**So the LORD spoke kind and comforting words to the angel who talked with me (*1:13*).** These words constitute something of a problem in that the Angel of the LORD had addressed the LORD but the LORD replies to the interpreting angel. Although the Angel's prayer had been offered to God the Father (compare 3:2), it is unlikely that the Father is to be considered as speaking here. It is the Angel who answers, sure that the plea implicit in his questions will have a favourable response. There is nothing incongruous in such a change from the LORD to the Angel, in that both are divine. The same change occurs in other passages of the Old Testament where the Angel of the LORD is found (Ex. 3:2, 4; Judg. 6:12, 14). The description of his speech as 'kind and comforting words' may perhaps be intended to recall the words of Isaiah 40:1, 'Comfort, comfort my people, says your God'. The assurance of God's presence brings relief even in the most overwhelming circumstances. 'Even though I walk through the valley of the shadow of death, I will fear no evil, for you are with me; your rod and your staff, they comfort me' (Ps. 23:4).

*The LORD's Jealousy (1:14-15).* The remaining verses give greater detail about what the kind and comforting words were. **Then the**

**angel who was speaking to me said, "Proclaim this word" (*1:14*).**
The message of comfort and consolation is not just for the angelic
figures, or even for the prophet. He is to act as the LORD's spokesman
and convey the message to the community. The message to be given
is of course from the LORD himself. **I am very jealous for Jerusalem
and Zion.** Literally, it is 'I am jealous <with> great jealousy'.
Jealousy is often misunderstood because it leads to wrong reactions
by sinful humans (Prov. 6:34; 27:4; 2 Cor. 12:20; Gal. 5:20). But in
God it is seen in a proper fashion as the reaction of love when it sees
the bond of love threatened either by external factors or by the
weakening affection of the other partner (see also on 8:2). God's love
for his people is not a weak emotion (Ex. 34:14; Deut. 29:20). His
anger is aroused when the relationship is threatened, and when others
take improper action against those who are his. He is determined to
promote the well-being of his people against any who would interfere
with the city called by his name, the place where he had chosen to put
his name. He had remembered Zion even though their rebellion had
forced him to chastise them. He was intolerant of any rivalry or
unfaithfulness.

There is therefore a corresponding reaction on the LORD's part to
those who are wrongfully threatening his people. This is brought out
in the Hebrew, where verse 14 ends with the words 'great jealousy'
and verse 15 begins with 'great anger'. **But I am very angry with
the nations that feel secure (*1:15*).** This is a reference to the nations
that were oppressing Jerusalem, particularly the Persians, but also
those in Samaria and Edom that were hostile to the rebuilding efforts
in Jerusalem. They were at ease and certain that nothing would
disturb their prosperity. The word is also used of the careless or carnal
security of those who have no fear of God before their eyes ('the
proud' in Ps. 123:4; 'complacent' in Isa. 32:9, 11; Amos 6:1; 'at rest'
in Jer. 48:11). **I was only a little angry,** that is with Judah when she
was punished. 'A little' may also possibly be understood as a
temporal expression, 'I was angry only for a little time.' **But they
added to the calamity.** Although they had been given by God a role
in carrying out his sentence against his people, they had exceeded
what it was proper for them to do. They were so intent on conquest
and plunder that they took full advantage of the situation, not

realising that there were divine limits on how far they were permitted to go (Isa. 10:5-27). In this way they incurred divine wrath on themselves.

Knowing this also helped the Jews reassess their national experience. The LORD had truly undertaken to fight against them 'with an outstretched hand and a mighty arm in anger and fury and great wrath' (Jer. 21:5). But what had befallen them was more than had been divinely authorised in just retribution for their sin. Perhaps this explains why the Angel of the LORD is shown on a red horse, as indicating his avenging jealousy on behalf of his people. He was ready to subdue and destroy all their foes.

*The LORD's Promises (1:16-17).* **Therefore (*1:16*)** introduces the divine resolution of the situation. First there is the declaration that the LORD's presence will once more be known among the people. **This is what the LORD says: 'I will return to Jerusalem with mercy'.** The verb is literally 'I have returned'. There is, however, a Hebrew idiom known as the 'prophetic perfect' in which the verb form that is usually associated with the past is used of a future event which is so certain that it is conceived of as already completed. The NIV is probably correct in finding that idiom used here. The past translation does also make sense. It could refer either to the LORD as having returned in the presence of the Angel of the LORD, or to the return of his Spirit (Hag. 2:5).

In whatever way the return is understood, it is an answer to the prayer of 1:12. 'Mercy' is God's deep, unconditioned love. Because of their sin, any such compassion had been withdrawn from them at the time of the Exile (Isa. 27:11), but he is the one who again has compassion, or displays mercy (Ps. 102:14; Mic. 7:19). He is like a father showing compassion on his children (Ps. 103:13), because he is the LORD who 'longs to be gracious to you; he rises to show you compassion' (Isa. 30:18).

Next there are three specific promises.

*(1)* **There my house will be rebuilt.** The people need not worry that their efforts to rebuild the Temple will be frustrated by their enemies' opposition. There is a divine guarantee that their work will reach a successful conclusion. This happened four years later. 'The

temple was completed on the third day of the month Adar, in the sixth year of the reign of King Darius', that is, 12th March 515 B.C. (Ezra 6:15).

*(2)* The work of rebuilding extends from the Temple to the whole city. **'And the measuring line will be stretched out over Jerusalem,' declares the LORD Almighty.** The line was used to measure distances, or around circular objects (1 Kgs. 7:23), while the plumbline was employed for vertical drops (Isa. 28:17). Jeremiah had given a description of the rebuilt city in which the measuring line was used to determine its perimeter (Jer. 31:39), and it seems to be such use by a surveyor (rather than carpenter or builder) that is intended here. Perhaps the picture is one of plots being measured off in the ruined city so that a major building programme could proceed. Such activity started under Nehemiah (Neh. 2:5) but reached its peak around 200 B.C. when many buildings were constructed. A later period of expansion occurred under Herod the Great (37-4 B.C.).

*(3)* The third promise goes beyond Jerusalem to bring the other cities of Judea into the picture of prosperity. **Proclaim further: This is what the LORD Almighty says: 'My towns will again overflow with prosperity'** *(1:17)*. It is a picture of such increase in size that they can no longer be contained within their original limits. Compare the picture of Jerusalem in 2:4.

But there is a further element. **The LORD will again comfort Zion and choose Jerusalem.** While it is possible to treat these words as recapitulating the thought with which the message began in the previous verse, it seems to point to something else. The LORD had more in store for his people than material blessings. These signs of his favour anticipated the greatest gift of all that he would give them, his Son. He truly was 'the consolation of Israel' (Lk. 2:25). This was not something that was theirs by merit or right, but bestowed because God had sovereignly chosen them (Isa. 41:8-9). Their destiny was determined by the action of God, and because of that they could face the future with confidence.

God had not abandoned his people. Their perplexity can be resolved in the light of his watchful guard over them, and the intercession that is made on their behalf. From the fact of his choice there can be built up a glorious chain of consequences for their well-being (Rom. 8:30). Often there may be circumstances that puzzle us, just as the situation of their own day puzzled Zechariah's contemporaries. How had God let the nations get the upper hand and stay in power, especially when there were the promises that had already been given to Haggai that they would soon be shaken (Hag. 2:6-7)? But this was to test their faith and lead them to put their confidence in the promises of God. Outward appearances are never a sure indicator that all is well. What has to be taken into account is the LORD's judgment on the situation. His people's misery always evokes his care and concern (Ex. 3:7-9; Isa. 63:9).

*Study Questions*

**1:12** What is the basis of intercessory prayer? What is there in common between the church's intercession and the Lord's? Rom. 8:34; Eph. 1:16; 6:18; 2 Thess. 1:11-12; 3:1-2; 1 Tim. 2:1-2; 1 Jn. 5:14.

**1:13** How is comfort made available to the believer? Jn. 14:1; 2 Cor. 1:3-7; 2:7; 7:6-7; Phil. 2:1; 1 Thess. 3:7; 4:18; 2 Thess. 2:16.

**1:14** Is jealousy still an appropriate characteristic to attribute to God? How may we provoke him to jealousy? Ex. 20:5; Deut. 6:13-16; 29:19-20; 1 Kgs. 14:22; 1 Cor. 10:18-22; Jas. 4:4-5.

**Zechariah 1:18-21: Vision 2: Four Horns and Four Craftsmen**
The second vision that Zechariah is shown is closely related to the first. In it the anger of the LORD against those who oppressed his people had been expressed (1:15), but the consequences for those nations were not stated. In the second vision judgment is seen coming on those who had harassed and devastated the LORD's people.

There seems to be no break from the first vision as Zechariah proceeds, **Then I looked up** (*1:18*). Literally, this is 'and I lifted up my eyes and saw', a phrase which also occurs later (2:1; 5:1, 9; 6:1) to introduce visions Zechariah had. It is found in Daniel 8:3 and 10:5

as well. It conveys the picture of the prophet deeply engrossed in thinking about what he had just seen, when he becomes aware of something else and focuses his attention on a new vision that the LORD is setting before him.

There is an element of surprise in the statement **and there before me were four horns!** The word 'horn' refers to the growth on the head of an animal such as a ram or ox. Horns were used as musical instruments and also as containers. Because of their shape, the projecting corners of the altar were also known as horns (Ex. 30:2-3). But what is relevant here is that 'horn' is a widespread scriptural metaphor for strength and power (Ps. 18:2; 75:4-5; 89:17; 92:10; 112:9; Jer. 48:25; Lam. 2:3, 17; Mic. 4:13). How this arose can be easily seen, in that the horn is used by the animal to defend itself and also to attack. It is the horn that is displayed as a trophy when the hunter has captured a wild beast. In Daniel 7 and 8 horns symbolise the power of nations, and it is something similar that is intended here.

There is no mention made of any animals, but that need not surprise us – there was no mention of any riders on the horses in the previous vision. Zechariah only records what is significant for understanding the vision. It may have been the case that the horns he saw belonged to some dimly-perceived animals, but the stress is on the horns themselves. Hebrew has a word for 'a pair of horns', but it is not used here. So we are to think of four separate horns, not of two pairs.

Zechariah would have had no difficulty in identifying the horns as horns, but their significance eluded him. We thus find him again asking questions of the interpreting angel. **I asked the angel who was speaking to me, "What are these?"** (*1:19*).

**He answered me, "These are the horns that scattered Judah, Israel and Jerusalem."** The further explanation given in 1:21 shows that it is foreign powers that are being thought of. The unusual order in which Judah, Israel and Jerusalem are mentioned has given rise to much speculation. One might have expected Israel to be mentioned before Judah in that the Northern Kingdom with its capital at Samaria was overthrown earlier in 722 B.C. As it is here mentioned between Judah and Jerusalem, it has been suggested that 'Israel' does not refer to the former Northern Kingdom, but to God's chosen people, who are now to be found in Judah (see on Mal. 1:1). What is being said is then, 'Judah, even the true Israel'. But it seems more probable that despite the word order the reference is to the Northern Kingdom. It is mentioned in second place, because the focus of God's purposes is primarily on those who have survived in the south.

Should we then identify the four horns as four specific powers? Early Christian interpreters were aware of the possibility of references to Assyria, Babylon, Medes/Persians, and Greece, or possibly Rome. They did so by setting Zechariah's description against Daniel's earlier and specific description of the four beasts (Dan. 7). Zechariah could have used this material, though it is not certain when Daniel's prophecies became generally available in Judah. However, Zechariah does not follow up the references to the four. Elsewhere he uses the figure of the four winds to refer to a universal phenomenon (2:6; 6:1-8). So it is probable that only a general reference is intended to the antagonism that had been shown on every side to the people of God. They had to deal with widespread, not isolated, instances of hostility.

The visionary experience did not end with the representation of the hostility being shown on all sides to the people of God. That would hardly have been news, or conveyed comfort. We also read, **Then the LORD showed me four craftsmen (1:20).** Zechariah stresses that he became aware of these four figures because the LORD revealed them to him in a special way. This fits in with their role in the vision as being the ones who carry out God's purpose against the hostile nations.

Zechariah is able to recognise them as craftsmen. The Hebrew word is of fairly general application, and can describe artisans who are skilled in the working of wood (2 Kgs. 12:12), stone (Ex. 28:11), or most commonly metal (1 Chr. 29:5; Jer. 10:9). It is the last possibility that seems most relevant here. The men are probably some type of blacksmith, not because the horns they are going to deal with are metal, but because metal tools are needed to deal with them. Sometimes 'craftsman' or 'smith' is used with ominous implications, as for instance in Ezekiel 21:31 where 'men skilled in destruction' is literally 'smiths of destruction'. Here there are four of them— just the right number to match the hostile horns.

**I asked, "What are these coming to do?"** (*1:21*) indicates that it was more than the way they were dressed that enabled Zechariah to identify them as craftsmen. He is aware that they are carrying out some task—possibly because they had tools with them. It would seem that in the vision these men were coming to remove the horns of the animals. This would have been something that would be done when a wild animal was captured and going to be kept alive in captivity, or if its horns were to be used as a trophy in some way. It was probably also the case that tame animals with horns had the tips of them removed for safety reasons.

The angel who talked with him **answered, "These are the horns that scattered Judah so that no-one could raise his head".** The focus is now on the events that culminated in the capture and sack of Jerusalem in 586 B.C. The picture of being unable to raise the head is one of utter conquest and subjugation (Judg. 8:28). The horns are identified as the hostile powers that had wrought such havoc in the past. Their successes are going to be overturned.

**The craftsmen have come to terrify them.** Since 'them' is masculine, it does not refer to the horns (a feminine word in Hebrew), but to the nations represented by the horns. The craftsmen may be angelic figures, but more probably they represent the human agents through whom the LORD effects his purposes. This is what is behind the power politics and events on the world stage—the LORD is working out his purposes. What happens goes beyond the symbolic picture. The terror is obviously part of what is felt by the world powers as they see other powers arise to threaten their position and indeed go so far as to overthrow them. There is to be a fitting return for their own actions. The craftsmen as instruments of divine retribution have as their intention **to throw down these horns of the nations who lifted up their horns against the land of Judah to scatter its people.** The nations had used their power (horns) against the LORD's people. Now their horns are going to be cut off and cast on to the ground, as their power proves insufficient before the new challenge and they themselves are going to be at an utter loss to know what to do.

God has not promised his people that there will be no opposition to them. Quite the contrary: opposition is to be expected. There may be times when 'the church ... enjoyed a time of peace' (Acts 9:31), but typically each age has witnessed determined and powerful enemies rise up against the church. However, opposition is not the same as defeat. God is true to his promise that 'no weapon forged against you will prevail' (Isa. 54:17), and has raised up agents who effectively disposed of those who would scatter his church. In times of crisis faith is called on to trust in him, certain of his watchful concern (Acts 7:56) and awaiting his intervention in power.

*Study Questions*

**1:19** What attitude are we to expect the world to show to the church today? In what ways will its hatred express itself? How are we to react? Jn. 15:20; 2 Tim. 3:12; Jas. 2:6-7; 1 Jn. 3:13; Rev. 2:10.

**Zechariah 2:1-13: Vision 3: The Man with the Measuring Line**
The third vision, like the second, provides more detail about the future prospects of the restored people which had been outlined in the first vision. But, whereas the second vision had pointed to the fate awaiting those who had oppressed Judah, the focus is now on the LORD's return to Jerusalem with mercy, when it will be rebuilt and the towns of Judah overflow with prosperity (1:16-17). The main problem in interpreting the vision is to decide on the time and manner of its fulfilment. Is it in the centuries after Nehemiah had the walls of Jerusalem rebuilt? Or, is this an Old Testament picture of what is enjoyed by the church, culminating in the heavenly Jerusalem? Or, are we to expect a literal rebuilding of Jerusalem in some future millennial period? It is the second of these options that is adopted in this commentary, and a detailed argument for it is presented in the Appendix.

*The Vision (2:1-4a).* The previous scene has faded, and while the prophet was pondering its significance, another view presses itself on his attention. **Then I looked up (2:1)** uses the same phrase as in 1:18 to show that a divinely given vision interrupts Zechariah's train of thought. **There before me was a man with a measuring line in his hand!** Various views have been advanced as to the identity of this man. *(1)* Although the anonymous man of 1:8 is later specified as the Angel of the LORD (1:11), such an identification is improbable here. It is much more likely that the Angel of the LORD is to be identified with the 'another angel' of 2:3 who comes with the message of the LORD. *(2)* A strong argument for taking the man in this verse as the interpreting angel is the fact that Zechariah questions the man in the next verse, and that is the role assigned to the interpreting angel in other visions. There would then be no doubt that the 'young man' of 2:4 was a reference to the prophet himself. But it would be unwise to make a generally observed pattern in the visions a straight-jacket to confine the interpretation of each. If the figure is angelic, then it must be assumed that his mission is divinely assigned. This seems to be at variance with the divine message of 2:4 which presents Jerusalem as without walls, stretching beyond measurable boundaries. *(3)* It therefore seems preferable to take the man as a man, representing the restored community of the prophet's day as they assessed the task that lay before them in rebuilding Jerusalem.

Zechariah himself enters into the action of the vision (compare 3:5). No doubt encouraged by the visions he had already received, he eagerly seeks information about what was now being so vividly portrayed to his inner consciousness. **I asked (2:2)** relates to a question from the prophet directly to the man he was seeing in the vision. He does not ask him who he is, or what he is going to do. The expression for measuring line is different from that of 1:16, but its purpose was obviously the same. **Where are you going?** Zechariah wanted to know what was to be measured, and by implication why it was to be measured.

**He answered me, "To measure Jerusalem, to find out how wide and how long it is."** This was an unusual way to try to measure the size of a city in the ancient world. It seems to reflect the way Ezekiel had talked about the size of the renewed city (Ezk. 45:6), or the picture that Jeremiah had presented of the measuring line stretching out over the rebuilt Jerusalem (Jer. 31:38-40). There is no verb in the original corresponding to 'it is'. All that is said is 'according to what its breadth and according to what its length'. The man represents the community as they try to work out the extent of the work that had to be undertaken. Notice that although the focus of their rebuilding at this time was the Temple, there is no mention of the Temple in this vision at all. It is the city that the focus is on. The divine reassurance of 2:5 indicates that the people were feeling exposed, wondering if their efforts in building the Temple would be overthrown if there were no fortifications round the city; yet, rebuilding the Temple was stretching their resources, so what would the position be if they undertook even more substantial work such as rebuilding the walls? They were trying to build their lives on the divine promises regarding Jerusalem's restoration, and yet were being baffled as they tried to reconcile what they could do with what God had said. This was often because their thinking was the thinking of the past. It did not measure up to the challenges of the future. What good had Jerusalem's walls been in 586 B.C.? What mattered was the relationship between Jerusalem's inhabitants and the LORD.

Before the conversation could proceed further, there was an interruption. The way the Hebrew is expressed suggests that this next action did not arise out of what had preceded. No doubt the interpreting angel had been beside Zechariah (as I think we must assume is the case in each vision), but now he acts. **Then the angel who was speaking to me left** (*2:3*), the idea being that the prophet noticed him as he was in the process of leaving, **and another angel came to meet him.** The identity of the other angel is not stated. He comes with a corrective message from the LORD which has to be relayed to Zechariah. What is said reminds one of the kind and comforting words spoken by the Angel of the LORD (1:13). This favours an identification of this angel with the Angel of the LORD, that is, the covenant angel, who is none other than the Lord Jesus. As we shall see, this helps clarify 2:8-9.

The second angel **said to him** (*2:4*), that is, to the interpreting angel, **"Run, tell that young man".** The identity of 'that young man' has been disputed as between the man with the measuring rod in his hand and the prophet. If the young man represented the community, the difference between the two interpretations is not crucial. The point of informing Zechariah was so that he would pass on the message to the people in Jerusalem. The message has to be conveyed as a matter of urgency so that the prophet was not kept in suspense regarding the matter about which he was showing such intense interest, and so that wrong ideas about the action God was going to take would not spring up.

*The Divine Promise (2:4-5)* To challenge the incipient defeatism of the people and to counteract their restricted ideas of what the future held (as represented by the man with the measuring line), the LORD presents a threefold promise. This promise undoubtedly spoke to the immediate situation of Zechariah's day, but it cannot be contained within that period. It opens out from the prospects of the Old Testament church to include the wider vista of the New Testament church, of whom it is said, 'You have come to Mount Zion, to the heavenly Jerusalem, the city of the living God' (Heb. 12:22). Although in one sense the church has now arrived, and has come to Jerusalem, it is still waiting for 'the Holy City, the new Jerusalem' (Rev. 21:2), where these promises will be finally and completely realised.

   *(1) Expansion.* There had been many promises stating that after the devastation of the sack of Jerusalem, the people would return to the land and the city would be restored (Isa. 44:26; Jer. 30:18; Ezk. 36:10; Mic. 7:11). **Jerusalem will be a city without walls because of the great number of men and livestock in it.** The young man had been acting as if the future of Jerusalem could be measured. This message corrects the impression that Jerusalem was going to be limited and enclosed by city walls. 'A city without walls' renders a word that normally is applied to a village or rural settlement which was without fortifications and so in an exposed position, as in the description of 'a peaceful and unsuspecting people—all of them living *without walls* and without gates and bars' (Ezk. 38:11). In this case, however, the absence of walls does not signify exposure to danger, but rather the massive increase in numbers of people and animals to be found in the restored city, so that it could not be enclosed within walls. This was to counteract their fears arising from the fewness of their numbers (Neh. 7:4). Although the Jewish historian Josephus records that in the period after Nehemiah Jerusalem rapidly outgrew its former boundaries and its population increased substantially, that was but a precursor of the final fulfilment

of this prophecy. Jerusalem was the Old Testament embodiment of the people of God, and it is in terms of the then-existing realities that their future is set before them. Prophecy is not mere prediction that is formulated as if it were history written beforehand, and so requiring fulfilment in a mechanical way for it to be true. It is to be thought of rather as promise, which embodies a divine commitment as to its realisation, but the precise way in which this occurs will be appropriate to the total outworking of God's purposes. It is not that the terms of the promise are broken, but rather that they are fulfilled in an even more glorious way, because the New Testament church is not confined within the boundaries of one nation. 'The barrier, the dividing wall of hostility' found in the ceremonial law has been removed by Christ (Eph. 2:14). The church is no longer hemmed in by protective restrictions, but is open to all. As it takes on the mantle of Jerusalem, so the promises come true in it. At first it was in terms of the tremendous increase in numbers of the church in the New Testament era (Acts 2:41; 9:31), but it is finally realised only in that 'great multitude that no one could count, from every nation, tribe, people and language, standing before the throne and in front of the Lamb' (Rev. 7:9).

*(2) Protection.* Being without walls would not leave the city defenceless. In an emphatic statement the LORD asserts he himself would be all the protection the city would need. **'And I myself will be a wall of fire around it,' declares the LORD (2:5).** This looked back to the protection the LORD had given the people when they left Egypt. The pillar of fire and cloud had been positioned between them and the pursuing armies of Egypt so that there could be no contact between them and their enemies (Ex. 14:19-20). Now it is to be a wall of fire about the city which no hostile force could penetrate. Their security will be directly and divinely guaranteed by the God of Jacob who was their fortress (Ps. 46:7, 11). He was the one who made his city secure (Ps. 48:8). A similar picture of the protection the LORD extends to his own is to be seen in the chariots of fire all round Elisha (2 Kgs. 6:17). Truly no weapon forged against the servants of the LORD will prevail (Isa. 54:17), though in times of little faith there is an ever recurring need to be reminded of the LORD's commitment to his own.

That remains true in the present age. The church is founded on the rock, which even the gates of Hades will not overcome (Mt. 16:18). This is because of Christ's presence with his people to the very end of the age (Mt. 28:20), providing protection and power. This is true collectively in the destiny of the church, and individually of each member. But it must be remembered that the enjoyment of the promises of the covenant is always conditioned on covenant obedience. If his people reject him, the heavenly Father disciplines them (Heb. 12:4-13). That is why the full realisation of these promises awaits the holy city which nothing impure will ever enter (Rev. 21:27) to divert the people of God from obedience and so disturb their enjoyment of all God's provision for them.

*(3) Divine Indwelling.* The LORD also promises **I will be its glory within.** 'Glory' refers to the presence of the LORD (see on Hag. 2:9). It had on past occasions been accompanied by the luminous cloud that covered the Tent of Meeting when the glory of the LORD filled the tabernacle (Ex. 40:34-35). The glory-cloud, or Shekinah as the Jewish rabbis called it, also indicated the LORD's presence at the dedication of Solomon's Temple (1 Kgs. 8:10-11). Before the fall of Jerusalem the prophet Ezekiel had been permitted to see the glory departing from the ark of the covenant (Ezk. 9:3), from the Temple (Ezk. 10:19), and from the city (Ezk. 11:22-23). The promise given here is that the LORD's glory will return to his people—not just the Temple, but the whole city is involved. This is what had already been promised through Haggai (Hag. 2:7, 9). It was not the case that the special glory-cloud was present in the Second Temple, but the reality of God's presence with his people was just as really true as they obeyed him and re-erected the Temple. This promise, of course, finds greater fulfilment with the coming of Christ, whose was 'the glory of the One and Only, who came from the Father, full of grace and truth' (Jn. 1:14), and whose incarnation was the ultimate expression of God's presence with his people. He continues his presence and that of the Father with them through the Spirit (Jn. 14:23; 1 Cor. 3:6) until the dwelling of God is finally with men in the new Jerusalem (Rev. 21:3).

*The Need for Separation (2:6-9)* There are two easily identified sections in the rest of the chapter (2:6-9 and 2:10-13). What is not so clear is their connection with the preceding vision. It may be that these prophetic oracles were given to the prophet at other times, and subsequently recorded here by Zechariah because of their relevance to the theme of the third vision, that is, the divinely guaranteed security that is given to the rebuilt Jerusalem. But there is no indication in the original text that these messages are not part of the divine speech begun in 2:4. Indeed there is much merit in reading them closely with the vision as this helps clarify the otherwise puzzling references to 'me' in 2:8, 9, 11.

The LORD first of all emphasises what his promises for Jerusalem imply for those who had not returned from Babylon. The warnings extended to them would incidentally have confirmed to those who had returned that they had done the right thing.

**"Come! Come! Flee from the land of the north," declares the LORD** *(2:6)*. 'Come!' is rendered 'Woe!' in other contexts, but here, as in Isaiah 55:1, it seems to be encouraging, 'Come on!', coaxing out a response rather than commanding movement. The imperative that follows makes clear what they are being urged to do. It suggests that the situation they are in is one of danger. 'The land of the north' is a reference to Babylon. Not that Babylon was due north of Palestine, but rather that following the traditional trade routes to get there meant in the first instance going north from Palestine before turning east, so as to avoid traversing the desert.

The words **"for I have scattered you to the four winds of heaven," declares the LORD** may well raise the question how they are to flee from Babylon if they have been scattered everywhere as 'the four winds of heaven' implies (Jer. 49:36; Ezk. 37:9; Dan. 7:2; 8:8; 11:4; Mt. 24:31; Rev. 7:1). Undoubtedly the various deportations from the land involved them in living in quite an extensive area in Mesopotamia, and there were Jewish communities that had escaped to Egypt. The picture could thus be of a return to the land from many different places, which might collectively be described as Babylon, the place of exile. But it seems easier to translate not 'to' but 'as' or 'like the four winds of heaven', indicating the power and ferocity with which God had scattered them. It thus took a divine command

and divine power to warrant their return.  This they had.

**Come, O Zion! Escape, you who live in the Daughter of Babylon!** (*2:7*) continues the same message of the need to leave a situation that was dangerous for them.  'Zion' is here used in its spiritual sense to designate the community of those serving the Lord whatever their geographical location.  'Daughter of Babylon' refers to the inhabitants of the city.  As the Hebrew noun for city was feminine, it was a natural transition to personify cities as women (see 2:10 below).  The danger they were in at that time was not physical, but rather of becoming too comfortable in their surroundings and settling down and conforming to Babylonian habits and practices. The Lord wanted his people to come back to the land and to the city so that they could live in a way that pleased him and conformed to his law.  What was true then in a geographical and spiritual manner (for the Lord's spiritual blessings were specially focused on the promised land in the Old Testament era), still remains true for his people spiritually.  'Therefore come out from them and be separate, says the Lord. Touch no unclean thing, and I will receive you' (2 Cor. 6:17). Notice that Paul is here citing two Old Testament texts (Isa. 52:11; Ezk. 20:41) that were initially about the exiles leaving Babylon.  The same need for separation persists through the ages as the words of warning concerning the eschatological Babylon show:  'Come out of her, my people, so that you will not share in her sins, so that you will not receive any of her plagues; for her sins are piled up to heaven, and God has remembered her crimes' (Rev. 18:4-5).

The Lord gives them the added incentive to make this move, in terms of the protection he will extend to them.  **For this is what the Lord Almighty says** (*2:8*) uses the name 'Lord of hosts' (see on 1:3) to emphasise his control over all that would threaten his people.

The next three words, rendered in the NIV **after he has honoured me and has sent me,** are highly problematic.  Literally they are, 'after (or afterwards) glory (or honour or weight) he sent me.'  And that seems to be as much as there is general agreement about.  Some of the more plausible interpretations include the following. *(1)* 'Weight' or 'weightiness' may be an idiomatic expression for persistent urging or insistence.  Whoever was sent had no option but to go.  It was required by God. *(2)* The phrase 'after glory' may indicate the purpose for which the person was sent. He was to obtain glory by carrying out the task of 2:9. *(3)* The phrase 'after glory' may indicate time. The particular time indicated would then depend on identifying the speaker.

Although many take the reference to be to the prophet himself, this seems to be ruled out by the nature of the mission described in 2:9 as 'I will surely raise my hand against them' and so punish the oppressing nations. That is a divine task. So the best explanation of the first person references is that the speaker is the Angel of the LORD who can both speak as the LORD and yet be distinguished from him. This would also explain the way in which in 2:4 it is the Angel who begins to speak, and yet the message continues in 2:5 as direct divine speech.

The wonder of the coming Saviour was also made known to the Old Testament church by means of the portrayal of the Servant of the LORD in Isaiah's prophecy. There the Servant uses similar language when he says of the LORD, 'He has sent me' (Isa. 61:1). Here too he tells of his divinely bestowed mission. It may be that this is to be understood as one by which God's glory will be vindicated and the Servant will gain glory for himself. But I am inclined to elucidate the reference to 'glory' in 2:8 in the light of 'I will be its glory within' (2:5). After the 'glory', that is when the Temple has been built and God has come to his people in the person of the God-man who was dwelling among them, the Messiah has yet another mission to perform. The Father entrusts all judgment to the Son because he is the Son of Man (Jn. 5:22, 27). In Isaiah 61:2 these two aspects of his mission are mentioned consecutively 'to proclaim the year of the LORD's favour, and the day of vengeance of our God.' But in the synagogue at Nazareth Jesus deliberately stopped before the second phrase, and so divorced the two phases of his Messianic ministry (Lk. 4:17-21; see on Mal. 3:2). It is the day of vengeance that is the topic here. It is a recognised Hebrew idiom to use a past tense in prophetic contexts to indicate a future action which is seen as so certain it is as if it were already done. What is said is then, 'After I have come to be among my people as the divine presence, there is another mission on which I will come when I am sent to punish the enemies of the LORD and his people.' This yields a similar sequence to the NIV where 'he has honoured me' (understood of Christ) would refer to the resurrection and ascension (Phil. 2:9; Heb. 2:9), and his 'being sent' to what he is charged to do after that.

**He has sent me against the nations that have plundered you.** The nations had gone beyond what was divinely permitted (1:15), and so the LORD's retribution will come on them. 'He will pay back trouble to those who trouble you' (2 Thess. 1:6). The covenant bond between the LORD and his people secures his action on their behalf. **For who ever touches you touches the apple of his eye.** 'The apple of the eye' is a Hebrew expression for the pupil of the eye. Being very sensitive and easily injured it is looked after with particular care (Deut. 32:10; Ps. 17:8; Prov. 7:2). The idea is not just that those who act against the LORD's people inflict injury on themselves (that is, touch their own eyes), but that they assault the LORD himself and so bring divine wrath on them. There is an intense relationship and identity of interest between the LORD and his people so that he considers actions against them as against himself (Ps. 105:13-15; Isa. 63:9; Mt. 25:45; Acts 9:4). This is one of many biblical expressions for the protecting care the LORD takes of his own. They are designed to give his people confidence as they grapple with difficult situations and hostile adversaries.

**I will surely raise my hand against them (2:9).** These are words of power and authority. The gesture is one of a judge lifting or waving his hand to indicate the dismissal from his presence of the parties involved (Isa. 11:15, where 'raise' is translated 'sweep'). A similar expression denotes the commencement of divine action against the Egyptians (Isa. 19:16). God's hand against the enemies of his people was often seen in particular providential interventions on their behalf, such as against Egypt (Ex. 15:6), against the Philistines (1 Sam. 7:13), against Nineveh (Nah. 1:8), and against Babylon (Dan. 5:30-31). Such special action foreshadowed the time 'when the Lord Jesus is revealed from heaven in blazing fire with his powerful angels. He will punish those who do not know God and do not obey the gospel of our Lord Jesus' (2 Thess. 1:7-8).

When the LORD through the Messiah acts on behalf of his own and overthrows their enemies, **then you will know that the LORD Almighty has sent me.** This would be an encouragement to faith in each particular situation, but the final vindication and worldwide acknowledgment of Christ awaits the day when at the name of Jesus every knee in heaven, earth, and under the earth will bow (Phil. 2:11). It strengthens faith when what has been foretold actually comes to pass (Jn. 13:19; 16:4).

*The Coming Glory (2:10-13)*  The closing section of the chapter develops the promise of the LORD's coming made in 2:5 as a source of encouragement for the people. They should rejoice now in the anticipation of his presence with them. But the prophecy looks beyond God's being with them as they worship in the rebuilt Temple. It looks forward to the way he will come to them in the Messiah (2:10), and beyond that to his second coming when there will be an international recognition of the sovereignty of the LORD (2:11) who will dwell with his people in the heavenly Jerusalem (2:12). The scene of future glory contrasted starkly with the reality of Zechariah's day when the people felt themselves to be insignificant and without influence on the events taking place around them, and was intended to strengthen and encourage the people in the tasks before them.

**"Shout and be glad, O Daughter of Zion. For I am coming"** **(2:10).** The description 'Daughter of Zion' does not refer to a group that is part of, or other than, Zion or Jerusalem. It is rather a Hebrew poetic mode of expression for the population of these places as a whole (Isa. 1:8; Lam. 1:6). Zion is used to indicate the city and people as a specifically religious community consisting of those who are loyal to the LORD (Ps. 2:6; 87:2; 132:13), and as such is applied to the church of all ages (Heb. 12:22; Rev. 14:1).

It is always a time of exuberant joy when God's salvation is experienced (Ps. 9:14; 48:11; Zeph. 3:14-18). The commands given here are for present exultation in the future prospect of the LORD's presence with them. They can only be obeyed through the faith that is 'fully persuaded that God had power to do what he had promised' (Rom. 4:21). That faith now acclaims the king who will surely fulfil the commitment he has undertaken. The thought is resumed in the words, 'Rejoice greatly, O Daughter of Zion! Shout, Daughter of Jerusalem! See, your king comes to you' (9:9).

**"I will live among you," declares the LORD.** 'Live' renders the verb that is used for the LORD's presence with his people by means of the tabernacle, the word for which also comes from the same root. God had taken his people out of Egypt so that he might live or dwell among them (Ex. 29:45-46). The people were looking for the resumption of that blessing with the renewed Temple. But its fulfilment involves far more than a physical building. It anticipates the coming of Christ as the temple-presence of God with his people (Jn. 2:19-21), and the establishment in the church of the temple of the Holy Spirit (1 Cor. 6:19), which is the temple of the living God (2 Cor. 6:16). See further on 2:5 and Haggai 2:9.

**Many nations will be joined with the LORD in that day and will become my people (*2:11*).** The religion of the Old Testament was never exclusivist. The promise to Abraham that 'all peoples on earth will be blessed through you' (Gen. 12:3) re-echoes through subsequent revelation. The Servant of the LORD was told, 'It is too small a thing for you to be my servant to restore the tribes of Jacob and bring back those of Israel I have kept. I will also make you a light for the Gentiles, that you may bring my salvation to the ends of the earth' (Isa. 49:6). 'Join' is an Old Testament idiom used of non-Israelites who bind themselves as converts in association with the LORD's people (Est. 9:27; Isa. 14:1; 56:3, 6). When the people returned from Babylon, they felt as if they were aliens coming to the LORD for the first time, and talked in the same way of binding or joining themselves to the LORD in an everlasting covenant (Jer. 50:5). Unlike some other passages in the Old Testament where this binding leaves the Gentiles in subordinate status to the Jews (Isa. 14:2; 60:10; 61:5), here they are viewed as fully incorporated as 'my people' (Ps. 22:27-29; Isa. 2:2-4; Eph. 2:18-19; 1 Pet. 2:9-10). The geographical and racial boundaries of God's people will no longer be significant, what will matter is true heart loyalty to him. Isaiah envisages the barriers between Israel, Egypt and Assyria being abolished, and Egypt called 'my people' (Isa. 19:23-25).

**I will live among you** again repeats the promise of verse 10, now pointing beyond the first coming of Christ. **You will know that the LORD Almighty has sent me to you** are crucial in the understanding of this passage. Whoever is speaking has to be different in some sense from the LORD Almighty, and yet the speaker is one whose presence with the people of God is closely linked with the LORD's own presence with them. This can be understood of none other than Christ himself. He is the one who is sent to provide his people with the blessings of the covenant. Of course the people of Zechariah's day did not have revealed to them all we now know about the incarnation. They understood this in terms of the Angel of the LORD who had already played such an important role in their history (Isa. 63:9).

**The LORD will inherit Judah as his portion in the holy land and will again choose Jerusalem (*2:12*).** It is only here in the Old Testament that the phrase 'holy land' occurs with respect to Palestine. It is in an eschatological context which looks forward to the LORD conveying to his people all the blessings of his covenant election of them. The holiness is a separation to the LORD's service which will not then be marred by any backsliding.

Problems arise in determining precisely who are being said to enjoy the LORD's favour in this time of future blessing. When the Old Testament prophets were permitted glimpses into the future, it was presented to them in terms that they, and the people of their time, could have some grasp of. The church was then geographically and ethnically restricted to Judah and to the descendants of Abraham. The descriptions of future blessing were consequently couched in language that referred to them. However, the New Testament repeatedly shows that the promises then made have been more than fulfilled in the New Testament church, to which there is no hesitation in ascribing the titles previously used exclusively of Israel (Gal. 3:29; 6:16; 1 Pet. 2:9-10). Paul speaks of this as a mystery, something that had not previously been known but had now been divinely revealed. 'This mystery is that through the gospel the Gentiles are heirs together with Israel, members together of one body, and sharers together in the promise in Christ Jesus' (Eph. 3:6).

There is therefore no need to imagine some future Jewish age of blessing in which the Old Testament predictions come literalistically true. To do so involves absurdities such as the restoration of sacrifices of blood (Ezk. 45:13-25, which is opposed to Heb. 10:12). The abundant provision that came with Christ more than fulfilled what the prophets had pointed to in Old Testament language.

In one passage, however, namely Romans 11, Paul discusses another mystery regarding the salvation of all Israel (Rom. 11:26).

There are various interpretations of this passage, but it is significant to note that Paul's discussion of God's future provision for ethnic Israel does not involve talk of their restoration to the land or the establishment of physical Jerusalem as a world capital of some sort. These Old Testament pictures have been taken up in the greater reality of the church. It may, however, be the case that Paul there talks of a time of immense gospel blessing for the Jewish people—not apart from Christ, but in terms of the only way of salvation now open equally to Jew and non-Jew. Even if that is so, it does not seem to impinge upon the interpretation of this passage where what is being spoken of is the LORD's interest in and choice of his people, whether of the many nations of the preceding verse or of ethnic Israel.

The passage ends on a resounding and majestic note. **Be still before the LORD, all mankind (2:13)**. 'Mankind' is literally 'flesh', a term frequently used in Hebrew to emphasise how weak and transient even the strongest and most long lived are. Unlike the New Testament usage, 'flesh' does not refer to mankind as rebels against God, but as his creatures, whose 'flesh' indicates that they are 'a passing breeze that does not return' (Ps. 78:39). This is brought out very clearly in the well-known passage of Isaiah: 'All men (literally, flesh) are like grass, and all their glory is like the flowers of the field. The grass withers and the flowers fall, because the breath of the LORD blows on them. Surely the people are grass. The grass withers and the flowers fall, but the word of our God stands for ever' (Isa. 40:6-8). In the presence of divine power and authority such flesh must display reverent silence and awed respect (Ps. 46:10; 76:7-9; Zeph. 1:7; Hab. 2:20).

In response to his people's prayers the Judge of all the earth comes to 'judge the world in righteousness and the peoples with equity' (Ps. 98:9). **Because he has roused himself from his holy dwelling!** 'Rouse' speaks from a human perspective of God showing himself to be active in the world (Ps. 44:23; 59:5; 78:65; Isa. 28:21). 'His holy dwelling' refers to heaven (Deut. 26:15; Ps. 68:5; Jer. 25:30). We often think that God is remote and indifferent, because he does not act when and how we expect. But the message being given by Zechariah is that we ought to look beyond the present and see ourselves as part of the outworking of the total and grand promises and purposes of God.

Our perception of the church is frequently coloured by our knowledge of our local fellowship with which we are familiar. We are aware of its (and our) blemishes and failures. So often we hardly seem to have started to face up to the agenda set before us. Sometimes our attitudes are defensive and backwards looking. We are prone in measuring Jerusalem to confine it within the forms and practices of the past. This chapter calls on us to rethink our attitudes in the light of the divine promises to the church. We are to align our outlook to God's, separating from worldly tendencies that would imprison us and grasping the glorious provision that God has made for his people. To realise our potential we have to build with confidence in him. As ever, the life to be lived is one of faith.

*Study Questions*

**2:5, 8** What other images does the Bible use to express God's care for, and interest in, his people? Ps. 18:2; 103:13; Isa. 49:15-16; Mt. 10:29-31; Jn. 10:27-30; Heb. 2:17-18.

**2:6-7** Separation is still required of the believer. How is it to be achieved? Ps. 1:1-2; 1 Cor. 5:9-13; 2 Cor. 6:14-18; Eph. 5:11; 2 Thess. 3:14; Jas. 4:7.

**2:10** What are the sources of joy for God's people? How is this joy to be expressed? Neh. 8:2; Ps. 4:7; 16:11; 149:2; Isa. 35:10; 56:7; Rom. 5:11; Gal. 5:22; 1 Pet. 1:8.

## Zechariah 3:1-10: Vision 4: Snatched from the Fire

The fourth vision deals with the problem of Israel's sin. It was all very well that God had made such great promises concerning her future, but was she in a position to be the recipient of them? Not only was there the legacy of her own past failure to live as God's people; there was also their present awareness of their on-going sin and failure. This formed a barrier in the way of their joyfully accepting the promises of God. It is this subjective condition of the people—of how they saw themselves as standing before God—that is now dealt with. They are shown that there is a God-appointed and God-accepted priesthood to mediate on their behalf. This looks forward to the coming Messiah.

*The Vision (3:1-5).* **Then he showed me *(3:1)*** is a different style of introduction from those of the other visions. This and other changes in the way the vision is related are just elegant variations to avoid monotony. They certainly do not constitute valid grounds for questioning the authenticity of the vision. Who the subject of the sentence is is not stated. It might be either the LORD (as in 1:20) or the interpreting angel (as in 1:9). As the interpreting angel does not appear elsewhere in the vision, perhaps his role is that of introducing it as a whole.

There are then introduced the three main characters who feature in the vision. **Joshua the high priest** at the time of the Return is mentioned also at 6:11, and in Haggai (1:1, 12, 14). As 'Jeshua' he appears in various places in Ezra and Nehemiah (for instance, Ezr. 2:2; 3:2; 4:3; 5:2). His grandfather Seraiah had been high priest at the time of the capture of Jerusalem in 586 B.C., and his father had been taken captive to Babylon. Joshua himself was born in Babylon and returned to Palestine. Although his name is mentioned frequently enough, nothing is really known about him as a person. Nothing that he said or did is recorded.

It is not Joshua personally that is significant for this vision. It is the fact that he is the high priest. This meant not only that in his official standing he represented all the priesthood of Israel, but that he represented the people themselves. What happens to Joshua here is of vital importance for the whole community he represents, as well as for himself.

Joshua is said to be **standing before the angel of the LORD**. Since that is an appropriate posture for one in the presence of a superior, it has led some to interpret the scene as a heavenly assize at which Joshua is being arraigned and at which Satan is acting as prosecutor. But the phrase 'to stand before' is also used on a number of occasions in the Old Testament as a technical term for priestly service. The tribe of Levi was set apart 'to carry the ark of the covenant of the LORD, to stand before the LORD to minister and to pronounce blessings in his name, as they still do today' (Deut. 10:8; see also 2 Chr. 29:11; Jer. 33:18; Ezk. 44:15). It is therefore not amiss to think of Joshua as here performing his official duties. This may have been in connection with the regular sacrificial offerings that had been restarted twenty years previously (Ezr. 3:5), or it may be that it is the future worship of the Temple then under restoration which is in view. But it is not what can be naturally seen by the human eye that is portrayed. By means of the vision we are given a divine picture of the spiritual realities with which that worship is concerned.

At the centre of that worship—and of the vision—is the Angel of the LORD. He represents the LORD; indeed, he is the LORD. His presence sanctifies (Ex. 3:5; Josh. 5:15); he speaks as God (Gen. 22:12) and is identified with God (Judg. 13:22); he accepts divine worship (Josh. 5:13-15; Judg. 6:20-22; 13:19-21). He is the Angel of the LORD's presence who has a close and compassionate interest in the affairs of the LORD's people and extends divine help to them in times of distress (Ex. 14:19; 23:20-21; Isa. 63:9). This being was the means of educating the Old Testament church in some of the wonders of the incarnation. Here, as in the previous visions, what he does coheres with the role he is assigned in the divine plan of salvation.

But we are told there is a third character present, **and Satan standing at his right side to accuse him.** 'Satan' means 'an adversary' or 'accuser'. Here he is specifically identified as '*the* adversary*', whose character and role become ever clearer throughout the Old Testament, until in the New Testament he is clearly seen as the one who leads the fallen angels in their opposition to the Messiah (Mt. 12:24; Acts 26:18; Eph. 2:2; 6:12; Rev. 12:9). Here it is specifically his role as the accuser of the LORD's people that is emphasised (Job 1:6-12; 2:1-8; 1 Pet. 5:8; Rev. 12:10). Precisely what these accusations were is not stated, but they obviously related to Joshua's condition (3:3). He is unfit to stand before the LORD and worship him. And if that was true of their representative, then it was equally true of the people. How could the Holy One accept the worship of rebels? They are unworthy to appear before the LORD and to receive his blessing. And the charge is true! Witness the silence of Joshua. He has nothing to say in his own defence, or that of his people.

However, **the LORD said to Satan** (*3:2*). As the text goes on to speak of the LORD in the third person, it is evident that the speaker is none other than the Angel of the LORD, himself identified with the LORD and also uniquely qualified to speak in the LORD's name. He intervenes in his character as the strong Defender who takes up the cause of the helpless against their adversaries (Ps. 12:5; 68:5; Prov. 23:11; Isa. 19:20; Jer. 50:33). Though his own accusing conscience has left Joshua speechless, his defender is not so baffled. **The LORD rebuke you, Satan!** It is a solemn word, made even more so by the way in which it is left to the LORD himself to carry out the rebuke. One is reminded of the way a similar matter is expressed in Jude 9. It is the LORD who will act to vindicate his own character and purposes (Ps. 135:14). Although the attack is ostensibly against his people, in reality it is the LORD himself who is being challenged.

This is brought out clearly when the solemn prayer is repeated. **The LORD, who has chosen Jerusalem, rebuke you!** Notice the language used corresponds to the representative character of Joshua. It is not 'the LORD who has chosen Joshua' but 'the LORD who has chosen Jerusalem'. (For 'choose' see on Hag. 2:23.) It was because Satan's accusations were directly opposed to that revealed choice that they were reprehensible. Satan was seeking to thwart God's purpose, or to suggest that in some way the divine choice of Jerusalem (1 Kgs. 11:13, 32; Ps. 132:13-16) was wrong. The LORD's rebuke is not merely an expression of displeasure or disapproval at the sentiments expressed by Satan. It is accompanied by divine power to give effect to the rebuke. 'He rebuked the Red Sea, and it dried up' (Ps. 106:9; Mk. 4:39).

The reason for the LORD's rebuke is made clear by means of a rhetorical question. **Is not this man a burning stick snatched from the fire?** The question urges recognition of the true state of affairs. Joshua and the people have been undergoing the horrific experience of being in the fire, which symbolises divine punishment. A similar description is found in Amos 4:11. They were not able to remove themselves from the fire. They would have been totally consumed had not the hand of divine mercy been outstretched to rescue them before they were burned to ashes. As it is, it is not surprising that those so recently snatched from the fire are like a charred and blackened stick. (How many of these must have been picked up by the Jews as they cleared the rubble from the Temple site!) Their appearance, however, testifies to the mercy and grace of their Saviour. What they had been does not debar them from appearing before the LORD. Rather their presence bears testimony to his divine election and grace. Say not, 'How polluted they are!', but rather marvel at the redeeming power and purpose of the LORD!

A further description of Joshua is then given to make the situation clear. **Now Joshua was dressed in filthy clothes as he stood before the angel** (*3:3*). 'Filthy' is a very strong word expressive of utterly disgusting muck. Some even suggest that the word indicates 'smeared with human excrement'. Not even the impoverished circumstances of the restored community would have warranted the high priest literally conducting the worship of the sanctuary in such apparel. No high priest would have dared appear in such a way to minister before God. This is a vision, and Joshua's dress is symbolic of the spiritual condition which he, and the people he represented, were in. They were spiritually polluted. No specifics are detailed of what constituted this pollution. It is difficult to be precise as to whether it was the past sin of their fathers, or their own present sin in not having rebuilt the Temple. Perhaps it is not right to be too specific. It is the reality of their sinful condition that is stated—and that of course was precisely the problem afflicting tender consciences in Israel. They were prepared to confess, 'All of us have become like one who is unclean, and all our righteous acts are like filthy rags' (Isa. 64:6). God had given them great promises, but they were painfully aware of their own unworthiness to inherit those promises, and of the inability of the priests to rectify the situation on their behalf. How could they deal with the legacy of their past?

However, the Angel takes action that Joshua (and Israel) cannot take for themselves. He does not allow the high priest to remain in such unfitting dress. **The angel said to those who were standing before him, "Take off his filthy clothes"** (*3:4*). Literally, it is 'the angel answered and said.' This does not indicate a reply to some question or statement made, but a response to the situation in general. The Angel was aware of Joshua's sorry state, and took steps to rectify it. Those he addressed were the angels who served as his attendants (Isa. 6:2).

What is being described is not merely a change of outward apparel but of spiritual standing (Isa. 11:5; 61:10). This is clearly stated in the explanatory words addressed to Joshua. **Then he said to Joshua, "See, I have taken away your sin, and I will put rich garments on you."** The Angel—who is after all the Lamb who takes away the sin of the world (Jn. 1:29)—does not proceed on the basis of dismissing or minimising the disruption and pollution caused by sin, but by dealing with it effectively. It is a divine prerogative to forgive sin and to hurl iniquities into the depths of the sea, never to intrude again into the relationship between God and his people (Mic. 7:18-19; Isa. 43:25; Ezk. 36:25). This declaration uses language which suggests that Joshua's sense of guilt had been a burden weighing him down, and now that it is declared removed he knows where he stands in relation to God and is able to serve him effectively (2 Sam. 12:13; Ps. 32:1-2; 51:9; Isa. 6:7). The word 'sin', or iniquity, denotes what was twisted or bent away from the truth. It was used to refer not only to the act of wrong-doing, but also the guilt that derives from it ('the *guilt* of my sin', Ps. 32:5) and the punishment that inevitably follows ('punishment', Gen. 4:13). So the declaration here spoke powerfully to Joshua and to the situation of the community. What mattered was not where they had been or what they had done, but what God had done for them and what he thought of them (1 Cor. 6:11).

The official dress of the high priest had been divinely designed to give him dignity and honour (Ex. 28:2). It was richly and intricately worked, as the descriptions in Exodus 28 and 39 make clear. The word used here 'rich garments' is not the normal description of the high priest's garments. It is only found elsewhere of the finery of women ('fine robes', Isa. 3:22). It may be that this emphasises the extent of the change in his appearance, as well as indicating that he is now properly clad for his official task. Not only is he accepted, he is also divinely equipped for his role (Rev. 7:14; 19:8).

There is on-going dispute as to how the next verse should begin. Following early translations of Scripture, many consider that it should begin 'Then he said', referring to the Angel of the LORD. This is an easier reading than the Masoretic text (the standard Hebrew text) which has **Then I said** (*3:5*). It is difficult to see how the more difficult reading could have arisen unless it was in fact original. The versions, considering it to be a mistake, substituted the easier reading for it. Zechariah is thus drawn into the action of the vision. The nearest parallel to this is in Isaiah 6:8, where the prophet intervenes in the heavenly scene presented to him, and says, 'Here am I. Send me!' On this occasion, however, Zechariah is not offering his services, but revealing his intense desire that what is going on should be carried through to completion. He had not had to ask what the vision meant. Its meaning had been obvious to him, and since it concerned something about which he felt strongly, he is drawn into the action of the vision, as previously at 2:2.

Orders had been given for the clothes of the high priest to be changed, but nothing had been said about the high priest's distinctive headdress. So Zechariah requests, **Put a clean turban on his head.** The NIV rendering may be misleading as to the tone of this request. It is not a command, either to the attendant angels, or to the Angel of the LORD, but, in accordance with the prophet's station, an indirect request through the Angel, literally, 'Let them set'. 'Turban' is not the usual word for what the high priest wore on his head. It may denote something grander ('diadem' in Isa. 62:3). The usual head-dress consisted of a linen strip wound round the head and tied to it was a plate of pure gold with the inscription: HOLY TO THE LORD (Ex. 28:36). This was explicitly connected with Aaron's function as the first high priest. 'It will be on Aaron's forehead, and he will bear the guilt involved in the sacred gifts the Israelites consecrate, whatever their gifts may be. It will be on Aaron's forehead continually so that they will be acceptable to the LORD' (Ex. 28:38). The prophet, acting in the interests of the people, requested this addition, so that there would be no doubt about Joshua's acceptability as the one presenting the offerings of the people.

**So they put a clean turban on his head and clothed him.** After both the Angel of the LORD and the prophet had spoken, the other angels who were around carried out the task allotted them, and **while the angel of the LORD stood by** is added to indicate his approval of the prophet's request. Nothing took place unless he permitted it.

*The Divine Testimony (3:6-10).* **The angel of the LORD gave this charge to Joshua (3:6).** Having been clothed anew and so ceremonially fitted to carry out his office, Joshua is then solemnly warned of what else was needed to carry out his role as high priest. It was not just a matter of external accoutrements, but of spiritual qualifications. These were requirements of God, for **this is what the LORD Almighty says** (*3:7*).

Although the Hebrew text might be understood differently (with four conditions and only the last clause representing the outcome) most translators understand verse 7 to have two conditions, and three consequences. The two conditions are: **If you will walk in my ways and keep my requirements.** The first of these relates to personal holiness (for 'walk' and 'way', see on Mal. 2:6,8). 'Requirement' is a word that is often used of the duties required of a priest or Levite (Lev. 8:35; Num. 1:53; 31:30; Ezk. 40:45-46). So the second condition points to what was specifically required of him as he executed the office of high priest. Obedience in his personal living and also in the demands of his office were both required to fit him out for the role assigned him (1 Kgs. 2:3). All had to be attended to faithfully; nothing was to be omitted.

Of the consequences that would flow from this obedience the first two are closely linked together: **then you will govern my house and have charge of my courts**. 'House' is unlikely to refer here to the community as a whole (10:6; Jer. 31:31). If it did, this would be a prophecy of the role the high priest was to play in coming centuries when the civil affairs of Judah were very much under his control (6:11). Here, however, the focus is on the religious life of the community, and 'house' is a synonym for the Temple, and specifically the central sanctuary, which was in process of being rebuilt (see on Hag. 2:15). The courts were the area around it. We do not have much detail of how these were organised at this time, but the courts were the areas where worshippers assembled and sacrifices were offered. The promise related not only to what was going on at that time in the ruins of the Temple, but also to what would occur when the structure was finished.

The third consequence is more problematic: **I will give you a place among these standing here.** Literally, it is 'I will give to you goings (or walkings) among (or between) these standing.' It might be taken in two ways. The 'walkings' could refer to Joshua's life (see on Mal. 2:6). Those who were standing around were the angels who were in the heavenly court, and it may be that Joshua was being assured of their protection as guardian angels (Gen. 32:2; Ps. 34:7; 91:11; Heb. 1:13). That would have been a factor in the uncertain times when opposition was having to be faced. On the other hand the specific thrust in this vision is Joshua's role as priest, and so it is more plausible that Joshua is being assured that if he maintains his integrity then he will be given permission to enter into the heavenly court, into the very presence of God, and there to fulfil his priestly role by interceding on behalf of the people.

There is then delivered a message which is of wider significance than that given to Joshua in the preceding verse. Joshua still remains at the focus of what is said, but in fulfilling his office, he was foreshadowing the one to come, who would be the ultimate High Priest. This role culminates in the enacted prophecy of 6:12-13. In this passage the revelation moves on from the particular details of Joshua's life to the consummation of the blessing, which, however obscurely intimated here, is to be found only in Christ. Notice that Jesus is the Greek form of the Hebrew name Joshua.

Some argue that the beginning **Listen (*3:8*)** indicates a separate oracle taken from somewhere else and only secondarily added here, but this seems unnecessary in that the focus of the address is still the high priest. These words are still governed by 'This is what the Lord Almighty says' in 3:7. They are uttered by the Angel on the Father's behalf. The command to listen is singular and addressed to the **high priest Joshua**, along with whom are mentioned **your associates seated before you.**

Undoubtedly there has been a change of scene, as we are no longer seeing the spiritual realities of worship. Joshua is now at the centre of the group of men. Are they priests? Although there is nothing that directly asserts this, it is the common view in that they **are men symbolic of things to come.** But the original is more terse than that, 'men of sign (or, wonder)', and there may be a certain backward reference. Joshua is in the midst of a group who have returned from the Exile. As such, they are all signs of God's redeeming grace. That they were brought from Babylon signalled that the Lord had not abandoned his purposes for his people, and on that basis they could still expect much to come. Furthermore, if they were also priests, then it was being emphasised that what they did and were in that capacity pointed forward to what was yet to be fulfilled in God's purpose. Their thoughts are re-directed from their present endeavours to the one in whom all that they foreshadowed would be realised. Whatever blessing they would enjoy was not for their own sake, and should not give them an inflated sense of their own importance. The key to the LORD's blessing was the one to come, and it was their weighty responsibility to carry out their tasks as fitting representatives of him.

**I am going to bring my servant, the Branch.** There are here two Messianic titles which were well known in Zechariah's day.

*(1) My servant:* It was Isaiah who supremely used this designation for the one the LORD appointed to bring salvation (Isa. 42:1-4; 49:1-7; 52:13-53:12). By undergoing suffering and rejection the Servant would carry through the LORD's purposes and deliver Israel. He would also be a light for the Gentiles, to bring God's salvation to the ends of the earth (Isa. 49:6).

*(2) The Branch:* This designation, denoting a shoot or growth, goes back to David's meditation on the covenant blessings promised him by the LORD. 'Is not my house right with God? Has he not made with me an everlasting covenant, arranged and secured in every part? Will he not bring to fruition my salvation and grant me my every desire?' (2 Sam. 23:5). 'Bring to fruition', literally 'cause to shoot or branch', is a verb from the same root as the noun 'branch'. The image is not that of one more branch growing from an existing tree, but of new growth that shoots up from the root. The metaphor was taken up by Isaiah to indicate the one through whom the promises made to David would be achieved. 'In that day the Branch of the LORD will be beautiful and glorious' (Isa. 4:2). A similar word referring to growth that is green and fresh (also translated 'branch') is used to convey the same idea. 'A shoot will come up from the stump of Jesse; from his roots a Branch will bear fruit' (Isa. 11:1). The expression is used to point to the ultimate and true descendant of David, son of Jesse, through whom the LORD will fulfil all his covenant promises (Jer. 23:5-6; 33:15-16). It would be in him that what had been anticipated by their recent deliverance from Babylon and what had been divinely foreshadowed by their priestly duties would be realised.

**See, the stone I have set in front of Joshua!** (*3:9*) introduces a verse which is difficult to interpret with certainty. However, the situation of the times with the Temple being rebuilt indicates that in the first instance reference is being made to a significant stone in the Temple—either the foundation stone or the capstone which will bring the building to completion (4:7). But we have also to take into account the spiritual significance of the literal stone before Joshua. There have already been mentioned two names of the Messiah, and it seems probable that here there is a third. It might look back to the words, 'The stone the builders rejected has become the capstone; the LORD has done this, and it is marvellous in our eyes' (Ps. 118:22-23), which is cited and applied to Christ in Matthew 21:42 and Acts 4:11. Alternatively, the reference might be to 'So this is what the Sovereign LORD says: "See, I lay a stone in Zion, a tested stone, a precious cornerstone for a sure foundation; the one who trusts will never be dismayed"' (Isa. 28:16), which is cited in 1 Peter 2:6. In either case, the Temple under construction looked forward to the presence and work of Christ (2:10).

But what are we then to make of **There are seven eyes on that one stone?** The NIV footnote suggests an alternative rendering, 'There are seven facets on that one stone,' but there is no obvious connection between a stone with seven sides and the building of the Temple. Others understand the Hebrew word 'eye' to be in fact another word with a similar spelling and which means 'spring of water'. They take the word translated 'engrave' in its primary meaning 'open'. The stone is then the source of seven springs from which the LORD opens their openings to remove the sin of the land. This interpretation certainly coheres with the burden of sin and pollution which is the theme of the vision, and with the purifying work of Christ (13:1). But this view has not yet been adopted by any major translation.

The safest way forward seems to be to note what is said in 4:10, 'These seven are the eyes of the LORD, which range throughout the earth'. It is not that there are seven eye shapes on the stone, but 'seven' is being used to indicate completeness and perfection. Notice the analogous phrase 'the seven spirits of God' (Rev. 3:1; 5:6), which does not undermine the unity of the Spirit. The eyes of the LORD (2 Chr. 16:9) are looking with great and special interest on this one, unique stone. He knows all about it, and the care he extends to it/him will be like that shown to the promised land: 'It is a land the LORD your God cares for; the eyes of the LORD your God are continually on it from the beginning of the year to its end' (Deut. 11:12). Such an understanding is reinforced by Ezra 5:5 when after the intervention of local Persian officials in the Temple building project, it is said that the work was not stopped while official enquiries were made because 'the eye of their God was watching over the elders of the Jews'.

It is less certain what is referred to by the next statement **and I will engrave an inscription on it.** It is not stated what the inscription might be. The best suggestion is that it refers to the engraving of HOLY TO THE LORD on the gold plate on the high priest's turban (Ex. 28:36). This has been indirectly referred to in the vision (3:5). So this would anticipate the consecration of the Branch to the unique role the LORD assigned him as the representative of his people.

Through the Messiah's ministry the LORD will fulfil the promise anticipated in the priestly role of Joshua and his companions. **I will remove the sin of this land in a single day,** literally 'one day'. The repetition of 'one' from 'one stone' earlier emphasises the uniqueness of the event (compare the idiom in 14:7). It cannot be understood of anything other than the crucifixion. 'This land' in the first instance refers to Judah, but only as it symbolises the people of God.

**In that day (3:10)** continues to describe the time when the LORD's salvation is revealed. It is a picture of the peace brought by the gospel, though as often in the Old Testament there is not a clear distinction made between the first and second comings of the Lord. The description of everyone under his own vine and fig-tree is first found in connection with the peace and prosperity of Solomon's rule (1 Kgs. 4:25). It seems to have been a fairly common idiom, being found also on the lips of the Assyrian commander besieging Jerusalem (Isa. 36:16). Micah used it to describe the result of the nations turning to the LORD, noting that when this happened no one would make them afraid since their security would be divinely guaranteed (Mic. 4:4). Here the familiar description is extended from one of individual peace, security and contentment to one of fellowship and friendship. **'Each of you will invite his neighbour to sit under his vine and fig-tree,' declares the LORD Almighty.** This beautiful picture of harmony is designed to represent spiritual blessings. It is not that the material blessings promised are unreal, but they were pledges of the total inheritance God bestows on his people. Social tensions and frictions will be overcome, and mutual forbearance and love will prevail. In measure that has already been achieved in the body of Christ, but the full measure of bliss has yet to be achieved for perfection has not yet come (1 Cor. 13:10).

This vision has much to encourage God's people in every age. Joshua was a type of the great High Priest to come, who would stand before the LORD and represent his people. Throughout his life Satan would be permitted to deploy all his malign skill against him—and especially in the hour 'when darkness reigns' (Lk. 22:53). The victory the Angel bestowed on Joshua here is based on the victory that he himself would win over the adversary. Though Satan attacked Jesus without restraint, he was unable to succeed in deflecting Jesus from his purpose or undermining his achievement. By his death he destroyed 'him who holds the power of death—that is, the devil' (Heb. 2:14). His victory was won on behalf of all who are his, and so he is able to extend to them a right standing before God (Rom. 4:23-25) and give them garments of salvation and a robe of righteousness (Isa. 61:10).

## Study Questions

**3:4** How is clothing associated with redemption in the New Testament? Mt. 22:11-14; Lk. 15:22; Gal. 3:27; Col. 3:10; Rev. 3:4-5; 7:14; 19:7.

**3:7** How are personal holiness and office in the church related? 1 Tim. 3:1-13; 4:16; 2 Tim. 2:20-21; Tit. 1:6-9.

**3:9** What do the following passages teach about the removal of sins? Isa. 53:5, 10; Gal. 3:13; Heb. 9:14; 1 Pet. 2:24; 1 Jn. 4:10.

## Zechariah 4:1-14: Vision 5: By My Spirit

The fifth vision proceeds to deal with another aspect of the troubles affecting the community. The fourth vision had focused on the spiritual obstacles in the way of their effective action, and ended with references to the Messiah who, as the Branch that would come from the house of David, was God's appointed instrument for dealing with their spiritual needs. The fifth vision follows on from this by showing how those given a new standing before the LORD should work in his cause. It looks particularly at the role of Zerubbabel, the civil leader of the community. He had political problems to contend with, chief amongst which was the need to expedite the Temple building project in the face of opposition, low morale and lack of resources. This vision is concerned with giving consolation to the community and with establishing the credibility of what Zerubbabel was undertaking. It finishes with a Messianic prophecy in which both the king and priest are involved.

*The Vision (4:1-5)*. In the previous vision the interpreting angel (1:9) had taken a very low profile. Perhaps he is to be thought of as one of the members of the heavenly court and thus not available for his usual role as Zechariah's informant and guide. This may explain **Then the angel who talked with me returned** (*4:1*), as referring to the return of the angel after his virtual absence from Zechariah's side during the previous vision. On the other hand the Hebrew may equally be understood as referring not to returning, but repeating an action: 'the angel who talked with me *again* **wakened me**', implying that this was something that had occurred previously. This is not to be understood as implying that Zechariah had fallen asleep. The words **as a man is wakened from his sleep** carefully guard against that interpretation. It was rather that the concentration of his mental faculties that was required to permit him to see and appropriate the divine vision was such that when one returned to an ordinary state of wakefulness the difference was as great as that between ordinary wakefulness and being in sleep. No doubt also the prophet had been absorbed in pondering over what he had seen.

**He asked me, "What do you see?"** (*4:2*). Events follow a different course from the earlier visions, where Zechariah had asked for clarification about what he was seeing (1:9, 19; 2:2). Here the angel questions Zechariah before any details of the vision are related. Perhaps this was part of the way in which he was stirred up. A similar technique is used in other places (Jer. 1:11, 13; Amos 7:8; 8:2) so that the prophet may grasp what is revealed to him and be in a better position to set it before the people.

Zechariah had no difficulty recognising and describing what it was that was presented to him. **I answered, "I see a solid gold lampstand with a bowl at the top."** The word translated 'lampstand' is *menorah*, traditionally rendered 'candlestick', but this was a misapprehension since candles as such were not involved. Rather it was a stand or support for lamps. The one Zechariah saw seems to have been differently shaped from those in the Tabernacle or Temple. There the lampstand had an upright central stem with three branches rising on either side of it to the same height. At the top of the central stem and of the six branches were seven lamps all at the same level (Ex. 25:31-38; 37:17-24). When lit, these provided light in the Holy Place.

Archaeological investigations have shown the later existence of lampstands consisting of hollow pottery cylinders, perhaps a metre high, at the top of which a bowl capable of holding oil would have been placed. Such bowls had spouts pinched in their rim so that they would hold and retain a strip of fabric which would act as a wick. When greater light was needed, the bowl was formed with more spouts for wicks round its rim. Zechariah's lampstand might have been similarly shaped—though it was of solid gold rather than pottery—and the phrase **with seven channels to the lights** might refer to such pinched channels for holding the wicks. **Seven lights on it** certainly suggests it was different from the tabernacle lampstand. It may be the lamps were arranged round the central bowl with a pipe leading the oil to each of them. Seven is often used to indicate perfection (3:9), and the lampstand was designed to give light that was completely adequate.

The phrase 'with seven channels to the lights' is literally 'seven and seven pipes (or channels) to the lamps that are on top of it.' The idiom 'seven and seven' has been variously interpreted as indicating one to each of the seven (hence the NIV rendering) or that there were fourteen or even forty-nine pipes. Descriptions of the lampstand can therefore involve intricate patterns of plumbing! It is unlikely that there was more than one channel to each lamp, but if more are needed, then certainly two would suffice to convey the idea of an abundant supply.

Whatever the detail of the construction of the lampstand, its interpretation is made abundantly clear in Scripture. The details are different in Exodus 25 and again in Revelation 1 where John sees 'seven golden lampstands' (Rev. 1:12) which are later interpreted as 'the seven churches' (Rev. 1:20). The lampstand represents the community of God's people. It is made of gold to indicate how precious they are in his sight. Their function is to give light in the world (Mt. 5:14-16; see also Phil. 2:15), first as the church in Old Testament Israel and then as the New Testament church comprising both Jew and Gentile.

There is then added the significant information, **Also there are two olive trees by it, one on the right of the bowl and the other on its left (*4:3*)**. It is not entirely clear how we are to view the olive trees in relation to the lampstand. It may be that all are set on the same level, but 'by it' may also be rendered 'above it' and the description in relation to the bowl which was at the top of the lampstand may suggest that the trees are to be viewed as higher up and at the level of the bowl. In this way they provide the oil for the bowl, as mentioned later (4:12).

**I asked the angel who talked with me (*4:4*)** is literally 'I responded and said' (compare 4:11). Zechariah is reacting to the whole situation presented to him with curiosity. **What are these, my lord?** does not of course relate to the identification of the objects. That was not the problem Zechariah had; it was their significance he could not grasp and about which he asks again later (4:11).

**He answered, "Do you not know what these are?" (*4:5*).** Literally, 'The angel who was talking with me answered and said to me.' The angel's response constitutes somewhat of a rebuke to Zechariah. It implies he should have been able to work out at least some of the significance of what he was seeing. The tone of mild surprise is reminiscent of Jesus' reply to his disciples, 'Don't you understand this parable? How then will you understand any parable?' (Mk. 4:13), or of what he said to Nicodemus, 'You are Israel's teacher, and do you not understand these things?' (Jn. 3:10). But the prophet makes no pretence that he can understand what is being shown him. **"No, my lord,"** I replied.

*Zerubbabel's Success (4:6-10).* **So he** answered and **said to me, "This is the word of the LORD to Zerubbabel"** (*4:6*). One might have expected an explanation of the vision to be given at this point, but that has to wait until 4:11-14. Since the picture should have been understood at least in part, it is the application of the vision that is given next. What Zechariah has seen should convey a message to Zerubbabel as he grappled with the difficulties facing him.

    **'Not by might nor by power, but by my Spirit,' says the LORD Almighty.** 'Might' and 'power' are very close synonyms. 'Might' refers to material wealth and military capability, while 'power' refers to the exercise of it. Together they represent the full extent of human resources which could be deployed to deal with a difficult situation. As Zerubbabel looked at what was available to him in organising the building of the Temple, he might well have compared what he had to the lavish provision David had set aside for Solomon—'a hundred thousand talents of gold, a million talents of silver, quantities of bronze and iron too great to be weighed, and wood and stone' (1 Chr. 22:14; 29:2). He might also have thought of the mighty men available to David and Solomon to protect their realms against external threat. The restored community had no comparable economic or military resources.

    But that was not the way forward for the LORD's people. Their destiny was not going to be determined by what man can muster to deal with problems. The challenges facing them can only be overcome by the strength given by the LORD. 'But'—the distinction is stronger than that—'But rather by my Spirit'. This is not a reference to the regenerating work of the Spirit, but to his external acts. He played a role in creation (Gen. 1:2). God's Holy Spirit was guiding and sustaining the people at the time of the Exodus (Isa. 63:11, 14). It is the same Spirit who intervenes to provide divine power whenever God's people need to be protected and built up, and whenever God's cause on earth needs to be advanced (Mic. 3:8; Hag. 2:5). This is the way in which the LORD Almighty (1:3) works so that it can be seen that success for his people comes from him alone, and they are to look to him for the help and resources that they need when confronted by seemingly impossible situations. There is a greater power with them than with their adversary. 'With him is only the arm of flesh, but with us is the LORD our God to help us and to fight our battles' (2 Chr. 32:8). 'For though we live in the world, we do not wage war as the world does. The weapons we fight with are not the weapons of the world. On the contrary, they have divine power to demolish strongholds' (2 Cor. 10:3-4).

The next verse dramatically declares that the problems besetting Zerubbabel as God's agent will be swept aside. **What are you, O mighty mountain?** (*4:7*) issues a challenge to whatever opposes God's purposes. From a human perspective there may seem to be insuperable impediments—a great mountain of them—but it is the divine perspective that ultimately counts. Isaiah showed how every obstacle would be cleared from the path of the coming LORD, every mountain and hill being made low (Isa. 40:4). In Jeremiah the figure of a mountain is used specifically of Babylon, 'the destroying mountain' (Jer. 51:25), which had done so much wrong in Zion. Perhaps then this challenge is not issued just to obstacles in general, but particularly to those parties that had already tried to make life difficult for the Jews. 'Then the peoples around them set out to discourage the people of Judah and make them afraid to go on building. They hired counsellors to work against them and frustrate their plans during the entire reign of Cyrus king of Persia and down to the reign of Darius king of Persia' (Ezr. 4:4-5). It was around this time that Zerubbabel had to cope with the official inquiries being made by Tattenai, governor of Trans-Euphrates (Ezr. 5:3-5).

But he had not to cope with these difficulties on his own. As David had exultantly exclaimed, 'With your help I can advance against a troop; with my God I can scale a wall' (Ps. 18:29). So Zerubbabel will also know the power of God working on his behalf. **Before Zerubbabel you will become level ground**. Moving forward in faith to complete the divinely assigned task, he will find that the threats of the enemies are nullified by the action of the LORD's power. The promise has been given that the opposition will be overcome. 'You will become' is an English supplement. The Hebrew is terse—'Before Zerubbabel to level ground'—and brings out the peremptoriness of God's sovereign command. He speaks and it is done (Ps. 33:9).

**Then he will bring out the capstone to shouts of 'God bless it! God bless it!'** The capstone is 'the foremost stone' or 'the principal stone'. Generally the most important stone in an ancient building was the foundation stone, but here it is the completion of the building that is specially marked, perhaps when Zerubbabel superintends the placing of a stone at the top of an arch or gateway, marking the completion of the Temple. It would have been previously prepared and then brought out from the workshop or quarry to fit into its allotted place. With jubilation the people will cry out, 'Grace! Grace to it!' extolling God's freely given blessing on the work now completed, and imploring that he continue to look with favour on the Temple and all that was represented by it. The joy of the people is specifically mentioned in Ezra 6:22 where it is associated with the LORD having changed the attitude of the king of Assyria (used as a general term to refer to the ruling power in Mesopotamia), so that he assisted them by making supplies available.

**Then the word of the LORD came to me (*4:8*)** marks off what follows from the preceding divine word which had been relayed by the interpreting angel. If we understand this to have been spoken directly to Zechariah by the Angel of the LORD, it helps to clarify the following verse.

**The hands of Zerubbabel have laid the foundation of this temple; his hands will also complete it (*4:9*).** This conveys an assurance to Zerubbabel of the completion of the project which has been started. In Ezra's narrative Zerubbabel is not personally mentioned in connection with the completion of the Temple, which is ascribed to the elders of the Jews in general (Ezr. 6:14). But this does not warrant claiming that this prophecy was not fulfilled.

**Then you will know that the LORD Almighty has sent me to you.** These words might be understood as Zechariah's claim to the people that fulfilment of this very specific prophecy will validate his divine warrant for coming to them as a prophet. But it seems more likely that the speaker is the LORD, or more specifically, the Angel of the LORD, who was sent to give assistance to the LORD's people. ('You' is plural and refers to the people, not to the prophet.) When their project is successfully accomplished, then the people will know that the LORD's blessing was resting on them.

**Who despises the day of small things?** (*4:10*) is not to be understood of the sneering attitude of their opponents. (See Neh. 4:2-4 for how they would express themselves on a later occasion). Rather what we have here is another reference to the despondency that affected the returned community when they reflected on the magnitude of the task facing them (Ezr. 3:13; Hag. 2:3). It was not that these people were hostile to the project; it was just that they claimed to be realists and did not see how it could be done. They had faith, but it was deficient in that it failed to grasp how dependent they were on God and how it was through him alone that the project would be successfully completed.

Their attitude was going to be transformed as the work progressed. **Men will rejoice when they see the plumb-line in the hand of Zerubbabel.** This may describe the situation as Zerubbabel checked on the progress of the work. An alternative understanding is to take 'plumbline' to refer to 'separate stone', the one set apart as the capstone in 4:6. When the Temple is finished, even those of little faith will have grounds for rejoicing. The more the work progresses, the more their discouraging fears will be dispelled, being replaced by joy and wonder at what the LORD has achieved (Ps. 118:22-24).

There are then added words which are difficult to understand, and translations vary. But there is much to commend the approach of the NIV, which takes the words as a parenthetic explanation. **These seven are the eyes of the LORD, which range throughout the earth.** This looks back to 3:9, and declares that this is the practical impact of the LORD's close supervision of all that occurs on earth. The project that he approves of will not lack his care and protection until it is completed.

*Further Explanation (4:11-14).* There has, however, been a feature of the vision that has not yet been adequately explained, and Zechariah again renews his earlier inquiry (4:4). **Then I asked the angel, "What are these two olive trees on the right and the left of the lampstand?"** (*4:11*). However encouraging the message that had been relayed to him, he still had not grasped what function the trees performed. He looks more closely at them, and rephrases his question in such a way as to bring out further details of what he was seeing. **Again I asked him, "What are these two olive branches beside the two gold pipes that pour out golden oil?"** (*4:12*).

'The golden oil' is literally 'the gold', identifying the oil by its colour. Olive oil was one of the staple crops of Palestine, being frequently mentioned along with grain and new wine as the principal products of the land (Deut. 7:13; 11:14; 12:17; 14:23; Neh. 5:11; Jer. 31:12; Hos. 2:8; Joel 1:10; Hag. 1:11). Oil was used for many purposes—in cooking, as a skin cleanser and cosmetic, in various medicinal compounds, and for lighting. The extraction of the oil from the olives was carried out in various ways according to the purity required.

Zechariah here mentions 'two olive branches beside the two gold pipes', and this raises the matter of how these features relate to the total vision. It is a vision. Perhaps real olive trees have branches that are not all equally fruitful, but that is not the point here. It is from one particular branch of each tree that oil is provided for the lampstand. The 'pipes' (or emptiers) are different from the channels mentioned earlier (4:2). They are the means by which the oil that drips from the branches is conveyed into the bowl at the top of the lampstand.

Again the angel expresses surprise that Zechariah had not been able to work it out (4:5). **He replied, "Do you not know what these are?"** (*4:13*). The prophet is still baffled. **"No, my lord," I said.**

**So he said, "These are the two who are anointed to serve the Lord of all the earth"** (*4:14*). 'The two who are anointed' is literally 'the two sons of oil' and refers to Joshua and Zerubbabel (there is no thought of one having precedence over the other) in their roles as God's appointed officers for his people. Though the word used for 'oil' usually refers to it as a natural, unprocessed product, and not in the highly refined form associated with anointing, the reference is clear. Both priests (Ex. 29:7; 40:15) and kings (1 Sam. 10:1; 16:1; Ps. 89:20) were anointed with oil to indicate their being set apart to special office. It is not in their personal, but their official capacity, that they are referred to here. 'To serve' is literally 'standing by'. It pictures them as servants of the Lord, the ruler, of all the earth (note the word translated Lord is *Adonai*, see on Mal. 3:1), waiting to hear what he commands and ever ready to execute his will. As they live up to the roles assigned to them, they prefigure the Coming One who alone perfectly and completely carried through the task of priest and king which the Father allotted him. This was how the LORD would be present with the community and in particular in the restored Temple.

Not only are they anointed with oil, they are also branches which dispense oil. It is the LORD who makes the olive trees to grow and be fruitful. But the priest and ruler are divinely appointed channels for conveying the blessing of the Holy Spirit to the lampstand, the church. Oil signified the Holy Spirit, as can be seen from passages such as 'So Samuel took the horn of oil and anointed him in the presence of his brothers, and from that day on the Spirit of the LORD came upon David in power' (1 Sam. 16:13) and 'The Spirit of the Sovereign LORD is on me, because the LORD has anointed me to preach good news to the poor' (Isa. 61:1). From the anointed ones the influence and power of the Spirit pervades the church, enabling it to maintain its role of providing light in the world of darkness, no matter what the opposition that threatens to subvert it. In this they foreshadowed Christ through whom the Holy Spirit came in fulness to the church.

There are two ways in which the church is presented in this chapter. The Temple represented God's dwelling with his people, and this is never achieved apart from the activity of the Holy Spirit. He is the only effective church builder, able to overcome obstacles and to claim hearts and lives for God's service. Often he begins his work in small ways so that it may be clearly seen that its success is not from human endeavour but by divine blessing. He worked through an Abraham who was 'as good as dead' (Rom. 4:19); through a David who was 'only a boy' (1 Sam. 17:33, 42); through twelve men like Peter and John, 'unschooled, ordinary men' (Acts 4:13). It is the LORD who is able to make 'worm Jacob' and 'little Israel' into a threshing-sledge able to reduce the hills to chaff (Isa. 41:14-16). We must be careful not to judge the potential of an enterprise by its small beginnings. What matters is that it has the blessing of God's Spirit. Without him the church is ineffectual and frustrated, and will never grow.

But the church is also represented here by the lampstand. It has the task of giving light to the world. Whenever the church has been unfaithful to its commission and preached human speculation and the currently received wisdom of the world rather than the oracles of God, it has spread darkness and not light. 'If the light within you is darkness, how great is that darkness!' (Mt. 6:23). It is not only the Pharisees who have proved to be blind guides, leading blind men (Mt. 15:14). So has the church, whenever it has tried to provide its own oil for the lampstand. It needs the continuous supply of the Spirit to give it understanding of the truth and the ability to apply it to the circumstances of the day. This is the church's basic resource, procured for it by the risen Christ. 'Exalted to the right hand of God, he has received from the Father the promised Holy Spirit and has poured out what you now see and hear' (Acts 2:33).

## Study Questions

**4:6** How does God provide his people with the power they need to accomplish what he requires? Acts 9:31; 16:5; Phil. 2:12-13; Col. 1:11; 2:7; Heb. 13:9.

**4:7** Zerubbabel was a type of Christ: that is, in fulfilling his God-appointed duties he foreshadowed Christ. In what ways do the challenge and promise of 4:7 foreshadow Christ? Jn. 14:30; Col. 2:15.

**4:10** In assessing projects what factors do we have to take into account? Gen. 24:50; Mk. 4:26-29; Lk. 12:13-21; Acts 5:38-39; 18:21; Phil. 1:15-18; Jas. 4:13-15.

**4:14** What role does anointing play in the experience of the believer? Ps. 23:5; 2 Cor. 1:21-22; 1 Jn. 2:20, 27.

## Zechariah 5:1-4:  Vision 6:  The Flying Scroll

Previous visions encouraged the covenant community by presenting the constituent elements of the gospel: the sovereign choice of God (3:2), the free justification of the sinner (3:4), the empowering of the Spirit to all holy endeavour (4:6, 14), and the Messiah through whom the basis of acceptance with God would be achieved (3:8-9). Inspired by these truths, the leaders of the community may set an example for all to follow. But there is another aspect to the situation. Covenant blessings may not be enjoyed without covenant obedience. Rebuilding the Temple was a worthwhile project, but it was not the only requirement of the LORD. A restored Temple had to be accompanied by a restored lifestyle, totally in accordance with his requirements. This vision and the next serve warning that the LORD will not look with impunity on those who make light of his requirements.

**I looked again (5:1).** Again the phrase is 'lifted up my eyes and looked' (1:18), indicating that after the intensity of the visionary experience granted to him, the prophet had become introspective and absorbed with his thoughts, until something caused his attention to be focused elsewhere.

**There before me was a flying scroll.** He had no difficulty identifying the object that was before him. Scrolls had been used for centuries for writing. They were long strips of material, made from specially prepared animal hide, or from the split core of the papyrus plant from Egypt. The stalks were laid criss-cross in two or three layers, and might be written upon both sides (Ezk. 2:10; Rev. 5:1). In Zechariah's day it seems probable that both materials would have been in use in Palestine. For ease of storage scrolls would be rolled up. Often this was done by attaching sticks to the ends of the scroll and winding the material round them. As it was read, a scroll was rolled from one stick to the other so that only a small portion would be visible at any time.

But though the scroll was recognisable as such, what was unusual was the fact that it was 'flying', not laid on a table, or preserved in a pottery storage jar, or yet in someone's hands for reading—but in the air, and as the next verse makes clear, unrolled. It seems to have been like the banners sometimes used in aerial advertising. The objective would have been the same; it was something that had to be taken note of by all—in Jerusalem and throughout the land (5:3).

**He asked me, "What do you see?" (5:2).** The unidentified speaker is the interpreting angel. The situation differs slightly from 4:2 in that Zechariah has already identified what is before him, but by quizzing the prophet, the angel leads him to consider the significance of the vision. As a prophet, Zechariah was not just to look in wonder at it. The vision conveyed a message which he had to comprehend and then proclaim to the people.

**I answered, "I see a flying scroll, thirty feet long and fifteen feet wide."** We do not know how Zechariah was able to work out the dimensions of the scroll. Perhaps the angel told him. But by describing it in this way he shows that the scroll was unrolled and capable of being read as it moved through the air. The length of scrolls was limited by the amount of material that could be conveniently rolled round one stick. A longer book of Scripture, such as Isaiah, would have been recorded on a scroll by itself. Some scrolls might well have been about thirty feet long. Zechariah, of course, gives the dimensions in cubits, traditionally the distance from the elbow to the tip of the middle finger (around eighteen inches, or somewhat under half a metre). 'Twenty cubits long and ten cubits wide' is, as the margin shows, about 9 metres long and 4 metres wide.

What is surprising about the dimensions of the scroll is the width relative to the length. Normally a scroll would be about 10 inches wide, that is 25 centimetres, but this one is half as wide as it is long! We are deliberately told about this unusual feature. Perhaps the intention was simply to emphasise that it was of banner size, and so would appear ominous as it went through the air. But it has been noted that the dimensions are the same as those of the Holy Place in the tabernacle (Ex. 26:15-28). (The fact that that was also the size of the portico or entrance porch of Solomon's Temple [1 Kgs. 6:3] seems accidental, as the portico had no special significance.) A feature drawn from the Tabernacle might be employed in a similar way to the use of the lampstand in the previous vision. What the scroll represented was determined by the standards of the sanctuary. That was what was significant for the covenant people.

The interpreting angel does not seem to expect Zechariah to be able to work out the significance of what he has seen and tells him straightaway. **And he said to me, "This is the curse that is going out over the whole land"** *(5:3).* The use of 'curse' brings us into the area of the covenant (see on Mal. 3:9). The covenant created a bond between the LORD and his people. To maintain that bond-relationship they had to obey God's commands. Such obedience brought blessing. If they disobeyed the LORD's commands, they violated the covenant relationship and incurred the curse of divine displeasure. This had been vividly brought before the people in the ceremony where the blessings were proclaimed from Mount Gerizim and the curses from Mount Ebal (Deut. 11:26-29; 27:12-13; Josh. 8:33-34). Here the curse is specifically the judgment that was threatening those who disparaged the requirements of God in their living.

It is not clear whether the curse is going 'over the whole land', or 'over the whole earth'. The Hebrew could mean either. As the covenant curse was of course a threat to those who are in covenant relationship with the LORD, it would seem that 'land' is a more reasonable translation, but we have to remember that the people had been dispersed throughout the Middle East, and the LORD looked for the obedience of those scattered abroad as much as of those who had returned to Judah. However, Zechariah's ministry at this time seems specifically concentrated on the problems of the returned community, and so it seems better to follow the NIV.

What was written on the scroll is not stated, but the implications of its message are. **According to what it says on one side, every thief will be banished, and according to what it says on the other, every one who swears falsely will be banished.** Two commandments are selected as representative of the whole covenant requirements of God. The eighth commandment focuses on the social relationships within the community (Ex. 20:15), and the third commandment (Ex. 20:7; Lev. 19:12) stands for all God's covenant requirements of behaviour directed towards himself. False swearing involved the use of God's name in connection with falsehood, or entering into a solemn commitment with no intention of keeping it. They were prepared to say 'As surely as the LORD lives', but had no respect for the truth (Jer. 5:2).

The imposition of the covenant curse would come impartially on all who violated the demands of the covenant. The verb 'be banished' seems to have conveyed the basic notion of 'be poured out', and was used with good and bad implications. Its more common use is positive to denote being freed or cleared of a charge, and so declared innocent. But it is used negatively in Isaiah 3:26, where it describes the land as 'destitute', that is, with its inhabitants poured out of it. A similar meaning is appropriate here—taken, or poured, from the land of promise by divine judgment.

The curse of the broken covenant was no idle threat. **The LORD Almighty declares, 'I will send it out' (5:4).** The following clauses show that 'it' here refers to the curse rather than the scroll. There should be no doubt. The LORD will not treat with impunity those who have slighted his covenant. **It will enter the house of the thief and the house of him who swears falsely by my name. It will remain in his house and destroy it, both its timbers and its stones.** This seems to reflect on Persian modes of punishment. When Darius permitted the work to proceed in Jerusalem, he decreed that 'if anyone changes this edict, a beam is to be pulled from his house and he is to be lifted up and impaled on it. And for this crime his house is to be made a pile of rubble' (Ezr. 6:11). If that happened to those who countermanded the edicts of an earthly king, how much more so will the curse fall on those who have made light of the edicts of the King of Heaven. The description emphasises the thoroughness of divine judgment, extending even to the destruction of the stones of their homes. Even the Temple stones had largely survived the fire lit by the Babylonians. But this will be like the fire of the LORD which came down from heaven on the altar Elijah built 'and burned up the sacrifice, the wood, the stones and the soil, and also licked up the water in the trench' (1 Kgs. 18:38). There are no half measures when God acts. 'The LORD'S curse is on the house of the wicked, but he blesses the home of the righteous' (Prov. 3:33).

The holiness of God should be reflected in his people. 'As obedient children, do not conform to the evil desires you had when you lived in ignorance. But just as he who called you is holy, so be holy in all you do; for it is written: "Be holy, because I am holy"' (1 Pet. 1:14-16). The consequence of this was that in building the Temple and thus seeking to have God dwell in their midst, the Jews had to ensure that all evil was expelled from the land. 'You are not a God who takes pleasure in evil; with you the wicked cannot dwell' (Ps. 5:4). The same requirement still holds. 'We are the temple of the living God' (2 Cor. 6:16), and there can be no alliance with wickedness and the wicked one.

*Study Question*
**5:3** What is a curse? How does it operate? What is the difference
between human and divine curses? Gen. 3:17; Deut. 11:28; Job 2:9;
Mk. 11:21; Lk. 6:28; Gal. 3:10.

## Zechariah 5:5-11:  Vision 7:  The Woman in the Basket

The theme of the seventh vision follows on closely from that of the
flying scroll. The restored people will not automatically enjoy the
blessings of the covenant. All that was symbolised by the restored
Temple would be spoiled unless they responded to the LORD with a
total commitment. That was the requirement of the covenant: 'Love
the LORD your God with all your heart and with all your soul and with
all your strength' (Deut. 6:5). It was not just a matter of outward
behaviour. At issue was the basic motivation of the people. There
were those who would carefully avoid theft and perjury. But were
they completely loyal to the LORD, or had worldly gain come to
dominate their thinking and their living? This vision looks forward
to a situation of a second Exile where those who pursue worldly
advantage and material profit are removed from the land. The people
of God in every age must devote themselves to him, seeking first his
kingdom and righteousness (Mt. 6:33).

It would appear that the interpreting angel had left Zechariah, and
so to mark the start of a new vision, **Then the angel who was
speaking to me came forward and said to me (5:5).** The interpreting angel approaches the prophet, who is once more absorbed in what
had been revealed to him, and has to refocus his attention on what is
now taking place. **Look up and see what this is that is appearing.**
It is as if the prophet is looking at a scene set out before him, and
something is coming closer from a distance. It is not said from where
it is moving out, or how it is moving.

Zechariah does not seem to be able to make out what it is that can
be seen. **I asked, "What is it?" (5:6).** There seems to have been
genuine grounds for his puzzlement, because the angel does not
upbraid him for his inability to understand (4:5), but immediately
gives an answer. **He replied, "It is a measuring basket."** The angel
identifies what is coming as an 'ephah', which was a basket used for

measuring and storing grain. A variety of materials—woven straw or pottery—were probably used to make such containers, and we do not know what precise size they were, but something of a capacity of two-thirds of a bushel (that is, about five gallons or 22 litres) seems not to have been uncommon.

As is later made clear (5:7), this ephah contains a woman. Some suggest the woman may have been smaller than usual, perhaps even a figurine, and so able to fit inside an ordinary size basket. The presence of a figurine, however, slants the interpretation of the passage towards idolatry. Since that was not one of the problems facing the restored community, it is more appropriate to think of the basket as larger than normal. It may have been this unusual size that caused Zechariah's difficulty in working out what it was.

But the interpreting angel does not merely identify the object Zechariah can see; he also gives its significance. **And he added, "This is the iniquity of the people throughout the land."** There is a textual problem here because, with one exception, all the Hebrew manuscripts read 'This is their eye' rather than 'This is their iniquity', though the latter is found in early translations of Zechariah. The difference between the two is a matter of the length of a stroke in a Hebrew letter, so it is easy to see how they could be confused. Perhaps there is not too great a difference of meaning between the two readings here. 'Eye' is a versatile word in Hebrew, and can refer to what presents itself to the eye, that is 'appearance' as in the NIV margin (Lev. 13:55; Num. 11:7). If, as I shall argue, the ephah stands for commercial trading and desire for material advancement among the people, it is not far-fetched to say that the ephah is the way they appear.

Following the rendering adopted by the NIV and many modern translations, the ephah represents the iniquity that was widespread throughout the land. For iniquity, see on 'sin' (3:4). Note that the other main element in the vision—the woman—has not yet been mentioned, and so she is not yet being identified with the sin of the land. That is symbolised by the basket, which was in shape, if not in size, like the ephah that was used in trading.

The ephah, though not the largest of Old Testament measures, was the most common way of measuring dry goods, and so often stands for measurements in general (Deut. 25:14). It was difficult to standardise weights and measures in the ancient world, and so those who were determined to get rich by fair means or foul found it very tempting to have two measures—a large one to use when they were buying, and a small one to use when they were selling (Prov. 20:10, 23). This had been a prevalent act of commercial malpractice in the materialistic culture that had captured the hearts of pre-exilic Israel and Judah, and hastened their downfall (Amos 8:5; Mic. 6:10-11). Many considered that observance of worship at the sanctuary was a hindrance in the pursuit of profit (Amos 8:4), and were prepared to use any means at all to become rich (Amos 2:6; 5:11; Hos. 12:7-8).

Unfortunately, the same wrong attitude still gripped the community after the Exile. Seventy-five years later, Nehemiah tells how he saw men farming and trading on the Sabbath (Neh. 13:15-18). They were also withholding the portions of the Levites (Neh. 13:10) and defrauding God of the offerings that were his due (Mal. 3:8). Their desire for gain and worldly prosperity had again come to dominate their living, and they were prepared to defraud labourers of their wages and oppress the less fortunate members of society to advance themselves (Neh. 5:1-5; Mal. 3:5). Despite all this they still professed loyalty to the LORD and engaged in the worship of the Temple. This outlook had had its origins in the newly returned community (Hag. 1:3-11). Through the preaching of Haggai and Zechariah it had been overcome to the extent that work on the Temple had been resumed, but it remained a very real threat to the integrity of the covenant bond between the people and the LORD. The ephah sums up the materialistic ambitions that were corrupting the people.

The vision does not, however, end there. **Then the cover of lead was raised** (*5:7*). It is not said who did this: it might have been the angel, or it may have been raised from within. There is no other record of circular lead covers being used to cover the opening of an ephah; so this is a second unusual feature apart from the ephah's massive size. **And there in the basket sat a woman!** The Hebrew emphasises that it was 'one woman', perhaps she was crouching in the confined space.

The angel immediately recognises what is involved. **He said, "This is wickedness"** (*5:8*). 'Wickedness' is a general word covering all that is the opposite of righteousness. It may be distinguished from guilt or iniquity as the principle of evil is from the consequences that follow from it. It is difficult to be certain why a woman is used to signify wickedness. It is improbable that it reflects on the role that Eve played in the Fall (Gen. 3). It may just be a natural personification in Hebrew where the word 'wickedness' is of feminine gender. In that case the woman and the ephah would point to the inner origin of wickedness and the acts of exploitation arising from it. Alternatively, the woman may be a development of descriptions such as 'Daughter of Zion' (2:10) to describe the community as a whole. There are a number of passages, generally uncomplimentary, where the prophets personify the nation in this way (Jer. 3:6-14; Ezk. 16; 23). Here the woman would represent not the nation as a whole, but those within it who were committed to what is wrong and entangled in the lifestyle summed up by the ephah.

The woman wants to be active among the restored community, but the angel is able to confine her. **He pushed her back into the basket and pushed the lead cover down over its mouth.** It was not easily done. There was a struggle. The phrase rendered 'the lead cover' is not the same one as found previously, but is now literally 'stone or weight of lead', to show that she was effectively imprisoned within the basket by the heavy closure. There was to be no escape from the confinement that God had imposed on her.

But the vision does not stop with the confinement of evil. **Then I looked up—and there before me were two women (5:9).** It was not just that they were there. They also were 'appearing', or 'coming forth', as the ephah had done (5:1). It is said that they were coming **with the wind in their wings.** The female figures were therefore not simply women, but creatures that also had wings, and they were moving even more swiftly because the wind was bearing them along. That they are women seems to derive principally from the fact that it is a woman who is confined. There is also some evidence from ancient Near Eastern art that it was traditional to portray half-human half-animal figures as female, particularly those with wings. The task requires two of them because the iniquity found in the land is so great.

Zechariah gives even greater detail about their wings. **They had**

**wings like those of a stork, and they lifted up the basket between heaven and earth.** The white stork is a common migratory bird in Palestine (Jer. 8:7), and the point of the comparison seems to be that the large size of their wings would make it easy for them to carry out their task of raising the basket and taking it away. Opinions differ as to whether there is any other significance in the mention of the stork. It was an unclean animal (Lev. 11:19), and so the thought might be that they were a fitting means of removing an unclean object. On the other hand, the Hebrew word for stork means 'faithful one' (this is supposed to arise from its kind treatment of its young), and it might signify that they were the agents of the faithful God who, keeping true to his covenant promises, removes the evil from among his people.

**"Where are they taking the basket?" I asked the angel who was speaking to me (5:10).** The basket had been lifted high off the ground, and as storks are migratory birds, it was natural for the prophet to ask regarding its final destination. He does not ask anything about the women with wings because their function was obvious.

**He replied, "To the country of Babylonia" (5:11).** The original reference is to 'the land of Shinar'. Shinar is used by the prophets to refer to Babylon (Isa. 11:11; Dan. 1:2), probably because it retained the sinister overtones of the mention of Shinar in Genesis as the place where opposition to God and his cause was located (Gen. 11:1-9). Babylon was also renowned as a commercial centre in the ancient world (Rev. 18:11-20). It was thus an appropriate symbol to denote the destination of those who through pursuit of earthly riches had opposed the LORD's cause and his ways.

What is more, the angel's reply emphasises that it is **to build a house for it** that it is being taken to Shinar. 'House' here seems to be a temple rather than just a dwelling (Hag. 1:2). It is not just that such wickedness is going to reside there. It will have a suitable temple prepared for its worship in Babylonia. **When it is ready, the basket will be set there in its place.** This is to be a permanent arrangement. 'Place' also fits in with the picture of this being a temple, as it is the word used for the stand on which various pieces of Temple equipment were to be found (e.g. 1 Kgs. 7:27-31).

There are a number of respects in which this vision looks forward to the dispersion of the Jews throughout the nations after the fall of Jerusalem in A.D. 70. But even more significant is the analysis it provides of the spiritual decline among the restored community of Zechariah's day. Many among the Jews who had returned from the Exile were looking for temporal prosperity. When it did not come as they hoped, they sought to make the most of the situation they found themselves in. Grasping after gain they lost their grasp of spiritual fundamentals, and became worldly and materialistic in their outlook. Idol worship as such may have been absent in the restored community, but idolatry appeared in the more insidious and subtle form of greed (Eph. 5:5; Col. 3:5). Setting our minds on earthly things is something that we have always to be on our guard against (Phil. 3:19). We may draw back from obvious transgression such as theft or perjury, but it is very easy to become like the men in the parable of the great banquet who find their latest acquisition of land or oxen a greater priority than the affairs of the kingdom (Lk. 14:15-24). Even though their activity gains them the whole world, that is all the reward they will get when the Son of Man comes (Mt. 16:26-27). If they are in the ephah, then they will be carried away with it, because they have shown that Money is their master (Mt. 6:24). 'If anyone loves the world, the love of the Father is not in him' (1 Jn. 2:15). Instead we should emulate Moses who 'regarded disgrace for the sake of Christ as of greater value than the treasures of Egypt, because he was looking ahead to his reward' (Heb. 11:26).

*Study Questions*

**5:6** What modern equivalents can you suggest for the ephah or measuring basket as a symbol of a lifestyle dedicated to wealth no matter what?

What attitude should we adopt towards wealth and acquiring possessions? Job 31:24-28; 42:10; Ps. 37:16; 49:16-20; Prov. 11:4; 15:16-17; Mk. 10:17-27; 1 Tim. 6:17-19.

How should we engage in business? Lev. 19:35-36; Lk. 3:12-14; 2 Cor. 8:21; Col. 3:22; 1 Thess. 4:11-12; 1 Pet. 2:12.

### Zechariah 6:1-8:  Vision 8: The Four Chariots

The final vision brings the series to an end by returning to the same theme as was found in the first: the LORD's supremacy over the whole earth, and the outworking of his providential control for the good of his people.  The similarity of theme is reflected in the similarity (but not identity!) of the imagery.  The intervening visions had been concerned with Israel's own relationship with the LORD, and now that that has been dealt with, it is time to resume what had seemed to be the delayed intervention promised in the first vision.  The LORD's people could not expect to see their foes vanquished and the kingdom of God ushered in until their own relationship with the LORD had been put on a right footing.  God's timetable is not determined by the need to punish the peoples who reject his rule, but by the need for his own people to be purified and ready to enjoy all he has prepared for them. When that is accomplished, he will ensure that no outside power will disrupt their peace and their enjoyment of fellowship with him.

**I looked up again (*6:1*).** Zechariah uses the same phrase as before (1:18) to indicate the start of another vision.  **And there before me were four chariots.**  In the first vision the prophet had seen horses which had patrolled the earth.  Now the time for reconnoitring was past.  Action was called for, and it is chariots that are presented to his view.  Although used for the conveyance of kings and other notable persons, these were principally military vehicles.  They symbolise the LORD's power (Isa. 66:15; Hab. 3:8).  That there are *four* of them seems to refer to the worldwide scope of their mission (2:6; 6:7).

The chariots are described as **coming out from between two mountains—mountains of bronze!**  There are two ways of identifying these mountains.  As the vision is one of judgment, it is often suggested that they are Zion and the Mount of Olives.  This would fit in with the scene described in 14:4.  There is also a long-standing Jewish and Christian tradition identifying the Kidron Valley on the east of Jerusalem with the Valley of Jehoshaphat mentioned by Joel (Joel 3:2, 12).  The name is not connected with King Jehoshaphat, but is a symbolic use based on the fact that Jehoshaphat means 'the LORD judges'.  If Zechariah's visions were seen against a known background, mention here of the Kidron would resume the setting of the first vision (1:8).  Also if this last vision occurred towards morning, the valley and mountains bathed in the light of the rising sun might account for the reference to bronze. But it was not just the coming of a new day that was presented to the prophet, but of a new era in the fortunes of God's people.

Another, and probably preferable, approach is to note that in this verse the chariots are said to be 'coming out' and that in 6:5 the horses associated with them are described as 'going out', the same word in the original. The horses are coming out from the presence of the LORD, and so the chariots must be also. The mountains mentioned in verse 1 are therefore to be understood as being at the entrance into the divine presence, standing guard over it, just as the two bronze pillars guarded the entrance to Solomon's Temple (1 Kgs. 7:12). When God promised to strengthen Jeremiah and protect him, he undertook to make him not only a wall, but a *bronze* wall (Jer. 1:18). So here the emphasis on the mountains being of bronze conveys the impregnability and immovably fixed character of the LORD's kingdom. An entrance into it cannot be forced, and its foundation cannot be moved, being as unchangeable as God himself.

The focus of the prophet's description then changes from the chariots to the horses which were drawing them. (Presumably there were charioteers, but just as with the riders of the horses in the first vision [1:8], they are not explicitly mentioned.) The horses were of different colours. **The first chariot had red horses, the second black, the third white, and the fourth dappled—all of them powerful (6:2-3).** Red and white were also used to describe horses in the first vision (1:8), red being associated with bloodshed and war, and white with triumph and peace. Though black is not mentioned so often in Scripture, it would indicate mourning, scarcity, famine and death (Job 30:28, 30; Jer. 14:2 ['wail' refers to being dressed in black]; Mal. 3:14; Rev. 6:5-6, 12). The last description, rendered 'dappled—all of them powerful' by the NIV, is more problematic. On its own 'dappled' may have the same significance as 'brown' earlier (1:8), that is, a mixed set of conditions. But 'all of them' is a translator's supplement to indicate that 'powerful', which might be understood only of the fourth group, should be taken as describing all the horses. This makes better sense of the reference to 'the powerful horses' in 6:7. However, it is not certain that the last word does mean 'powerful'. Some understand it as part of a two-colour description of the last group 'dappled gray' (NRSV), which might be explained in terms of the pale horse of Revelation 6:8 which is ridden by Death and is given power to kill by sword, famine and plague, and by the beasts of the earth.

Many interpreters have tried to relate the four chariots to great empires of the past: perhaps, Babylon, Persia, Greece and Rome. Such specific interpretations failed to do justice to the details of verse 6. Even though there are aspects of the colours we do not fully understand, a more general approach seems preferable. These colours represent various providences of God. To sustain the people as they worked on the Temple, they are shown that all the varied conditions to be found on earth are under the control of the LORD as he works out his pleasure among the affairs of men.

**I asked the angel who was speaking to me, "What are these, my lord?" (6:4).** (For 'my lord', see on 1:9.) Given the difficulty interpreters have had with the details of this vision, even after the following explanation has been given, it was not surprising that Zechariah needed help in comprehending what he saw.

**The angel answered me, "These are the four spirits of heaven" (6:5).** As the NIV margin notes, the Hebrew word may be translated either as 'spirits' or 'winds'. The conception of the four spirits of heaven, presumably angelic beings, is not found elsewhere, and is not without difficulty. On the other hand, 'the four winds of heaven' are used to represent powerful forces, especially of God's judgment (Jer. 49:36; Dan. 7:2; Rev. 7:1). One symbol—the chariots and their horses—is being explained by another, more obvious symbol. These are the forces which shape events in the world.

What is more they are forces that carry out the LORD's purpose throughout the earth. **Going out from standing in the presence of the Lord of the whole world** shows that they had been waiting obediently and expectantly to do his bidding, and now they are acting in accordance with his commands. For 'standing' and 'Lord of the whole world', see on 4:14. The decrees of the Sovereign Ruler will not be frustrated.

**The one with the black horses is going towards the north country, the one with the white horses towards the west, and the**

**one with the dappled horses towards the south (6:6).** Verse 6 begins awkwardly in Hebrew, and some have suggested that a reference to the red horses going towards the east has been omitted. But it is not certain that there ought to be a reference to the four points of the compass. As is noted in the NIV margin 'towards the west' is literally 'after them', an additional consonant having to be added to the Hebrew to get the meaning 'after the sea', which would refer to the Mediterranean and be a reference to westwards movement. It is quite possible that there are two chariots which move towards the north, that is, in the direction of the enemies of the people that would be found in Mesopotamia (Jer. 3:18; 6:22; 25:9; 46:10). The chariot sent to the south would be directed against the other traditional enemy of Israel, namely Egypt. The fact that nothing is said of the chariot with red horses might be accounted for by it having already gone in all the disturbances of previous years in Mesopotamia. The destiny of the enemies of the LORD's people is in his hands. He will deal with them as best promotes the good of his own cause.

The construction at the beginning of 6:7 shows that it is not to be understood as following on from the previous verse. That had described a specific mission of the chariots and horses. Now there is added graphic detail about a more general mission of all the horses. **When the powerful horses went out, they were straining to go throughout the earth (6:7).** It is difficult to take 'powerful' here as applying only to the fourth chariot (see discussion of 6:3 above.) When all the horses came out from the presence of the LORD, they were eager to be about their more general tasks, but they were restrained until the appropriate time. It is not at the first sign of revolt that the LORD strikes those who rebel against him, but when the measure of their sin is full (Gen. 15:16; Mt. 13:30; 23:32; 1 Thess. 2:16). When that time has come, we find **and he said, "Go throughout the earth!" So they went throughout the earth.** It is not clear who the speaker is. It might be the interpreting angel, but taken in connection with what follows it is preferable to identify the speaker as the Angel of the LORD. The thrice repeated 'throughout the earth' emphasises the universality of God's dominion. 'Acknowledge and take to heart this day that the LORD is God in heaven above and on the earth below. There is no other' (Deut. 4:39).

**Then he called to me (*6:8*).** 'Call' does not describe the action of one close by, as the interpreting angel who was speaking with Zechariah would have been. Rather we are to think of this as uttered by the same speaker in the previous verse, who goes on to talk of 'my Spirit', and so must be identified as the Angel of the LORD.

**Look, those going towards the north country have given my Spirit rest in the land of the north.** The Angel of the LORD calls the prophet's attention to what is being accomplished in the north. 'Those going towards the north' refers specifically to the horses, whose mission can be determined from their colour, and not the chariots (the genders are different in Hebrew). They are on a mission of vengeance, and when they have imposed the LORD's judgment on those who have oppressed his people, the white horses will bring a period of stability and God's Spirit will be at rest, his anger against them having been appeased. It is the language of anticipation that is used. The commission that had been given them was so sure to be carried through that it is spoken of as already realised.

The final vision emphasises divine initiative and control over all events that occur on earth. It presents two aspects of divine intervention: what was specifically being done in Zechariah's day (6:6, 8), and the more general truth of his on-going control over all things.

Sceptics in every generation have asked, 'Where is this "coming" he promised? Ever since our fathers died, everything goes on as it has since the beginning of creation' (2 Pet. 3:4). But such an attitude may only be maintained by deliberately forgetting what has already occurred. The chariots of God's judgment have already gone out on numerous occasions to overthrow empires and expose the emptiness of the claims of those who pit themselves against him. God has not loosened his control over what happens on earth, but it is governed by the spiritual goals he has set himself (2 Pet. 3:9) and not by a need to vindicate himself against the scoffing of the ignorant.

*Study Questions*

**6:1** How does Scripture show the futility of setting ourselves against God? Ps. 2:4-5; Isa. 10:15; 29:16; 45:9; Rom. 9:20-21.

**6:7** How should we react to the fact of God's universal sovereignty? 1 Chr. 29:11; Ps. 22:28-29; 47:7; 96:10; Jer. 10:10; 1 Tim. 6:15-16; Rev. 11:17; 19:6.

## Zechariah 6:9-15: The Crowning of Joshua

In form this section (6:9-15) is an appendix to the eight visions. On several previous occasions explanations and applications had been added to the visions that Zechariah saw (2:6-13; 3:6-10; 4:6-10). These verses seem to be a similar expansion of the message, not however of one vision, but of them all. In such circumstances, to call them an appendix is to understate their significance. This section is the grand climax to the visions. Zechariah is commanded to crown Joshua the high priest. This is a symbolic act looking forward to the Branch of David's house who will be the Messiah and unite in himself the offices of priest and king that had been kept separate in Israel. It is his twofold work that is the basis for the promises found in the visions.

*The Symbolic Crowning (6:9-13).* **The word of the LORD came to me (6:9).** It is Zechariah who speaks, and uses the formula that indicates reception of a divine message, not a visionary experience (1:1; 7:1; 8:1). What follows, though arising out of the material of the visions, is quite distinct from them. The prophet does not see anything, but is commanded to act in a certain symbolic fashion. We are not told when this took place in relation to the visions of 15th February 519 B.C., but it is reasonable to think of it as occurring very shortly thereafter.

The message is very tersely expressed. It would have occasioned no difficulty for someone familiar with recent events in Jerusalem, but lacking this background makes it obscure for us. **Take <silver and gold>** (*6:10*). The text does not specify what Zechariah has to take, but the mention of 'silver and gold' in the following verse makes this a reasonable supplement. **From the exiles Heldai, Tobijah and Jedaiah.** These three men were not among the exiles who had originally returned from Babylon. They seem to have returned recently, bringing material for the Temple reconstruction.

At a later date, the Persian king Artaxerxes spoke to Ezra of two types of assistance: that from state funds, 'the silver and gold that the king and his advisers have freely given to the God of Israel', and that from the Jews' own contributions, 'all the silver and gold you may obtain from the province of Babylon, as well as the freewill offerings of the people and priests for the temple of their God in Jerusalem' (Ezr. 7:15-16). Darius' decree at this time shows that the Persian authorities were prepared to assist the project out of state revenues, but using funds from the provincial rather than the central treasury (Ezr. 6:8). As these men had come from Babylon, it makes it unlikely that they were acting as official emissaries from the Persian government, bringing state help. They were bringing funds collected by the Jews themselves. Zechariah later mentions the praise accorded them (6:14); so perhaps they themselves had organised the collection.

**Go the same day to the house of Josiah son of Zephaniah.** The Hebrew is repetitive and emphatic: 'You yourself go on the same day and go to the house of Josiah son of Zephaniah.' It would seem that after he had received the material Zechariah was to go to this house. Perhaps Josiah was a goldsmith who could make the crown that was required. Alternatively, it was at his house that the party from Babylon were staying before they completed their task by handing the material they had brought over to the authorities in Jerusalem. The Hebrew adds **who have arrived from Babylon** at the end of the verse. This makes its reference somewhat more ambiguous than in the NIV, where it is placed after the names of the party. It might also be the case that Josiah had arrived as one of the party from Babylon, and because he had a house in Jerusalem, they were staying there with him. It would have been quite clear to anyone who knew the local circumstances in Jerusalem. 'The same day' indicates that the prophet was not to delay in carrying out his commission, perhaps so that there would be not be any opportunity for suspicions to arise as to why he had received the precious metals. It would have been sacrilegious theft to have used material intended for the Temple for any other purpose than one the LORD had appointed.

**Take the silver and gold and make a crown** (*6:11*). The word 'crown' in the original is a plural noun, but it is improbable that more than one crown is meant. Sometimes plurals are used in Hebrew to indicate a superlative, so that the idea would be of the ultimate or supreme crown. The mention of the two metals, moreover, makes it likely that what is described is a crown consisting of multiple rings of metal. Presumably there must have been at least two rings, one of silver and one of gold. It was therefore an item of considerable intricacy and magnificence (Rev. 19:12), and its dual construction accords with the dual role of the one crowned. It is also the case that the word used for 'crown' is not the same as that used for the high priest's headdress. It never refers to priestly apparel, but is a sign of royal or princely rank, as well as being used metaphorically (2 Sam. 12:30; Ps. 21:3; Song 3:11; Prov. 4:9; 14:24). It is therefore a matter of surprise that Zechariah is instructed **and set it on the head of the high priest, Joshua son of Jehozadak.**

So surprising is this that many commentators have argued that the text has become corrupt and it should be Zerubbabel, the civil ruler of the people, that is mentioned here. No ancient text supports this contention. Further, if Zechariah had in fact crowned Zerubbabel, it would most probably have been misconstrued by the Persians as indicative of revolt. What he did to a priestly figure would have been more readily accepted as a religious ceremony. It might also have been misunderstood by the Jews themselves. Since Zerubbabel was of Davidic descent, they might have thought that he was personally the Messiah, the promised descendant of David through whom the LORD's promises about his kingdom would come true. But it is the priest who is crowned, not personally or permanently, but in a symbolic action as the one representing the Messiah. Joshua becomes a temporary Melchizedek, combining priesthood and kingship in one person (Ps. 110:1-4; Gen. 14:18).

Such a union of the offices of king and priest had previously been forbidden. When King Uzziah tried to burn incense on the altar of incense, he was punished for his usurpation of the priests' role (2 Chr. 26:16-21). Now it is shown that both these functions are going to be combined in the one person. This was the truth that had been prophesied by David in Psalm 110 where the LORD's anointed king was also declared to be a priest after the order of Melchizedek, who had been both king of Salem and a priest of God Most High. That truth is now restated in much clearer terms. In that it is the priest who wears the crown, and not the prince some item of priestly garb, there is demonstrated that it is the priestly role of the Messiah that is primary. It is only when he has completed this role to the satisfaction of the Father that he is invested with his Mediatorial kingship.

An explanation of what was happening was then given to Zechariah to relay to Joshua. **Tell him this is what the LORD Almighty says: 'Here is the man whose name is the Branch'** (*6:12*). The declaration is literally, 'Behold a man! Branch his name.' This places less emphasis on Joshua personally than the NIV rendering suggests. Joshua and his associates had already been called 'men symbolic of things to come' (3:8), and here too it is what Joshua foreshadowed that is significant. Joshua as thus crowned is a representative or typical figure: he is the one who looks forward to the Messiah, the coming priest-king. 'Branch' as a Messianic title has already been used in 3:8, and here there are outlined five noteworthy features about the coming one.

*(1)* In a play on the title 'Branch' it is said **he will branch out from his place.** This does not relate to the extension of the Messianic kingdom throughout the earth, but to the genuine origin of the Messiah within Israel. It picks up the idea of the appearance and growth of the Messiah himself as the horn the LORD causes to grow for David (Ps. 132:17, using the same root). 'From his place' has been variously interpreted, but it seems to point to the Messiah as a legitimate descendant of David. He will not be a foreigner (Deut. 17:15), but would be of David's own line (2 Sam. 7:12). This might have been obscured by the symbolism, where Joshua, of the tribe of Levi, was crowned. The priest-king will be of Judah, of the house of David.

There seems to be another idea also present in the statement. In Joshua's day the fortunes of the house of David were at a low ebb, and the people were suffering from a crisis of confidence. The promise given to them is that the Messiah will grow up 'from his place', that is, from wherever he is and from whatever conditions prevail in Israel at his birth. No matter how depressed the state of the house of David, his power to be what the Branch or sprout really should be will not be limited by time or circumstance. Though he grew up before the LORD 'like a tender shoot, and like a root out of dry ground' (Isa.

53:2), one whose origins in Nazareth of Galilee are a cause for suspicion and contempt (Jn. 1:46; 7:52), he will spring up with power.

(2) Specifically it is said that the Branch will **build the temple of the LORD**. This fact is emphatically repeated at the beginning of the next verse. **It is he who will build the temple of the LORD (6:13)**. Since the rebuilding of the Temple in Jerusalem was already under way, that cannot be what is referred to. Indeed, it is a misconception to think that this refers to any physical temple at all. It is confounding symbol with reality to think that the descriptions of passages such as Isaiah 2:2-4 or Ezekiel 40–42 require the Messiah to undertake an actual reconstruction programme in an earthly Jerusalem. He himself pointed out that the Temple was not a matter of a building of stone, but rather of what his bodily presence with his people signified (Jn. 2:19-22). The Lord's presence is now maintained with his people through the indwelling of the Spirit. 'Don't you know that you yourselves are God's temple and that God's Spirit lives in you?' (1 Cor. 3:16; see also 1 Pet. 2:4-5). There is no Temple in the New Jerusalem because it is all Temple (Rev. 21:22). This is the provision made by the Messiah for his church, 'built on the foundation of the apostles and prophets, with Christ Jesus himself as the chief cornerstone' (Eph. 2:20). It was only by the work of Jesus, the 'one greater than the temple' (Mt. 12:6), that the building could be founded, and it is by his power it grows to completion.

(3) Because of the accomplishment of his task, it is said of the Branch that **he will be clothed with majesty**. 'Majesty' relates to the awe-inspiring splendour that is characteristic of God whose glory covers the heavens (Hab. 3:3) and who is clothed with splendour and majesty (Ps. 104:1; 96:6). It is also used—but less often—in a derivative sense in connection with those on whom God confers such splendour as his representatives (Num. 27:20, where 'authority' renders the same word as applied to Moses and Joshua; Jer. 22:18, of Jehoiakim as king). The Messiah, being in very nature God (Phil. 2:6), had divine glory before the world began (Jn. 17:5), but what is spoken of here is his investiture with the majesty of his mediatorial kingship on completion of his mission. 'After he had provided purification for sins, he sat down at the right hand of the Majesty in

heaven' (Heb. 1:3). 'We see Jesus ... now crowned with glory and honour because he suffered death' (Heb. 2:9). It is emphasised that the Branch himself will receive this honour.

*(4)* He **will sit and rule on his throne.** Sitting was not a posture associated with the Old Testament priesthood. Their task was never completed. No seat was provided for them in the Tabernacle or in the Temple. But here the victor is seen after the battle has been won. His task is completed, and seated at the Father's right hand as the Saviour of his people, he awaits his enemies being made a footstool for his feet (Ps. 110:1). This was what Gabriel announced to Mary: 'He will be great and will be called the Son of the Most High. The Lord God will give him the throne of his father David, and he will reign over the house of Jacob for ever; his kingdom will never end' (Lk. 1:32-33). It is a mediatorial reign which he has been given by the Father. As he himself testified, 'All authority in heaven and on earth has been given to me' (Mt. 28:18), and when the end comes, 'he hands over the kingdom to God the Father after he has destroyed all dominion, authority and power' (1 Cor. 15:24).

*(5)* And **he will be a priest on his throne** emphasises that it is not just as king that the Messiah is enthroned. As Mediator, he is also a priest. But this is not in the sense of continually making offerings on behalf of his people. 'Christ was sacrificed once to take away the sins of many people' (Heb. 9:28), and so unlike the Aaronic high priest he does not 'enter heaven to offer himself again and again, the way the high priest enters the Most Holy Place every year with blood that is not his own' (Heb. 9:25). The Branch has made the definitive sacrifice to atone for sin, and his priestly work now consists of pleading the effectiveness of that offering as he makes intercession on behalf of his own. 'Because Jesus lives for ever, he has a permanent priesthood. Therefore he is able to save completely those who come to God through him, because he always lives to intercede for them' (Heb. 7:24-25).

The concluding comment **And there will be harmony between the two of them** is rendered very lamely by the NIV. More literally the text reads, 'counsel of peace will be between the two of them.' 'Counsel' is not used in Hebrew to refer to a relationship between two parties, as if priest and king will be able to get on well together. It points rather to a course of action. In Isaiah 53:5 'the punishment that brought us peace' is literally 'the punishment of our peace'. Similarly here, 'counsel of peace' here is that deliberate policy which procures peace. It is in his combined role of priest and king that the Prince of Peace (Isa. 9:6; Mic. 5:5), 'making peace through his blood, shed on the cross' (Col. 1:20) reconciled heaven and earth, and procured the blessings for sinners that grant them peace with God (Rom. 5:1-2).

*Further Blessings (6:14-15).* The concluding two verses of the chapter do not elaborate further on the achievement of the Branch, but list three further blessings that are bestowed, some immediately, some at a later date.

*(1)* **The crown will be given to (*6:14*)** perhaps conveys the wrong idea, namely that it will be handed over to them. Literally, it is 'the crown will be to ... as a memorial in the temple of the LORD'. That is, it will be kept in the Temple to act as a perpetual tribute to those who had come with such gifts. The names of the men involved **Heldai, Tobijah, Jedaiah and Hen son of Zephaniah** show two changes from verse 10: that of Helem in the Hebrew for Heldai (see NIV footnote), and Hen for Josiah. The best explanation that has been advanced for this is that these were alternative names for the same persons. Josiah/Hen may be mentioned along with the other three either because he too was one of the party who had come from Babylon with the contributions, or because of the artistry with which he had made the crown.

*(2)* The concluding verse of the chapter has three statements. **Those who are far away will come and help to build the temple of the LORD (*6:15*).** This is a prophecy and seems not to relate to the present work, nor to be confined to the Jews in exile. Those who had come from far off bearing gifts were themselves precursors of the coming worldwide impact of the gospel. It is a further anticipation of the involvement of all nations in the work of constructing the spiritual temple in which God and his people will be found dwelling together in harmony (Isa. 56:6-8; 57:19; Acts 2:39). The NIV 'help to build' is an attempt to convey an unusual phrase in the original 'to build in the temple of the LORD'. Perhaps it indicates that what they

are doing was secondary and supportive with respect to the work of the Branch (6:13). The ideas of those far off coming and of their being involved in Temple building are also linked by Paul in Ephesians where he calls the Gentile converts 'you who once were far away' (Eph. 2:13) and 'you who were far away' (Eph. 2:17), but who are now part of the united new 'holy temple in the Lord', 'a dwelling in which God lives by his Spirit' (Eph. 2:21-22). This is the way in which these Temple promises are realised.

*(3)* The statement **and you will know that the LORD Almighty has sent me to you** raises the problems that have been encountered on earlier occasions (2:9, 11; 4:9). While it is possible to make a case for them to refer to Zechariah himself, it is preferable to see here also a reference to the Angel of the LORD. The ingathering of the nations will provide abundant proof of the divine warrant of the Messianic mission.

There is then a promise to the people as a whole. **This will happen if you diligently obey the LORD your God.** The language is somewhat compressed, and 'this' is a supplement indicating the blessings just enumerated and especially their own understanding of them. It seems unlikely to refer to the Messianic blessings as a whole, because the Messiah would come despite the unbelief and lack of recognition of the Jewish people. 'He came to that which was his own, but his own did not receive him' (Jn. 1:11). By their denial of him, they brought not on themselves the blessing of the LORD, but his curse. 'Yet to all who received him, to those who believed in his name, he gave the right to become children of God' (Jn. 1:12). The enjoyment of covenant blessing is always conditioned on covenant obedience (3:7; Isa. 3:10).

The Old Testament age was one when God instructed his people by means of types and symbols. In this section it is clearly revealed that the people were not just to be satisfied with the outward forms of worship. They are encouraged to perceive the spiritual realities represented by them. They are shown that their own Temple restoration project was only a stage in the building of a spiritual temple by the Messiah. What they were doing foreshadowed a grander reality of which they were already part, but which would only be fully seen in the future.

There was also the prophetic crowning of Joshua to be interpreted. None of their hopes would be realised without the Messiah who was the key to God's purposes of salvation. The Branch would fulfil both what the Aaronic priesthood typified and what the line of David pointed forward to. As priest, he would offer the complete atoning sacrifice and so have absolute authority to forgive sin and remove guilt. As king, he would have power to provide for his people's needs and to rule over them and their enemies. In both capacities his provision is uninterrupted and perpetual. 'Because Jesus lives for ever, he has a permanent priesthood' (Heb. 7:24) and 'his dominion is an everlasting dominion that will not pass away, and his kingdom is one that will never be destroyed' (Dan. 7:14). There is no tension between priest and king, because both offices are combined in one person. The priest who forgives is also the king whose power can break the power of sin, and with the past atoned for we can look forward to the future through the provision he continually makes for us.

## Study Questions

**6:12** How does the New Testament develop the idea of God's people being a temple? What consequences arise from this? 1 Cor. 3:9-17; 6:18-20; 2 Cor. 6:14-18; Eph. 2:19-22; 1 Pet. 2:4-8.

**6:13** What does Christ do as king? Mt. 25:31-34; Rom. 14:9; Eph. 1:20-22; Phil. 2:9-11; Heb. 2:7-8; 1 Pet. 3:22; Rev. 5:5; 17:14.

## ZECHARIAH'S SERMON (Zech. 7:1–8:23)

### Zechariah 7:1-14:  A Question of Fasting
In chapters 7 and 8 we are no longer in the world of visions and symbolic action. Here we have a narrative concerning an incident that took place two years after Zechariah's night visions. The Temple was by then half-completed, and people were wondering about how this should affect their pattern of living and worship. By asking if it was permissible to stop certain fasts which had been instituted in the

aftermath of the fall of Jerusalem, they exposed themselves to a searching divine critique of their heart motivation. As Zechariah relays God's word to them in this chapter, their situation is portrayed negatively. But that is not all that is said to them. Chapter 8, which is closely linked with this one (see on 8:19), presents the situation of the people in a more positive light— as that of recipients of the promises of God.

**In the fourth year of king Darius** *(7:1)* shows that again (Hag. 1:1; Zech. 1:1, 7) there is no escaping the fact that the people were under foreign domination. Though they are restored to their land, they have not totally escaped from the consequences of their national sin. However, the LORD was still sending his message to them through the prophet. **The word of the LORD came to Zechariah on the fourth day of the ninth month, the month of Kislev.** This brings us to 7th December 518 B.C. Nearly two years have elapsed since the visions were granted to Zechariah (1:7). Work on the Temple had resumed on 21st September 520 B.C. (Hag. 1:15) and would be completed on 12th March 515 B.C. The structure was thus half-completed at this time. The use of Kislev, the Babylonian name for the month, acts as another reminder of the changed circumstances of the people (1:7). The phrase for the divine word coming to the prophet is not followed immediately by the message that was given. Instead further background details are first given. The phrase 'the word of the LORD came to Zechariah' is found also at 7:4, 8; 8:1, 18, and indicates the major breaks in this prophetic address.

*The Question (7:2-3).* **The people of Bethel had sent Sharezer and Regem-Melech, together with their men** *(7:2).* It is difficult to be certain how this verse should be understood. It is possible to take Bethel-Sharezer as a compound name, and translate, 'Bethel-Sharezer had sent Regem-Melech, together with his men'. This involves omitting the 'and' before the second name, and opens up the possibility that what is being described is the arrival of a delegation from Babylon. The NIV's approach is, however, as good as any. We know that Bethel had been inhabited by some of those returning from exile (Ezr. 2:28; Neh. 7:32; 11:31). The NIV understands 'Bethel' as a reference to these people, and takes 'his men' as a Hebrew idiom referring to those who accompanied the two men.

It was Jacob who had given Luz the name Bethel, which means 'house of God' (Gen. 28:19)—the Hebrew form of this expression is never used to refer to the Jerusalem Temple. Bethel's sacred associations, as well as its site 12 miles north of Jerusalem, no doubt influenced Jeroboam I, when, after the breakup of the kingdom in 931 B.C., he put one of his golden calf idols there to function as an alternative to the Jerusalem shrine (1 Kgs. 12:29). There had thus been a history of hostility between Bethel and Jerusalem over the ensuing centuries. But now the people of Bethel are seen turning their backs on the past, and acknowledging that it is to Jerusalem they must turn for guidance in divine matters.

They send two representatives. Their names are of Babylonian origin, and presumably they were among those who had returned from the captivity. In accordance with their instructions they come **to entreat the LORD.** The origin of the expression rendered 'entreat' is obscure. It used to be explained as coming from stroking someone's face as a gesture of appeasement, but, if so, this notion had been forgotten by Biblical times. Three times it is found in secular contexts of approaching someone of power or influence with a view to gaining their favour (Job 11:19; Ps. 45:12; Prov. 19:6). Otherwise it is used of approaching God for mercy (Ps. 119:58) or for help in time of trouble ('intercede', 1 Kgs. 13:6; 2 Kgs. 13:4; Jer. 26:19). Here it indicates seeking divine assistance with the question that is troubling them, and so they come to those whom the LORD had appointed for such circumstances (Deut. 17:9-11; Ezk. 44:23-24; Mal. 2:7). **By asking the priests of the house of the LORD Almighty and the prophets (7:3).** Probably the full title given to the priests is a reflection upon those of whom people from Bethel had in the past asked advice. The prophets would be figures like Haggai and Zechariah (Ezr. 6:14).

**Should I mourn and fast in the fifth month, as I have done for so many years?** To express their grief, during the Exile the Jews instituted various fasts associated with the disastrous events of the fall of Jerusalem and its aftermath. Another fast is mentioned in 7:5, and a list of four is given in 8:19. The fast of the fifth month was connected with the burning to the ground of the city and Temple, and the razing of the city walls, in August 586 B.C. (2 Kgs. 25:8-9; Jer. 52:12-14). But though the people had instituted these fasts themselves, without any divine warrant, it was not on that account that fault was found with them.

In many ways the question that is asked is a natural and proper one. The people had now been brought back by the LORD to the land. Was it not then inappropriate to continue mourning the past? The Temple was in process of being rebuilt; was not the time near when fasting because of its destruction should come to an end? Perhaps it is possible to detect a note of their distaste and impatience in the words 'for so many years', but on the face of it, it seems a reasonable inquiry.

*The Divine Rebuke (7:4-7).* **Then the word of the LORD Almighty came to me (*7:4*).** The priests do not seem to have been prepared to answer the question, but the fact that the matter had been raised provided an opportunity for the LORD to bring forward his agenda for dealing with the current spiritual attitude of the people. The question about the fast never receives a direct answer, but the people are instructed to look more deeply at themselves and to pay attention to what the LORD had said in the past—they should then be able to work out the answer for themselves. In many ways the thrust of the message here is identical to the call for repentance that Zechariah issued in his first message (1:1-6). Notice that here Zechariah abandons the impersonal style adopted in 7:1 and identifies himself as the one who composed this record.

**Ask all the people of the land and the priests (*7:5*).** 'All the people of the land' here refers to everyone apart from the priests. The whole of the returned community was to be challenged as to its attitude. Perhaps the priests, who had given no answer, were as uncertain in their thinking as any. **When you fasted and mourned in the fifth and seventh months for the past seventy years.** The question uses different, more intense words for 'mourn' and 'fast'. In verse 3 the word for 'fast' had been 'abstain, keep oneself away from', and what one was renouncing had to be deduced from the context. Here 'fast' specifically refers to afflicting the body by depriving it of food as a sign of grief (Neh. 1:4; Est. 4:16). In verse

3 'mourn' referred to the shedding of tears, either from joy (Gen. 29:11; 33:4) or from distress. Here 'mourn' indicates to engage in the often elaborate rituals associated with grief for the dead, including beating on the breast (Isa. 32:12) and uttering dirges and shrill wailing cries.

As well as the fast of the fifth month (7:3), mention is now made of another fast, instituted in the seventh month to commemorate the assassination of Gedaliah by a group of extreme patriots (Jer. 41:1-3). After the fall of Jerusalem, the Babylonians had appointed him governor of Judah, with responsibility for the poorest in the land who had not been taken into exile (Jer. 40:7). Fear of reprisals after his death had led the group of Jews associated with him to seek refuge in Egypt, contrary to Jeremiah's entreaties (Jer. 43:1-3). His death had thus intensified the desolation of the land. As this had taken place immediately after the fall of Jerusalem, possibly in the following year, a period of approximately seventy years had elapsed since then (see on 1:12).

But the question is not focusing on the origins of their fasts, but the religious motivation behind them. The matter is put quite pointedly. **Was it really for me that you fasted?** Fasting was engaged in at times of sorrow and crisis (2 Sam. 12:16; Mt. 9:15), particularly national crisis (2 Chr. 20:3; Jer. 36:9). As a spiritual exercise, it was accompanied by confession of sin (1 Sam. 7:6), by repentance and by a recognition of an individual's true standing before God. 'Return to me with all your heart, with fasting and weeping and mourning' (Joel 2:12). 'I proclaimed a fast, so that we might humble ourselves before our God' (Ezr. 8:21). This was also the feature emphasised in connection with the only divinely appointed, stated fast in the Old Testament. It too was in the seventh month, on the Day of Atonement, when the people were to 'deny themselves' (Lev. 16:29, 31), or 'humble (or, afflict) themselves' (Ps. 35:13; Ezr. 8:21).

This note of contrition and self-humiliation seems to have been absent in the practice of the exiles. They were sorrowing for what they had lost, but in an exercise of self-pity, rather than with due recognition of the righteousness of God's judgment against them and their nation. They should rather have acknowledged that they were rightly afflicted by God. Fasting was an exercise designed to induce a right perception of their spiritual condition as before God. The people seem to have entered into it in a spirit that focused on themselves and lamented their own woes without adequately considering what the LORD wanted of them in inward and outward conformity to his covenant standards (Isa. 58:3-9). They wanted restored to the land, but without a true spiritual desire to experience what that signified—namely, drawing close to the LORD. So although their actions were religious rites, God emphatically asks if it was 'really for me' that they did it.

**And when you were eating and drinking, were you not just feasting for yourselves?** (*7:6*). 'Feasting' renders a repetition of 'eating and drinking'. 'For yourselves' is not expressed in the original, but it is an appropriate supplement to bring out the sense. Such activities were of course entirely proper. People have to eat and drink for nourishment. In this context, however, the reference seems to be to the eating and drinking associated with solemn religious festivals. Whether they were depriving themselves of food, or whether they were celebrating a religious festival, they were doing so without true religious motivation. All their living ought to be dedicated to God (1 Cor. 10:31), and until that was so, fasting and feasting were alike an abomination to him (Isa. 1:11-17). These questions were designed to stir up their consciences that they might repent of their externalism and self-righteousness. Note that this applied as much to the priests (7:5) as to the people.

The question that follows seems rather abrupt. **Are these not the words the LORD proclaimed through the earlier prophets?** (*7:7*). It obviously leads into the following lesson from their history (7:8-14). But it is appropriate here in that the people were questioning the need for fasting and humbling themselves before God now that he had brought them back and the Temple was being rebuilt. 'The earlier prophets' were those who had ministered before the Exile (1:4). Zechariah was far from the first to have addressed the people with a call for repentance, for inner change not outward ritual (1 Sam. 15:22-23; Isa. 1:11-17; Jer. 7:21-24; Hos. 6:6; Amos 5:21-27; Mic. 6:6-8). The teaching of the past meant that they could not plead ignorance as an excuse for their behaviour.

What was more, the ministry of those earlier prophets had been at times of national prosperity **when Jerusalem and its surrounding towns were at rest and prosperous, and the Negev and the western foothills were settled.** The Negev was the southern part of the land which, although dry as its name implies, was not desert in Biblical times. The western foothills were the lower slopes between the central plateau and the coastal plain. It was a region of plenty, where much of the food of the land was grown. When conditions were good in the past, God had still sent his prophets to warn the people that their attitude towards him was wrong. Those same messages constituted a warning to the later community also. Even the stark contrast with the material conditions of their own day should have reminded them of the need to cultivate a right attitude towards God. Their desire to do away with the fasts—a thing of little significance in itself—betrayed an inner forgetfulness of the circumstances that had led to them, and of their own failure to walk humbly with their God.

*Lessons from the Past (7:8-14).* **And the word of the LORD came again to Zechariah (*7:8*).** It is difficult to be certain how much time passed between Zechariah's original response to the question and this new message coming from God. Perhaps there was just a brief pause for the people to ponder the message they had heard, before they are reminded in greater detail of what had been said before.

**This is what the LORD Almighty says (*7:9*).** This is the standard translation of this very common clause, but in this instance it would probably be better to render 'said' rather than 'says', as verse 11 shows that these words were particularly addressed to past generations. Of course, they were still valid—that was the point of Zechariah's message—but what we have here is, in the first instance, the word that the LORD had sent to the people through the former prophets.

**Administer true justice of God.** This was a personal requirement as well as one that affected the conduct of public officials. Their behaviour in such matters revealed the state of their hearts and the character of the nation (1 Sam. 24.:13; Mt. 12:34; Lk. 6:45; 1 Jn. 3:10). The LORD uses their outward behaviour as an index of their covenant loyalty, for he had always required of his people, 'Do not pervert justice; do not show partiality to the poor or favouritism to the great, but judge your neighbour fairly' (Lev. 19:15). Furthermore, the norms of the covenant were not abstract ideals but a description of their covenant overlord himself, who as Judge of all the earth does right (literally 'justice', Gen. 18:25) and who 'loves justice' (Ps. 33:5). They were not to be deflected from his standards and were to follow justice, and justice alone (Deut. 16:20). The prophets had frequently brought these requirements of the Mosaic covenant to the attention of the people (Isa. 58:3-10; Jer. 21:12), perhaps nowhere more eloquently than in the well-known words of Amos, 'But let justice roll on like a river, righteousness like a never-failing stream!' (Amos 5:24).

**Show mercy and compassion to one another.** Literally, it is 'a man to his brother', emphasising the reasoning that lay behind this. Both were members of the same community, united by their loyalty to the LORD, and therefore the relationship between them should be worked out in terms of the covenant bond that they had in common. 'Mercy' is here the word (*hesed*) that is particularly used to describe the relationship of love and kindness characteristic of the covenant. It is conditioned on, and patterned after, the covenant love of the LORD himself, going beyond the strict terms of any engagement. It is with such feelings of compassionate sympathy that Israel was expected to behave towards other members of the covenant community, loving mercy (Mic. 6:8). For 'compassion', see on 'mercy' (1:16).

**Do not oppress the widow or the fatherless, the alien or the poor (*7:10*).** This presents the sort of behaviour ruled out for those who were merciful and compassionate. These categories of people were very open to being cheated, oppressed, or simply forgotten about in ancient society. The widow and the fatherless were those who had lost not only the breadwinner in their family and so were liable to be in economic straits, but also the one who would stand up for their rights and protect them. The alien was one who was temporarily resident from another land and who did not have full citizen rights in the country he was staying in. That did not mean he had no rights at all, and the Old Testament is very careful to stress the rights of the alien in the land. The poor were those who from some misfortune or other were economically deprived. These vulnerable groups in society had been the object of the LORD's special protection

from the start (Ex. 22:21-22; Deut. 10:18-19; 15:7-11; 24:14-18).
The fact that Israel had experienced such deprivation in Egypt was
used to reinforce the obligation on them to act sensitively towards
others in similar circumstances.

But though it entered the praise of Israel that 'the LORD watches
over the alien and sustains the fatherless and the widow' (Ps. 146:9),
and though it became part of the proverbial wisdom of the people not
to exploit the poor or encroach on the fields of the fatherless (Prov.
22:22-23; 23:10-11), their practice often fell short of the covenant
ideal. The prophets were frequently sent to remonstrate with the
people and their rulers on such matters (Isa. 1:23; 10:2; Amos 2:6-7;
4:1; 5:11-12; Mic. 2:1-3; 3:1-4; Mal. 3:5).

**In your hearts do not think evil of each other.** Here again the
phrase 'each other' renders 'a man his brother', bringing out clearly
the covenant motivation that should underlie their thinking and
action. It is not just a matter of having a poor opinion of their
neighbour, or ill-feeling towards him, attributing base motives to his
action. The translation of the virtually identical expression in 8:17,
'do not plot evil against your neighbour', makes clear that it is
malicious scheming to deprive a neighbour of his rights that is
particularly condemned here (Ps. 21:11; Mic. 2:1).

Zechariah himself then adds an account of how the people had
responded to the LORD's message in the past. **But they refused to
pay attention (7:11).** This was a deliberate act on their part, not
merely of not giving attention to the message that was being
presented, but of refusing to act on it. They had heard it, but they
deliberately decided to do nothing about it. They refused to listen to
the LORD's words, emend their ways and repent (Jer. 5:3; 8:5; 11:10).
**Stubbornly they turned their backs.** Literally, 'they gave a
shoulder of stubbornness.' The picture is that of an animal persistently refusing to allow the yoke to be placed on it, but the body
language is clear—whether of man or beast—'We don't want to
know' (Hos. 4:16; Neh. 9:29). **They stopped their ears.** This is a
metaphor from blocking the ear so as not to be disturbed by noise. As
far as they were concerned, the LORD's word was an intrusive sound
which would only disturb them. The people were utterly intransigent
in their attitude.

**They made their hearts as hard as flint (*7:12*).** They hardened their heart, blocking off any spiritual response to what the LORD was saying to them. The result of their intransigence was that they **would not listen to the law or to the words that the LORD Almighty had sent by his Spirit through the earlier prophets.** The 'law' they disdained refers to the law of Sinai, as the similar passage in Nehemiah 9:29-30 makes clear. But the LORD did more than set the covenant standards before the people when he gave it to them through Moses at the start of their national existence. Repeatedly he sent the prophets as the messengers of his covenant to warn the people of where their transgressions were leading them (2 Chr. 36:15-16; Jer. 7:25; 25:4; 26:5). The prophets did not think up this message by themselves, but were given it by the Spirit (Num. 11:25-26; 1 Sam. 10:6; 2 Chr. 15:1; 18:23; Neh. 9:30; Ezk. 11:5). Peter specifically identifies the Spirit in connection with the inspiration of the prophets as 'the Spirit of Christ in them' (1 Pet. 1:11). Their attitude was therefore essentially the same as the later rejection by the Jews of the Word made flesh (Jn. 1:11).

But the people perverted God's well-intentioned warnings to them. By not responding to them, they made their downfall inevitable, for the LORD could not look with impunity on the treatment that his people were according to his words and to his messengers. **So the LORD Almighty was very angry.** The people of Zechariah's generation did not need to have that all spelled out to them. The realities of the Exile and its aftermath still governed their daily living.

The consequence of this behaviour is now spelled out. Their refusal to respond led to the withdrawal of access to God (Jer. 11:14; 15:1). **'When I called, they did not listen; so when they called, I would not listen,' says the LORD Almighty (*7:13*).** The change back to direct divine speech is not as smooth as the translation makes it appear. 'When I called' is literally 'when he called'. Zechariah is so conscious of relaying the LORD's message even when he himself is speaking, that he can merge without embarrassment into directly relaying the divine speech. The LORD had called on the people to repent, but they had not heeded his warnings. However, the calamity that comes upon them impels them to cry out in despair to the LORD, but the opportunity for averting the disaster has passed. It had become too late, for they had spurned the LORD's plea for repentance. The LORD's retribution is not arbitrary, but righteous and proportionate to the offence. 'Then they will call to me but I will not answer; they will look for me but will not find me. Since they hated knowledge and did not choose to fear the LORD, since they would not accept my advice and spurned my rebuke, they will eat the fruit of their ways and be filled with the fruit of their schemes' (Prov. 1:28-31).

The judgment of God ensued. **I scattered them with a whirlwind among all the nations, where they were strangers (7:14).** Right from the beginning this had been set out as one aspect of the curse of the broken covenant (Lev. 26:33; Deut. 28:64). The LORD's judgment came as an irresistible storm carrying all before it (Isa. 66:15; Jer. 23:19; Nah. 1:3). 'Where they were strangers' is literally 'whom they did not know' (Deut. 28:33). The reality of this did not need to be spelled out for the generation who returned from Babylon, but that had been twenty years before. Memories are short, and there would have been many who were too young to have had personal experience of Babylon.

**The land was left so desolate behind them that no-one could come or go.** The land was the place of God's favour. It was the land of his selection, promise and gift. The good land had been described to them in glowing, rapturous terms (Deut. 8:7-9). But their sin had caused it to be so devastated by the enemy that it was not possible to travel about it in safety. The picture may be that of such an absence of habitation that the traveller could find no place to lodge at night, or it may point to the wild state of the land, with wild beasts and groups of marauders threatening the traveller. See on 8:10, and compare the situations described in Judges 5–6 and 2 Chronicles 15:5. **This is how they made the pleasant land desolate.** It was as a consequence of their own actions that this had befallen them. The purpose is not to vindicate the LORD's way of acting with his people in the past. This is being stated as self-evident. The purpose is that they learn the lesson of what had happened before, and not permit the same attitudes and wrong-headed thinking to permeate their national living again.

We can see that things moved far from the first question about observing a fast to consider the basic attitudes that were being revealed. This is often the way when we approach God. We do not perceive what our real problem is. The matter that perplexes us may well be the symptom of something much deeper, which has to be dealt with first of all.

Are we sure that our conduct can stand up to scrutiny? When we worship God and engage in specifically religious duties, are we giving him the first place in our thinking that is rightfully his? Do we have the same awareness of God and what he wants in our everyday conduct? We may not think of ourselves as oppressors (7:10). Surely that is only true of tyrannical rulers or criminal organisations? But oppression occurs whenever we see others who are vulnerable or ignorant and take advantage of it to our own benefit (Jas. 2:5-6; 5:4-6).

God is still calling us and we are still responsible for our answer. Now that he who spoke before by the prophets has spoken to us through his Son, should we not be even more ready to respond?

*Study Questions*

**7:5** What sort of fasting is acceptable to God? Isa. 58; Mt. 6:16-18; Mk. 2:18-22; Lk. 5:33-39; 18:12. What lessons can be learned from this for other spiritual exercises? Mt. 15:7-9.

**7:12** What does the New Testament teach about the role of the Spirit in giving God's word to the prophets? Acts 11:28; 21:11; 1 Cor. 12:7-11; 1 Pet. 1:11; 2 Pet. 1:21; Rev. 2:7; 10:7.

**7:13** Review what Scripture says about the dangers of not responding to God's warnings. Prov. 1:28-31; Mt. 24:36-42; Lk. 16:31; Rom. 2:4-5; Heb. 12:17.

## Zechariah 8:1-23:  Favour Restored

In the previous chapter Zechariah had pointed to the spiritual emptiness that affected the thinking of the people. He had been instructed to show the close links that existed between their attitudes and those of previous generations, and to remind them of how that had led to the desolation of the Exile. But God did not seek the repentance and reformation of his people only by threatening them with punishment if they strayed. In this chapter he encourages them by reminding them of his commitment to them, and urges them to advance and enjoy the inheritance he has promised them. Both warning and encouragement have a role to play in stirring up the people of God to renewed obedience.

Chapter 8 is noted for its tenfold repetition of **This is what the LORD Almighty says** (*8:2, (3), 4, 6, 7, 9, 14, 19, 20, 23*). This repetition solemnly emphasises God's commitment to his promises, and his ability to carry them through to completion. There is also the twice repeated statement **Again the word of the LORD Almighty came to me** (*8:1, 18*), which breaks the statements into a group of seven and a group of three. While it is possible to argue that this structure is an artificial way of bringing together prophecies that were originally given on a number of separate occasions, the fact that 8:19 resumes the theme of fasting seems to favour the conclusion that this chapter is to be taken as a continuation of chapter 7, and these oracles were part of the teaching Zechariah gave on that occasion. The use of the numbers three, seven and ten points to the completeness of the LORD's promises and provision.

*(1) The LORD's Jealousy:* **This is what the LORD Almighty says: "I am very jealous for Zion"** (*8:2*). Zechariah had already mentioned the LORD's jealousy in 1:14. This verse is introduced here as a summary of the background circumstances that underlie all that is to follow. There had been times when this jealousy worked for judgment against the people because of their waywardness which God could not allow to undermine his relationship with them (Ps. 78:58). But now this jealousy is operative for their good. It will not allow anyone or anything to disrupt his desire to see them blessed (Ezk. 36:5-6; Joel 2:18; Nah. 1:2). Zechariah is assuring the disheartened people of the fundamental fact of God's disposition towards them for good, and his determination to see all that he has promised to them come true. Nothing will be allowed to interfere with his purpose. The basic thought is repeated in **I am burning with jealousy for her,**

literally, 'I am jealous for her <with> great heat'. The word 'heat' is generally used to convey the intensity of anger, but here it emphasises the intensity of the divine commitment. There is nothing lukewarm or half-hearted about the LORD's attitude towards his people—and that should be true of the other side of the relationship as well.

Zion was originally the fortified mound or stronghold of Jerusalem, and was located on the ridge between the Kidron and the Tyropean valleys. When David captured it, he made it his capital and built his royal residence there (2 Sam. 5:7-9). With the coming of the ark, Zion became known as the dwelling place of the LORD (Ps. 9:11; 74:2), and when the ark was later removed to the Temple, built just to the north, the name Zion was transferred to the new site. It is thus especially used to denote Jerusalem not as a political centre, but as the place the LORD has desired for his dwelling (Ps. 132:13) and 'the city of the great King' (Ps. 48:2). The fundamental distinguishing fact about Zion was the divine presence. Zion was also used to describe the place of the LORD's future redemption (Isa. 4:5; 28:16; 33:5, 20; 62:1), where he will come as Saviour (Isa. 24:23; 59:20). The name of the place is frequently extended to denote its inhabitants (Isa. 51:16).

(2) *The LORD's Return:* **This is what the LORD says** (*8:3*) is the only one of the ten times the phrase is used in this chapter without 'Almighty', literally, 'of hosts' (1:3). It is difficult to see any particular reason why it is omitted here. **I will return to Zion and dwell in Jerusalem.** The LORD had been seen by the prophet Ezekiel withdrawing his presence from the Holy City (Ezk. 9:3; 10:19; 11:22). The verbs 'return', 'dwell' and 'be called' are all perfects, presumably prophetic perfects, describing a certain future event (see on 1:16). For further comment, see on 2:5. The rupture of the covenant bond caused by the sin of the people inevitably led to God abandoning them to devastation at the hands of the nations. But though they had given up on their covenant commitment, the LORD had not. Here he promises that he will return to them and the former relationship will be restored. The restored city will be worthy of the name, 'THE LORD IS THERE' (Ezk. 48:35).

When this occurs is a matter of considerable dispute. Some argue that prophecies such as this had their fulfilment in the period between the Exile and the first coming of Christ; others that they await a future millennial period when there will be a time of unparalleled blessing for the Jewish people; but it is best to take these promises as finding their true reference not in anything distinctly Jewish, but in the church of Christ, embracing both Jew and Gentile (see Appendix). There was a sense in which such blessing as was enjoyed by the returned community in the centuries after Zechariah's time was a partial fulfilment of these promises. But it was at best very incomplete, and we are not doing justice to the full and absolute language of Scripture if we try to restrict the fulfilment solely to those times.

In his ministry of encouragement the prophet was directed to point the people forward to the time of the fulfilment of God's blessing. Living as they did before the coming of Christ, neither the prophet nor the people could appreciate every aspect of what would then occur. It was described to them in terms of the people of God and of their situation as known to them. But the New Testament has shown that these promises, couched in the language and perception of the Old Testament, have their true reference in the people of God from all nations. It is not that those who were his people were rejected from the enjoyment of such blessings. This Paul emphatically rejects in Romans 11:1-2. Furthermore, although God's presence with his people was realised in an altogether fuller way with the coming of Christ and the subsequent sending of the Spirit, the Holy City, which is the church of all the saints, still awaits her Lord's return to experience the presence of God with her in all its fulness (Rev. 21:3).

The prophet is shown the time when the LORD's presence with his people will be so obvious that it will be universally recognised. **Then Jerusalem will be called the City of Truth.** It is not stated who will do this calling, whether the people themselves or others. The implication is that the title will be fully justified. Jerusalem seems to have been accorded the title 'the faithful city' in recognition of the privileges extended to her (Isa. 1:21). When her fortunes and status, or more precisely those of her inhabitants, are divinely restored, the prophets see various names being applied to her: the City of Righteousness, the Faithful City (Isa. 1:26), the City of the LORD (Isa. 60:14); the LORD our Righteousness (Jer. 33:16); THE LORD IS THERE

(Ezk. 48:35). These all present aspects of the impact of the LORD's presence with his people. 'Truth' refers to what is certain and dependable. It is a characteristic of the LORD that he is the God of truth (Ps. 31:5), and so his word and laws that he has revealed to his people are also truth, or true (Ps. 119: 30, 43, 151, 160). Consequently, truth also characterises those who have put their trust in God and pattern their conduct after his standards (8:16; Ps. 15:2; 26:3; 86:11).

**The mountain of the LORD Almighty will be called the Holy Mountain** refers to Zion. It had been called the Holy Mountain previously (Ps. 2:6; Isa. 27:13; 56:7; Joel 2:1; 3:17—the same words are also rendered 'holy hill'). What is different is that at the LORD's return it will truly live up to that description. 'Holy' in the first instance indicates set apart for divine use or service (Ex. 19:23; 40:10; Num. 16:5, 7, 38). As regards God himself it refers to his being set apart from creation (Ps. 99:2-3), particularly in the ethical sphere (Ps. 99:4-5). In the same way his people are holy in that they are privileged to be set apart to serve him (Ex. 19:6; Deut. 7:6), and on that basis are enjoined, 'Be holy because I, the LORD your God, am holy' (Lev. 19:2; 1 Pet. 1:16). Zion is set apart by the LORD's presence there (Ex. 3:5; Josh. 5:15), and also by the conduct of those who inhabit it.

The LORD's presence with his people is seen to sanctify the city and the mountain, effectively transforming the way his people live, not just in an outward ceremonial respect as previously, but in inner reality also. This is, of course, begun with the indwelling of the Spirit in the church (Jn. 14:23; 2 Cor. 6:16), but is only completely and finally true in the New Jerusalem, where God lives with his people (Rev. 21:3) and from which all that is impure, shameful and deceitful will be banished (14:20-21; Rev. 21:27).

*(3) The City's Prosperity:* Zechariah then presents a picture of the conditions which will be experienced in the new city—a picture which draws on the past of the people and contrasts with their present. **This is what the LORD Almighty says; "Once again men and women of ripe old age will sit in the streets of Jerusalem"** *(8:4)*. There is emphasis placed on the fact that it is 'once again'. It is looking back to a time in the history of the city when it enjoyed

prosperity and security, probably the days of David and Solomon (1 Kgs. 4:25; 10:27). In a world where the ravages of war and the shortages of famine had greatest impact on the young and the old (Isa. 65:20), absence of such horrors is seen in the presence of old folk, both male and female ('ripe' is an addition by the NIV translators; the original is simply 'old men and old women'), enjoying undisturbed relaxation in the sun. In ancient cities the space between the houses was very narrow. 'Streets' does not refer to these alleyways, but to larger squares which occurred where routes intersected, and particularly to the plazas that were to be found near the city walls. **Each with cane in hand because of his age.** In these places of public concourse the old would find a place to meet once their working days were over. This must have contrasted very sharply with the situation that prevailed in Jerusalem in Zechariah's day. Very few of the elderly among the exiles would have felt up to undertaking the journey back. The small returned community would have been principally composed of fitter younger members.

The health of the whole community is shown not only by the presence of the aged, but also **The city streets will be filled with boys and girls playing there** *(8:5)*. Again, it is in the squares or plazas of the city that we find the young have located a spot large enough to play in. This is a city without fear, and without economic hardship. The young have the opportunity to enjoy themselves.

This had obviously happened before in Jerusalem. It would in measure happen again. But this beautiful picture of contentment and satisfaction ultimately points to the undisturbed bliss of New Jerusalem, where 'he who sits on the throne will spread his tent over them. Never again will they hunger; never again will they thirst. The sun will not beat upon them, nor any scorching heat' (Rev. 7:15-16). It does not take the rebuilding of an ancient city at some future date to fulfil what is promised here. Features of ancient society were used to speak meaningfully to the people of Zechariah's day and to portray to them the blessedness of the eternal provision of God for his people. As they saw what divine blessing was to bestow on them, they would be encouraged to persevere. 'Blessed are the people of whom this is true; blessed are the people whose God is the LORD' (Ps. 144:12-15).

*(4) No Reason for Incredulity:* **This is what the LORD Almighty says: "It may seem marvellous to the remnant of this people"** *(8:6).* 'The remnant of the people' are of course the descendants of the community which had experienced God's judgment (Ezr. 9:8, 13; Isa. 10:20; Jer. 23:3; Mic. 2:12; Hag. 1:12). They considered God's promises of prosperity to be quite out of touch with the everyday realities around them (Hag. 1:5-11; 2:15-19). What was 'marvellous' was what was hard to do, something that seemed incapable of realisation. Such scepticism breeds when the situation is assessed only in terms of worldly resources and possibilities, and faith fails to grasp the reality of God's power (Gen. 18:14; Num. 11:23; 2 Kgs. 7:2; Mk. 10:23-26). The attitude to be adopted is always that of Abraham, the father of the faithful. 'He did not waver through unbelief regarding the promise of God, but was strengthened in his faith and gave glory to God, being fully persuaded that God had power to do what he had promised' (Rom. 4:20-21).

**At that time**, literally, 'in those days', seems to look forward to the time of realisation. Even if the incredulous attitude of the people persists right up to when the LORD fulfils his promises, their lack of faith does not detract from his power. **"But will it seem marvellous to me?" declares the LORD Almighty.** The repetition of LORD Almighty (see on 1:3) calls on them to consider just what he does have under his control. He is the one who is lord and master of all the created realm and is able to direct it to accomplish his purposes. What his wisdom has planned will not be frustrated by any lack of power or resources. His power 'enables him to bring everything under his control' (Phil. 3:21). 'Nothing is impossible with God' (Lk. 1:37). So they are not to be downhearted because of the seeming difficulty of the accomplishment of the promises. Rather they are to focus in faith on what the LORD has committed himself to do.

*(5) The Covenant Bond Restored:* **This is what the LORD Almighty says: "I will save my people from the countries of the east and the west"** *(8:7).* The word used for 'save' points primarily to deliverance from a situation of peril to one of safety. That is what the LORD had done at the time of the Exodus (Deut. 33:29), from the Philistines (1 Sam. 7:8), and from Babylon (Jer. 30:10). But to what does this

further salvation refer? In Zechariah's day it would undoubtedly be understood against the background of the continuing dispersion of most of the people throughout the Persian empire (Est. 3:8; 9:20). There is no need to find difficulty with the mention of the west, on the grounds that the people had been exiled to Babylon and Mesopotamia, which would be covered by the mention of east. Many had in fact gone to Egypt (2 Kgs. 23:34; Jer. 43:7; 44:15). 'The east and the west' are here mentioned in a figure of speech that denotes the whole extent of the dispersion.

But though the LORD did gather them 'from the lands, from east and west, from north and south' (Ps. 107:3), many still remained abroad. How then is this prophecy to be fulfilled? There is no need to invent some future age of exclusively Jewish blessing in which 'the LORD will reach out his hand a second time to reclaim the remnant that is left of his people from Assyria, from Lower Egypt, from Upper Egypt, from Cush, from Elam, from Babylonia, from Hamath and from the islands of the sea' (Isa. 11:11). That has already happened in type, and what remains to be fulfilled of the promise as regards the Jews is taken up and more gloriously fulfilled in the ingathering of all nations to the LORD. This had been already seen by Isaiah who spoke of the Root of Jesse standing as a banner for the peoples, the nations rallying to him, even at the same time as he gathered the exiles of Israel (Isa. 11:10-12). The LORD has not two peoples, but one. What was said to his people in Old Testament times and partly fulfilled then, is not forgotten, but advanced to an extended fulfilment involving God's scattered people from every nation (Jas. 1:1; 1 Pet. 1:1). As Peter reminded his Jewish audience, 'The promise is for you and your children, and for all who are far off, as many as the Lord our God shall call to himself' (Acts 2:39, NASB). It is in this way 'that many will come from the east and the west, and will take their places at the feast with Abraham, Isaac and Jacob in the kingdom of heaven' (Mt. 8:11).

**I will bring them back to live in Jerusalem (8:8).** The place where the LORD has promised to reveal his presence is the place where his people should also be found, enjoying all that that presence means for them. At that time there will be a restoration of the covenant bond that links the LORD and his people. **They will be my people and I**

**will be faithful and righteous to them as their God.** Literally it is 'they will be to me as a people and I will be to them as God in faithfulness and in righteousness'. It is not certain that the final phrase rendered 'faithful and righteous' by the NIV qualifies only God's relation with his people, and not also theirs with him. Undoubtedly it is the divine commitment that makes the relationship inviolable, in a way that it had not been in the past. But based on this it seems reasonable to take these words as qualifying both sides of the relationship. 'Faithfulness' is the same word as is translated 'truth' in 8:3, and denotes the reliability and constancy of the bond that is forged. 'Righteousness' is a word with many shades of meaning. Basically it denotes conformity to a norm, and so here it asserts that all that is required of the covenant relationship will obtain (see on Mal. 4:2).

This description of the covenant bond between the Lord and his people spans the epochs from the time of Moses through the present era of the New Covenant to its consummation in the New Jerusalem. 'I will walk among you and be your God, and you will be my people' (Lev. 26:12; Jer. 32:38; 2 Cor. 6:16). 'I will be their God, and they will be my people' (Jer. 31:33; Heb. 8:10). 'My dwelling-place will be with them; I will be their God, and they will be my people' (Ezk. 37:27). 'Now the dwelling of God is with men, and he will live with them. They will be his people, and God himself will be with them and be their God' (Rev. 21:3).

*(6) The Changes from the Past:* The next divine word is longer than those that preceded, taking in 8:9-13. It focuses principally on the immediate past, and encourages the people to remain active and obedient by declaring that the Lord will reverse the conditions that affected them.

**This is what the Lord Almighty says: "You who now hear these words spoken by the prophets who were there when the foundation was laid for the house of the Lord Almighty"** *(8:9).* This very long description of the people does not just identify them as those who had heard the words of Haggai and Zechariah, the two prophets who we know were active at the time of the laying of the foundation (Ezr. 5:1), but also gives the reason for the command that follows. 'Now' renders 'in these days', when they had then heard the promises of the word of the LORD relayed to them. They should continue to work with a positive attitude, without hesitation or lingering doubts. For a discussion of when the foundation was laid, see on Haggai 2:18. **Let your hands be strong so that the temple may be built.** This reflects the message that was originally given them (Hag. 2:4).

**Before that time (*8:10*)** is literally 'before those days' referring to the time when decisive action was taken to restart the Temple building project. The sentence begins 'for', indicating that what follows is the reason why they should be motivated positively towards the work in hand. Previously **there were no wages for man or beast.** It had been a time of economic hardship (Hag. 1:6-11; 2:16-18). **No-one could go about his business safely because of his enemy** is an effective rendering of 'for one going out and for one coming in there was not peace from the enemy'. There is difficulty in identifying the 'enemy'—were they foreigners, or from within the community? The NIV certainly suggests the latter, by beginning the next clause 'for', literally 'and'. However, the word rendered 'enemy', one who harasses and torments, may also refer to a foreigner, and so it is preferable to find here mention of two sets of obstacles to safety. The peoples whose territory bounded that of the small returned community viewed it with hostility and subjected it to harassment (Ezr. 4:1-5). It was hazardous to move out of and into the land while trading, and this would complicate keeping in touch with the Jewish communities in Mesopotamia.

But the economic depression affecting the land also meant that there was increased tension within the community. **I had turned every man against his neighbour.** It was a time of edginess and strain because things were not going well. Rather than a spirit of helpfulness towards one another and a sense of communal purpose in restoring the land and the Temple, there had developed a spirit of infighting (Jer. 9:4-5; Mic. 7:5-6). This had been part of God's chastisement of his people for getting their priorities wrong. It should have alerted them to the fact that there was something fundamentally faulty with the way they were living.

**But now (*8:11*)** indicates that a new epoch is about to begin. **"I will not deal with the remnant of this people as I did in the past,"**

**declares the LORD Almighty.** 'In the past' is literally 'as <in> the former, or initial, days'—another way of referring to the same period as 'those days' (8:10). The original expression is very terse, 'But now not as <in> the former days I to the remnant of this people.' It seems to cover both the LORD's attitude towards them and the way in which he providentially dealt with them. Because of his gracious interposition on their behalf, and certainly not because they had of their own accord come to their senses spiritually, things are going to change (Isa. 12:1; Hag. 2:18-19).

The change will be principally seen on their farms, which were the main source of income. Previously their harvests had been disastrous (Hag. 1:11; 2:16-17), but now that will be reversed and **the seed will grow well (8:12).** The phrase is simply 'the seed of peace/prosperity'. It may, as in the NIV, be taken as a description of the total transformation of the yield from their farms, or it may be another description of the vine which is mentioned next. The prosperity of God's land of promise was closely linked to the spiritual attitude of the people. Since they had heeded the prophetic warnings and taken up the task of rebuilding, God will bless them in all their ways.

**The vine will yield its fruit, the ground will produce its crops, and the heavens will drop their dew.** This again contrasts with the situation that Haggai had described. As in Ezekiel's description of the blessings of the covenant of peace, the 'showers of blessing' are literal (Ezk. 34:26). If the rains failed to come at the right time in Palestine, the winter grass and harvests would fail. 'Dew', 'the precious dew from heaven above' (Deut. 33:13), was equally necessary for sustaining vegetation in the summer. Without it the late crops shrivel up and there is no fruit harvest (Hag. 1:10). **I will give all these things as an inheritance to the remnant of this people.** For remnant, see on 8:6. Their changed economic conditions were a sign not only of divine favour, but specifically of the blessing that was theirs in terms of the covenant inheritance the LORD gave to his people (Ex. 32:13; Deut. 12:10; Ob. 17).

The restoration of their fortunes is then summed up. **As you have been an object of cursing among the nations (8:13)** relates to their being taken away into Exile and their land being devastated. It is the curse of the broken covenant in general (Deut. 28:15-68). It seems to cover both the idea that they were cursed by the nations (Ps. 44:13; Jer. 24:9; 25:9-10), and also the idea that the nations used them as a standard of cursing for others, as if to say, 'May your condition be like that of Judah and Israel.' The order **O Judah and Israel** clearly shows the priority of those from the south among the covenant returnees. But it does indicate that there were some from the ten tribes who returned at this time. They had of course been in exile for over a century and a quarter longer, and so the upheaval involved would have been far greater for them. Their presence picks up the theme of the reunited people (Ezk. 37:15-19).

**So will I save you.** For 'save' see 8:7. The LORD's action will be in inverse proportion to the intensity of the degradation they had experienced. He will act to restore their fortunes, but that is not an end in itself. The LORD's people had a specific role to perform. **And you will be a blessing.** It is not 'you will receive a blessing', but rather a reflection on the terms of the covenant with Abraham (Gen. 12:2-3). They will be blessed by God so that they will be able to fulfil their proper function. This theme is expanded on in 8:20-23 in terms of their mission to the nations.

But for the present there is a task before them. **Do not be afraid, but let your hands be strong.** The pathway to blessing and usefulness is by way of obedience to the task in hand. They are called on to be active in the duty presently assigned to them, and to wait with expectation to see how God will use their obedience to further his purposes. The grand future vision is not to dazzle and enthral us to such an extent that it robs us of willingness to be active immediately.

*(7) The LORD's Determination:* The next section is specifically linked by an initial 'for' to indicate that what follows supplies additional grounds for the people to be confident that the promised changes would occur. **This is what the LORD Almighty says: "Just as I had determined to bring disaster upon you"** *(8:14).* 'You' is plural, and refers to the whole nation. Again the LORD looks back to their previous history and what had happened in the period leading up to the capture and devastation of Jerusalem. That was not to be interpreted merely at a secular level of the territorial ambitions of Nebuchadnezzar. It had been the direct consequence of the deliberate

decision of the LORD who has all things under his control. 'Determined' is a word often used by Jeremiah to indicate the LORD's fixed decision to punish (Jer. 4:28; 23:20; 30:24; 51:11-12). He had brought the calamity of the capture and sack of Jerusalem upon them, and the Hebrew links this immediately with the words **when your fathers angered me.** Many times God had mercifully drawn back from imposing the curse of the broken covenant on them, but the recalcitrance of the previous generations and their refusal to respond despite repeated entreaties so judicially angered the LORD that 'there was no remedy' (2 Chr. 36:16). **He showed no pity.** ' "You have rejected me," declares the LORD. "You keep on backsliding. So I will lay hands on you and destroy you; I can no longer show compassion" ' (Jer. 15:6; Ezk. 24:14). His words had taken hold of their fathers (1:6).

But now in a surprising and gracious turn of events, that past determination to punish, from which there was no turning back, is made the basis of confidence in the resolution that there will be future blessing. **So now I have determined to do good again to Jerusalem and Judah (8:15).** 'Now' is once more the phrase 'in these days', and the 'again' is to be taken with 'determined' rather than 'do good'. The LORD has again come to a determined conclusion, but now it is a matter of doing good. 'As I have brought all this great calamity on this people, so I will give them all the prosperity I have promised them' (Jer. 32:42; 31:28). These blessings had been partly listed at 8:12. Because of this divine determination upon which they can rely, they are again exhorted **Do not be afraid.** They are to show the willingness of faith that moves forward trusting in the LORD's provision and promises (Zeph. 3:16-17; Lk. 12:32).

But there is more to it than that. There is now explicitly indicated where their obedience fits in to this provision of divine blessing. It does not procure the blessing for them, as if it had not been graciously given by God. But their continued enjoyment of the blessing depends on their true and loyal response to the commands of their covenant king. This had been spelled out to them from the beginning by Moses. It was after they had been saved from Egypt that he said to them, 'And now, O Israel, what does the LORD your God ask of you but to fear the LORD your God, to walk in all his ways, to love him, to serve the LORD your God with all your heart and with all your soul, and to observe the LORD's commands and decrees that I am giving you today for your own good?' (Deut. 10:12-13; 11:8). So when they are brought back by God to the land, they are to produce fruit in keeping with repentance (Lk. 3:8).

**These are the things you are to do (*8:16*).** 'Things' may also be rendered 'words', recalling the similar use to refer to the Ten Commandments, which in Hebrew are the Ten Words (Ex. 34:28; Deut. 4:13; 10:4). This fits in with the covenant relation that is being set out.

The matters raised correspond to those already set out in 5:3 and 7:8-10. **Speak the truth to each other.** 'Truth' forms one of the themes of this section (8:3, 8, 18). It is the characteristic that underpins the fabric of society, when an individual's word and undertaking may be relied on. In this way stable relationships may be built up (Ps. 15:2; Zeph. 3:13; Eph. 4:25). **And render true and sound judgment.** The legal framework of society also needs to be above reproach to ensure social cohesion. 'Sound judgment' is 'judgment of peace', that is a judgment that is so manifestly fair and correct that it immediately commends itself and is therefore accepted. Justice must be seen to be done (7:9). **In your courts** refers to the 'gates' of the city, where there were often stone benches. At these it was customary for public affairs to be transacted and justice to be dispensed (Gen. 23:18; Deut. 21:19; Ruth 4:1, 11; 1 Kgs. 22:10; Jer. 1:15).

Having spoken of the positive requirements of the covenant for the social fabric of the community, attention is then turned to what is to be avoided. **Do not plot evil against your neighbour (*8:17*).** Their inner attitudes were to be right (Mt. 15:19). The rights of fellow members of the covenant were to be respected. **And do not love to swear falsely.** It is not only the practice of giving false information regarding another, or entering into solemn engagements with no intention of carrying them through, that is proscribed. It is that attitude towards life that delights, loves to get the better of another, no matter how foul the means used to do so. **"I hate all this,"** **declares the LORD.** It is not merely said, 'That is wrong.' The matter is personalised. This is the basis of Biblical ethics. It is not motivated by conformity to an abstract standard of what is right and proper. It is motivated by relationship to a person, and to the likes and dislikes of God. He is the one whose preferences dictate what is right and proper, and obedience is motivated by a desire to please and honour him. Compare this with the list of what the LORD hates in Proverbs 6:16-19. Notice that idolatry is not mentioned by Zechariah. This fits in with the view that the Exile had purged this from the nation.

The enjoyment of God's covenant blessings is never independent of faith and obedience on the part of the recipient. There is a divinely decreed link of blessing with obedience, and suffering with disobedience. 'Now if you obey me fully and keep my covenant, then out of all nations you will be my treasured possession' (Ex. 19:5). Whoever looks for the blessing without the obedience of faith is self-deceived. 'The man who says, "I know him," but does not do what he commands is a liar, and the truth is not in him' (1 Jn. 2:4).

*(8) The Question Answered:* The words **Again the word of the LORD Almighty came to me (*8:18*),** mirroring as they do those of 8:1, show that Zechariah here introduces a break into the sequence of divine messages. This seems to be done so that attention may be focused on the matter that gave rise to this message—that of whether the fast of the fifth month should continue to be observed (7:3). What has been said so far constitutes a necessary introduction to the answer, for the question has to be seen in its right context. There were far more serious and fundamental matters to be dealt with, and indeed once that was recognised, their queries were already well on the way to being answered.

**This is what the LORD Almighty says: "The fasts of the fourth, fifth, seventh and tenth months" (*8:19*)** sound ponderous and solemn, if not ominous, in the original. At first, mention had been made of the fifth month (7:3). Then there had been added the fast of the seventh month (7:5). Now there are two more: the fast of the fourth month, which arose because on the ninth day of the fourth month the wall of Jerusalem had been breached (2 Kgs. 25:3; Jer. 39:2), and the fast of the tenth month, which commemorated the fact that on the tenth day of the tenth month Nebuchadnezzar had started the siege of the city (2 Kgs. 25:1-2; Jer. 39:1; 52:6-7). These four events were a litany of the grievous blows suffered by the people. They summed up the disasters that had affected them.

They are mentioned, however, to show that under the LORD's

transforming grace their days of mourning would be ended (Ps. 30:11; Isa. 12:1). Their fasts **will become joyful and glad occasions and happy festivals for Judah.** What the LORD is about to do will revolutionise every aspect of their national existence, so that the whole rationale of the fast days will be done away with. They will become feast days. 'Joyful' relates primarily to social occasions at which there are festivities, such as weddings or banquets. 'Glad' is a more general word indicating happiness. The phrase 'happy festivals' occurs only here but well indicates the transforming hand of the LORD at work. It is not explicitly said that the fasts will be done away with, but it is clearly indicated that circumstances will be so changed that they will have become totally inappropriate (Isa. 61:3, 7; 65:18-19). Enjoying God's presence with them, 'How can the guests of the bridegroom fast while he is with them?' (Mk. 2:19).

But there is a word, one might almost say of warning. **Therefore**, or simply 'But', **love truth and peace.** The language is emphatic: 'It is truth and peace you are to love.' This is the response of gratitude, recognising that all has come from the LORD, and in a spirit of self-dedication they are to strive to do his will. For 'truth' see 8:3. 'Peace' here is not just absence of war and economic prosperity, but the gift God gives his people of living in harmony with him (Num. 6:26; Ps. 85:8). The pathway to enjoyment of the blessings of the LORD's restoring grace is as ever the pathway of obedience.

It is not certain what the Jews of Zechariah's day did as regards keeping these fast days. They are still observed in the Jewish calendar, but there is evidence to suggest that, having lapsed, they were re-instated after the destruction of the Temple in A.D. 70 .

*(9) The Universal Blessing:* The blessings the LORD will provide are seen as flowing out from Judah and Jerusalem to encompass all nations. **This is what the LORD Almighty says: "Many peoples and the inhabitants of many cities will yet come"** *(8:20).* The LORD's speech begins in a way that strongly emphasises the 'yet'. Perhaps we could render it, '<It will> yet <be the case> that many peoples ...' It refocuses attention from the immediate circumstances of the restored community to the time of universal blessing that still awaits the people of God. The passage is reminiscent of Isaiah 2:2-

4 and Micah 4:1-5 (compare also 2:10-12; 14:16-19).

The fact that the inhabitants of many cities are mentioned seems to reflect on the situation of Judah in the prophet's day when the land was largely uninhabited. So great would be the blessing to be enjoyed in Jerusalem, that people would be prepared to leave places of security and prosperity to come there. Indeed it will be a matter of urgency on their part that they do so. **And the inhabitants of one city will go to another and say, 'Let us go at once to entreat the LORD and seek the LORD Almighty'** *(8:21)*. They are not content with going themselves, they exhort one another to do so. For 'entreat', see on 7:2. **I myself am going** indicates how eager they are to know the only true God and enjoy a right relationship with him.

**And many peoples and powerful nations will come to Jerusalem** *(8:22)*. Their going towards Jerusalem is of course motivated by the fact that God has been pleased to reveal himself in a special way there. If the nations would have dealings with the LORD, then they must go to Jerusalem. This of course expresses the truth in its Old Testament guise. Now that the worship of God is no longer localised in that way, the truth of this prophecy is fulfilled not in spatial terms, but in coming to the community where the LORD's presence by his Spirit is to be found. There they intend **to seek the LORD Almighty and to entreat him,** reversing the order of the phrases from 8:21.

*(10) Salvation is from the Jews:* The final saying in the series brings out two additional features of this international turning to the LORD. It will be accompanied by a recognition of the rights and privileges of the Jews, and it will be motivated by reports about how the LORD has blessed them and how he is to be found in their midst. **This is what the LORD Almighty says: "In those days ten men from all languages and nations will take firm hold of one Jew by the hem of his robe and say, 'Let us go with you, because we have heard that God is with you'"** *(8:23)*.

Controversy surrounds precisely when and how these final two prophecies, and others like them, are to be fulfilled. Such a universal recognition of the LORD who had made Israel his people did not occur in the inter-testamental period. We may see something of this blessing being achieved in the group of 'Parthians, Medes and

Elamites; residents of Mesopotamia, Judea and Cappadocia, Pontus and Asia, Phrygia and Pamphylia, Egypt and the parts of Libya near Cyrene; visitors from Rome (both Jews and converts to Judaism); Cretans and Arabs' assembled on the day of Pentecost (Acts 2:9-11). Figures such as the Ethiopian eunuch (Acts 8:26-39) and Cornelius (Acts 10) show the blessing spreading out to all the nations. Those were the start of the realisation of this blessing. Salvation was from the Jews, and spread out from Jerusalem to the ends of the earth (Acts 1:8), enlightening the world by presenting the gospel of the one who had been appointed 'a light for the Gentiles' (Isa. 42:6; 49:6).

Before the coming of Christ, Jerusalem was the exclusive centre of the revealed religion of the one and only God. The turning of the nations to him, which takes place under the gospel, is therefore presented in symbolic terms taken from Old Testament times (Isa. 66:18-23; Zech. 14:16). But the reality thus depicted is taken up and attained in a far more grand way in the expansion of the church. The terms of the prophecies are not falsified, but more than fulfilled. There is a superabounding element to the work of God brought about by the arrival of Christ. He pointed to this quite clearly when he said to the Samaritan woman, 'Believe me, woman, a time is coming when you will worship the Father neither on this mountain nor in Jerusalem. You Samaritans worship what you do not know; we worship what we do know, for salvation is from the Jews. Yet a time is coming and has now come when the true worshippers will worship the Father in spirit and truth, for they are the kind of worshippers the Father seeks. God is spirit, and his worshippers must worship in spirit and in truth' (Jn. 4:21-24). We can see this change glimpsed at in Malachi 1:10-11. It is out of keeping with these statements to view such prophecies as having to be fulfilled in terms of some millennial Jerusalem. Their fulfilment has already begun in the spreading influence of the church, and will be completed in the day when the Lord returns for his own—both Jew and Gentile.

*Study Questions*

**8:6** How may we avoid adopting an incredulous attitude towards God's promises? Mk. 10:23-26; Rom. 4:20-21; Heb. 3:12-15; 10:32-39; 12:1-3.

**8:17** What are we to learn from the truth that love motivates Christian obedience? Jn. 14:15, 23; 15:10-12; 1 Jn. 3:10; 2 Jn. 6.

**8:20-21** God 'rewards those who earnestly seek him' (Heb. 11:6). How is that done? 2 Chr. 30:18-19; Ps. 119:2, 10; Prov. 8:17; Mt. 7:8; Jn. 4:23.

## THE MESSIANIC PROSPECT
### (Zech. 9:1-14:21)

Zechariah does not record for us that the Temple was completed; that is to be found in Ezra 6:13-22. However, the completion of the Temple was not the end of the story. What was to happen next? It is the message for the subsequent period that is taken up in Zechariah 9-14.

These chapters have been the occasion of much perplexity and debate. There is an undoubted change in the approach and style of the material. Unlike the earlier chapters which mention Zechariah by name (1:1, 7; 7:1), there is now no specific reference to the prophet, nor are dates recorded for the various messages. Whereas the structure, if not the meaning, of chapters 1-8 is evident, the basis on which material in chapters 9-11 and 12-14 has been ordered is far from clear. Such factors have often been taken as sufficient grounds for supposing that other authors were responsible for the concluding chapters of Zechariah.

There are, however, many themes in Zechariah 1-8 that are taken up again in chapters 9-14. The focus is on the future of the LORD's people as described under the title of Jerusalem and Zion (1:12-16; 2:1-13 as compared with 9:8-10; 12:1-13:1; 14:1-21). The need is for the community to be cleansed of their spiritual defilement (3:1-9; 5:1-11 as compared with 10:9; 12:10; 13:1-2; 14:20-21). There is also a place for the nations in the fulfilment of the purposes relating to God's kingdom (2:11; 8:20-23 as compared with 9:7, 10; 14:16-19).

So the break at Zechariah 9 is not unlike that occurring at Isaiah

40, and similar reasons may be advanced for the changed style and approach. These centre round the possibility that these chapters relate to revelation that was given at a later period and for a different purpose. Their focus is no longer on building the Temple or resettling in the land. Indeed they are not dated, and it is difficult to relate them to any particular set of historical circumstances. The diverse results of attempts to find a specific background for their origin testify to the inconclusive nature of such approaches. But it is obvious that the chapters do relate to the general circumstances after 515 B.C.— not to the need for obedience in relation to a specific project, but the need for stamina to keep going in a period of great change all around and seemingly little encouragement for the people of God.

It was a time of disillusionment. The people seem to have interpreted the promises that had been given them as signalling that there would be a speedy arrival of a time of blessing and national prosperity. Now they had to be sustained in the face of their circumstances. The Chronicler, who probably composed his history about a century after the completion of the Temple, was led to strengthen the people by reminding them of their place in history, and how God had blessed obedience in the past. His retrospective view was designed to develop present confidence, and overcome their identity crisis: 'Who are we? What is it that we are suppose to be doing? Why?' Their lack of confidence led to many irregularities and acts of disobedience in their living. The ministries of Ezra, Nehemiah and Malachi testify to the many matters that had to be exposed and rectified.

Zechariah's later ministry falls at an earlier period than this, perhaps fifteen to twenty years after the completion of the Temple and forty to fifty years before Malachi. Departure from the standards of the covenant was not then as open as it later became. The task given to Zechariah was to encourage the people to remain true to the LORD by showing them what still lay in the future. This was not achieved by presenting an optimistically unreal picture of their future prospects, but by looking forward realistically and presenting some basic Scriptural truths. Though there seemed from their perspective to be delay, the future glory is no less certain. Themes that had been touched upon in passing in the earlier messages are now dealt with more extensively, and the Messianic focus of the prophetic message is seen even more clearly. These chapters are frequently employed in the Gospels and in the book of Revelation, where they are in part fulfilled by Christ's first coming and in part await his return.

It has to be recognised that even among those who have a conservative approach to Scripture there exists a great diversity of opinion as to how unfulfilled prophecy should be interpreted. There are those who argue that prophecies that are yet to be fulfilled will be fulfilled with as great attention to detail as was evinced in the fulfilment of prophecies relating to the first coming of Christ. In particular this requires that every mention of Jerusalem, Zion or Judah must relate to an outward, national embodiment of these Old Testament entities, which thus have to be restored at some future time. However, quite apart from the fact that the New Testament fulfilment of prophecy is often not as literal as is claimed, we have also to make due allowance for the way in which the New Testament interprets Old Testament prophecies as fulfilled in the destiny of the church encompassing both Jew and Gentile. The wall of partition between Jew and Gentile has been broken down, never to be raised again, and so there can never again be a specifically Jewish people of God in a rebuilt Jerusalem. There may yet be a time of special blessing for the Jews when they come to know Christ on a scale not yet precedented: but that is within, not apart from, the one church of Christ. There is further discussion of these questions in the Appendix.

Zechariah was permitted to see what lay in the future for the people of God. This was presented to him in Old Testament terms, for those were the realities that he and the people he ministered to knew and understood. We have to ask whether what he relates has already occurred, or whether it awaits fulfilment. Sometimes this is difficult because, as is often true in Old Testament prophecy, there was not a clear understanding of the twofold coming of Christ, and so what pertains to one coming may be merged with what pertains to another. In general, however, it seems that in chapters 9-11 Zechariah is presenting what would happen in the closing years of the Old Testament church, and in chapters 12-14 his focus is principally on the period from Christ's ascension through to his return.

# THE FIRST BURDEN: PRISONERS OF HOPE
## (Zech. 9:1-11:17)

This burden looks forward to the future of the covenant people in the period between the fall of the Persian Empire and the first coming of Christ. In chapter 9 there are described two times of deliverance for God's people. In the first (9:1-8) destruction is divinely sent upon their neighbours, but effectively warded off from them. Jerusalem alone of the major cities of Palestine emerged unscathed. The other deliverance (9:13-17) is set against the background of a conflict with Greece, which is subdued by the LORD going forth like a whirlwind. As a result of this his people shine forth like a diadem. Between these two accounts there is introduced the peaceful king whose dominion would be worldwide and who would accomplish much (9:9-11). Despite their depressed circumstances his people should even now be able to capture some of the joy that will be known when he comes.

Chapter 10 develops the promises of prosperity with which the previous chapter closed, emphasising the gift of good leadership that the LORD will bestow on his people (10:3-5) and the strength they will be endowed with (10:6-12).

Chapter 11, however, presents a complete contrast, not blessing, but judgment (11:1-3). This comes about because the people of God calamitously reject the good shepherd he sends to them (11:4-14). Part of their judgment is that having rejected the good shepherd they will have a worthless and foolish one to rule them (11:15-17).

## Zechariah 9:1-8: The LORD's Irresistible Advance

After the Temple was completed, the restored community were challenged to display continuing faithfulness to God during a period when there was no immediate fulfilment of the divine promises. The people had hoped for much, and the delay caused them doubt and lack of confidence. Zechariah's later prophecies were given to strengthen their wavering faith and encourage them to get the divine dimension back into their living. God's promises will certainly come true, and those who are his should live with confidence in his commitment to ensure the safety and heritage of his people.

In this section God is portrayed as the divine warrior who will subdue those who are hostile to him and to his people. In the list of those overwhelmed by the divine advance it is significant that there is no mention of such traditional enemies of the Jews as Edom, Moab or Ammon. Their territories lay to the east of the Dead Sea, and were not considered to be part of the land of promise. Similarly the fate of Egypt and Mesopotamia is not mentioned. The focus is on Palestine, the land of promise, which the LORD will reclaim for himself. In 9:1-4 he is envisaged as being in the north of Palestine. In the matching second section (9:5-7) it is in the south of the land that he is active. The significance of all this is brought out in 9:8, where the LORD is found in his Temple, ruling over and protecting his people in the land he has given them.

There are various views as to how this prophecy has been or will be fulfilled. The distinguished Jewish historian, Josephus (A. D. 37-100 ), wrote a twenty-volume work *Jewish Antiquities,* in which he recounted the history of his people from earliest times down to his own day. There we find many remarkable parallels between what Zechariah prophesied here and what happened at the next major convulsion of the ancient world when the Greeks, who had held the Persians at bay for many years, were united under Alexander the Great (356-323 B.C.). At the start of a ten-year campaign in which he extended his empire from Greece to the borders of India, in 333 B.C. Alexander was victorious over the Persians at Issus, in the far northeastern corner of the Mediterranean. Force-marching his troops, he surprised and routed the numerically superior Persian army, and then moved south to take Egypt, passing down the eastern Mediterranean coast to do so. His treatment of Damascus, Tyre, Philistia and Jerusalem corresponds closely to what Zechariah described a century and a half before.

But it would be wrong to take this portion simply as a prophecy of Alexander and what he did as the LORD's instrument in the affairs of the land. There is no mention of Alexander or any human agency at all. The emphasis in this passage is on the fact that it is the LORD that is at work. He determines the outcome of the events of history, and this culminates in the Messiah. We are summoned to look beyond Alexander's day. What happened then is used to teach concerning the LORD's cleansing and restoration of his inheritance, which ultimately issues in the inviolable security of 'Never again will an oppressor overrun my people' (9:8). That was not true of Jerusalem after Alexander's day, but it in measure applies now of Christ's church which the gates of Hades will not overcome (Mt. 16:18), and it is a security that in the future is enjoyed totally in the New Jerusalem.

*Advance Through the North (9:1-4).* **An Oracle (9:1)** is a word over which there has been extensive debate that is still unresolved. Does the word denote a message from God, or is its main thrust the fact that it is a message of judgment, a message with an ominous note? Translators are divided. NRSV, REB and NIV prefer 'oracle', but NKJV and NASB have 'burden' with 'oracle' in the margin. In this passage they are also undecided whether the word should be taken independently as a title, corresponding to a similar title at 12:1, or whether it should be rendered 'the burden of the word of the LORD' (NASB, NKJV) as the Hebrew accentuation would suggest. Separating it off as a title is preferable if the rendering is merely 'oracle' because 'oracle of the word' is redundant. Nonetheless, the threatening note of what follows warrants the rendering 'burden'. For further discussion of this word, see comments on Malachi 1:1.

**The word of the LORD is against the land of Hadrach.** 'The word of the LORD' here involves more than a prophetic message which has been divinely given. It looks forward to the content of that message being realised. This is not because of some magical property inherent in the word itself, but because the word expresses the purpose of the God whose power is supreme and who 'does as he pleases with the powers of heaven and the peoples of the earth' (Dan. 4:35).

Since Hadrach is not elsewhere mentioned in Scripture, its location constituted an on-going problem for commentators, until Assyrian records showed that there was an Aramean city-state of Hatarikka north of Hamath, at least until the eighth century B.C. The identification of Hadrach and Hatarikka is now generally accepted. It would thus be the northernmost site mentioned in this list of places, lying not far from the upper reaches of the Euphrates. The point of mentioning it here seems to be that the Jews were expecting the revitalisation of their fortunes to encompass the restoration of the land to its promised limits 'from the river of Egypt to the great river, the Euphrates' (Gen. 15:18). This then is a vision of the LORD's judgment coming upon those hostile people who occupied the land he had granted to his people. The LORD is acting to fulfil the covenant promises.

The same message **will rest upon Damascus,** 180 miles (290 km) further south than Hadrach, which was the capital of Aram (Syria). The fact that the resting-place of the word is to be there is not an indication of blessing, but rather of the fate that is to going to be imposed on those people. The Arameans were long-standing enemies of Israel (1 Kgs. 20:1; 2 Kgs. 10:32-33), and judgment was often pronounced against her by the prophets (Isa. 17:1-3; Jer. 49:23-27; Amos 1:3-5). At this time Damascus was the seat of the Persian governor of the province of Trans-Euphrates. This is judgment to come upon the occupying power. No indication is given here of what is to happen to Damascus, or why. But it is clear that she will be unable to resist what the LORD has determined. Alexander in fact devastated the city on his way north from Egypt.

The next clause may be variously understood. The NRSV rendering 'For to the LORD belongs the capital of Aram, as do all the tribes of Israel' rests on a double emendation of the Hebrew that is without versional support. Two interpretations of the Hebrew are to be found in the NIV, one in the text **(for the eyes of men and all the tribes of Israel are on the LORD)** and another in the margin ('For the eye of the LORD is on all mankind, as well as on the tribes of Israel'). The second rendering expresses the truth that what is happening occurs because the providential government of the LORD extends over all the earth and not merely over the affairs of his chosen people (Ps. 33:13-19; Prov. 15:3, Deut. 11:12; 1 Kgs. 9:3). As Jeremiah put it, 'Great are your purposes and mighty are your deeds. Your eyes are open to all the ways of men; you reward everyone according to his conduct and as his deeds deserve' (Jer. 32:19). So the LORD who sees all will render just recompense to all for their actions.

While this interpretation fits the context, the first rendering—that of the NIV text—is undoubtedly the more natural way to translate the Hebrew. The clause would then express the reason for the LORD's announcement of his impending judgment on those lands. People everywhere expect him to be true to his word that he will punish those who are his enemies. The world as well as his own people are watching to see his justice executed. The LORD sends this message that he will act in accordance with his word to reinforce that expectation.

However, 'are' in 'are on the LORD' is a translator's supplement, which could equally well be 'shall be'. When the LORD's judgment comes upon those lands, everyone, Jew and Gentile, will focus on what he is doing. It will be so terrifying that all will be struck with awe and consternation. The outworking of the word of the LORD cannot be ignored, or viewed with indifference. 'In that day men will look to their Maker and turn their eyes to the Holy One of Israel. They will not look to the altars, the work of their hands, and they will have no regard for the Asherah poles and the incense altars their fingers have made' (Isa. 17:7-8). 'When his judgments come upon the earth, the people of the world learn righteousness' (Isa. 26:9). In all this there is anticipated the reality of that day when 'every eye shall see him' (Rev. 1:7).

The catalogue of those on whom the LORD's word of judgment is imposed continues. **And upon Hamath too, which borders on it (9:2).** Hamath lay 125 miles (200 km) to the north of Damascus. Lebo Hamath, traditionally rendered as 'the entrance of Hamath', was frequently mentioned in connection with the boundaries of the land of promise (Num. 13:21; 34:8; 1 Kgs. 8:65; 2 Kgs. 14:25; Ezk. 47:15). It probably lay just to the north of the territory controlled by Damascus, and will share its fate.

Then the focus shifts south to Phoenician territory on the coast west of Damascus, in the area of modern Lebanon. **And upon Tyre and Sidon** the word of the LORD will come. Sidon, the more northerly of the two cities, was situated 25 miles (40 km) south of modern Beirut, and Tyre as far south again. Israel had often been on friendly terms with these two city states that dominated Phoenicia. Solomon entered into a treaty with Hiram of Tyre, who provided materials and technical skill for the erection of the Temple (1 Kgs. 5:1-12; 7:13-46). But later links with Phoenicia during the dynasty of Omri, however economically beneficial they might have been, were spiritually disastrous. Ahab, Omri's son, married the daughter of the king of Sidon, who actively promoted Baal worship (1 Kgs. 18:19).

**Though they are very skilful.** Although Tyre had originally been a colony of Sidon, 'skilful' or 'wise' is singular, perhaps reflecting the much reduced status of Sidon by this period. The Phoenicians were, of course, renowned traders (Ezk. 27:12-24), and 'skilful' refers to their ability to make money. 'By your wisdom and understanding you have gained wealth for yourself ... By your great skill in trading you have increased your wealth' (Ezk. 28:4, 5). But that very wealth proved a snare to them by encouraging pride and self-confidence. Their desire for profit involved them in ruthless and unprincipled action (Ezk. 28:16; Amos 1:9).

**Tyre has built herself a stronghold (9:3)** involves a word play in Hebrew between Tyre, which means 'rock' (*tsor*) and the word 'stronghold' (*matsor*). The city was originally on the land, but there was also an island about a mile offshore which was extensively fortified, and surrounded by a double sea-wall. This formed the new city, 'surrounded by the sea' (Ezk. 27:32), and called 'fortress of the sea' (Isa. 23:4). **She has heaped up silver like dust, and gold like the dust of the streets.** There is no disparagement of this wealth as such. Just as in the description of Jerusalem of Solomon's day (1 Kgs. 10:27), it is the commonness, the unremarkable nature of the presence of silver and gold, that is being brought out. They had amassed gold and silver in their treasuries (Ezk. 28:4). As the leading commercial and naval power of the time, Tyre thought she could ensure her own security. But when the LORD decided her time had come, all her entrenched might was worthless.

Tyre's wisdom was a purely worldly one, and could not withstand the purposes of God. **But the Lord** (*Adonai*, see on 4:14) **will take away her possessions and destroy her power on the sea, and she will be consumed by fire (9:4).** 'Destroy her power on the sea' points to the end of her success as a maritime trading power. It might also be rendered 'destroy her wealth in the sea', which would picture the ruined city falling into the sea and associate the source of her strength and wealth with her downfall. The new city of Tyre on its island had successfully withstood sieges in the past. It had survived a five-year siege by the Assyrians (701-696 B.C.), and though the

Babylonians under Nebuchadnezzar had taken the city on the main-land, the island fortress was uncaptured after 13 years (585-572 B.C.). But it was not so with Alexander the Great. He built a mole out to the island fortress and was able to overthrow the city in seven months (332 B.C.) and burn it before sweeping south in his campaign. What happened then is an illustration of the truth that 'wealth is worthless in the day of wrath' (Prov. 11:4), and Tyre like Babylon stands for all that human wealth achieves apart from God, and which will ultimately be swept away (Rev. 18).

*The Southern Campaign (9:5-7).* The Philistines occupied the coastal plain of southern Palestine to the south of Joppa, and had some sort of joint rule under the lords of their five cities—from north to south, Ekron, Ashdod, Ashkelon, Gath and Gaza (Josh. 13:3). They were traditional enemies of Israel, achieving most success in the days of Samuel and Saul. David defeated them and made their cities vassal states. However, they continued to be a source of trouble in later times (2 Chr. 21:16-17; 26:6), and are the subject of prophetic denunciation (Amos 1:6-8; Jer. 25:20; 47:1-7; Zeph. 2:4-7; Ezk. 25:15-17). In these prophecies no mention is made of Gath which seems to have been ruined from the days of Uzziah (2 Chr. 26:6; Amos 6:2).

Although descriptions are given of the reactions and fate of the various cities, it would seem that in measure they apply to them all. **Ashkelon will see it and fear (9:5)** records how the news of Alexander's capture of the seemingly impregnable Tyre caused shockwaves further south. Indeed Ashkelon and Ekron seem to have been so demoralised that they submitted to Alexander without resistance. **Gaza will writhe in agony** may well refer to the five-month siege before it too fell to Alexander—a delay that intensely irritated one whose main weapon was speed and decisiveness. **Ekron too, for her hope will wither.** Although Ekron was not besieged, her experience is described in similar terms. Was her hope that of continuing independence, or of Tyre stopping Alexander in his tracks, or of being spared the worst by submission? **Gaza will lose her king** may be a reference to Alexander's cruel treatment of her king, but because 'her' is a supplement, it probably indicates that

Gaza was deprived of a native ruler entirely. Ancient conquerors often left local kings to rule under their overall control. After being delayed for five months besieging Gaza, Alexander was in no mood to allow the city the privilege of having such a subordinate ruler, as it had had under the Persians. **Ashkelon will be deserted.** The verse returns to the first city mentioned and prophesies that it would be uninhabited, completing the picture of devastation and ruin.

**Foreigners will occupy Ashdod (9:6).** Those whose descent is of uncertain provenance (the word is found elsewhere only in Deut. 23:3) will take over the remaining Philistine city. The native population would be removed. **And I will cut off the pride of the Philistines.** There is a change to divine speech, as God explains what he will do. There is no reference elsewhere to the Philistines as being particularly arrogant in their demeanour. Perhaps what is meant is that the losses to be inflicted on them (particularly if the descriptions apply to all the cities) would be such as to deprive them of all that set them apart from others, their national identity and existence.

There is then, however, a surprising turn of events. Although the Philistines are to be subjected to judgment, the LORD has also gracious intentions towards them. But this good does not come to them irrespective of their character. First he proposes to remove from them the pagan practices to which they tenaciously clung. **I will take the blood from their mouths, the forbidden food from between their teeth (9:7).** This refers to heathen sacrifices where blood was consumed—something that was strictly prohibited in Israel (Lev. 17:10). The 'forbidden food' or 'detestable things' are not just the Philistines' sacrifices to pagan deities, but the subsequent consumption of part of the offering including the blood (Jer. 7:30; 13:27; 32:24). The LORD will bring such abominable practices to an end.

**Those who are left will belong to our God.** There is an element of surprise. 'It (Philistia) too shall be a remnant for our God' (NRSV) brings out the additional thought in the original that the preservation of the Philistine remnant will have parallels to the divine preservation of the remnant from Israel. 'Remnant' was virtually a technical term for the restored people of God, but his mercy is extended beyond the Jews. The Philistines are to be brought into positions of prominence, as they will **become leaders in Judah.** 'Leaders' is used of princes of tribes of Edom and the Horites (Gen. 36:15, 16; Ex. 15:15; 1 Chr. 1:51), and refers to one with status as a head of a family. This would not apply to all the Philistines but is part of the picture here that the favour extended to them will not make them subordinate in status to the remnant of Israel. **Ekron will be like the Jebusites** takes Ekron, the most northerly of the Philistine cities, as an instance of what will happen to them all. The Jebusites were the original inhabitants of Jerusalem, who were incorporated into Israel during the period of David and Solomon, for instance Araunah (2 Sam. 24:18; note also 1 Kgs. 9:20-21).

This incorporation of the Gentiles within the people of God fits in with the message given to Zechariah earlier (2:11; 8:20-23). It is a reminder of the universalism of the Old Testament, whereby the covenant blessing would extend to more than the natural descendants of Abraham (Gen. 12:1-3). This theme is often found in the Psalms (Ps. 67; 87; 117; 148) and the prophets (Isa. 2:2-5, 11; 19:23-25; Amos 9:12; Mic. 4:1-5; Joel 2:32). But it is not an undiscriminating universalism. Though it goes beyond boundaries of race, there is no thought of acceptance of, or compromise with, paganism. The LORD incorporates them within his people after he has purged them of their pagan ways.

This verse also warns us against a one-dimensional perspective on the prophecy. Although there are features in it that can be related to the time of Alexander the Great, there is nothing in the prophecy which compels it to be interpreted of that time exclusively. Indeed, in directing the prophet (and the people) to look forward, the LORD brings in other related aspects of the future. There is no record of the transformation of the Philistines described in 9:7 as taking place in the time of Alexander. During the period of the Maccabees (2nd century B.C.) mention is made of a hostile Philistine force (1 Macc. 3:41*), of Judas Maccabee pulling down Philistine altars and images in Ashdod (1 Macc. 5:68), and of the destruction by Jonathan Maccabee of a Philistine temple to Dagon at Ashdod (1 Macc. 10:83-84). Thereafter the Philistines disappear from historical records,

---

* This, and the following references, are to the books of the Maccabees. They are not inspired Scripture, but are still of value as sources of historical information about the inter-testamental period.

perhaps being absorbed into the Jewish and Greek populations of the area. An initial fulfilment of the prophecy is no doubt to be found in Philip's preaching at Azotus (Ashdod) (Acts 8:40), and in Peter's ministry in Lydda and Joppa, on the fringes of former Philistine territory (Acts 9:32-43). But the ultimate fulfilment is to be found in that scene where there is gathered 'a great multitude that no-one could count, from every nation, tribe, people and language, standing before the throne and in front of the Lamb. They were wearing white robes and were holding palm branches in their hands' (Rev. 7:9).

*The Ultimate Security (9:8).* Having cleansed the land, the divine warrior comes to Jerusalem. There had been previous invaders from the north, such as the Assyrians and Babylonians, and the word of the LORD had been that, because of their sin, his chosen people would not be exempt from their depredations (Isa. 10:5-6; Jer. 1:14). But now the picture is one of the LORD's determination to treat them in an obviously different way. **But I will defend my house against marauding forces.** The LORD gives the assurance that he will 'defend' or 'camp around' to protect them (Ps. 34:7). 'My house' may refer to the Temple (1:16; Mal. 3:10) as the symbol of the LORD's presence with his people. But though preserved from Alexander, it was desecrated by Antiochus Epiphanes in 167 B.C. and destroyed by the Romans in A.D. 70. It is therefore preferable to take 'my house' as a reference to the people as a whole (Hos. 8:1; 9:15; Jer. 12:7; Num. 12:7). Those who are his will know his protection and deliverance.

'Marauding' renders 'one who passes through and one who returns'. The phrase only occurs four times in the Old Testament, here and in Zechariah 7:14 (being thus an indication of the interconnection between the two parts of the book), and also in Exodus 32:27 and Ezekiel 35:7. It may refer to Alexander going through Palestine, and then returning from Egypt. At that time Alexander treated the city with respect. Josephus relates that when Alexander had captured Gaza and was advancing towards Jerusalem, those around him expected it to meet the same end. So too did Jaddua the high priest. But he put on his robes of office and, accompanied by the other priests and many of the population, went out to meet Alexander. Rather than the expected rebuff, he received a warm welcome, as Alexander declared that back in Macedonia he had seen the high priest in a dream and that he had promised him success against the Persians. As a result, Alexander was well disposed towards the Jews. Not all are convinced about the historicity of Josephus' narrative, but there is no denying that at a time when the other major cities of Syria-Palestine were ravaged, Jerusalem escaped unscathed. (See also on 2:5.)

But, as the next sentence shows, there is more involved in this prophecy than that. **Never again will an oppressor overrun my people, for now I am keeping watch.** The last clause may also be rendered, 'Now I have seen with my eyes'. It is reminiscent of Exodus 3:7, 'The LORD said, "I have indeed seen the misery of my people in Egypt. I have heard them crying out because of their slave drivers, and I am concerned about their suffering."' 'Slave drivers' is the same word as 'oppressor' here. The LORD confirms that he is aware of what was happening to his people and is determined to prevent them from being reduced to the circumstances that they had experienced in Egypt and again more recently in Babylon. That did not come true in the period after Alexander. The Jews experienced great suffering under Antiochus Epiphanes, and later they were under the control of Rome. The language looks forward to the final security of the people of God.

Zechariah is extending a message of hope to the people of his day. The reality of Persian domination affected every aspect of their living, and the promises they had been expecting to come true were still unfulfilled. But Haggai's prophecy of the nations being shaken would be realised (Hag. 2:7, 22). What happened at the time of Alexander was a foreshadowing of the protection God would extend to his church in time to come, to those 'who through faith are shielded by God's power until the coming of the salvation that is ready to be revealed in the last time' (1 Pet. 1:5).

*Study Questions*

**9:4** Scripture often reminds us of the worthlessness of material prosperity. Why is this so? Prov. 11:4; 16:8; Lk. 12:16-21; Rev. 3:17-22.

**9:5** Hope plays an important part in life. How does the hope of the believer and unbeliever differ? Job 27:8; 31:24-28; Ps. 33:18-22; 49; Prov. 10:28; Rom. 5:2; 8:24; Eph. 2:12.

**9:8** In what ways does God act to defend and preserve his people? What should we look for in times of danger or perplexity? Ps. 34:15-22; 37:23-33; 41:1-3; Rom. 8:28-39; 1 Cor. 10:13; 1 Pet. 3:12-13.

### Zechariah 9:9-17:   The King and his People

The previous section set out the LORD's providential action to defend his people and rid the land of all that offends him and mars their inheritance. It also told of his coming to be in their midst to protect them. Many of the features could be paralleled in what happened in the time of Alexander the Great, but the prophecy took in more than was ever bestowed through his instrumentality. The theme is not that of the Messiah in comparison with Alexander, but the Messiah as the embodiment of God's saving purpose. It is with him alone that the fulness of divine blessing is pre-eminently associated, when the long-awaited king of Davidic descent delivers the LORD's people and secures their inheritance.

*The King (9:9-10)*. Following on from the LORD's presence in the Temple (9:8), the prophet is shown the Messianic king entering Jerusalem. As he relates this wonderful scene to the people, he urges them to express their appreciation of its significance by giving voice to joyful acclamation. There are two commands given: **Rejoice greatly, O Daughter of Zion! Shout, Daughter of Jerusalem! (9:9)**. 'Daughter of Zion' (see on 2:10) and 'Daughter of Jerusalem' are personifications of the LORD's people, the believing members of the covenant nation. What is described is a scene of great excitement and intense emotion that bursts out into exultant cries. As the people recognise the one for whom they have been waiting so long, their response knows no bounds (2:10).

**See, your king comes to you.** 'Your king' in relation to Judah or Israel is either the LORD himself (as in Isa. 43:15) or a Davidic king (2 Sam. 3:17). Here it is the ultimate king who would 'reign on

David's throne' (Isa. 9:7), the Son of God who was also king of Israel (Jn. 1:49). He would not be a foreigner, but one whose rule over them would be legitimate (Deut. 17:15; Mt. 1:1). It is not just that he comes 'to you' but that his presence is to their benefit and advantage. How this would be is then described in greater detail.

*(1)* He is **righteous**. Kings were often arbitrary and unfair in their actions—not least Alexander whose vanity often caused him to act inequitably. But the rule of the Messiah will be fair and just, because he himself desires to do God's will and has his law within his heart (Ps. 40:8). The character of his official actions is determined by his inner attitude towards God (Jn. 5:30). Such righteousness had long been associated with the Messiah (2 Sam 23:3; Ps. 45:6-7; Isa. 11:3-5; 32:1; 45:23; 53:11; Jer. 23:5; 33:15). In his reign the injustices and perplexities of this world would be eliminated, and equity would prevail. In particular, the Messianic king would meet and fulfil all the requirements of the covenant.

*(2)* He is also one **having salvation**. The translation of this word has caused problems. It could mean 'saved', that is, the Messiah himself is one who has experienced salvation. That would refer to the fact that he needed help from the Father to endure all he underwent (Lk. 22:41-43), and especially the fact that it was the Father who raised him from the dead (Rom. 10:9; Eph. 1:20). It need not rule out the additional thought that because he was saved as the representative of his people, that salvation becomes theirs also. But more probably the verb form used in Hebrew conveys the idea that he 'shows himself as one who saves'. He is one who provides deliverance (Deut. 33:29). This is the thought that was found by the earliest translations, a Saviour. It was this that determined his mission on earth: 'The Son of Man came to seek and to save what was lost' (Lk. 19:10). So the strictness of his rule as regards standards of equity is matched by the help which he extends to those in need. As Isaiah had done two centuries before, the ideas of righteousness and deliverance are combined (Isa. 45:8; 46:13; 51:4-5), but notice that this is ascribed to the coming king, not to the priest.

*(3)* He is also described as **gentle**. The Hebrew term covers a variety of ideas and may also be rendered 'poor' in an economic sense (as in 7:10), 'oppressed' (11:7), 'afflicted' by evildoers (11:11),

'lowly', or 'humble'. It describes one who knows suffering and misery, and who lives in outwardly insignificant circumstances. When such earthly misfortunes are rightly improved on, they foster an attitude of humble dependence on the LORD (Isa. 66:2), and of taking him as a refuge (Ps. 14:6). The spirit of the humble sets them apart from those whose eyes are haughty (Ps. 18:27) and from proud mockers (Prov. 3:34). What they have experienced makes them sensitive to the situation of others. Even if they could, they would not employ force to get their way. Hardly a characteristic of earthly kings! What is described here reflects on the priestly role of the Messiah, which Zechariah has already mentioned (Zech. 6:9-15). It is this attribute that is reflected in Jesus' claim 'I am gentle and humble in heart' (Mt. 11:29), in his earthly poverty (Mt. 8:20; Lk. 9:58), indeed in the humiliation of all his earthly life (Isa. 53:1-3; Phil. 2:6-8).

This lowliness is exemplified by the fact that he is **riding on a donkey, on a colt, the foal of a donkey.** In earlier centuries the donkey had been the animal ridden by all classes, for instance Solomon (1 Kgs. 1:38)—and Absalom once used a mule (2 Sam. 18:9). After the time of Solomon, the horse had been the animal ridden by kings and nobles to emphasise their rank (cf. Jer. 17:25). This accorded with the horse being a military animal, and so ridden in triumphal processions. The use here of a donkey shows the unpretentious nature of the Messiah's reign. He comes alongside his people, identifying with them, and not as a harsh overlord, intent on emphasising his own status (as Alexander did with the magnificent animal he rode). The use of a donkey also reflects on one of the earliest Messianic passages, which says of Shiloh, or the one whose right it is to wield the sceptre of Judah, that 'he will tether his donkey to a vine, his colt to the choicest branch' (Gen. 49:11).

This prophecy was recognised as being fulfilled when Jesus rode into Jerusalem a week before his crucifixion (Mt. 21:1-5; Jn. 12:12-16). But it would be wrong to think of it as only fulfilled then. What is presented here is in fact a characterisation of the whole of our Lord's earthly life. Indeed, it would not have needed such a detailed and precise fulfilment for the prophecy to have been true, because it is principally setting out the character of the Lord. It was with this in mind that Jesus deliberately took steps to enact this prophecy. He had previously gone out of his way to avoid regal acclamation by the Jews (Jn. 6:15), because he knew that their ideas of Messianic kingship were misconceived. They were looking for a popular leader who would expel the Romans from their land and lead them on to political domination of the world. But this passage so clearly ran counter to their ideas and asserted his own conception of what being the Messiah involved that he fulfilled it to assert his claim to be Israel's true king.

The LORD then speaks of what he will do through the Messiah. **I will take away the chariots from Ephraim and the war-horses from Jerusalem, and the battle bow will be broken (*9:10*).** 'I will take away' is literally 'I will cut off' (rendered 'destroy' in Mic. 5:10-13) and suggests that the change has to be divinely imposed on the people. The former southern kingdom of Judah is represented by its capital, Jerusalem, and the northern kingdom of Israel by Ephraim, one of its principal tribes. Both are mentioned, not as if they still existed, but to indicate that the whole people are reunited and involved in the LORD's blessing. The changes described apply to north and south alike. It is not as if chariots are left in Jerusalem and war-horses in Ephraim: the whole people will be without both. This does not mean that they are thereafter defenceless and vulnerable to any hostile attack. Rather the presence of the Messiah in their midst means that no one would be able to assail them and so they could live at peace, without recourse to armaments (Hos. 1:7). He who came as the king on a donkey did not establish his kingdom by worldly power, and will not have it maintained that way either.

Many find this prophecy fulfilled by the political extinction of the Jews after the fall of Jerusalem in A.D. 70. They had hoped to assert their independence from Rome. Instead they were overwhelmed and scattered. But it is unlikely that the prediction refers to what happened to the Jews when they refused to recognise the Messiah, and continued blindly on the course they had chosen for themselves. 'Jerusalem' and 'Ephraim' are the people of God in the Old Testament, and the prophecy is fulfilled in the New Testament people of God. No longer found as a theocratic state, the church of Christ is to renounce military force as the means of achieving its ends. That stage is past. The LORD has decisively removed that option from his church. 'My kingdom is not of this world. If it were, my servants would fight to prevent my arrest by the Jews. But now my kingdom is from another place' (Jn. 18:36). The sword with which battle is to be waged is 'the sword of the Spirit, which is the word of God' (Eph. 6:17; 2 Cor. 10:4).

**He will proclaim peace to the nations.** The idiom of 'proclaiming peace' does not mean that the Messiah commands it to exist, but rather that he declares that he has established the conditions for true peace. This proclamation takes place through the preaching of 'the message God sent to the people of Israel, telling the good news of peace through Jesus Christ, who is Lord of all' (Acts 10:36). This peace is not merely an absence of earthly strife, but the realisation of that true prosperity that can only come about in the kingdom of the Messiah. It is primarily the message of peace with God through the atoning work of Christ (Rom. 5:1; Eph. 2:14-17), which forms the basis of all the blessings of the kingdom. The command to submit to him in faith and to enter his kingdom is not confined to the Jews, but extends to all the earth.

It is the universality of the Messiah's reign that is emphasised in words taken from Psalm 72:8. **His rule will extend from sea to sea,** originally meant from the Mediterranean Sea to the Persian Gulf, but it became an expression for 'everywhere'. **And from the River,** that is from the Euphrates as the northernmost limit of the land of promise (Gen. 15:18), **to the ends of the earth**, a figure of indefinite extension. The alternative rendering 'to the end of the land' (NIV footnote) would point only to the border with Egypt as the traditional southern limit of the promised land. But the view has now become much more extensive than that.

In this presentation of the Messiah's coming and kingdom there is, as is frequently the case in the Old Testament, a merging of what pertains to the first coming of Christ with what refers to his second coming. It is a prophecy that reaches out from his first coming to embrace the whole activity of his people (Lk. 24:47; Acts 1:8) until he comes again. As Peter tells us, 'Concerning this salvation, the prophets, who spoke of the grace that was to come to you, searched intently and with the greatest care, trying to find out the time and circumstances to which the Spirit of Christ in them was pointing when he predicted the sufferings of Christ and the glories that would follow' (1 Pet. 1:10-11). There was then still a considerable measure of difficulty in ascertaining how prophecy was going to be fulfilled. It is only in the light of what has already been accomplished that we are able to see what is still to come true when our Lord returns again.

*The People (9:11-12).* The focus of the prophet's message now moves from the Messiah and the future extent of his realm to the present condition of the LORD's people. They are not unconnected, for the glorious vision of their coming king should enhearten them despite the gloominess of their current circumstances, and should reinvigorate them to persevere, come what may.

**As for you (9:11)** is a hanging construction, which gives strong emphasis to the subject of what follows. The pronoun is feminine, and refers back to Daughter of Zion and Daughter of Jerusalem at the beginning of 9:9. No matter how desperate the circumstances his people were in, the LORD promises them deliverance. **Because of the blood of my covenant with you,** literally 'of your covenant', refers to the way blood was shed when the covenant was inaugurated (Ex. 24:8). That blood, which foreshadowed the blood of Christ shed to establish the new covenant (Mt. 26:28; Heb. 9:11-28), established a bond between the LORD and his people. Even though the people had frequently violated the terms of their engagement to be the LORD's— 'We will do everything the LORD has said; we will obey' (Ex. 24:7)—he still graciously recognises the union that exists with them (Isa. 49:14-16; Jer. 31:20). On that basis he is prepared to act for their good. He will not forget Israel (Isa. 44:21; Rom. 11:28-29).

**I will free your prisoners from the waterless pit.** 'Your' is again feminine singular and refers to Zion. A pit was a cavity that was hollowed out of rock. It was generally bulb-shaped with a narrow neck and plastered sides, and was designed to hold water for use in the dry season. Sometimes pits were put to other uses, such as holding prisoners. Joseph was thrown into a waterless cistern by his brothers (Gen. 37:24), and Jeremiah, confined in one which had not totally dried out, sank into the muddy sediment at its base (Jer. 38:6). It was a hopeless situation, from which one could not free oneself (Ps. 40:2).

It required outside intervention if there was to be any prospect of relief.

Two views are taken of the significance of this sentence. One view notes that the verb is literally 'I have freed', and sees in the 'waterless pit' a metaphor for the hopelessness of the exile, from which the Jews were released only by divine intervention. The next verse then urges those who had not yet returned to Palestine to do so, in the light of a coming time of divine blessing.

The other view is reflected in the NIV translation. Though the verb is past in form, there is a common Hebrew idiom known as a *prophetic perfect* (see on 1:16) which uses this to denote a future event that is so certain it is as if it had already happened. 'The waterless pit' is not just the past experience of exile in Babylon, but the misery and distress the people were currently in. Trapped by the power politics of their day, they had become increasingly dejected by their helplessness and ineffectiveness. The LORD assures them that because of the continuing reality of his covenant bond with them, he will deliver from their forlorn state.

The LORD urges them, **Return to your fortress (9:12).** In Psalm 40:2 the rock is the opposite of the slime, mud and mire of the pit. Here the 'fortress', a strong, fortified site, serves the same purpose. But what is this fortress? It cannot be a literal reference, as there were no fortified sites in Palestine at the time. The rebuilding of the walls of Jerusalem awaited the coming of Nehemiah (Neh. 1:3). The figure of speech might be drawn from the hilly nature of Palestine itself which provided many natural refuges, but Palestine was pre-eminently the land of God's presence, and this fortress looks to the security he provides. 'We have a strong city; God makes salvation its walls and ramparts. Open the gates that the righteous nation may enter, the nation that keeps faith. You will keep in perfect peace him whose mind is steadfast, because he trusts in you. Trust in the LORD for ever, for the LORD, the LORD, is the Rock eternal' (Isa. 26:1-4).

**O prisoners of hope,** 'prisoners of the hope', shows that even in their distress they are unique in that future release is made possible by their covenant relationship with the LORD who is the hope of his people (Ps. 71:5; 146:5; Lam. 3:25-26). If by faith they lay hold of that possibility, they will have returned to their spiritual stronghold, and be in a position to enjoy the benefits the LORD will bestow on them (Ps. 130:7-8). **Even now I announce that I will restore twice as much to you** points to the fulness of blessing which will come from the restoration of their fortunes. Because of who he is, the LORD can make that promise 'now' or 'today' when outwardly matters are so bleak and discouraging. There will be a double share of his blessings to compensate them for past sorrow (Isa. 40:2; 61:7). But the correspondence between 'return' and 'restore', literally, 'cause to return', shows that the path to spiritual security and enjoyment of the blessings of the covenant is that of obedience to the commands of the God of the covenant.

*The Coming Victory (9:13-17).* The military language of the following verses forms an unexpected contrast with the prediction of verse 10. The fulfilment of this prophecy seems to occur in the period between Alexander the Great and the coming of Christ. The truth being expressed is the counterpart to that of 9:8. The LORD will deliver his people, but they themselves have a vital role to play. The obedience required so as to enter into enjoyment of the covenant involves being valiant for the truth and fighting the good fight of faith. Although the blessings are secured only by divine intervention, the people are not simply passive recipients of God's bounty, but are used by him to gain the victory.

**I will bend Judah as I bend my bow and fill it with Ephraim (9:13).** 'Bend' is literally 'tread on'. The foot was used to bend the bow prior to fitting the arrow. The picture is of God as a Divine Warrior using Judah and Ephraim as bow and arrow. The LORD will use his people to conduct an offensive campaign. The terms of it are spelled out by the LORD who controls the destinies of nations: **I will rouse your sons, O Zion, against your sons, O Greece.** Greece is Yawan (the word is related to Ionia, the Greek area on the coast of Asia Minor) and is mentioned as comprising peoples of distant lands (Gen. 10:2, 4; Isa. 66:19—applied to distant, unknown people on the edge of civilisation). Greek influences began to affect Jewish life from the time of Alexander the Great. The most intense conflict occurred under his successors, one of whom Antiochus Epiphanes (175-163 B.C.) introduced the cult of Olympian Zeus into the

Temple, set up a pagan altar and sacrificed a pig on it (167 B.C.).
Opposition to this was organised by the Maccabees and led to almost
a century when the Jewish state was virtually independent. This
struggle was part of the ongoing hostility between the people of God
and the seed of the serpent (Gen. 3:15), and the LORD roused his
people to engage in what was a spiritual conflict, and not simply a
matter of political independence. **And make you like a warrior's
sword** refers to his people being equipped and used by the LORD in
the battles of those days. Such physical warfare is now no longer part
of the church's task (9:10), but that does not mean that the battle is
any less intense.

But the battle on earth is not conducted apart from divine
intervention. 'The LORD strong and mighty, the LORD mighty in
battle' (Ps. 24:8) will be active on his people's behalf as a man of war
coming to defend them. **Then the LORD will appear over them
(9:14).** This is the language of theophany. It may well reflect how
'the cloud of the LORD was over the tabernacle by day, and fire was
in the cloud by night' (Ex. 40:38) during the wilderness journeys of
Israel. He is the one who will wonderfully interpose on behalf of his
people so that his presence with them will be abundantly evident. **His
arrow will flash like lightning.** The LORD's presence with his
people is compared to a storm (Ps. 18:7-15; 77:17-18; 144:5-6; Hab.
3:8-15). The help he gives them will be swift and powerfully
effective (Hab. 3:11).

**The Sovereign LORD** involves a combination of the two words
*Adonai*, Lord, and *Yahweh*, LORD, often rendered in other translations
Lord GOD. Although the double name is found throughout Scripture,
it is especially common in the prophets, particularly Ezekiel, who
accounts for over two-thirds of the three hundred or so times it is
used. It is an ascription of supreme authority to the covenant LORD.
He is the one whose mandate extends to all things. In this capacity
**he will sound the trumpet,** the signal for the troops to gather and the
battle to commence (Num. 10:9; Judg. 3:27; 6:34; 1 Sam. 13:3-4).
**He will march in the storms of the south.** The storms coming in
from the deserts to the south east of Palestine are used for a figure of
fierce and devastating action (Job 37:9, Isa. 21:1; 29:6). When the
LORD unleashes his power, all is swept away before him.

**But the LORD Almighty (*9:15*)**, the LORD of hosts, who has all forces in the universe at his disposal, will not only be a devastating presence for his enemies to come to terms with, he **will shield them**, that is, his people, as he had shielded Jerusalem from the Assyrians ('defend' in Isa. 37:35; 38:6). They will experience his complete protection as the covenant God (Gen. 15:1; Deut. 33:29; Ps. 3:3; 7:10; 18:2; 59:11; 84:11), and because of the help they derive from on high, they will be victorious. 'With God we shall gain the victory, and he will trample down our enemies' (Ps. 60:12).

**They will destroy** is literally 'they will eat'. The comparison is with a ferocious beast of prey consuming its kill. 'The people (that is, Israel) rise like a lioness; they rouse themselves like a lion that does not rest till he devours his prey and drinks the blood of his victims' (Num. 23:24; Mic. 5:8). They will also **overcome with slingstones** views the people as David-like defeating their enemies just with a sling (1 Sam. 17:40). But 'with' is a supplement, and a more satisfactory rendering is they 'will trample on slingstones'. The weapons their enemies have hurled at them are seen as spent and exhausted, and they victoriously walk over them as if they signified nothing at all.

**They will drink** has 'blood' supplied after it by the translators of the Septuagint (see Num. 23:24 cited above, and also Ezk. 39:17-20). But the picture could equally be of a victory banquet, where they will be ecstatically joyful and **roar as with wine**, the 'as' indicating that it is not in fact a drunken orgy that is envisaged. Rather the people will be so exuberant at the victory granted them that their rejoicing knows no bounds. The NIV takes the following words as one comparison. **They will be full like a bowl used for sprinkling the corners of the altar.** The bowl was the one in which the sacrificial blood was collected (Ex. 27:3; Lev. 1:5). The point of the comparison is the completeness of their success. It also hints that the warfare they have been engaged in was specifically holy warfare, determined and guided by God and set apart to accomplish his purposes. The blood that has been shed is dedicated to the LORD. The NIV footnote indicates there may be two comparisons: 'they will be full like a bowl, like the corners of the altar'. In that case the second comparison would focus on how blood-stained they had become through fierce fighting.

Their success comes about because of the LORD's assistance. **The LORD their God will save them on that day as the flock of his people (*9:16*)**, that is the people who constitute his flock (Ps. 100:3; Ezk. 34:22; Mic. 5:4; 7:14; Lk. 12:32; Jn. 10:27). He looks after them and provides for them completely (see on 11:4-14; 13:7). **They will sparkle in his land like jewels in a crown** contrasts them to their enemies whose weapons (slingstones as compared to the stones or jewels in the crown) lie useless on the ground (9:15). This language stretches far beyond any victory the Jews achieved under the Maccabees, and looks forward to the final victory of God's people.

**How attractive and beautiful they will be! (*9:17*)**. Literally, it is 'For what his goodness and what his beauty!' where 'his' could refer back to 'people', but much more probably picks up '*his* land', which in Hebrew is at the end of the preceding verse. The LORD's goodness refers to the blessings he bestows on all creation (Ps. 145:7) and especially on his covenant people (Ps. 31:19). Though the Messiah is certainly spoken of in terms of beauty (Ps. 45:2; Isa. 33:17), it is often felt to be an awkward epithet for God. 'His beauty' may, however, be readily understood not as the beauty God possesses but as the beauty he gives to those he makes jewels in his crown. We then have here an exclamation of wonder at what the LORD has done for his own. 'What goodness and beauty he has bestowed!' **Grain will make the young men thrive, and new wine the young women** looks to the bounty of the LORD's provision as giving prosperity to the land (Isa. 62:9; Joel 2:26; 3:18; Amos 9:13-14). For 'grain' and 'new wine', see Haggai 1:11. The description ties in with that of the blessing to be enjoyed in Jerusalem (8:5). The material blessings described are mentioned as part of the total abundance enjoyed through divine favour.

Despite their present dejection the people are drawn forward to consider all that will be provided for them. It is not just that the Messiah will certainly come, but that his coming and their future are bound together. His provision is abundant and overflowing. As we have a spiritual appetite for what our Lord's second coming will involve for his people, so these promises will encourage us when we are perplexed or in danger. Our efforts to advance his cause often seem to be becalmed, just like those of the Jews of Zechariah's day, but we are to strive to have a clear vision of what is at the end of the road, so that we will be ready to press onwards.

*Study Questions*

**9:9** Consider how the character of the Messiah should also be found in his followers. Mt. 20:26-27; Jn. 13:5-17; 1 Cor. 11:1; Eph. 5:2; Phil. 2:5-7; 1 Pet. 2:21.

**9:13** How should the church witness to those whose aims and interests are not in submission to God? Acts 8:4; 1 Cor. 9:19-23; 2 Cor. 6:6-7; Gal. 6:10; 1 Pet. 2:15; 3:1.

**9:15** God is the shield of his people. In what circumstances is this truth particularly precious? Gen. 15:1; Ps. 5:12; 18:2; 33:20; 91:4; Prov. 2:7; 30:5; 1 Cor. 10:13; 1 Pet. 1:5.

## Zechariah 10:1-12:   The LORD who provides

This chapter is so closely connected with what precedes that it is difficult to decide where a break should be made. Chapter 9 had closed with a description of the abundance of the blessings the LORD bestows, and this theme is developed in a transitional section (10:1-2) which sets out the role of prayer in receiving blessing. The description of the people as the LORD's flock (9:16) pervades this chapter, and the introduction of the associated imagery of the shepherd (10:2-3) prepares the way for its more extensive use in chapter 11. Throughout the emphasis is on the provision the LORD alone can make: fertility (10:1-2), leadership (10:3-5), restoration (10:6-12).

*The LORD of Fertility (10:1-2).* The command **Ask the LORD for rain in the springtime** *(10:1)* does not warrant the assumption that the prophet was speaking at a time of drought, or that the people had particularly neglected this duty. The imperative is rather a rhetorical device to impress on them the need to live in conscious dependence on the LORD if they were to enjoy the blessings of the covenant.

Continuing the language of 9:17, where agricultural prosperity is used to represent all the blessings of God, the prayer for rain is but one instance of the people recognising that all is under divine supervision and control. It is the outworking of the spiritual principle set out by Moses, 'So if you faithfully obey the commands I am giving you today—to love the LORD your God and to serve him with all your heart and with all your soul—then I will send rain on your land in its season, both autumn and spring rains, so that you may gather in your grain, new wine and oil' (Deut. 11:13-14). Neglect of this had already caused the people to lose their way spiritually (Jer. 5:23-25).

The autumn rains provided the moisture required for the crops to germinate, whereas the spring rains were those required for the crops to swell. Generally both rains are mentioned together (Deut. 11:14; Jer. 3:3; Joel 2:23; Jas. 5:7). If any significance is to be found in the mention here of the spring rains alone, it would be that the autumn rains of blessing have already been provided in the return from the exile, and that what the people need now is the second stage of blessing that would come from the spring rains. This would fit in with the use made elsewhere of showers of rain as a symbol for spiritual blessing (Isa. 27:3; 32:15; 55:10-11; Ezk. 34:26; Hos. 10:12).

**It is the LORD who makes the storm clouds.** 'The storm clouds' are elsewhere taken as 'lightning', as a precursor of rain (Jer. 10:13; Ps. 135:7). As Baal the Canaanite god was thought of as the god of rain and fertility, this assertion could well involve a warning against seeking blessing from illicit sources, a theme developed further in verse 2. **He gives showers of rain to men** (literally 'to them') emphasises the abundance of the divine response to the petition made for what he is ready to bestow upon those who ask him. **And plants of the field to everyone.** The problem in the past had been that Israel had 'not acknowledged that I was the one who gave her the grain, the new wine and oil, who lavished on her the silver and gold which they used for Baal' (Hos. 2:8).

Verse 2 begins 'for', and provides a further reason for living in dependence on God. Other sources of help cannot help at all. This constitutes a warning against getting involved in pagan practices (Jer. 14:22). There are brought together here four words 'deceit, lie, false and vain' that are characteristic of the prophetic polemic against idol worship. **The idols speak deceit (10:2)** refers to the teraphim, household gods that were used to tell the future (Gen. 31:19; Judg. 17:5; 1 Sam. 15:23; Ezk. 21:21). But all they can proclaim is false (Isa. 41:29), empty and fraudulent. **Diviners see visions that lie** refers to those who sought omens and dreams to foretell the future (Ezk. 13:9, 23; Mic. 3:6), a practice that had been forbidden in Israel (Deut. 18:9-14). **They tell dreams that are false, they give comfort in vain.** Those who relate dreams have only what is insubstantial, empty and deceiving ('lying' in 1 Kgs. 22:22 and Jer. 23:26; see also Lam. 2:14) and, as they couch their words to favour those whose fortunes they are telling, what they say is 'in vain', mere breath, no sooner uttered than blown away (Jer. 27:9-10; 29:8-9).

The question that arises is the extent to which this fits in with the post-exilic situation, when idolatry is generally considered to have been eradicated from the nation. It is also possible to translate the verbs of this verse as referring to the past, and so to see the pre-exilic situation used as a warning that such conduct is no way forward. But though open, national adherence to pagan cults was a thing of the past, there is evidence to suggest that various superstitions and false practices lingered on. Nehemiah tells of the false prophet Shemaiah who tried to trick him, and the prophetess Noadiah and others who tried to intimidate him (Neh. 6:10-13). Malachi mentions sorcerers (Mal. 3:5). It may be that the dejection of the people exposed them to the temptation to revert to the practices of their fathers, which were still current in the heathen communities around them.

**Therefore the people wander like sheep oppressed for lack of a shepherd.** The consequence of superstitious practices had been the Exile ('the people wandered'), or the current malaise of spiritual uncertainty. 'Wander' refers to being continually on the move from one encampment to another. Relying on false teachers as their guides, they will be 'tossed back and forth by the waves, and blown here and there by every wind of teaching and by the cunning and craftiness of men in their deceitful scheming' (Eph. 4:14). Their action is like a flock of sheep moving about without fixed aim. 'Oppressed' is hardly appropriate to sheep: the reality is breaking through the figure. They are liable to be victimised because they are without a shepherd. 'Shepherd' was used to describe a leader, usually the king. The people were at the mercy of charlatans because they lacked the guidance of one 'to go out and come in before them, one who will lead them out and bring them in, so that the LORD's people will not be like sheep without a shepherd' (Num. 27:17; see also Jer. 13:20; Ezk. 34:5; Mic. 2:12; Mt. 9:36).

*The Gift of a True Leadership (10:3-5).* There is a formal link between verses 2 and 3 in the use of the word 'shepherd', but it is now the LORD who speaks, and it is not about the absence of a true, native ruler of his people, but about the impact of foreign shepherds on them. Their behaviour has enraged the LORD (Jer. 25:34-38; 49:19). **My anger burns against the shepherds, and I will punish the leaders (*10:3*).** 'Leaders' is literally 'he-goats' as those who give guidance to the herd (Isa. 14:9; Ezk. 34:17). This may be the same group as the shepherds, or it may refer to nobles and influential people. The Hebrew word rendered 'punish' denotes the action of a superior with respect to those under him. When they have been remiss in their duties it involves punishment, 'I will punish the leaders' (Ex. 20:5; Amos 3:2), but where action is needed by the superior to right wrongs and provide for the needs of his subordinates the same verb conveys the notion of 'care' (Ruth 1:6; Ps. 8:5): **for the LORD Almighty will care for his flock, the house of Judah.** The shepherd of his people looks after their needs. Judah is here mentioned not over against the North, but as standing for and being the centre of the restored community, particularly as the Messiah will come from that tribe (see next verse). The LORD will **make them like a proud horse in battle**, literally 'the horse of his majesty'. It conveys not only the idea of a changed condition, from oppressed flock to a richly ornamented royal stallion, but of being such to the renown of the LORD and fit to serve his purposes. 'In battle' may be part of the picture, the comparison being with a royal war-horse, or it may lead into the picture of the LORD's people being involved in battle against his enemies.

The LORD now acts to provide true leadership for his people. Four times in verse 4 the word 'from him' is repeated, the first time being rendered by the NIV as **from Judah (*10:4*)**, identifying the reference as to the people. This accords with the fact that Judah had been divinely ordained to possess the sceptre and the ruler's staff (Gen. 49:10). In this way also proper leadership would be provided for the people, as had been required in the case of a king. 'He must be from among your own brothers. Do not place a foreigner over you, one who is not a brother Israelite' (Deut. 17:15). (While it is grammatically possible to refer the pronoun in 'from him' to the LORD who had just been mentioned in the Hebrew text in the phrase 'the horse of his majesty', this is less likely.)

It is preferable to take the elements of this description (at any rate the first three items) as indirect Messianic prophecies. Zechariah was not led to point directly to the Messiah, but to divinely provided leadership for the Jews, probably including the Maccabees who championed the cause of Judah in the intertestamental period. Insofar as such leaders lived up to the divine requirements of their office, they foreshadowed the perfect leader and ultimate king. He alone is able to match up completely to the description.

*(1)* The first achievement of good leadership is to provide stability. **The cornerstone**, or 'corner', refers to the large stone which lies where two walls meet and joins them firmly together. It is vital to the integrity of the structure, and determines the position of the rest of the building. The term 'corner' was used of outstanding leaders (Judg. 20:2; 1 Sam. 14:38; Isa. 19:13). But it is pre-eminently a title of the Messiah who is the foundation that firmly and truly establishes his people against falsehood. 'You boast, "We have entered into a covenant with death, with the grave we have made an agreement. When an overwhelming scourge sweeps by, it cannot touch us, for we have made a lie our refuge and falsehood our hiding-place." So this is what the Sovereign LORD says: "See, I lay a stone in Zion, a tested stone, a precious cornerstone for a sure foundation; the one who trusts will never be dismayed"' (Isa. 28:15-16; see also Ps. 118:22; Zech. 4:7; Eph. 2:20; 1 Pet. 2:4).

*(2)* There is then a reference to the reliability of leadership. **From him the tent peg** can refer either to a peg used to secure the tent ropes into the ground (Ex. 27:19; 35:18; Judg. 4:21,22), or else to a peg used either in a tent or in a wall on which things were hung (Ezk. 15:3). Although it was a far more significant item in the east than it might seem to us, its importance here derives from the saying found

in Isaiah when God says of Eliakim, the successor of the unworthy Shebna as steward of the royal household, 'I will place on his shoulder the key to the house of David; what he opens no-one can shut, and what he shuts no-one can open. I will drive him like a peg into a firm place; he will be a seat of honour for the house of his father. All the glory of his family will hang on him: its offspring and offshoots—all its lesser vessels, from the bowls to all the jars' (Isa. 22:22-24). Christ as the true son of David used part of this description of himself (Rev. 3:7), and the description is ultimately of him as the true holder of the key of the house of David, the one by whom the glory of the Father is unshakably displayed.

*(3)* The third attribute of a successful leader is the ability to protect the realm and defeat adversaries. **From him the battle-bow** is an obvious reference to the military prowess of the leaders the LORD will raise up from Judah. This too finds its final reference in Christ the mighty warrior, the Lion of the tribe of Judah (Rev. 5:5). This aspect of his kingship will not be apparent until his second coming when he rides out 'as a conqueror bent on conquest' with a bow in his hand (Rev. 6:2) and 'he treads the winepress of the fury of the wrath of God' (Rev. 19:11-16; Isa. 63:2-4). 'He will crush kings on the day of his wrath' (Ps. 110:5) and his sharp arrows will pierce the hearts of the king's enemies (Ps. 45:5).

*(4)* The fourth phrase **from him every ruler** is a very difficult expression. 'Ruler' is commonly used of one who acts harshly or oppressively, employing force to keep another in check ('oppressor' in 9:8). It is disputed whether it has any other sense. Some have taken it as describing the harsh action of the people (possibly also of the Messiah) when victorious over their foes. Others have argued that the word is used in a good sense, which is the interpretation adopted by the NIV. In Hebrew the word **together** is taken as part of verse 4 (see NIV footnote), and the picture is of a number of rulers who act in concert. The provision the LORD makes for the leadership of his people is one that is united, able to take joint action to achieve their goals.

Under this united, heaven-sent leadership the people will defeat their enemies. **They will be like mighty men trampling the muddy streets in battle *(10:5)*.** 'Trample' is used elsewhere of hostile forces showing no respect for the possessions of others (Isa. 63:18; Jer.

12:10). It is a picture of men who have let nothing impede them in their pursuit of victory. Although a different verb is used, it recalls the picture of trampling on slingstones (9:15). 'Mighty men' is from a root that recurs in 'strengthen' (10:6, 12). The secret of their power and success is revealed as divinely given. **Because the LORD is with them, they will fight and overthrow horsemen.** 'Overthrow' is literally 'make to be ashamed'. They will be able to frustrate the tactics of even the most formidable troops. Cavalry were not normally part of Israelite armies, and formed the most feared part of enemy forces (Dan. 11:40). In the time of the Maccabees the Jews were successful against such forces.

*The LORD's Strengthening (10:6-12).* The theme of this section is indicated by the repetition of 'I will strengthen them' (10:6, 12). This divine empowering is the means by which the fortunes of his people will be restored. But when will this be accomplished? Particular attention is paid to the survivors of the northern tribes who had been deported from Samaria by the Assyrians in 722 B.C., and some have suggested that this relates to the ten lost tribes being reincorporated into Israel at some future date. However, during the period of the Maccabees many from the northern tribes forgot their former animosity towards the South, and returned to settle in Galilee, becoming to all intents Jews. There is no scriptural support for the idea that the ten tribes remain in some way still hidden. But though these prophecies were fulfilled in the events of the inter-testamental period, it is obvious that the description of verses 10-12 moves beyond that to a much greater return, when the Messiah finally releases all who are his from spiritual bondage, and brings them into the freedom of his final kingdom. Once more, behind the Old Testament descriptions that were accessible to Zechariah's hearers, and which came partially true in that epoch, there lies a New Testament fulfilment which embraces far more than was immediately obvious then. This fulfilment is not contrary to the terms of the original prophecy, but more than realises it precisely because the coming of Christ signals the forward movement of God's redemptive purpose from what had been largely local and national to what transcends national and racial boundaries.

**I will strengthen the house of Judah and save the house of Joseph (10:6).** The description 'house of Joseph' covers the whole of what had been the Northern Kingdom of the ten tribes that had broken away from the South on the death of Solomon in 931 B.C. The two major tribes among them were Manasseh and Ephraim, descendants of the sons of Joseph. Although the future prospect had so far been described in terms of the south, that is Judah (10:3), it was the LORD's purpose to reunite his people (Ezk. 37:15-28). It seems that few descending from the northern tribes had returned with Zerubbabel, but God still remembered them (Jer. 31:20). So while the descendants of Judah who had returned are promised strength to cope with the situation they find themselves in, the house of Joseph is promised salvation, that is deliverance from the misery and distress imposed on them in their exile as punishment for their sin.

God does not forget any of his people, but promises to act graciously towards them. **I will restore them because I have compassion on them.** The verb 'I will restore them' has an unusual form, which is traditionally understood as a conflation of two ideas, 'I will bring them back' (NKJV, NRSV, NASB), and 'I will make them dwell'. 'I will restore them' (NIV, REB) tries to convey both thoughts: return and residence. This is brought about by the LORD's compassion, that is, his deep feeling of pity towards those whom he regards as his own (1:12, 16; see also Ps. 103:13; Mic. 7:19). It is not a sign of any merit on their part, but of God's sovereign resolution to have compassion on whom he will (Ex. 33:19). **They will be as though I had not rejected them** indicates a return to conditions that had existed before the LORD's judgment fell on them. The covenant bond is stated in the words **for I am the LORD their God,** and this is the basis for the response to their prayers. **I will answer them** involves a complete reversal of the threat of 7:13. Now their prayers are heard.

The people of Ephraim will be in no way second to Judah in the future prosperity of the nation, and the same blessings are promised to them. **The Ephraimites will become like mighty men (10:7)** reflects the blessing of Judah in 10:5. 'Like a mighty man' here may also pick a reference to the strengthening, making mighty again of Judah in verse 6. **Their hearts will be glad as with wine** may be compared with what is said in 9:14. The victory that is granted to them will cause them great joy. **Their children will see it and be joyful; their hearts will rejoice in the LORD.** This rejoicing is as intense as that described in 9:9. It is not just because of the victory they have gained, but in specific acknowledgment of the LORD who had bestowed that victory (Ps. 92:4).

Verses 8-12 begin by giving greater detail about how the LORD's restoration will come to Ephraim, but as the prophet is shown this, the vista opens out to include more than what happened in the period before Christ's advent. Using images drawn from past deliverances that had been extended to the church of old, the prophet describes the final gathering of all God's people when the Son of Man 'will send his angels and gather his elect from the four winds, from the ends of the earth to the ends of the heavens' (Mk. 13:27).

Verse 8 begins without any connecting word, and so the events described are not subsequent to those of the preceding two verses, but rather an elaboration of them. **I will signal for them and gather them in (10:8).** 'Signal' is literally 'whistle' as in Judges 5:16, 'the whistling for the flocks'. The picture is of a shepherd who has decided to gather his flock, and so uses his familiar whistle to call them to himself. **Surely I will redeem them** indicates the action the LORD will take to rescue them from those who hold them captive. Redemption refers to the total transformation of an individual's situation through the payment of a ransom price. It was the paradigm of salvation for Israel, looking back as it did to what the LORD had done for them at the time of the Exodus. 'Remember that you were slaves in Egypt and the LORD your God redeemed you' (Deut. 15:15; 24:18).

**They will be as numerous as before** refers to a great increase in their population. 'As before' is literally 'they will be many as they were many'. It looks back to the substantial growth of Israel in the captivity of Egypt (Ex. 1:7, 12; Deut. 26:5), and anticipates that happening once more (Ezk. 36:10, 11). It does seem that during the period of the Maccabees Galilee again became populous. But that foreshadowed the blessing given to the church in New Testament times when there is a vast influx from all nations into the people of God (Isa. 49:19-21; 54:1-3; Rev. 7:9).

**Though I scatter them (10:9)** is more literally 'sow them' and does not refer to a forcible scattering as in the Exile or later after the fall of Jerusalem to the Romans in A.D.70. It seems to indicate a time of increase in numbers (Hos. 2:23; Jer. 31:27). The fact that this is **among the peoples** rather than the more hostile term 'nations' fits in with this as a description of the spread and increase in number of the people throughout the Dispersion. But though God permitted them to be found in so many places, **yet in distant lands they will remember me** shows that their condition is not hopeless. They will turn to the LORD (Deut. 30:1-3; 2 Chr. 6:36-39). **They and their children will survive** or simply 'live' a reference to the prophecy of Ezekiel 37:14, 25. **And they will return,** the verb which covers both physical movement back to the land, and spiritual movement back to God from whom they had backslidden.

**I will bring them back from Egypt and gather them from Assyria (*10:10*).** This does not describe a literal movement from these lands—after all, Assyria had ceased to exist long before Zechariah's day, and there is no historical record of an exile from the North to Egypt. It is true the name 'Assyria' may be used to refer to the Babylonians, and subsequently the Medes and Persians who assumed control of Babylonian territory (Ezr. 6:22; see also on 4:7). But Assyria here is not intended to convey where the people were geographically to be found, but rather indicates the conditions they had to contend with. Egypt and Assyria are mentioned as typical of the powers that had harassed and oppressed the people in the past. Egypt was the first power to oppress Israel, and Assyria is mentioned rather than one of the later Mesopotamian powers because of the focus on Ephraim, which had been taken captive by Assyria. The LORD assures the people of Zechariah's day that he will bring them out of every situation in which they are oppressed and enslaved by worldly powers. Ultimately this leads to that gathering of the church of all ages which joins in singing the song of Moses which is also the song of the Lamb (Rev. 15:3).

**I will bring them to Gilead and Lebanon.** Gilead was the territory on the east of the Jordan that had formerly belonged to the ten northern tribes. Their territory stretched over eastwards to the Mediterranean at Lebanon (Mic. 7:14). They thus return to their full inheritance. As had been previously mentioned, their numbers will have increased very significantly (10:8). **There will not be room enough for them** is hyperbolic speech which shows they are an oppressed remnant no more, but enjoying all the LORD has blessed them with.

Verse 11 begins in the Hebrew 'He shall pass through the sea' (NKJV) and this may be taken as referring to the divine action at the Exodus where the pillar of cloud/fire, as the symbol of the LORD's presence with his people, preceded them (Ex. 13:21,22). The LORD will again miraculously intervene on behalf of his people. **They will pass through the sea (*10:11*)** follows the Septuagint's reading, and it also indicates a future deliverance patterned after the Exodus. The sea is specified as being one **of trouble**, or 'affliction' because of the perplexity it caused the Israelites when they first came there (Ex. 14:9-12). They thought there was no way forward—a view that many of Zechariah's contemporaries seem to have shared. The Hebrew is grammatically difficult, but it may be taken as a name, Sea Affliction, or as a descriptive phrase, 'with affliction' (NKJV). But the LORD's help will be again extended to his church at a time when, humanly speaking, they seem trapped by the enemy.

**The surging sea will be subdued.** At the Exodus 'the sea looked and fled', as the Psalmist put it (Ps. 114:3; Ex. 14:16, 21-22), because of God's presence and power. The same thing will happen again to any obstacles that impede his people's progress. **And all the depths of the Nile will dry up.** The reference to the Nile, rather than the Jordan (Josh. 3:13; Ps. 114:3-5), is unexpected. It shows we are dealing with imagery, and is an example of the resources that the world relies on and boasts itself in (here the annual inundation of the Nile on which the prosperity of Egypt depended) being really under the control of God who can do with them as he wishes. **Assyria's pride will be brought down.** Assyria's pride is here used in a bad sense. She boasted in her invincibility (2 Kgs. 19:22-24; Isa. 10:8-13; 37:23-25), and her cruelty was immense (Nah. 2:11-12; 3:1, 19). She had already passed from the world scene at the end of the seventh century B.C., and is here referred to as an instance of what will befall all political and earthly power that sets itself against the people of God and his purposes. **And Egypt's sceptre will pass away.** 'Sceptre' is an emblem of dominion and authority. Again the people of the LORD are being told that they can look forward to an end of all rule that is exercised against them.

The promise of verse 12 shows that these changes in the fortunes of the LORD's people with respect to their adversaries are accompanied by spiritual renewal among them. Although **I will strengthen them in the LORD** *(10:12)*, is grammatically connected with Ephraim, the whole of the LORD's people are now in view. It is not a matter of outward military strength, but inward spiritual renewal. In view of the subsequent **declares the LORD** some have found the third person reference 'in the LORD' awkward, but it is possible in Hebrew style (Hos. 1:7). **And in his name they will walk,** that is, 'walk to and fro' (1:10, 11; 6:7), unimpeded as representatives of the LORD, who bear his name (see on Mal. 1:6) and act on his behalf. This is true of all who are 'strengthened with all power according to his glorious might' (Col. 1:11) 'through his Spirit in your inner being' (Eph. 3:16). They fulfil the pledge 'We will walk in the name of the LORD our God for ever and ever' (Mic. 4:5), and enjoy the promise 'Blessed are you, O Israel! Who is like you, a people saved by the LORD? He is your shield and helper and your glorious sword. Your enemies will cower before you, and you will trample down their high places' (Deut. 33:29).

It is generally agreed that these prophecies were at best only partially fulfilled in the history of the Jews in the period before the coming of Christ. It is often forgotten how many Jews, both in Palestine and throughout the Dispersion, in faith accepted Jesus as the Messiah and formed the core of the Christian church. Paul explicitly repudiates the idea that God has rejected his people. 'At the present time there is a remnant chosen by grace' (Rom. 11:5). Furthermore, those that had stumbled had not fallen beyond recovery (Rom. 11:11), and he envisages a time when they will again be accepted and their fulness bring great riches to the church as a whole (Rom. 11:12, 15). This only occurs through faith in Christ, for there are not two ways of salvation or two peoples of God. The two have been made one, and the barrier has been destroyed (Eph. 2:14). It is not to be re-erected in the interests of some theory of prophetic interpretation. Both Jew and Gentile enter into the blessing that the prophet here portrays for the future of the one people of God.

Once more the future has been revealed to encourage steadfastness in the present. It is the same approach that Paul employs when he describes the final victory over death and concludes, 'Therefore, my dear brothers, stand firm. Let nothing move you. Always give yourselves fully to the work of the Lord, because you know that your labour in the Lord is not in vain' (1 Cor. 15:58). To avoid encouraging curious prying into the future, precise details are omitted, but the grand vista, drawing on the LORD's past displays of redemptive power, inspires a positive attitude towards the future that leads us away from despair over where we are and what is to come of us. 'In this hope we were saved. But hope that is seen is no hope at all. Who hopes for what he already has? But if we hope for what we do not yet have, we wait for it patiently' (Rom. 8:24-25).

## Study Questions

**10:1** We are not tempted to ascribe rain and good harvests to Baal, but we do often think in terms of natural causes. Show how we too need to live in conscious dependence upon God. Ps. 65:9-13; 145:15-16; Mt. 5:11; 6:25-34; Acts 14:17; 17:28; Jas. 1:17; 5:17-18.

**10:2** What are the dangers of false prophecy? How may we guard against them? Jer 14:13-16; 23:14-21; Mic. 3:5-7; Mt. 7:15, 22-23; 2 Cor. 11:3-4, 13-15; 2 Pet. 2:1-3, 13-22.

**10:4** What may we deduce from the characteristics required in Old Testament leaders of those needed in the church today?

**10:6** What qualities does Scripture ascribe to God's mercy? Ex. 33:19; Ps. 25:6; 41:4; Isa. 55:7; Dan. 9:18; Mic. 7:18, 20; Lk. 1:78; Eph. 2:4; 1 Pet. 1:3; Jude 21.

**10:12** How is hope strengthened by considering God's promises about the future? Rom. 8:14; 15:13; Phil. 3:20-21; Tit. 2:12-13; Heb. 10:25.

## Zechariah 11:1-3: The Devastating Judgment

Zechariah's later prophecies were primarily designed to inspire hope and resolve in the people of his day by giving them insight into the future purposes of God, and so enabling them to rise above the discouragements and baffling circumstances of their own time. By seeing their lives in terms of the future prospect when the Messiah would come and the divine promises be realised, they would recapture the eagerness that should characterise those destined to enjoy such an inheritance (1 Cor. 1:7), and be strengthened in their 'faith and love that spring from the hope that is stored up for you in heaven and that you have already heard about in the word of truth' (Col. 1:5).

But the future held more than glory. There was a darker side. While the prophet would encourage, he cannot do so contrary to the truth. Furthermore, the people needed to be warned of the dangers ahead. These are dramatically introduced here. Many details of what the prophet says cannot be interpreted with certainty, but the overall picture is clear. First, he enigmatically presents a picture of catastrophe sweeping south through Palestine (11:1-3). Then he shows why this catastrophe awaits the Jews. It is the LORD's judgment on them for rejecting the good shepherd he had sent to them (11:4-14). Instead the people would be ruled by a foolish and worthless shepherd (11:15-17).

There is considerable diversity of opinion about the significance of this catastrophe. The basic options seem to be twofold: (1) this is a completion of the doom of the opponents of the people of God described in chapter 10, and the trees mentioned here are to be viewed as standing for foreign powers whose destruction is prophesied; and (2) this is a description of judgment falling on the people of God, and as such it stands as an introduction to the rest of chapter 11. In favour of the first style of interpretation is the fact that tall, stately trees are used as symbols of rulers elsewhere in Scripture (Ezk. 31:3-9; Isa. 10:33-34; Ezk. 20:47-48; 17:22-24; Dan. 4:22). The lion is used to symbolise the princes of Israel (Ezk. 19:5-9), while shepherd is throughout this section of the book a metaphor for the ruler. The problem with this approach lies in establishing a reason for Lebanon and Bashan being chosen to represent the nations hostile to Israel. The use of Egypt and Assyria in that way in 10:10-11 is easily accounted for, but Gilead and Lebanon in 10:10 are viewed as part of the inheritance to which the people return, and the Jordan valley (11:3) is most naturally seen as part of the land of promise. In this way it is easier to take this as a description of a catastrophic judgment which sweeps over the nation from the north. Full details are not given about it. What is to be asked is rather why this should happen.

The prophet uses vivid poetic imagery, with compressed and allusive language. **Open your doors, O Lebanon!** (*11:1*) addresses Lebanon as if it were a city or a fortress. It lay to the north of the boundary of the former kingdom of Israel but was within the bounds of the territory allocated in the covenant (10:10; Deut. 11:24). The origin of the disaster will be in the north, but it is not clear whether it is caused by a devastating storm or invading army. The hilly region of Lebanon was renowned for its cedars, and here it is being told that it may as well be prepared for their destruction, **so that fire may devour your cedars.**

The prophet engages in further personification, addressing a tree which has been variously identified as the cypress, juniper, or an evergreen such as the pine or fir. It is a tree that was found in the area of Lebanon, but was not so costly as the cedar. **Wail, O pine tree, for the cedar has fallen** (*11:2*). The cry of sorrow and anguish is to be uttered because of the destruction of the cedars and what that implies for the fate of everything else. There then follows a conjunction, 'for' or 'because'. **The stately trees are ruined!** The rest of the forest has become involved in the destruction and there is a call for a lament. This lament spreads east of the Jordan to Bashan which was renowned like Lebanon for its wooded areas (Isa. 2:13), and also for its pasture for cattle. **Wail, oaks of Bashan; the dense forest has been cut down!** is an injunction for the cries of loss and despair to spread further throughout the land. There was no longer an obstacle in the way of movement further south. Indeed, the trees may have been cut down precisely to make armaments with which to attack the cities in the rest of the land (Deut. 20:20).

Throughout verses 2 and 3 certain words are repeated, or very similar words are used in the Hebrew. This feature brings out the prolonged and intense nature of the catastrophe. 'Wail' occurs twice in verse 2 and again in verse 3; 'ruined' is found in verse 2 and twice in verse 3 (the first of these is rendered 'destroyed' by the NIV); and in verse 3 'listen to' is repeated. **Listen to the wail of the shepherds; their rich pastures are destroyed!** *(11:3)*. This continues the description of the devastation of the land, whether by natural catastrophe or by enemy action, and the weeping over the resultant loss. The shepherds are no longer able to support their flocks because the pasture has been ruined. **Listen to the roar of the lions; the lush thicket of the Jordan is ruined!** The thicket of the Jordan refers to the dense growth of bushes and trees on the banks of the Jordan, and moves the description further south from Bashan, which was on the east bank at the north of the river. The lions are crying out because their lairs and hunting grounds have been taken away from them. Their habitat has been ruined. As we have seen, shepherds and lions might both be used of human rulers, but there is no need to go beyond a dramatic and graphic picture of severe devastation spreading south across the land.

The picture itself is of physical disaster, especially as it affects the most stately and powerful aspects of natural life in the land (the cedars, oaks, lions). Apart from the shepherds, there is no overt mention of people, or cities. But the backcloth that has been drawn is such that it is difficult to envisage anything other than the whole land being in ruins. If this is how the land and animals are affected, what can possibly become of the people? What heinous offence against God has been committed to give rise to this? These three verses give no hint of the answer, but what follows in the rest of the chapter makes it clear that this devastating judgment has come upon the land because of the Jews' rejection of Christ. This prophecy is fulfilled in the events of A.D. 70 when the Romans destroyed Jerusalem, and then later the fortress at Masada, with horrifying loss of life.

*Study Question*

**11:1** It is very easy to shut our eyes to the consequences of our actions and think that God will not respond. What areas of our national and individual life today might be subject to a warning of God's impending judgment?

## Zechariah 11:4-14:  The Good Shepherd

In approaching this section we are coming upon an admittedly obscure portion of Scripture, and yet one which we cannot easily pass by because of its citation in the New Testament, even though that actually adds difficulties of its own to the situation.  Later references do, however, have this advantage: they rule out any interpretation which is inconsistent with a Messianic application of the passage.

The first matter on which we have to take a view is the nature of the passage: is it vision, or is it an acted parable?  An acted parable would involve Zechariah dressing like a shepherd, taking two staffs, and acting out what is described here.  Ezekiel is the prophet best known for such enactments (Ezk. 4–5; 12), but Zechariah himself was involved in this in the crowning of Joshua (6:9-15).  A strong argument in favour of such an approach is that in 11:7, 11 the prophet reports his obedience to the commands given.

But there are difficulties when others are drawn into the action. The payment of the thirty pieces of silver (11:12) is more easily understood as described than as acted out.  The prophet would then be describing a vision in which he himself was involved, and which had allegorical significance.  On either approach, what Zechariah did had a symbolic reference, anticipating the work of Christ and the reception given to him.

The second matter is the role of the prophet.  He was of course God's spokesman, and it is in that capacity that he speaks and acts in 11:8, 10 and 14.  The question that is often asked is whether the prophet also represents the Messiah.  There seems to be no good reason for doubting that he does.  What Zechariah as the LORD's representative does foreshadows what the Messiah will do and undergo in the same capacity.  He is the one who can truly claim, 'I am the good shepherd' (Jn. 10:11, 14; Heb. 13:20).  It is through him that the LORD fulfils his promise, 'I myself will search for my sheep and look after them.  As a shepherd looks after his scattered flock when he is with them, so will I look after my sheep' (Ezk. 34:11-12).

*The Divine Commission (11:4-6).*  The introductory formula **This is what the LORD my God says** (*11:4*) emphasises the prophet's involvement in what is to be described, and also his close relationship with God. He is given the command to act as a shepherd, and the flock represents the people (Ps. 80:1; 95:7; 100:3; Ezk. 34:31). It cannot be addressed directly to the Messiah in prophetic vision because of the parallel statement in 11:15 regarding acting like a foolish shepherd (note there 'take *again*'). **Pasture the flock marked for slaughter.** 'Pasture' is from the same root as the word 'shepherd'. It denotes carrying out all the duties a shepherd would perform in caring for his flock (see 11:16 for these set out in terms of what the foolish shepherd does *not* do). But this flock is 'marked for slaughter', literally 'flock of the slaughter', which may be understood in two ways. It may point directly to the destiny God intends for them because of their sin, or it may be their situation at the hands of their oppressors that is referred to. The latter seems preferable in the light of the next verse, 'Their buyers slaughter them.' They are already being massacred, and the LORD appoints the prophet (representing the Messiah) to intervene on behalf of the people in their plight. His ministry of protection and care towards them is an expression of the LORD's own sympathy and commitment.

Although the description, **their buyers slaughter them and go unpunished (*11:5*)**, might refer to foreign rulers who were enslaving the Jews, it seems instead to apply to internal exploitation and oppression at the time the prophet is describing. The three groups mentioned—buyers, sellers, shepherds—are the powerful classes in the land, who repeatedly act in this way. They were able to do as they pleased because they were the authorities and would not act against themselves (Mic. 3:1-3, 9). **Those who sell them say, 'Praise the LORD, I am rich!'** They each make hypocritical pretensions to piety even as they act with ruthless selfishness (Hos. 12:8; Mt. 23:14). They were out to feed themselves (Ezk. 34:2) and had no qualms of conscience about trading in the lives of their fellow countrymen, either to one another or to foreigners (Neh. 5:1-13; Jer. 34:8-11). **Their own shepherds do not spare them.** Their civil and spiritual rulers felt no twinge of pity at all for the people, and treated them without mercy or consideration for their welfare. Again the Hebrew expression is such as to emphasise that this is true of each of them individually. The situation Isaiah had described had returned again. 'Israel's watchmen are blind, they all lack knowledge; they are all mute dogs, they cannot bark; they lie around and dream, they love to sleep. They are dogs with mighty appetites; they never have enough. They are shepherds who lack understanding; they all turn to their own way, each seeks his own gain' (Isa. 56:10-11).

For (*11:6*) shows why this state of affairs will arise. **"I will no longer have pity on the people of the land," declares the LORD.** 'Have pity' repeats the same verb rendered 'spare' in the previous verse. This can only be understood in the light of their rejection of the good shepherd, which has still to be described. The people are going to repeat the spiritual mistakes of their forefathers. The same tragic course of conduct had been enacted prior to the fall of Jerusalem in 586 B.C. The LORD had had pity on his people and had repeatedly sent prophets to alert them to the gravity of their situation. Their reaction had been to mock and despise the warnings, and the time came when it was recorded, 'there was no remedy' (2 Chr. 36:15-16; see also Ps. 78:32-41). Their persistent misbehaviour had exhausted God's patience. Last of all he has sent his Son. 'I will send my son, whom I love; perhaps they will respect him.' But they did not (Lk. 20:14-15). There is no remedy but the outpouring of divine wrath.

The nation is left to its own devices. **I will hand everyone over to his neighbour and his king.** This is literally 'into the hand of his neighbour and into the hand of his king', so as to be under their power and at their mercy. Internal strife had characterised an earlier period of divine abandonment (8:10), and it returned in the years before Jerusalem fell to the Romans. There was much factional disagreement and fighting. When the city was under siege, the Jews themselves burned the supplies that should have fed them. Their feuds weakened their ability to withstand the enemy. And this was the king they had chosen for themselves. 'We have no king but Caesar' (Jn. 19:15) haunted them with a vengeance. Having rejected the LORD's Anointed, they had to endure the fearful destruction and carnage their self-chosen king brought to their land.

**They will oppress the land** is literally 'beat it to pieces with repeated blows'—an apt description not only of the internal tensions, but also of the calculated and unrelenting pressure of the Roman forces. **I will not rescue them from their hands** declares that the

LORD will permit no respite for that generation. It does not mean that the Jews are finally and irrevocably abandoned by the LORD, any more than the judgment of 586 B.C. had done. But there was to be no escape at that time from the devastation.

*The Ministry of the Good Shepherd (11:7).*  After the LORD's commission, which partly anticipates the declarations of subsequent verses, Zechariah records his obedience to the command given him. **So I pastured the flock marked for slaughter (*11:7*)**, meaning that he took care of it, saw to its welfare, and acted on its behalf for good. This prefigured Jesus of Nazareth who 'went around doing good and healing all who were under the power of the devil' (Acts 10:38; see also Mt. 11:4-6). For 'the flock marked for slaughter' see on 11:4 above. **Particularly the oppressed of the flock.** As 11:11 shows, this denotes a group within the people as a whole who were piously waiting upon the LORD and who were oppressed on account of their loyalty to him. See the discussion of 'gentle' at 9:9. 'Yet I am poor and needy; may the Lord think of me. You are my help and my deliverer; O my God, do not delay' (Ps. 40:17). The downtrodden were especially the objects of the prophet's ministrations as he presented beforehand the mission of him who was sent to the lost sheep of Israel (Mt. 15:24).

**Then I took two staffs.** Shepherds in the East commonly had two staffs ('your rod and staff', Ps. 23:4), one a stout cudgel to ward off attacking predators from the flock, and the other corresponding more to the traditional idea of a shepherd's staff with a crook at the end to help rescue the sheep from difficult situations. The two staffs are given symbolic names which sum up the two main aspects of the shepherd's ministry. The prophet called the one staff **Favour**, 'pleasantness', a symbol of the LORD's care and protection of his people, providing them with fellowship with himself and all the bounty of his covenant (Ps. 23; 27:4-5; 90:17). The other staff he called **Union**, literally a plural expression, 'bindings' or 'ties', expressing the unifying effect of Christ's ministry, 'there shall be one flock and one shepherd' (Jn. 10:16), particularly here in connection with the union of Judah and Israel (11:14). These two aspects of union and blessing had been brought together previously by Ezekiel

in connection with the coming rule of David as the LORD's servant
over his people (Ezk. 37:15-28). With both these blessings, **I
pastured the flock** (repeating the expression at the beginning of the
verse), acting as the representative of the LORD caring for his people.

*The Estrangement of Shepherd and Flock (11:8-11).* Zechariah then
enigmatically records **In one month I got rid of the three shepherds (*11:8*).** Many attempts have been made to ascertain in what
historical connection this prophecy might have been fulfilled. The
variety of conflicting hypotheses regarding which three specific
rulers are intended and whether they were Jewish or foreign, undermines confidence in historical interpretations of the passage. There
are two more general hypotheses that are of some merit. One is to
argue that the three shepherds referred to are not three specific
persons, but the three great offices within Israel—prophet, priest and
king. The other is that 'three' is a complete number (as in the sins of
the nations, Amos 1-2), indicating all rulers whatever. 'In one
month' could well indicate within a relatively short period of time.
The prophecy would then be one of the speedy removal from the
Jewish nation of all vestiges of internal authority and rule, as
happened after the collapse of A.D. 70.

There is a problem with this in that the expression is generally
regarded as indicating an action that was for the good of the people.
That is why the NIV uses a paragraph break in the middle of the verse
to set this statement off from the judgment that follows. It is possible
to argue that the removal of the holders of these offices would have
been a boon to the people if the shepherds were corrupt and their
removal led to a reduction in oppression or in the opportunity for the
people to seek the LORD. It is more plausible, however, to question the
assumption that this statement is intended to be beneficial. It is rather
the first part of the withdrawal of divine favour from the people by
removing those who ruled over them and maintained their national
identity and existence. But it must be admitted that all interpretations
are tentative.

**The flock detested me, and I grew weary of them.** The NIV has
inverted the order of the Hebrew clauses, which state 'My soul was
weary with them, and their soul also detested me', presumably to

show that the divine attitude is a reaction to the people's perverseness. Both parties are affected by deep-seated emotions. The LORD's soul is described as 'shortened', a Hebrew idiom for being vexed, disappointed and no longer patient (Num. 21:4; Judg. 10:16; 16:16). Despite the care that was being bestowed upon the sheep by the Shepherd, they were unresponsive and renounced him. 'But my people would not listen to me; Israel would not submit to me. So I gave them over to their stubborn hearts to follow their own devices' (Ps. 81:11-12). The people's reaction is expressed by a verb that occurs only here, indicating nausea and disgust. This well describes the attitude the Jews took to Christ both before the crucifixion (Isa. 53:3) and in their opposition to the early church (1 Thess. 2:14-16).

The prophet as the representative of the Shepherd-King of the people says, **I will not be your shepherd (*11:9*),** or rather rendering the verb as the NIV has done previously in the passage 'I will not pasture you.' The focus is on his action rather than his rights and status. He judicially hands them over to their fate which had been anticipated in 11:6. **Let the dying die.** The shepherd will no longer tend those in need of care. They are abandoned to the outcome of their folly. **And the perishing perish** refers to the fate of those that are cut off and disclaimed as being no longer of the flock. They will know all that is involved in being separated from the Shepherd's care. There is then an even more sombre note, where the language of shepherd and flock is completely eclipsed. **Let those who are left eat one another's flesh.** Josephus tells us that cannibalism occurred during the Roman siege of Jerusalem. By withholding his shepherding, the people are left to the inevitable consequences of their chosen course—and that is always downwards (Gen. 6:5-6).

The thoughts expressed in this verse are not just the expression of Old Testament sentiments. Such dire language is also found on the lips of Christ (Mt. 23:29-39). In particular he reflects on their unwillingness to respond, and the devastating judgment that would come on them. 'O Jerusalem, Jerusalem, you who kill the prophets and stone those sent to you, how often I have longed to gather your children together, as a hen gathers her chicks under her wings, but you were not willing. Look, your house is left to you desolate' (Mt. 23:37-38).

The prophet then relates a symbolic action which vividly portrayed what was to come upon the people. **Then I took my staff called Favour and broke it, revoking the covenant I had made with all the nations (*11:10*).** Which covenant this was has caused perplexity. But 'covenant' denoted a sovereign imposition of an overlord, and is used of the LORD holding in check forces hostile to his people (Ezk. 34:25; Hos. 2:18). Here it refers to the way in which the LORD as ruler of all nations had acted to impose bounds on what the nations were permitted to do to his chosen people. If the people had remained obedient to their covenant obligations, then the LORD would have ensured that the nations remained in awe of them and did not covet their territory (Ex. 34:24; Deut. 2:25; 11:25; Josh. 2:11). The response of the nations would not have involved any formal recognition on their part of limits being placed on their actions by the LORD. It was an involuntary response on their part to the LORD's providence. The staff Favour denoted his protection from hostile powers, and its being broken signified an end to that defence. When his guarding hand was lifted, their enemies were left unhindered from invading the land.

**It was revoked on that day (*11:11*).** 'On that day' refers to the time when the relationship between the good shepherd and Israel was sundered by his refusing to be their shepherd and symbolically breaking his staff Favour. As regards Zechariah, the reality he is prefiguring was, of course, still future. However, in terms of the action of the vision, what is related is past. When all restraining influences on the conduct of the nations have been removed, this will constitute an indisputable sign for those with the right perception. **So the afflicted of the flock who were watching me knew it was the word of the LORD.** It is not said of all the flock but of 'the afflicted' (the same expression as 'the oppressed of the flock', 11:7). This applies to those who are described by Jesus when he said, 'Blessed are the poor in spirit, for theirs is the kingdom of heaven. ... Blessed are you when people insult you, persecute you and falsely say all kinds of evil against you because of me' (Mt. 5:3, 11). They were those who would receive him and believe on his name (Jn. 1:10-13). They are pictured as 'watching me', that is Zechariah. This may have been part of Zechariah's visionary experience, or it could refer to a

group who had gathered round the prophet as he acted out his
commission to represent the shepherd to come. His sheep know his
voice (Jn. 10:4) and pay attention to his warnings. The faithful have
therefore insight denied to others, being able to interpret 'it', the
events of their day, in the light of his teaching, and consequently not
treating what was happening as mere historical change, but as
directly attributable to divine action. They were able to act appropri-
ately because Jesus had warned, 'When you see Jerusalem being
surrounded by armies, you will know that its desolation is near. Then
let those who are in Judea flee to the mountains, let those in the city
get out, and let those in the country not enter the city. For this is the
time of punishment in fulfilment of all that has been written' (Lk.
21:20-22). There is indeed some evidence that the Jewish Christian
community in Jerusalem did in fact escape to Pella in the mountains
of Trans-Jordan just before the armies of Rome surrounded the city.

*The Rejection of the Good Shepherd (11:12-14).* The prophet's
message now goes back to bring out in greater detail what was
involved in the Jews' detestation of the shepherd the LORD sent to
them. **I told them** *(11:12).* Though grammatically the easiest
reference for 'them' is to the afflicted of the flock, 'them' must refer
to the flock as a whole. The shepherd asks for his pay. The metaphor
is of course breaking down here: the sheep were really people, and the
one who has provided for them and cared for them is entitled to
receive a just reward. He puts the onus of giving a reward on them
so that they are forced to evaluate what he has done for them. **If you
think it best, give me my pay; but if not, keep it.** As in the Parable
of the Tenants, it was appropriate that the owner of the vineyard be
given of its produce (Lk. 20:10). What the Lord wished from the
people was the response of repentance, gratitude and love (Mt. 4:17;
Gal. 5:22), but they were blind to their obligations (Mt. 21:43; Mk.
11:13-14, 20-21; Lk. 13:6-9). He did not demand payment or reward
in the spirit of a hired help, but set them a spiritual test. It would have
been less insulting had they refused to pay him, but instead they
awarded a price that equated his worth with what a slave-owner
would have received as compensation for a slave gored to death by
someone else's ox (Ex. 21:32; Hos. 3:2). **So they paid me thirty**

**pieces of silver.** 'Paid' literally points to the silver being 'weighed' (Jer. 32:9-10) as coins were only gradually becoming accepted as a means of exchange (Ezr. 2:69; 8:27; Neh. 7:70). The insult was directed at the LORD as much as at his servant.

The LORD did not permit his servant to formulate his own response to this despicable behaviour. **And the LORD said to me, "Throw it to the potter"** (*11:13*). 'Throw' is an expression of contempt, 'toss' or 'fling'. It is used of a carcass mauled by wild beasts, which is 'thrown' to the dogs (Ex. 22:31), of idols 'thrown away' to rodents and bats (Isa. 2:20), or of a corpse being shamefully treated (Jer. 26:23). The following ironic words clearly indicate the scorn being expressed: **the handsome price at which they priced me!** The significance of the potter is not clear. Since what the potter produced was cheap and easily replaced, it may be a proverbial expression for 'toss away as insignificant', though there is no direct evidence for such an expression. Moreover what follows shows a real potter was involved.

Zechariah reports his obedience in the vision. **So I took the thirty pieces of silver and threw them into the house of the LORD to the potter.** The significance of this taking place in the house of the LORD, the Temple, is that that was the centre of the theocracy and what is done there is seen as a public transaction between the LORD and his people in that both sides are present to witness it. The people thought nothing of the shepherd, but they were not permitted to dismiss him and his wages as a minor and trivial matter. It was given the public status it required. Whether we are to imagine the potter as being by chance in the Temple, or whether he is a minor Temple functionary (many earthenware pots would have been needed there, 14:20) is not made at all clear.

This prophecy is clearly stated by the New Testament to be fulfilled in the events surrounding Judas' betrayal of Christ. 'When Judas, who had betrayed him, saw that Jesus was condemned, he was seized with remorse and returned the thirty silver coins to the chief priests and the elders. "I have sinned," he said, "for I have betrayed innocent blood." "What is that to us?" they replied. "That's your responsibility." So Judas threw the money into the temple and left. Then he went away and hanged himself. The chief priests picked up the coins and said, "It is against the law to put this into the treasury, since it is blood money." So they decided to use the money to buy the potter's field as a burial place for foreigners. That is why it has been called the Field of Blood to this day. Then what was spoken by Jeremiah the prophet was fulfilled: "They took the thirty silver coins, the price set on him by the people of Israel, and they used them to buy the potter's field, as the Lord commanded me.'" (Mt. 27:3-10).

Two problems arise in connection with this citation.

*(1)* Matthew ascribes the words to Jeremiah. Some explain this by maintaining that the gospel citation is a conflation of Zechariah 11:12-13 and Jeremiah (particularly 19:1-13 and 32:6-9). In attributing the combined quotation to the greater author, Matthew was using an ancient citation technique, which can also be found in Mark 1:2 where a conflation of Malachi 3:1 and Isaiah 40:3 is attributed to Isaiah alone. But it has to be acknowledged that this explanation is not fully satisfactory here precisely because 'field' and 'potter' do not occur together in Jeremiah.

Alternatively, it may be that this is not a conflated citation, but one that reflects Zechariah alone, and that another ancient practice can explain the mention of Jeremiah. We know that the scrolls on which ancient writings were kept were often named after the first book in them. This can be seen in Jesus' use of 'the Law of Moses, the Prophets and the Psalms' (Lk. 24:44), where 'Psalms' stands for the whole of the third section of the Jewish canon, the Writings. Many ancient Hebrew scrolls have Jeremiah in first place among the prophets, and Matthew's use of Jeremiah here may indicate no more than an ascription to the second part of the Jewish canon, the Prophets.

*(2)* The fact that there are divergences between Zechariah and what Matthew records is often found to be disturbing. This seems to arise from our modern practice of putting quotation marks round Matthew's citation and expecting it to match identically the passage cited, and that the prophecy be fulfilled in precise detail. It is better to think of Matthew's citation as an interpreted quotation. There are changes needed to Zechariah 11:13 to show the prediction as subsequently fulfilled. 'And the LORD said to me' (Zech. 11:13) becomes 'as the Lord commanded me' (Mt. 27:10); 'at which they

priced me' (Zech. 11:13) becomes 'the price set on him by the people of Israel' (Mt. 27:9); 'So I took the thirty pieces of silver' (Zech. 11:13) becomes 'They took the thirty silver coins' (Mt. 27:9); '[I] threw them' (Zech. 11:13) becomes 'and they used them' (Mt. 27:10), but note also 'Judas *threw* the money into the temple' (Mt. 27:5).

There are points of obvious diversity nonetheless: there is no mention of a field in Zechariah; it is not the shepherd who receives the silver coins but his betrayer; he also is the one who throws the money. But though some Old Testament prophecies concerning Christ were fulfilled in a direct way (Mt. 2:6), this was not true of all, as Matthew's own citations show (Mt. 2:15, 17-18, 23). This is particularly so when it is a visionary experience that is being fulfilled. The substance of Zechariah's message came remarkably true: the insulting value the Jews through their leaders placed on Christ; the identity of the price; the involvement of the Temple in what became of the money; and the fact that a potter eventually received it in exchange for a field. There can be no doubt that this is not accommodation of facts to the ancient prophecy, but the outworking of the intended implications of the original message.

The breaking of the first staff had signified the disruption of the covenant ties between the nation and the LORD; the breaking of the second signifies the disruption of the ties that bound the nation together. In this way all the blessings of the covenant are removed from the people. As the prophecy is not set out in chronological sequence, there is unlikely to be any significance in the fact that this staff is broken now, apart from the fact that the tie with the LORD was more fundamental and the basis on which their social order rested. **Then I broke my second staff Union, breaking the brotherhood between Judah and Israel (*11:14*).** For Union, see on 11:7. In the centuries after the Exile, Israelites had at various times returned to Palestine, and the old hostility between north and south had passed away. There had existed a true 'brotherhood' (a word only found here) in terms of the ties that should have characterised the internal relationships of the covenant people. Obedience to the standards of the Mosaic law is frequently motivated by the fact that they were brothers ('one of your countrymen', literally, 'your brother with you', Lev. 25:39; 'a fellow Hebrew', literally 'your brother, a Hebrew,' Deut. 15:12; see also Deut. 15:3, 7-11). David extolled the situation that prevailed when such brotherhood was realised. 'How good and pleasant it is when brothers live together in unity!' (Ps. 133:1). But now that is divinely shattered. It is not that there will be re-established two rival kingdoms, but a new disintegration of their national life inflicting even deeper wounds than the schism of Jeroboam. This is reflected in 11:4 and 9, and could be seen in the internal dissension and feuding of the Jewish community in the years up to A.D. 70.

This poignant section of Zechariah's prophecy should not be read apart from John 10, where Jesus claimed, 'I am the good shepherd. The good shepherd lays down his life for the sheep' (Jn. 10:11). Immediately following his exposition of what it meant to be the good shepherd, we are told of the unbelief and rejection of the Jews (Jn. 10:19-39). So intense was their hostility that Jesus had to escape from their grasp and withdraw from Jerusalem to the region across the Jordan. Such a reaction is not confined to Christ's days on earth. Individuals and nations who continue to spurn him and his offer of salvation will find that the time comes when his long-suffering is at an end and he hands them over to the destiny they have brought on themselves.

*Study Questions*

**11:8-9** What lessons are to be learned from God's forbearance and patience? Ex. 34:6; Ps. 86:15; Isa. 48:9; Joel 2:13-14; Mt. 23:37-38; Lk. 13:6-9; Rom. 2:3-4; 1 Pet. 3:20; 2 Pet. 3:9.

**11:10** The nations are under the control of God. How then should we view national and international events today? Ps. 9:5, 15-20; 22:27-28; 66:7; 79:10; Prov. 8:15-16; Dan. 4:35; Jn. 19:11.

**11:14** What does Scripture teach about the brotherhood of the people of God? Gen. 13:8; Jer. 32:9; Jn. 13:34; 1 Cor. 1:10; 1 Jn. 3:14.

## Zechariah 11:15-17:  The Foolish Shepherd

Remarkably Zechariah's prophetic shepherding does not end with his visionary portrayal of the good shepherd.  He is again divinely commanded to act the part of a shepherd, but now one with a very different character.  **Then the LORD said to me, "Take again the equipment of a foolish shepherd" (*11:15*).**  'Again' does not imply that he had already done so, just that he had played the part of a shepherd the first time.  The shepherd's implements would have been things like a staff, a bag for food (1 Sam. 17:40) and a reed-pipe for calling sheep.  There is no reason to suppose that they would have been materially different from those of a good shepherd, though perhaps their appearance showed they were not as well cared for.  But it would especially be the use to which they would be put that was different.

'Foolish' does not principally indicate one lacking in intelligence or common sense, but rather points to someone without principles or fear of God.  He despises wisdom and discipline (Prov. 1:7, with NIV footnote explanation).  He 'chatters', that is, opens his mouth without thinking and says whatever crosses his mind (Prov. 10:8, 10).  He is proud and unwilling to accept advice, because he is always sure he is right (Prov. 12:15; 14:3).  It is therefore no surprise to be told that those who have become fools through their rebellious ways suffer affliction because of their iniquities (Ps. 107:17).  Such is the character of the ruler divinely set over the people who have rejected the good shepherd.  If they will not have the one God appoints for their good, then they will have one whose character reflects their own moral judgments.

Six characteristics of the foolish shepherd are listed.

*(1)* **For I am going to raise up a shepherd over the land who will not care for the lost (*11:16*).**  He will not have a true shepherd's compassion for those who are in process of being ruined or destroyed, having strayed off from the flock and got themselves into difficulties.  They will be left to fend for themselves.

*(2)* **Or seek the young,** who being weaker need special care.  The lack of such care sets the foolish shepherd apart from the LORD who 'tends his flock like a shepherd: he gathers the lambs in his arms and carries them close to his heart; he gently leads those that have young' (Isa. 40:11).

*(3)* **Or heal the injured.** The picture is that of sheep with limbs that have been broken through a fall.

*(4)* **Or feed the healthy,** 'those that are capable of standing by themselves'. This would have required least effort of all the duties of the shepherd, but even that he was not prepared to undertake.

*(5)* He will be selfish, as one who **will eat meat of the choice sheep.** This is similar to the indictment brought by Ezekiel: 'Woe to the shepherds of Israel who only take care of themselves! Should not shepherds take care of the flock?' (Ezk. 34:2, 8).

*(6)* He will be cruel, **tearing off their hoofs.** It is implied that he will go to any length to get some juicy morsel (here the marrow in their hoofs) for himself. He is not going to display any of the proper characteristics of a true shepherd but is going to act ruthlessly to exploit them (Ezk. 34:3-4).

It may be that some of the characteristics of this foolish ruler are to be found in Herod Agrippa I (A.D. 37-44), who set himself against the early church and was prepared to receive the god-like adulation of others (Acts 12:1, 23). But the denunciation which follows is expressed in such general terms that it may well be understood of all the rulers whom the Jews were subsequently put under, particularly Roman rulers. It may correspond to the description given of the fourth beast (world empire) described by Daniel as 'different from all the others and most terrifying, with its iron teeth and bronze claws—the beast that crushed and devoured its victims and trampled underfoot whatever was left' (Dan. 7:19). This was the king they had chosen for themselves (see on 11:6). But there is doubtless also here a foreshadowing of the lawless one (2 Thess. 2:3-4; Rev. 13:1-10).

**Woe to the worthless shepherd, who deserts the flock!** *(11:17)*. '*My* worthless shepherd' (AV, NRSV) is based on a different understanding of the Hebrew text. Although it is true that even evil rulers hold sway only by divine sufferance, the NIV rendering is grammatically preferable. 'Worthless' is often used of idols as incapable of achieving anything and deficient in what they represent (translated as 'idols' in Lev. 19:4; Ps. 97:7; Isa. 2:8, 20; 19:1; 31:7). This foolish shepherd is equally valueless and unable to contribute what a shepherd should to the welfare of the flock. 'Who deserts the flock' reminds one of Jesus' description of the hired hand who 'is not the shepherd who owns the sheep. So when he sees the wolf coming, he abandons the sheep and runs away. Then the wolf attacks the flock and scatters it' (Jn. 10:12).

**May the sword strike his arm and his right eye! May his arm be completely withered, and his right eye blinded!** God's justice matches the penalty to the crime. 'According to what they have done, so will he repay' (Isa. 59:18; Mt. 16:27). 'His arm' represents the power of the worthless shepherd. It should have been used to defend the flock, but having been perverted to exploiting them, the faculty that was misused will be completely taken away from him. 'His eye' represents the intelligence on which he prided himself. The capacity he had to guard the flock and be ready to act for their good was also misused, and of that too he is to be judicially deprived.

There is no neutral situation. Those who set themselves against the LORD and his Anointed One (Ps. 2:2) are not left to themselves. Rejecting the rule of the good shepherd does not mean having no shepherd. It is like the evil spirit returning to the unoccupied house, and taking seven others to dwell with him. 'The final condition of that man is worse than the first. That is how it will be with this wicked generation' (Mt. 12:45).

*Study Questions*

**11:15** What makes one a fool in God's sight? Prov. 1:7, 22, 32; 24:7; 28:26; 29:11; Eccl. 10:2-3; Mt. 23:17; Lk. 12:20.

**11:16** What can we deduce about the characteristics of a faithful minister from what is said here about the foolish shepherd?

## THE SECOND BURDEN: ON THAT DAY
### (Zech. 12:1–14:21)

The difficulties involved in interpreting this division of the prophecy are well known, but we are not left totally without clues as to how to proceed. Some commentators over-interpret the significance of the title found in 12:1 and argue that it indicates the start of what was originally another prophecy by a different author. However, the title was placed here by Zechariah to show that he considered what followed to be distinct from the First Burden and to have a significant unity in itself. The distinction is best expressed by saying that as Zechariah considered what had been divinely revealed to him about the future, he was aware of a difference in time perspective between the two Burdens. We can now see that the First Burden relates principally to events up to the first coming of Christ and his rejection by the Jews. The Second Burden focuses on what is to happen subsequently. There are, of course, overlaps. Previously the language in which the future of the Jews was anticipated held not a few instances of prevision of the more glorious future awaiting the redeemed people of God. And in this division, there are not wanting prophecies concerning Christ's first coming (12:10; 13:1; 13:7)—but the focus is on what happens from then on.

What then is described in the Second Burden relates to the experience of the church in the present age through to its consummation. This is often obscured by the fact that the language available to the prophet to relate what was revealed was limited to what was known in his own day. But what he says about Jerusalem, Judah or the house of David comes true not in any narrow way, but in terms of New Testament realities that fulfil the prophecies in a heightened sense. This is set out more extensively in the Appendix.

But when are these prophecies fulfilled? In these chapters there is an integrating stylistic feature in the repetition of the phrase 'on that day'. It occurs fifteen times in the Second Burden (12:3, 4, 6, 8, 9, 11; 13:1, 2, 4; 14:4, 6, 8, 13, 20, 22) and in 14:1 there is a related expression 'a day of the LORD'. Indeed that expression has often misled interpreters into thinking that these chapters describe the end of the age and the Second Coming of Christ. Undoubtedly 'the day of the Lord' (1 Cor. 5:5; 1 Thess. 5:2; 2 Thess. 2:2; 2 Pet. 3:10) or 'the day of the Lord Jesus Christ' (1 Cor. 1:8; 2 Cor. 1:14) anticipate the final judgment of all mankind when Christ returns, but that New Testament meaning cannot be simply read back into the Old Testament phrase.

'Day' does not signify that what is foretold here is going to occur in a single 24-hour period. As in English, 'day' is in Hebrew used in a variety of senses, one of which is a significant and important period of time, one characterised by common features that give it a unity, no matter how long it lasts. The precise features of the day have often to be understood from the context rather than from the expression. For example, 'the day of Jerusalem' (Ps. 137:7, NKJV) refers to the time of its downfall, and 'in the days of David' (2 Sam. 21:1, NKJV) to his reign. 'The day of the LORD' is not primarily eschatological, but points to a time when God intervenes significantly to re-order affairs on earth in a way that corresponds to what he wants. That may take place through temporal judgments on Babylon (Isa. 13:9) or Jerusalem (Lam. 2:22), or it may relate to the more distant, final judgment of God.

In this division of the prophecy 'day' relates to the coming age which Zechariah foresees in which the LORD acts decisively to establish the fortunes of his people. At first it is co-extensive with the whole of the present age, but in chapter 14 it becomes strictly eschatological. The nations are seen attacking Jerusalem, and the promise of divine intervention to defeat them is given (12:1-9). This outward act of deliverance is associated with inward cleansing and renewal of the people in a spirit of true repentance (12:10-13:1). The people turn from all that is false and expose whatever compromises faithful worship of the LORD (13:2-6). All this will come about because of the work of the true shepherd. But there are negative consequences too. His death leads to the flock being scattered and subject to suffering (13:7–9). However, chapter 14 shows that this is not to be their final destiny. Even when all seems to be lost, the LORD is true to his promise and intervenes to deliver his people, utterly overthrow their enemies and usher in the new age in which there will be complete devotion to him.

## Zechariah 12:1-9: Divine Deliverance

The introductory words **An Oracle. This is the word of the LORD concerning Israel (*12:1*)** are modelled on 9:1, and show that this is the beginning of a new section of the prophetic message. For a discussion of 'oracle' or 'burden', see on 9:1 and Malachi 1:1. The preposition rendered 'concerning' may also be rendered 'upon' or 'against'. The former translation seems preferable in that although much suffering is foretold for Israel, the message is not primarily one of doom for her, but for her enemies.

The use of Israel in this title is of considerable exegetical significance. Though in the period of the divided kingdom Israel was used to refer to the north, or Ephraim, after the return from the Exile Israel reverted to its original use for the one covenant people of God (Mal. 1:1). That is especially true in a verse such as this where it is found alone, and not paired with Judah as in 8:13 and 11:14. The fact that Judah and Jerusalem are repeatedly mentioned in the rest of the prophecy is because in the prophet's day it was there that the church of God was to be found. This does not detract from the validity of finding in the use of 'Israel' in the title a valuable hermeneutical bridge by which these chapters can be elucidated in terms of the New Testament Israel (Gal. 6:16).

The LORD is then portrayed in a three-part description, expressed in the original by participles. This was an idiom frequently used in praise of God, perhaps to show that his character and actions were unchanging. **The LORD, who stretches out the heavens, who lays the foundation of the earth, and who forms the spirit of man within him, declares.** The first two phrases show that the LORD, the one who has bound himself in covenant with Israel, is also the one who has created the universe, and who is therefore able to control it (Ps. 104:2; Isa. 40:12, 22; 42:5; 45:12; 51:13). His control extends beyond the inanimate realm because he is the 'God of the spirits of all mankind' (Num. 16:22; Gen. 2:7; Isa. 42:5). (For 'spirit', see Hag. 1:14.) Consequently, the hearts of all mankind are in his hand, just as is the king's. 'He directs it like a watercourse wherever he pleases' (Prov. 21:1; Ps. 33:13-15). If he accuses mankind, he says, 'Then the spirit of man would grow faint before me—the breath of man that I have created' (Isa. 57:16). The supremacy of such a God cannot be overthrown, and no obstacle will frustrate the execution of his declaration. Perhaps there is also the thought that as he is the Creator who in the beginning imposed his order on the universe, so too in the consummation he will impose his order on the disarray that sin has introduced into it.

*The Enemy's Disarray (12:2-4)*. The LORD declares what he is going to do. **I am going to make Jerusalem a cup that sends all the surrounding peoples reeling (*12:2*).** The judicial wrath of the LORD is often likened to a wine-cup which the wicked are made to drink and which renders them as incapable and incoherent as a drunk man (Ps. 75:8; Isa. 51:17-23; Jer. 25:15-16; Ezk. 23:32-34; Rev. 14:10; 16:19). The vessel described here is larger than an ordinary cup or goblet from which an individual would drink. It is a 'bowl' or 'basin' (2 Sam. 17:28), both because of the overwhelming nature of the judgment (Ob. 16; Hab. 2:16), and because so many were going to be made to drink from it. 'The surrounding peoples' are the nations who have come to besiege Jerusalem (12:3). This is a change from the conflict described in 9:13 where the enemy is Greece and not a number of peoples.

But what events are anticipated here? The description given here does not match anything in the experience of the nation of Israel after Zechariah's day. For instance, they were never able to gain such a sweeping victory over their enemies that they could be said to have 'consumed them right and left' (12:6). Although a siege of Jerusalem is described, it cannot be that of A.D. 70 because then the city was devastated, whereas here 'Jerusalem will remain intact in her place' (12:6). There are those who argue that what is foretold here is some future siege of a literal Jerusalem, but this is at variance with the way the New Testament treats the significance of Jerusalem as now continued in a spiritual sense in the universal church of God. So this depiction of a siege of Jerusalem portrays in Old Testament dress the reality of the ongoing hostility between the world and the people of God. 'And I will put enmity between you and the woman, and between your offspring and hers; he will crush your head, and you will strike his heel' (Gen. 3:15). But God is assuring his church that no matter how intense the conflict and how hard pressed they will be by the world's persecution, he will make them instrumental in overthrowing their persecutors (Ps. 118:10-12). 'The God of peace will soon crush Satan under your feet' (Rom. 16:20; Jn. 16:33; Rom. 8:37).

The second part of 12:2 has occasioned problems of translation. **Judah will be besieged as well as Jerusalem** implies that the surrounding land as well as the capital is inevitably going to be caught up in the events portrayed. However, the clause literally is, 'and also against Judah it will be in the siege against Jerusalem', and by identifying the unspecified subject of the verb as the cup of reeling, some have found here (and in 14:14) a statement of hostility between Judah and Jerusalem. While it is possible to interpret 12:5 as the leaders of Judah coming to realise their error, and then in 12:6 acting from within the enemy forces to destroy them, the basic notion of a division between the capital and its surrounding land seems forced, particularly as 'also' would lead us to expect a natural development of thought from the first statement, rather than such a perplexing one. The emphasis then is that not part, but the whole, of the people of God are going to experience this time of persecution.

**On that day** (*12:3*) has already been discussed in the introduction to the Second Burden. It is a phrase which occurs sixteen times in the final three chapters of Zechariah, and serves to indicate the cohesion of the events being described. They all belong to that time which was still future to the prophet—a time when the LORD's purposes for his people would be brought significantly forward. It points to that new age which has already come in Christ, and stretches forward to its consummation at his return (2 Cor. 5:17; 2 Pet. 3:13; Rev. 21:5). At that time the people of God on earth will experience the fury of the devil 'because he knows that his time is short' (Rev. 12:12). But though 'the beast and the kings of the earth and their armies gathered together to make war' (Rev. 19:19), they will be defeated by Christ. It seems that there will be a period of intense opposition against the church. Satan will deceive the nations in the four corners of the earth, and they will march to surround the camp of God's people, the city he loves (Rev. 20:7-9), but they will be divinely overthrown. Zechariah is here presented with glimpses of the destiny of God's people, and he is to relate them to his contemporaries that they might believe and take courage. If they are on the LORD's side, they are on the side whose victory is assured and whose enemies will be utterly overthrown.

**When all the nations of the earth are gathered against her** is found at the end of the verse in Hebrew (and in many English translations). Since the clause expresses attendant circumstances, it yields a more natural English order to bring it forward as in the NIV. This hostility is not to be viewed as mere politics. Jerusalem was 'the city of the Great King' (Ps. 48:2), 'the city of God, the holy place where the Most High dwells' (Ps. 46:4), and the actions of the nations are motivated by their attitude towards him. Their hatred of him leads them to make common cause against his people (Ps. 2:2; 48:4).

**I will make Jerusalem an immovable rock for all the nations.** The context shows that the image of the 'very heavy stone' that is hard to lift is not one of security, but of difficulty. Since the days of Jerome, it has been suggested that the stone was used in some sort of weight-lifting contest to establish the prowess of those who could lift it. Equally, the picture could be of a farmer trying to clear some ground, and coming across a very heavy stone in his field. **All who try to move it will injure themselves.** It is stressed that the injury is serious. The root is usually associated with cutting or gashing oneself, but here the idea seems rather of rupturing themselves or dislocating their backs when they try to lift it. The task of moving Jerusalem out of their way proves too great for the nations. The imagery has now moved beyond them losing control of their faculties to suffering severe self-inflicted injury. 'The wicked are ensnared by the work of their hands' (Ps. 9:16).

The LORD will directly interpose on behalf of his people. **On that day I will strike every horse with panic and its rider with madness (*12:4*).** The reference to cavalry is to the foremost troops of which the enemy seems to have no lack. But the LORD will render even the most formidable of their weapons completely ('every horse') useless against his city and people. 'Panic' comes from a root indicating astonishment and bewilderment. It here refers to a startled animal that has got out of control. The rider smitten with madness has also lost control of himself and is acting irrationally. He would turn on his own fellows (see 14:13). The words 'panic' ('confusion') and 'blindness' occur only here and in Deuteronomy 28:28, 'The LORD will afflict you with madness, blindness and confusion of mind.' (Apart from these two passages 'madness' occurs only in 2 Kgs. 9:20, of Jehu's chariot driving.) What had been part of the curse on covenant disobedience when Israel would be defeated by her enemies and be unsuccessful in everything she did, now falls on those who attack her. **I will keep a watchful eye over the house of Judah.** He will open his eyes not only to be aware of the situation of his people ('house of Judah' referring to all the people), but also to act with loving concern (Deut. 11:12; Ps. 33:18-19). **But I will blind all the horses of the nations.** The LORD's attitude towards their opponents is markedly different. He brings the curse of the covenant on them. 'Blind' is literally 'strike (emphatically repeating the earlier word) with blindness'. Their army is thrown into utter confusion.

*The LORD's Deliverance (12:5-9).* **Then the leaders of Judah will say in their hearts (*12:5*).** 'Leaders' (9:7) is an old word and some translations, suspecting its accuracy, emend it to 'clans' or 'families'. This makes better sense of 9:7, but it is possible to take the leaders in both verses as acting on behalf of the people. 'Heart' refers to the whole interior of man. It here indicates the genuine inner conviction of these leaders as they witness what is happening in the enemy forces, where the blinded horses are a danger to their riders and those near to them, and unable to mount an effective attack on the city. They attribute this unequivocally to the LORD. **The people of Jerusalem are strong because the LORD Almighty is their God.** The Hebrew reads 'Strength to me <are> the inhabitants of Jerusalem in the LORD of hosts their God'. The singular 'to me' may be taken as a collective reference to Judah. The NIV, with the support of a few Hebrew manuscripts and the early Jewish Aramaic rendering in the Targum, considers that a letter has been wrongly written twice giving rise to the word 'to me', and that originally it was 'to the inhabitants'. This is a confession that it is only from the LORD who controls all things that his people derive strength. Their success comes through the covenant bond that makes him 'their God' (see on 1:16; 3:2).

It is on the basis of this confession that the action of verse 6 proceeds. **On that day I will make the leaders of Judah like a brazier in a woodpile (12:6).** When the faith of the leaders is strong, they will be effective in their action for the LORD. The 'brazier' (or 'firepot' as it was translated in earlier editions of the NIV) would be used for carrying fire from one place to another. Obviously the fire coming into contact with pieces of wood would cause them to ignite. Similarly, **like a flaming torch among sheaves** pictures material that would rapidly ignite, the dry sheaves easily going up in flames (Ex. 22:6; Judg. 15:4-5; 2 Sam. 14:30). **They will consume right and left all the surrounding peoples** seems to point to their armies being able to gain an easy victory over their enemies. **But Jerusalem will remain intact in her place,** literally 'Jerusalem will still remain in her place in Jerusalem', where the first reference would be to the people personified and the second to the city. Though those around them are burnt up by the fire of God's judgment, the people of God remain unscathed and able to enjoy what the LORD has provided for them.

The message of the following two verses is that there will be order in the LORD's victory so that there will be no occasion for one part of his people to boast at the expense of others. **The LORD will save the dwellings of Judah first, so that the honour of the house of David and of Jerusalem's inhabitants may not be greater than that of Judah (12:7).** 'Dwellings' is literally 'tents', perhaps pointing to the more temporary structures that existed outside the capital. 'Honour' is primarily an aesthetic word referring to beauty, 'a beautiful wreath' (Isa. 28:5). It is also used in Exodus 28:2 of the eminence of the high priest as signified by his magnificent garments. 'Indeed there are those who are last who will be first, and first who will be last' (Lk. 13:30). The people will be united and not split by internal rivalry through the LORD's deliverance.

**On that day the LORD will shield those who live in Jerusalem (12:8).** This was the promise he had given in Hezekiah's day against the power of Assyria (see on 9:15). 'Like birds hovering overhead, the LORD Almighty will shield Jerusalem; he will shield it and deliver it, he will "pass over" it and will rescue it' (Isa. 31:5). But, as the next verse warns, this is conditioned on obedience to the injunction: 'Return to him you have so greatly revolted against, O Israelites' (Isa.

31:6). The expression of faith in 12:5 ensures the fulfilment of the covenant promise here.

The protection is not just for the leaders or the successful. **So that the feeblest among them will be like David** shows the impact of the LORD's help throughout the community. 'The feeblest' is the one in the besieged community who stumbles and is unable to stand properly, through tiredness, weakness or fear. He will be transformed into a warrior of renown and a national hero like David (1 Sam. 18:7). **And the house of David will be like God** may seem at first to be too extravagant language, but the addition of **like the Angel of the LORD** (only here in the NIV is the Angel capitalised) **going before them** shows in what sense it is to be taken. It is not a reference to the essential attributes of deity, but to the presence of God to help and guide his people, particularly as this had been known at and after the Exodus (Ex. 32:34; 33:15; Isa. 63:9). The Angel was a pre-incarnate appearance of the Son of God (see on 1:11), and in fulfilment of this prophecy he will again appear as the guide and ruler of his people.

**On that day** (*12:9*) again indicates the unity of the events being presented, and is to be understood of the final resolution of this world's tensions and conflicts. **I will set out to destroy all the nations that attack Jerusalem.** 'Set out' or 'seek' does not imply that this purpose will be frustrated. It is an expression of the LORD's determination, and gives to his people a promise to rely on when they see all things around them hopeless from a human point of view. The hold that evil has on humanity cannot be broken until there is this decisive conquest of it.

The church of God has many times been shown to be a cup that God uses to send others reeling and to be an immovable rock. Pharaoh thought he had Israel trapped, but the LORD provided an escape that led to the destruction of the Egyptian armies (Ex. 14). When the Philistines captured the ark of God, little did they realise how their trophy would turn into a source of danger, and how glad they would be to return it (2 Sam. 5–6). When the Babylonians were impiously using the vessels captured from the Temple, at that very time the sentence was written on the wall against them (Dan. 5). In the days

of the early church the persecutions strengthened rather than weakened it, and so it was said that the blood of the martyrs is the seed of
the church. Those who have sought to destroy the church have found
their efforts unavailing. So when the conflict is at its hottest—for
there will be conflict: the church is given no promise of easy
victory—we must judge the outcome not by the seeming strength of
the adversary, but by the presence of the LORD who 'will fight for you'
(Ex. 14:14).

*Study Questions*

**12:3** Scripture often illustrates the truth 'the wicked are ensnared by
the work of their hand' (Ps. 9:16): Ex. 14:5-7, 28; 1 Sam. 4:11; 5:1–6:12;
Dan. 5:2-28. Can you think of later instances in the history of the
church?

**12:5** The strength of the church comes from an active faith in God.
How should this be practised in times of conflict? 2 Chr. 13:12;
14:11; 20:12; 32:9; Ps. 20:7; 22:5; 34:6; 44:3; 2 Cor. 12:9.

**12:7** How may pride and rivalry cause tensions within the church?
Mk. 9:34; 1 Cor. 3:3-8; 8:2; Gal. 6:3; Phil. 4:2; 1 Tim. 6:3-5; 1 Jn.
2:16; 3 Jn. 9.

**Zechariah 12:10-14: Penitence and Revival**
The next section is a decided contrast to what preceded. There is no
mention of war or enemies or destruction. The focus is no longer on
the outward deliverance extended to the people of God, but rather on
the inner change that must be present for this deliverance to be
granted to them. What is portrayed is their changed perception of the
one they have rejected, and their repentance for their former attitude
to him. Bitter mourning affects all in the community at a time of
widespread spiritual revival.
    Many have understood this as a prediction of a time of specifically
Jewish revival corresponding to what Paul calls the 'fulness' of Israel

(Rom. 11:12) and their 'acceptance' (Rom. 11:15; see also Rom. 11:36). But it is doubtful if this should be read back into Old Testament revelation (see Appendix). It is preferable to continue to understand the references to Jerusalem and the people of Israel as references to the Old Testament people of God, and to find these predictions fulfilled in terms of the New Testament Israel, incorporating Jew and Gentile. Even those who interpret the passage as specifically fulfilled in a future Jewish revival acknowledge that the spiritual experience set out here is not confined to them, but is true of all believers. We then take it that what is portrayed here is that in the coming age of the Spirit the church will experience repentance and revival.

The speaker continues to be the LORD (12:1, 4). **I will pour out on the house of David and the inhabitants of Jerusalem (***12:10***).** 'House of David' (12:8) indicates the royal household, the descendants of David, presumably the highest classes in the land. But the predicted blessing is not confined to them. It also comes on all in Jerusalem, presumably the capital here standing for all the covenant people.

'Pour out' indicates the copious blessing that will be divinely bestowed. 'I will pour out my Spirit on all people' (Joel 2:28; see also Isa. 44:3; Ezk. 39:29). This was one of the predicted blessings of the end-time, which was inaugurated at Pentecost (Acts 2:15-21) but which is still only realised in part. What is bestowed is here more particularly defined as **a spirit of grace and supplication.** As the NIV footnote indicates, it may also be rendered 'the Spirit'. This is preferable in that it is not merely an inner disposition that is given, but the one who works effectively to transform the inner being (Jn. 3:6). The Spirit's action within the people is twofold. 'Grace' and 'supplication' are from the same root in Hebrew, and this choice of words indicates the interrelated nature of the blessing. *(1)* As the Spirit of grace (Heb. 10:29), the Spirit comes bringing the LORD's free favour. This produces an inner realisation of their spiritual rebellion and blindness which leaves them convicted of their sin. *(2)* As the Spirit of supplication, he works within them the additional reaction of seeking for forgiveness and further mercy from the LORD to maintain their relationship with him.

**They will look on me, the one they have pierced.** The verb 'look on' can refer either to bodily sight (Num. 21:9) or spiritual perception (Isa. 5:12). The surprising words 'on me' are supported by the ancient versions, and in this context can refer to none other than the LORD himself who is speaking. But in what sense can the people be said to have pierced the LORD? Two alternatives have been suggested. *(1)* 'Pierce' is here used as equivalent to 'scorn deeply' or 'insult'. In Leviticus 24:11, 16 'blaspheme the Name' is literally 'pierce the Name', though a different verb is used. *(2)* 'Pierce' refers to death (Num. 25:8; 1 Sam. 31:4. Isa. 53:5 uses a different word), the precise nature of which was only presented in merest outline to Zechariah. The verb implies a common action, and their subsequent repentance the recognition that the action was without justification. This fits in with the citation in John 19:37, 'As another scripture says, "They will look on the one they have pierced" '—again an interpreted citation to meet the circumstances of the fulfilment (see on 11:13). This is a prophecy of the sufferings of Christ, who through the uniqueness of his incarnation was able to bring it about that God could be wounded. Undoubtedly it was a prophecy whose significance was obscure until it was fulfilled.

The change of person in the next clause **they will mourn for him**, not 'for me', may indicate an awareness that though there is an identity between the speaker and the wounded one, there is also differentiation (see also on 13:7). That, however, may read too much into the Hebrew construction, where such changes of person are not uncommon. 'Mourn' refers to beating of the breast in deep distress. Note that John does not cite this part of the verse in connection with the crucifixion. It may be incipiently fulfilled in the reaction described in Luke 23:48, 'When all the people who had gathered to witness this sight saw what took place, they beat their breasts and went away.' Certainly this mourning is to be associated with the response to Peter's sermon on the day of Pentecost. 'When the people heard this, they were cut to the heart and said to Peter and the other apostles, "Brothers, what shall we do?"' (Acts 2:37). But this distress is shared by all who see what their sin has done to Christ. True repentance goes hand in hand with a correct appreciation of what took place on the cross. As one for whom Christ died, the individual acknowledges his personal part in piercing him. This induces deep sorrow, which is only mitigated by recognition of the fact that it was love which led to this identification of God with the sinner, and that Christ's sufferings are efficacious to atone for sin.

The mourning of those who recognise that it was their sin which led to the cross is described in terms of its intensity and its extent. Two comparisons are employed to bring out the depth of their distress. The first is with the anguish of a family, especially a Jewish family, over the death of **an only child** (Amos 8:10). They will **grieve bitterly for him as one grieves for a firstborn son.** Through the inner work of the Spirit what they have done has hit home to the people. 'Grieve bitterly' involves a metaphor from tasting what is sour as a way of expressing heart-crushing sorrow (Ruth 1:20; Isa. 38:15). It is reminiscent of what Egypt experienced when the last of the ten plagues came on it. 'Every firstborn son in Egypt will die, from the firstborn son of Pharaoh, who sits on the throne, to the firstborn son of the slave girl, who is at her hand mill, and all the firstborn of the cattle as well. There will be loud wailing throughout Egypt—worse than there has ever been or ever will be again' (Ex. 11:5-6).

The second comparison is with one of the most tragic instances of public mourning in the history of the covenant people, the death of King Josiah in 609 B.C. (2 Kgs. 23:29-30; 2 Chr. 35:22-25). **On that day the weeping in Jerusalem will be great, like the weeping of Hadad Rimmon in the plain of Megiddo (12:11).** Hadad-Rimmon was the name of a Canaanite fertility deity, who was held responsible for sending rain. There may have been seasonal rites of mourning to induce him by sympathetic magic to send rain to nourish the crops, comparable to the mourning for Tammuz denounced by Ezekiel (Ezk. 8:14). But to make that the basis of the comparison is grotesque. Far more plausible is the suggestion that Hadad Rimmon is a place name, compounded of names of Canaanite gods, and is to be located in the valley of Megiddo, near where Josiah was struck down. The place itself is not mentioned in Scripture, but the identification has been recorded since the days of Jerome (around A.D. 400). It would not be surprising if facts additional to those recorded in the Biblical history were still remembered by the people in Zechariah's day.

When Josiah died, 'all Judah and Jerusalem mourned for him. Jeremiah composed laments for Josiah, and to this day all the men and women singers commemorate Josiah in the laments. These became a tradition in Israel and are written in the Laments' (2 Chr. 35:24-25). Josiah's death involved a bitter loss of hope as the last reforming king of Judah was taken from them, and the possibility of averting the course of events which ended in the exile of 586 B.C. was lost. So too the rejection of the good shepherd had fearful consequences (11:9, 11, 14) for the Jewish people.

The extent of the distress is brought out in verses 12-14 which chant a solemn tale of the mourners who will be involved right across the land, not just the capital. **The land will mourn, each clan by itself, with their wives by themselves (*12:12*).** The separation of the clans or families, and the women by themselves, is to indicate the depth of the sorrow felt, and also the fact that it was not an event where the professional mourners were present to whip up the grief. There was no need for that, so deeply felt was the anguish. There then follows a list to emphasise the total involvement of the community. **The clan of the house of David and their wives, the clan of the house of Nathan and their wives, the clan of the house of Levi and their wives, the clan of Shimei and their wives, and all the rest of the clans with their wives (*12:12b-14*).** It would seem that the mention of David and his son Nathan (2 Sam. 5:14; see also on Hag. 2:20) is of the greater and the lesser branches of the royal family, and that of Levi and his grandson Shimei (Ex. 6:17) is of the greater and lesser lines of the priests. These are instances of the comprehensive nature of this mourning which will involve all the rest of the people too. What the NIV translation lacks is the repetition of 'by itself' or 'apart', which occurs eleven times in the Hebrew of 12:12-14. This repetition adds its own note of the dulling impact of grief to the deep personal anguish involved in it. 'The heart knows its own bitterness' (Prov. 14:10), and this separate mourning shows that this widespread spiritual awakening is not some mass hysteria which sweeps all along with it, but is composed of individual repentance and mourning so intense that it has to withdraw from public view.

There are two other New Testament references that require to be mentioned in connection with this mourning. 'At that time the sign of the Son of Man will appear in the sky, and all the nations of the earth will mourn. They will see the Son of Man coming on the clouds of the sky, with power and great glory' (Mt. 24:30). 'Look, he is coming with the clouds, and every eye will see him, even those who pierced him; and all the peoples of the earth will mourn because of him' (Rev. 1:7). These are not formal quotations of this passage, and the similarity of the language disguises how different the mourning is. It is not the grief of those brought to repentance, but the distress of those who recognise too late how misguided they had been in their attitude to Christ, who has now returned to judge the living and the dead.

This prophecy is a clear instance of a prediction that is fulfilled in various stages. The piercing referred to clearly took place on the cross after Christ had yielded up his spirit. The unbelieving Jewish nation had rejected its Messiah. The spear was indeed that of a Roman soldier. It was the unbelieving world as a whole that was represented there. But what of the mourning? It is the action of those who have been brought to a saving knowledge of Christ. It describes more than Jews. 'But I, when I am lifted up from the earth, will draw all men to myself' (Jn. 12:32). It is in this way that Christ builds his church throughout this age. Formerly through types and sacrifices he had drawn his people to consider what the final and completely acceptable offering for sin would be. Now in the proclamation of the cross he confronts us with the consequences of our sin, and causes his people to mourn over their long rejection of him. Throughout this age the church is the community that remembers and proclaims 'the Lord's death until he comes' (1 Cor. 11:26).

*Study Questions*

**12:10** How is the Spirit involved in a believer's prayers? Rom. 8:26-27; Gal 4:6; Eph. 2:18; 6:18; Jude 20.

**12:10-11** In what way is sorrow associated with repentance? Ps. 34:18; 51:17; Mt. 5:4; 26:75; Acts 2:37; 2 Cor 7:10; Heb. 12:17.

**Zechariah 13:1-6:  Cleansing from Sin**

Sorrow over sin is not an end in itself. Those who repent and come
to God find that he will 'revive the heart of the contrite' (Isa. 57:15)
and wipe out their sins (Acts 3:19). Zechariah is shown two aspects
of the process by which the people are purified from sin. There is
inner spiritual cleansing by which they are freed from the polluting
influences of sin within (13:1). It is also the case that the LORD works
in them and through them to remove all impurity from their lives
(13:2-6).

*Personal Cleansing (13:1)* **On that day a fountain will be opened
to the house of David and the inhabitants of Jerusalem** *(13:1)*.
The connection with what had gone before is maintained by the
phrase 'on that day' (12:6, 11), and also by the identity of those
spoken about, 'the house of David and the inhabitants of Jerusalem'
(12:10), the Old Testament embodiment of the church of God. They
have received the blessing of God's Spirit poured on them in such a
way that they truly repent. But no amount of weeping will solve the
problem of their sin. So this fountain is provided. A 'fountain' was
a source of flowing water obtained by digging. It was frequently used
in Proverbs in the phrase 'fountain of life' (Prov. 10:11; 13:14; 14:27;
16:22; also Ps. 36:9). In a similar prophecy in Joel 3:18 the word used
for 'fountain' is that of a naturally occurring source of water. Unlike
streams which frequently dry up in the heat of the east, a fountain
provides a perennial water supply. So here this fountain is 'opened'
in that action has been taken to provide a permanent and abundant
source of water.

   **To cleanse them from sin and impurity.** 'To cleanse' is not
expressed in Hebrew, but the thought is certainly there. Ritual
cleansings had been part of the ceremonial law. At their consecration
the Levites had been sprinkled with the water of cleansing to purify
them (Num. 8:7). Persons contaminated by contact with death were
sprinkled with water of cleansing prepared from the ashes of a red
heifer (Num. 19:9; Heb. 9:13). The ceremonial impurity denoted the
defilement of sin, and the water of sprinkling denoted its removal. In
Psalm 51 David had seen the need for thorough spiritual cleansing:
'Wash away all my iniquity and cleanse me from my sin ... Cleanse

me with hyssop, and I shall be clean; wash me, and I shall be whiter than snow' (Ps. 51:2, 7; see also Isa.1:16). The provision of this fountain of cleansing has been made in Christ. 'The blood of Jesus, his Son, purifies us from all sin' (1 Jn. 1:7). But Zechariah did not see as far as that. He was no doubt thinking of the laver of cleansing, and so was unaware of the link found in Revelation 7:14—'They have washed their robes and made them white in the blood of the Lamb'. It is water that is in Zechariah's fountain, not blood. The language is not that of sacrifice, but of ceremonial purification. It is the fact rather than the basis of cleansing that is stated.

It is not immediately evident how this prophecy about the fountain fits in with the other descriptions of what happens 'on that day'. Cleansing from sin was available to the Old Testament church, but its ultimate basis was prospective, looking forward to what Christ would accomplish. The fountain which provides cleansing in a new and effective way was definitively opened by the sacrifice of Christ (Heb. 9:9, 13-14). But if Zechariah is envisaging that initial opening of the fountain, there are difficulties in integrating this verse with the mourning of 12:10-14 on any interpretation of that passage. However, the Hebrew construction is not that for a simple action in the future, but may be translated, 'There will be an opened fountain'. What is foreseen is the era when it will be possible to look back to the cross, and when those who mourn over their sin will have access to the cleansing that has been procured by the completed work of the Mediator.

'Sin' renders the main Old Testament word for human failure to reach the standard God requires. The imagery behind the word can be seen in the way it is sometimes translated: 'miss' (Judg. 20:16), 'fails to find' (Prov. 8:36), 'miss the way' (Prov. 19:2), and 'fails to reach' (Isa. 65:20). 'Impurity' or 'uncleanness' is used of the ceremonial defilement of a woman in her period and at childbirth (Lev. 12:2) and in connection with touching a dead body (Num. 19:9-13), the 'water of cleansing' being of particular significance in this passage. It is used more generally of 'defilement' (2 Chr. 29:5) and 'corruption' (Ezr. 9:11). Impurity is abhorrent and pollutes. Together with sin it is mentioned here to cover every sort of offence and blemish that would debar an individual from approaching God acceptably, but through the fountain provision has been made for

cleansing from every type of defilement.   'Let us draw near to God
with a sincere heart in full assurance of faith, having our hearts
sprinkled to cleanse us from a guilty conscience and having our
bodies washed with pure water' (Heb. 10:22).

*Collective Renewal (13:2-6).* The personal and intensely individual
changes involved in repentance and mourning over sin (12:10-12)
and in spiritual cleansing (13:1) lead to a desire for holiness in all
things, because such great spiritual change cannot be confined to an
individual's inner life.  It leads to an altered perspective in every
aspect of living.  The prophet is shown this in terms of Old Testament
examples relating to idolatry (13:2) and false prophecy (13:3-6).
These had corrupted the national life of Israel, and represent all types
of ungodly and immoral behaviour that marred the profession of
God's people.  The LORD takes decisive action to remove them from
the life of the church.  Indeed, those who are renewed by God's grace
will strive to have all that is offensive to him eradicated from their
fellowship.

**On that day, I will banish the names of the idols from the land
(13:2).**  The word used for 'idols' represents them as things that are
carved or fashioned (Ps. 115:4), and so it is appropriate that they will
be 'cut off'. As this word is also used for being cut off from the
people, NIV renders it 'banish'. Not just the images will go, but their
names also. The 'names' of the idols are not just what their worshippers call them. They refer to the characteristics and powers attributed
to them. Mention of them by name or in any other way will be a thing
of the past. **"They will be remembered no more," declares the
LORD Almighty.**

It is often asserted that whatever else the Exile achieved, it rid
Israel of idolatry. But it may not be that this happened all at once. The
evidence of this verse, if nowhere else, suggests that it was a snare
that the returned community had to grapple with. We know that
mixed marriages were a problem in the days of Ezra and Nehemiah
(Ezr. 9:1-2; Neh. 13:23-27), and one consequence of this would be
pressure to adopt the practices of the surrounding nations. Undoubtedly the returned community had a new resolve to worship the LORD,
but that resolve was put to the test in many matters and there was not

an immediate victory in every aspect of their living. The reference to idolatry would not have struck them as a problem from the past. Indeed, it is one which will in transmuted form arise again (Rev. 9:20-21; 13:15).

**I will remove both the prophets and the spirit of impurity from the land.** This is an additional and related aspect of the situation. The false worship had its proponents, and they too would be removed from the worshipping community. 'Prophets' in this section refers to false prophets, there being no specific word for them in the Old Testament. They were active in promoting the false cults that were threatening the land. False prophets will continue to be a menace till the end of time (Mt. 24:24; Lk. 21:8; 2 Thess. 2:2; 1 Jn. 4:1). 'The spirit of impurity' refers to all the thought patterns contrary to the way of the LORD that they were bringing into the land. It is in contrast to the 'Spirit of grace and supplication' (12:10), and may well describe an active power of darkness rather than just a tendency. The false prophets were subject to external influences, but demonic ones. The operation of such a spirit is described by Paul in 2 Thessalonians 2:9-12.

It is not envisaged that the task of removing false worship will be easy. **And if anyone still prophesies, his father and mother, to whom he was born, will say to him, 'You must die, because you have told lies in the LORD's name'** *(13:3)*. 'Still' implies that this takes place after God's detestation of false worship has been made abundantly clear. This is not just the action of the deluded, but of the defiant. It is a measure of the prevailing commitment to the LORD's cause and the purity of his name, that even the bonds of natural affection will not prevent appropriate action being taken against any who still offend in this way. 'Lies' or 'falsehood' (see on 10:2) relate to what has no basis in fact, like the message of 'the prophets who tell lies' (Isa. 9:15; Jer. 5:31; 14:14; 23:25). The same word is also applied to idolatry ('fraud' in Jer. 10:14). What is envisaged here is not outright paganism, which would be prophesying in the name of other gods, but an unwarranted claim to speak in the name of the LORD (1 Kgs. 22:24; Jer. 23:16-22; 28:1-4). One post-exilic example of a false prophet, Shemaiah, is recorded in Nehemiah 6:10-13.

The penalty for such action was death. **When he prophesies, his**

**own parents will stab him.** In Deuteronomy 13:6-11 anyone who tried to entice an Israelite from the worship of the LORD was to be stoned to death. A close relationship was not to interfere with the imposition of this penalty—indeed the relatives of the offender were to throw the first stones. That emphasis is preserved here in that 'his own parents' is originally a repetition of the phrase 'his father and his mother, to whom he was born'. The death penalty was also imposed on false prophets (Deut. 18:20). Instead of stoning it is stabbing that is mentioned here. 'Stab' or 'pierce' is the same word as in 12:10. The attitude and action that had previously been shown towards the Messiah are now rightly displayed towards the impostor.

In 13:4-6 another description is given of how open espousal of what is contrary to God's revelation will be shunned. So total will the revulsion be among God's people against all that wrongly takes to itself the right to speak in the LORD's name, that the false prophets, who were often motivated solely by the desire to be popular and say just what the people wanted to hear (Isa. 30:10-11; Mic. 2:11), will repudiate their former activities and pretend that they had never happened at all. **On that day every prophet will be ashamed of his prophetic vision** (*13:4*). This does not ascribe true prophetic vision to these men, but when they spoke they would claim to have had matter divinely revealed to them. They would claim to be authorised spokesmen of God. But when their imposture will no longer be tolerated, the message that they had once made so much of, will now be a matter of acute embarrassment to them. **He will not put on a prophet's garment of hair in order to deceive.** The NIV supplement 'prophet's' is to show that the long robe was not made from skin, but woven from the hair of camels or goats. It was Elijah who had worn such a garment, and put it round Elisha his successor (1 Kgs. 19:19; 2 Kgs. 1:8; see also Mt. 3:4). It is unlikely that it was worn by all subsequent prophets. But these impostors, not having a genuine word from God, dressed up to appear to be latter day Elijahs, and so more readily dupe the gullible among the people. Such ploys will then be seen through, and so they will be avoided by those who had formerly used them.

**He will say, 'I am not a prophet'** (*13:5*). When challenged, such individuals will no longer be prepared to acknowledge their former activities. Instead they will claim, **I am a farmer**, literally, 'one tilling soil', and so perhaps 'farm worker', rather than one owning and working his own land. The following words are obscure, but reinforce his denial by claiming that his working on the land was a matter of long-standing. **The land has been my livelihood since my youth** is obtained by slight emendation of the Hebrew text. The other reading in the footnotes, 'a man sold me in my youth' is also not without problems, but it can be retained. It would then imply that so ashamed will the false prophets become of what they had been doing that they would rather present themselves as slave workers on the land than acknowledge their former occupation.

**If someone asks him, 'What are these wounds on your body?'** (*13:6*) is probably to be understood as occurring when his claims to be a farm-hand are put to the test. He takes off his upper garment to get on with the job, and suspicions are aroused because that would reveal the lacerations that had been made as part of the ecstatic performance of the false prophets (Deut. 14:1; 1 Kgs. 18:28; Jer. 48:37). 'On your body' is literally 'between your hands' or 'arms'. The phrase seems to be an idiomatic expression for anywhere on the chest or back. **He will answer, 'The wounds I was given at the house of my friends.'** This is not to be understood as referring back to verse 3. The friends are not his parents. That prophet was put to death. Nor is this in some way a Messianic prophecy foretelling the rejection of Christ. This is rather the cover story put up by the ex-prophet to account for the scars on his body. 'I got them in a drunken brawl with my friends.' There is an element of irony in the answer in that 'friends' or 'lovers' could be used to refer to false deities (Hos. 2:5, 13; Ezk. 16:36), and so the words may be heard as 'in the temples of false deities'. But this is no frank confession of his past, but an implausible excuse for the marks on his body. He will explain away anything that seems to link him with what he had been doing before, so utterly rejected is false prophecy and anyone who had anything to do with it.

The people who are blessed with the knowledge of their spiritual cleansing act in intense and absolute loyalty to the LORD to ensure that there is nothing in their land that is inconsistent with the acknowledgment of him as their covenant king. This comes finally true in the New Jerusalem of which it is said, 'Nothing impure will ever enter it, nor will anyone who does what is shameful or deceitful, but only those whose names are written in the Lamb's book of life' and 'Outside are the dogs, those who practise magic arts, the sexually immoral, the murderers, the idolaters and everyone who loves and practises falsehood' (Rev. 21:27; 22:15).

Their loyalty is particularly seen in their concern that nothing debase the word of the LORD. They are concerned to maintain purity of doctrine and practice. This is what Jude was concerned about when he urged those to whom he wrote 'to contend for the faith that was once for all entrusted to the saints' (Jude 3). There are false doctrines which undermine the faith, and which are propagated by those who secretly slip in among the church. They are to be exposed 'through the word' (Eph. 5:26) and excommunicated (1 Cor. 5:13) so that the church might become as Christ wants it 'a radiant church, without stain or wrinkle or any other blemish, but holy and blameless' (Eph. 5:27). It is by the exercise of such godly discipline the church readies herself for the coming of her Lord.

*Study Questions*

**13:1** What priority should we give to purity in our living? Gen. 35:2; Isa. 1:16-17; Mt. 5:8; Phil. 1:10; 2:15; 4:8; Tit. 1:15; 2:14; 1 Pet. 1:22; 1 Jn. 3:3.

**13:3** How may Christian commitment affect family relationships? Mal. 4:6; Mt. 10:21, 35-37; Mk. 10:13-16; Lk. 21:16; Jn. 19:26-27.

## Zechariah 13:7-9:  Through Many Hardships

This section begins with an abrupt shift in focus from the deceitful evasions of the false prophet to the sufferings of the Messiah. A similar dramatic change of theme occurred at 11:1 in the first Burden, and there, as here, served to throw what followed into greater prominence, introducing an aspect of the situation that had not been covered so far in the Burden—the death of the good shepherd and the consequences of that for his flock.

This is the only section of the second Burden in which the phrase 'on that day' does not occur. It differs from the other sections of the Burden in that it is written in poetry. Some have suggested that it is misplaced, and the New English Bible went so far as to print it after 11:17 on the grounds that it continued the shepherd theme. There is, however, no textual evidence to warrant such a transposition, and the undoubted affinity in theme is rather to be taken as evidence that corroborates the traditional view that both Burdens come from the one source. It may be that the phrase 'on that day' is omitted because the focus—at least initially—switches back to events connected with the first coming of Christ, and so prior to the period with which this Burden is concerned. On the other hand, its absence may be of no greater significance than that Zechariah could not easily add the phrase into the poetic structure of the prophecy when he was gathering together into the Burden the various revelations that had been given to him.

The citation of 13:7 in Matthew 26:31 and Mark 14:27 clearly demonstrates that it is the time of Christ's death that is in view. This reversion to an earlier period already foreseen (11:4-14) is made so as to contrast the false prophet and his wounds with the good shepherd and how he was afflicted. Previously he had been portrayed as contemptuously dismissed (11:12-13), but now the fact of his being pierced (12:10) is taken up. He will be killed—and that by divine appointment! His suffering presages what his followers will also have to undergo (13:8-9). So the fulfilment of this prophecy stretches out from the cross until the return of Christ, and is characterised both by the affliction of the church and by the fidelity of the purified remnant as through many hardships they enter the kingdom of God (Acts 14:22). The scene is then set for a fuller portrayal of their final deliverance in chapter 14.

**Awake, O sword, against my shepherd (*13:7*).** It is the LORD himself who is speaking, and who addresses the 'sword', which is mentioned as a common instrument of inflicting death (Ex. 5:21; Ps. 17:13; Ezk. 21:8-10; Rom. 8:35). Indeed it may stand for other weapons. In the narratives about the death of Uriah the Hittite, though mention is made of the 'sword' (2 Sam. 11:25; 12:9), he seems to have been shot by archers (2 Sam. 11:24). The 'sword' is also used as a symbol of judicial authority (Deut. 32:40-41; Jer. 47:6; Rom. 13:4). Here it is considered to have been asleep and so inactive. There was no reason in the conduct of him who was 'holy, blameless, pure, set apart from sinners' (Heb. 7:26) for the sword of divine justice to threaten him with punishment. That was the conclusion of Pilate: 'I find no basis for a charge against this man' (Lk. 23:4); the testimony of the criminal who was crucified along with him: 'This man has done nothing wrong' (Lk. 23:41); and the witness of Roman centurion at the cross: 'Surely this was a righteous man' (Lk. 23:47). It therefore required an explicit divine command to arouse the sword 'against my shepherd'. This metaphor for a ruler has already been extensively employed in chapters 10 and 11, and here explicitly connects back to the good shepherd portrayed in 11:4-14. It is against him in his capacity as the divinely appointed ruler of God's people that the sword is to be unsheathed. What awaits him is a consequence of the task he has undertaken of saving his people as their representative and substitute. Before it was recorded that the people pierced the shepherd, but now it is seen that it was really the LORD who was acting through them (Isa. 53:10; Jn. 19:11; Acts 2:23; 4:28).

The only understanding of this that suffices is that what we have here is substitutionary atonement. It had already been hinted at in Isaiah 53. 'He was pierced for our transgressions, he was crushed for our iniquities; the punishment that brought us peace was upon him, and by his wounds we are healed' (Isa. 53:5). Although Zechariah does not connect the Shepherd here with the suffering servant, nor yet with the Davidic ruler who was to come, these are strands of Old Testament revelation that were being brought closer and closer together, awaiting the day when all would be revealed.

The further description **against the man who is close to me** indicates something of the relationship that existed between the LORD and the shepherd. It is not the ordinary word for 'man' that is used here, but rather one that denotes man in his strength and at the height of his power (it is related to the word rendered 'mighty men' in 10:5). Perhaps this should not be stressed, as it may just be used as a poetic equivalent for the ordinary word. What is startling, however, is that a man should be described by God as 'close to me'. The word rendered in this way is found elsewhere in the Old Testament only in Leviticus (11 times, e.g. 6:2; 7:21; 18:20; 24:19) to indicate someone who is a very close relative or neighbour. The shepherd is thus one who dwells side by side with the LORD, has the same status as him as the man at his right hand (Ps. 80:17), and can only be the divine-human Messiah—the one who was with God and was God (Jn. 1:1). This truth is not yet fully spelled out, but it is more clearly expressed here than in the language of 12:10 where the use of 'me' and 'him' had in some way identified the pierced one with the LORD. **Declares the LORD Almighty** impresses the inevitability of this command being obeyed, coming as it does from the one who has power over all.

The LORD goes on to reveal the consequences of what will happen to the Shepherd for those who are his. **Strike the shepherd, and the sheep will be scattered** continues the poetic device of addressing the sword. The earlier use of a similar comparison— 'Israel scattered on the hills like sheep without a shepherd' (1 Kgs. 22:17)—expressed the scene in greater detail. When the shepherd is removed from them, the sheep will be exposed to hazards and enemies that will cause them to move off in every direction.

But who are the 'sheep' or 'flock' in this connection? Many refer it to the Jews, the sheep of this sheep pen (Jn. 10:26), and find the prophecy fulfilled in the dispersion of the Jews after the fall of Jerusalem. But note Jesus explicitly told the unbelieving Jews, 'You are not my sheep' (Jn. 10:26). Further, this conflicts with the general approach employed in this commentary, that there is no reference to the Jewish nation as such in this Burden, but rather what is said of Jerusalem and Judah, who were the Old Testament people of God, finds fulfilment in the New Testament Israel. More importantly, a reference to the Jewish dispersion conflicts with Christ's own use of the passage. In John 16:32 he warned his disciples, 'A time is coming, and has come, when you will be scattered, each to his own home. You will leave me all alone. Yet I am not alone, for my Father is with me.' Later that night he made it more explicit. 'This very night you will all fall away on account of me, for it is written: "I will strike the shepherd, and the sheep of the flock will be scattered."'

(Mt. 26:31). They were his 'little flock' (Lk. 12:32) and represent the New Testament Israel. There can be no doubt that the prophecy was fulfilled in the disciples' desertion of Jesus—but that probably does not exhaust the implications of the passage. In the persecution after Stephen's martyrdom the church was scattered (Acts 8:1, 4) and both James and Peter refer to the church as 'scattered' (Jas. 1:1; 1 Pet. 1:1), a condition that continues until the Lord himself returns.

**I will turn my hand against the little ones.** The 'little ones' may be a reference to the young of the flock, or the more helpless animals, but the parallelism of Hebrew poetry probably requires that it be taken simply as synonymous with 'the sheep', 'the flock' in the preceding line. They are the Lord's 'little flock' (Lk. 12:32). There is a division of opinion as to how these words are to be understood. Generally the phrase 'to turn the hand against' is used in the context of punishment (Ps. 81:14; Ezk. 38:12; Amos 1:8). Those who argue that the phrase may be understood in a positive way, that of providing protection, cite 'I will turn my hand against you; I will thoroughly purge away your dross and remove all your impurities' (Isa. 1:25). This does not substantiate the claim of the phrase being used of protection, but it does make clear what is intended here. The LORD is going to subject his church to a period of trials and opposition, but by way of purification. Jesus repeatedly warned his disciples of the persecution and difficulties ahead, 'Remember the words I spoke to you: "No servant is greater than his master." If they persecuted me, they will persecute you also' (Jn. 15:20), and 'They will lay hands on you and persecute you. They will deliver you to synagogues and prisons, and you will be brought before kings and governors, and all on account of my name' (Lk. 21:12). The history of the church shows that this came abundantly true.

**"In the whole land," declares the LORD (*13:8*)** does not refer simply to the earth. Old Testament references to 'the land' point to Palestine as the place inhabited by the people of God and where God himself was pleased to be present. In terms of its New Testament realisation this does not refer to any particular geographical location, but is an expression for the church wherever it is to be found. **Two-thirds will be struck down and perish** portrays a time of great suffering for the people of God, and may refer to the persecutions of the early centuries. **Yet one-third will be left in it.** The picture is not totally bleak. There will be survivors, but even then there will be further testing to be undergone. A similar process of multi-stage testing had been the experience of the Old Testament church (Isa. 6:13a).

**This third I will bring into the fire (*13:9*).** They have not escaped because of their personal merit, but because of the gracious purpose of God. 'Fire' indicates a time of suffering, not here punitive but reformative. **I will refine them like silver and test them like gold.** Trying, testing and proving experiences are to be expected. The death of the shepherd Messiah does not bring immediate heaven. For the figure of testing compared to refining, see on Malachi 3:3. This is the lot of believers in Jesus Christ. God views them as precious metals, but they need to be purified. 'In this you greatly rejoice, though now for a little while you may have had to suffer grief in all kinds of trials. These have come so that your faith—of greater worth than gold, which perishes even though refined by fire—may be proved genuine and may result in praise, glory and honour when Jesus Christ is revealed' (1 Pet. 1:6-7).

The result of all they have experienced is that there is a renewed and heighten appreciation of the covenant relationship. It is presented in a chiastic fashion—they, I, I, they—as is suitable to the interlacing of the bond between people and their God. **They will call on my name and I will answer them.** 'Call on the name of the LORD' indicates prayer to him as the true God (Gen. 4:26; 12:8; 1 Kgs. 18:24). This is in accordance with the LORD's advice to his covenant people: 'Call upon me in the day of trouble; I will deliver you, and you will honour me' (Ps. 50:15; see also Ps. 91:15; Ps. 107:6, 13, 19, 28). Indeed, Isaiah envisages the situation developing when God will say, 'Before they call I will answer; while they are still speaking I will hear' (Isa. 65:24). This close fellowship is an expression of the bond of the covenant (Ex. 3:10; 5:1; 19:5-6). **I will say, 'They are my people,' and they will say, 'The LORD is our God.'** This represents the enjoyment of the blessings and privileges of the New Covenant, 'I will be their God, and they will be my people' (Jer. 31:33; Hos. 2:23; see on 8:8).

We are here reminded that the Messiah suffered and that those who are his will also suffer. Previous prophecies had predicted prosperity and blessing (9:17; 10:12; 12:6, 9), but there is a darker side to the future of the church after the cross, just as there had been a darker side to the experience of the Jews in chapter 11. Paul talks of the sufferings of Christ flowing over into our lives (2 Cor. 1:5), of sharing in Christ's sufferings that we may share in his glory (Rom. 8:17), and of 'the fellowship of sharing in his sufferings' (Phil. 3:10). He even goes so far as to say of his sufferings, 'I fill up in my flesh what is still lacking in regard to Christ's afflictions' (Col. 1:24). We always need to remember how Peter exhorted believers in his own day. 'But rejoice that you participate in the sufferings of Christ, so that you may be overjoyed when his glory is revealed' (1 Pet. 4:13).

*Study Questions*

**13:7**   What do the following passages teach about Christ as the substitute for sinners?  Isa. 53:5; 2 Cor. 5:21; Gal. 3:13; Heb. 2:9; 9:28; 1 Pet. 3:18.

How is the relationship between God and 'the man who is close to me' clarified by New Testament teaching? Jn. 1:1; 10:30; 17:5; Phil. 2:6; Col. 1:15-17; 2:9.

**13:9**  In what ways does the church today 'suffer a little while' (1 Pet. 5:10)?

## Zechariah 14:1-11:  King Over the Whole Earth

It cannot be claimed that there is anything like unanimity among interpreters regarding the final chapter of Zechariah. Some consider it to have been fulfilled in the experience of the Jews in the age of the Maccabees. Others take it as awaiting literal fulfilment in terms of a rebuilt Jerusalem. But there is much to be said in favour of taking it as describing the culminating events in the experience of the church of God in the period from the first coming of Christ through to his second coming. This description is, as in the two preceding chapters, related in terms of the Old Testament embodiment of the people of God. Indeed it would seem that the attack on Jerusalem of chapter 14 is to be identified as the culminating assault of the nations on the city which had begun in 12:3-9. That had ended with the divine determination to save the city. Now further details are given of that deliverance.

Zechariah shows that the attack of the nations meets with considerable success, threatening the very existence of the city (14:1-2). But then the LORD intervenes on behalf of his people, granting them first escape and then deliverance (14:3-5). This will be a unique time without parallel in history (14:6-7), and ushers in the final, universal reign of the LORD (14:9-11).

Zechariah uses what is termed *apocalyptic language* in his presentation. This means that the events revealed to him are so overwhelming that only hints of what is involved can be given using language drawn from known events and realities, for what is being described far surpasses anything ever experienced before. It is therefore quite improbable to understand these descriptions as coming literally true. They are true, but the language they are using is to be likened more to that of a sketch or cartoon in which only certain elements are present, and not necessarily precisely portrayed. It is the language of symbol and metaphor that has to be employed to describe the unusual, indeed the unique. There is only one consummation of all things.

*The Final Assault (14:1-2).* **A day of the LORD is coming (*14:1*)** does not use the ordinary expression for 'the day of the LORD', but rather 'a day to/for the LORD', perhaps to mark the resumption in an intensified form of the theme of 'on that day' which is not found in 13:7-9. 'The day of the LORD' was an expression used by the prophets to mark a time when the LORD is seen to intervene on earth in a display of his power and majesty, overthrowing and judging all that has set itself against him and his people, and granting them the blessings he intends for them. The day of the LORD could refer to the overthrow in history of powers that oppressed Israel, but even then the descriptions are coloured by the climactic events of the second coming. It is a day when the LORD alone will be exalted (Isa. 2:17), when the

wicked will be punished for their sins (Isa. 13:11), when the deeds of
the nations will return upon their own heads (Ob. 15), but also when
salvation will be extended to Mount Zion and Jerusalem (Joel 2:32).
Perhaps the most ominous Old Testament description of that day is
to be found in Zephaniah 1:14-18. While the note of wrath and
judgment continues in New Testament references (Rom. 2:5; 2 Pet.
3:7; Rev. 6:17), joy and anticipation become more prominent in
descriptions of that day, because it has now become the day of
Christ's return (Jn. 6:39; 2 Cor. 1:14; 2 Tim. 4:8; 2 Pet. 3:12). See
also on Malachi 4:5.

**When your plunder will be divided among you** refers to the
plunder that has been taken from the people of Jerusalem ('your' is
feminine and refers to the city). This verse is a summary statement
which anticipates what is spelled out more fully in following verse.
The people will be overcome by their opponents and will have to
watch helplessly as their own possessions are leisurely shared out by
their conquerors before their very eyes ('among you'). It is a picture
of the seemingly hopeless situation of the people of God.

Why did this happen? It is not attributed to the superior forces of
the enemy, or even to the sin of the people. But in direct divine speech
the LORD reveals that it has occurred because of his overruling
providence. **I will gather all the nations to Jerusalem to fight
against it (14:2).** The nature of the international forces gathered to
destroy one city indicates that what is involved goes far beyond a
mere military or political campaign. The dispute is more basic than
that: it is the forces of the heathen aligned against the city of God.
'They marched across the breadth of the earth and surrounded the
camp of God's people, the city he loves' (Rev. 20:9). What is more,
the LORD has permitted it; indeed, he has caused it (see also Joel 3:2).
It was not that he had to stir up the nations to hatred and hostility
against his people—that was their attitude anyway. But the one who
is in control of all things permitted their fury to express itself so that
it would further his purposes by leading to their destruction. A
similar situation arose at the time of the Exodus when the LORD led
the Egyptians to pursue the Israelites to their own destruction (Ex.
14:1-4).

But whereas the Egyptian forces, though terrifying the Israelites, had not been allowed to come near them (Ex. 14:20), in the final conflict the devastation that is wrought upon the city is immense. **The city will be captured, the houses ransacked, and the women raped.** This is a description of what would happen when an ancient city fell to its enemies (similar expressions occur of the fall of Babylon, Isa. 13:16). But are we to understand by it something that happened to the literal city of Jerusalem? Zechariah is being shown the future of God's people, a future that opened out to encompass the church of the New Testament. It is at that level rather than with the future of a city in Palestine that we are to seek the fulfilment—with the whole Israel of God. The message is that the future of the church will involve a time when it will be surrounded by its enemies and seemingly overwhelmed by them. **Half of the city will go into exile, but the rest of the people will not be taken from the city.** These words show that what is being described certainly has not occurred in history. Neither at the capture of Jerusalem by Nebuchadnezzar nor at its capture by the Romans was half of the population left in the city. Under the metaphor of the pillaging of an ancient city, the church is presented as suffering grievously at the hands of her enemies, and yet there has been a remnant left. It is possible, but pedantic, to reconcile these figures with those in 13:8 on the basis of city suffering to a different extent from the rural area of Judah.

*Escape and Deliverance (14:3-5).* But the people of God will not be left helpless and scattered before their enemies. 'How awful that day will be! None will be like it. It will be a time of trouble for Jacob, but he will be saved out of it' (Jer. 30:7). We may well wonder why this salvation does not come sooner. Could not God have intervened before his people endured the suffering and grief described? Would that not have been more loving? But in this, as in much else, we have to accept that divine wisdom is greater than ours, and that there are divine priorities that take precedence over ours. The incident of the death of Lazarus is instructive in this regard. When Jesus had been informed that Lazarus was sick, he did not act immediately, but 'he stayed where he was two more days' (Jn. 11:6). This was not to traumatise Lazarus or his family, but 'for God's glory so that God's Son may be glorified through it' (Jn. 11:4). There was also the consequence that the faith of the disciples would be strengthened by Lazarus' resurrection (Jn. 11:15, 42).

So too in the final deliverance, the delay heightens the perception of the LORD's glory. When he does intervene, there can be no doubt that he alone achieves the victory. **Then the LORD will go out (*14:3*).** 'Go out' presents him as a king leading his people into battle (Num. 10:35; Judg. 4:14; 1 Sam. 8:20; 2 Sam. 5:24; Ps. 68:7). The LORD has so far permitted the nations to have their way, but now he goes out from heaven to intervene decisively and show that he is the one who is in control of all that happens on earth. He comes to **fight against those nations, as he fights in the day of battle,** a phrase describing engaging in the hand-to-hand encounters of ancient warfare. This is the warrior LORD who intervened at the Exodus to shatter the enemy, throw down those who opposed him and redeem his people (Ex. 15:3-18). True to his promise, 'I will be an enemy to your enemies and will oppose those who oppose you' (Ex. 23:22), the LORD had fought for his people on many occasions in their history (Josh. 10:14; Judg. 4:15; 2 Chr. 20:15). Now he comes to deal the final blow to his enemies (Rev. 19:11-16).

**On that day his feet will stand on the Mount of Olives, east of Jerusalem (*14:4*).** 'His feet' indicates a theophany, perhaps one where the presence of God causes the earth to shake (Ps. 68:8; 97:4; Mic. 1:3-4; Nah. 1:3, 5). The addition 'east of Jerusalem'—which was scarcely needed to locate this well-known hill—links this vision with that granted to Ezekiel when the LORD's glory left Jerusalem and 'stopped above the mountain east of it' (Ezk. 11:23). The LORD whose visible presence with his people had then ceased now returns in power, as was similarly forecast in Ezekiel 43:2. It is not of course to some reconstructed city that he comes, but to the New Jerusalem which is the reality symbolised in these visions. It is the city that bears the name 'THE LORD IS THERE' (Ezk. 48:35).

**The Mount of Olives will be split in two from east to west, forming a great valley, with half of the mountain moving north and half moving south.** The mountain lay to the east of Jerusalem and was a ridge about two miles long. It was higher than, and overlooked, the Holy Mountain of Zion, being separated from it by the deep Kidron Valley. As such the Mount of Olives presented an obstacle in the way of escape from Jerusalem to the east. This had been seen notably in the case of David as he fled from Absalom (2 Sam. 15:30). But now the LORD's presence in power means that the obstacle is transformed. It is split in two so that escape is easily effected through the newly created valley.

**You will flee by my mountain valley, for it will extend to Azel** (*14:5*). 'My' refers to the LORD whose action has just created this valley through the mountain. He tells the people how they can use it to escape. The footnote rendering in the NIV, 'My mountain valley will be blocked and will extend to Azel. It will be blocked as it was blocked because of the earthquake' follows ancient translations in understanding the Hebrew verb in a different way. It pictures their route being filled in by landslides so as to provide an even more easy escape. The location of Azel (in fact the Hebrew spelling is Azal here) is unknown. Some have identified it with Beth Azel mentioned in Micah 1:11. The text here requires some location to the east of the city.

**You will flee as you fled from the earthquake in the days of Uzziah king of Judah** (767-740 B.C.). Palestine is subject to earthquakes, and a major tremor occurs every fifty years or so. An earthquake of considerable magnitude had occurred in the days of the prophet Amos, in the mid-eighth century B.C., and he dates his book by it (Amos 1:1). Just as Zechariah had recalled the mourning over Josiah (12:11), so now he uses the panic on the occasion of that earthquake to make more vivid the way in which the delivered people will escape from the enemies.

The key statement in the description is left to last. **Then the LORD my God will come, and all the holy ones with him.** The prophet speaks in his own right to express his joy and satisfaction at what has been shown to him. Here is the vision of the coming of his God accompanied by his 'holy ones'. Some, referring to 1 Thessalonians 3:13 and Jude 14, particularly as translated in the AV, consider this a reference to redeemed humanity coming from heaven, as well as to angelic beings (see also Deut. 33:3; Ps. 16:3; Dan. 7:18, 21-22). But as the thought is of the LORD coming to his people to save them, the emphasis here is more readily taken as referring to his angelic retinue (Deut. 33:2; Ps. 89:5-7; Dan. 4:13, 17, 23; Mt. 16:27; 25:31; 2 Thess.

1:7; Rev. 19:14). 'With him' is literally 'with you'. It may be the prophet speaking directly to the one he sees in vision, but such a change of person does occur in the prophets in an idiom alien to English, and without such significance. It is not immediately stated what God has come to do, but the coming is undoubtedly to the city. The LORD has returned.

*A Unique Day (14:6-7).* In terms of the general approach to prophetic interpretation adopted in this commentary these verses (14:6-7) and the following ones (14:8-11) may be interpreted in two ways. **On that day** (*14:6*) may be understood more narrowly in terms of God's eschatological intervention on behalf of his people, or more broadly in terms of the circumstances that will prevail throughout the inter-adventual period. If the latter understanding is adopted, then the condition of the church in the present age is described as one neither of glowing prosperity nor total darkness, but something in between. One might have expected it to have faded away altogether, but by the LORD's intervention there have been revivals, and finally when all seems lost ('evening comes'), there is miraculously the light of deliverance. In the same way the following picture of the river of living water flowing out of Jerusalem may be taken to refer to the spread of the gospel and the extension of Christ's kingdom on earth, culminating in his return. On balance, however, I prefer the narrower understanding of the passage—that is, it relates strictly to the final intervention of God, because this seems to do justice to the uniqueness of what is described (14:7), and to the significance of 'living water' (14:8).

**There will be no light, no cold or frost** adopts a different reading from the (admittedly obscure) original, which is literally, 'there will not be light; the precious ones will congeal (grow dim)'. 'The precious ones' refers to the stars and heavenly bodies (the same root is used for the 'splendour' of the moon in Job 31:26). Their light is progressively withdrawn as part of the re-ordering of the universe associated with the day when 'the stars of heaven and their constellations will not show their light. The rising sun will be darkened and the moon will not give its light' (Isa. 13:10) and 'the sun and moon will be darkened, and the stars no longer shine' (Joel 3:15; see also

Isa. 24:23; Mt. 24:29; Rev. 8:12). As a result there is no light. This is a reversal of the creation order of God (Gen. 1:14-19; Ps. 136:7-9). Absence of 'cold or frost' would also fit in with a picture of the radical re-ordering of the created realm, particularly as described in the covenant with Noah (Gen. 8:22).

**It will be a unique day, without daytime or night-time (*14:7*)** continues the same picture, neither of light nor of darkness, but of murky gloom. 'A unique day' is literally 'one day' that stands out as the only one of its kind. As the lights that serve 'as signs to mark seasons and days and years' (Gen. 1:14) have been withdrawn, there is no way of telling when it is day or night. This is an occurrence quite without parallel. **A day known to the LORD** is one which he alone can understand. It is futile for others to try to work out how or when this will be (Mk. 13:32). **When evening comes, there will be light.** The whole course of nature is turned upside down. When one would have expected the gloom to turn into darkness, there is instead light. This is not the light of a restored sun, for the New Jerusalem 'does not need the sun or the moon to shine on it, for the glory of God gives it light, and the Lamb is its lamp' (Rev. 21:23; 22:5). This unique day ushers in the new heavens and the new earth.

*The Final Reign (14:8-11).* **On that day living water will flow out from Jerusalem (*14:8*).** Jerusalem was always poorly provided with water, but the renewed city is the source of a divinely provided supply. Zechariah here resumes the picture presented by Joel and Ezekiel of the Temple as a source of water (Joel 3:18; Ezk. 47:1-12). This is not just typical of physical change, but of the spiritual blessings that water represents. It is 'living' water flowing freshly from a spring or fountain, and symbolic of true spiritual life given in salvation (Jer. 2:13; Jn. 4:10; 7:38). This looks back to the river of Paradise, when 'a river watering the garden flowed from Eden' (Gen. 2:10), and it looks forward to Paradise restored. In the New Jerusalem there will be 'the river of the water of life, as clear as crystal, flowing from the throne of God and of the Lamb down the middle of the great street of the city. On each side of the river stood the tree of life, bearing twelve crops of fruit, yielding its fruit every month. And the leaves of the tree are for the healing of the nations' (Rev. 22:1-2).

Truly 'there is a river whose streams make glad the city of God, the holy place where the Most High dwells' (Ps. 46:4).

Unlike Ezekiel's river which flowed only to the east (Ezk. 47:1, an embarrassment for those who take both prophecies to refer to the same *literal* future event), the water splits **half to the eastern sea,** that is the Dead Sea, **and half to the western sea,** that is, the Mediterranean. In this way it is available for all the land. And it is available all the time, **in summer and in winter.** Many streams in Palestine were only winter torrents which dried up in the heat of summer, when the need for water was at its greatest. Not so this source of supply. It is available all the year round. There is no disruption of the bliss of the new creation 'for the old order of things has passed away' (Rev. 21:4).

There is then presented the basis on which this abundance of spiritual blessing will be achieved. **The LORD will be king over the whole earth (*14:9*).** Although the word 'earth' may also be translated 'land', and that at first seems to fit in with the Palestinian orientation of the surrounding verses, in fact 'earth' is required to do justice to the extensive scope of what is being described here. Many of the psalms had spoken of the reign of the LORD, 'the great King over all the earth' (Ps. 47:2; 93:1; 97:1; 99:1-2), and Zechariah is describing the time when his universal dominion will be openly and outwardly acknowledged on all sides. He at present rules all, but his authority is not recognised by a world in rebellion against him. The time will come when the LORD will not only be, but also be seen to be, the universal ruler. 'The kingdom of the world has become the kingdom of our Lord and of his Christ, and he will reign for ever and ever' (Rev. 11:15).

**On that day there will be one LORD, and his name the only name.** This too has always been the case, as was stated in the Shema, 'Hear, O Israel: The LORD our God, the LORD is one' (Deut. 6:4). What is now predicted is that there will be universal acknowledgment of this. 'Name' refers to all the character and attributes of the one who alone can truly say, 'I AM WHO I AM' (Ex. 3:14). They will be acknowledged as the only true authority and standard. He will be universally honoured as the unique one. Since all other claims to homage and worship of 'many "gods" and "many" lords' will be exposed and totally done away with, it will be seen that 'there is but one God, the Father, from whom all things came and for whom we live; and there is but one Lord, Jesus Christ, through whom all things came and through whom we live (1 Cor. 8:5-6).

The prophet next presents a picture of the dominance and supremacy of the final reign of God in terms of physical changes in Palestine. **The whole land, from Geba to Rimmon, south of Jerusalem, will become like the Arabah (*14:10*).** Geba was six miles north east of Jerusalem. Though it actually lay in the traditional territory of Benjamin, it was taken as the northernmost limit of Judah (1 Kgs. 15:22; 2 Kgs. 23:8). Rimmon was 35 miles south west of Jerusalem, and was on the southern border of Judah where the hill country merged into the Negev (Josh. 15:32; 19:7). This whole area surrounding Jerusalem is to be transformed, but it is not certain what is to be understood by the comparison 'like the Arabah'. The Arabah was the rift valley through whose first section the Jordan flowed from the Sea of Galilee to the Dead Sea. The Arabah continued south through the region round the Dead Sea to the Gulf of Aqaba. The traditional derivation of the word as 'plain' (now largely abandoned) has led some to find here the thought that the rest of the land becomes flat. Others have thought of it as agriculturally fertile (as the northernmost section of the Jordan valley is), linking it back to the flow of water in 14:9. But the most probable reference of Arabah is to land that is depressed below the level of surrounding territory. So this area around Jerusalem does not become flat or fertile (or infertile like the central and southern Arabah) but depressed. This accentuates what happens to Jerusalem.

**But Jerusalem will be raised up.** The one exception to this general levelling down of the land was the capital. The description of the exaltation of Jerusalem reminds one of Isaiah 2:2 and Micah 4:1, 'In the last days the mountain of the LORD's temple will be established as chief among the mountains; it will be raised above the hills, and peoples will stream to it.' The main differences are that Zechariah does not mention the Temple, and that the other prophets do not speak of the surrounding area being depressed. Their message, however, is the same. The physical preeminence of the king's city towering over the whole land is a spiritual metaphor for the dominance of the holy city when its king is present and all his people are gathered round him.

The same theme is developed in another way. The city is viewed as being rebuilt to the dimensions of its former grandeur. It will **remain in its place** (12:6), not being displaced from its true and proper site, and recovering from the havoc wrought by its enemies (14:1-2). This will extend **from the Benjamin Gate,** probably in the north east wall of the city, leading out to the territory of that tribe (Jer. 37:12-13) **to the site of the First Gate,** perhaps to be located in the northern wall of the city, **to the Corner Gate,** which lay in the west. **The Tower of Hananel** was the northernmost limit of the city's expansion (Neh. 3:1; 12:39), and **the royal winepresses** were presumably located in the south of the city, near the king's pool (Neh. 2:14) and the king's garden (Neh. 3:15). The whole city is involved in this elevated grandeur.

What is more, **it will be inhabited (*14:11*)**, literally, 'they (that is, the people of God) will dwell in it'. In the period after the return from the Exile, there seems to have been an on-going problem with population in Jerusalem. Many of those who returned preferred to live in the countryside and had to be forced to come to the capital (Neh. 7:4; 11:1-2). But there will be no problem about getting people to live in the capital when the king has returned to it. His presence will also ensure that **never again will it be destroyed**. This refers to the 'ban' which the LORD imposed on the cities of Canaan because of their great wickedness (Josh. 6:17-18; see also Mal. 4:6). The fate of God's people for their rebellion had been understood in similar terms (Isa. 43:28). But when the LORD returns to the city, 'no longer will there be any curse' (Rev. 22:3). His people will have been purified and will be ready to enter into his presence. **Jerusalem will be secure.** This is the confidence and undisturbed peace of those who have the LORD in their midst, and whose relationship with him is inviolate. Jeremiah predicted that when the righteous branch of David would reign in Jerusalem, Israel would live in safety (Jer. 23:5-6) and under the new covenant that is achieved (Jer. 31:40).

How often the church has been considered a spent force—and not only by its adversaries! In struggling with our lack of confidence, there are two things we can do. We may look within ourselves to find that 'the Spirit himself testifies with our spirit that we are God's children' (Rom. 8:16), and seeing what God has already done, we may gain confidence that 'he who began a good work in you will carry it on to completion until the day of Christ Jesus' (Phil. 1:6). Hope is also strengthened by looking forward. In passages such as this, Scripture encourages us to do so by providing glimpses of the glory that is yet to be. In this way we will be stirred up to that eager, almost impatient, expectation that characterises the whole creation as it waits for the sons of God to be revealed (Rom. 8:19, 23). Looking forward also helps us to regain a right, God-centred perspective on life. The emphasis is on what the LORD will do on that day, and on what he will be seen to be. It is the vindication of his name and the establishment of his rights that fires the soul of the faithful. What is lacking in Zechariah's Old Testament picture is the presence and role of Christ on that day. It awaited the clearer light of New Testament revelation to bring that clearly into focus, so that now 'we wait for the blessed hope—the glorious appearing of our great God and Saviour, Jesus Christ' (Tit. 2:13).

## Study Questions

**14:3** How should we react when we consider that God is delaying and not intervening when we think he should? Ps. 13:1; 40:1, 17; 69:3; 119:82; Isa. 25:9; Hab. 2:3; Lk. 18:7; Jn. 11:4-6; Heb. 10:37; Jas. 5:7; 2 Pet. 3:9.

**14:9** In what ways is God said by Scripture to be king? Ex. 15:18; 2 Chr. 20:6; Ps. 10:16; 59:13; 95:3; 103:19; 1 Cor. 15:24-28; 1 Tim. 1:17; Rev. 19:6.

## Zechariah 14:12-21:   The Final Contrast

Zechariah continues his description of the events of 'the great and dreadful day of the LORD' (Joel 2:31), but he does not follow a strictly chronological order.   He begins by looking back to what was involved in the LORD fighting against the nations that had captured Jerusalem (14:2-3).  His wrath will be poured out on those who have manifested their opposition to him by attacking his people (14:12-15).  It is, however, still envisaged that a remnant of the nations will be saved (14:16-19).  The final scene presented is that of the holy city, enjoying the peace of the LORD and totally devoted to his service, with even the most insignificant items dedicated to him (14:20-21).

*The Fate of the Wicked (14:12-15).*  Though the day of the LORD brings blessing for those who are his, it is also 'the day of judgment and destruction of ungodly men' (2 Pet. 3:7).  This truth is brought before the prophet in terms of the overthrow of the armies that had come against the holy city (14:2).  They had seemed invincible, but they cannot stand before the LORD. 'Though the wicked spring up like grass and all evildoers flourish, they will be destroyed for ever' (Ps. 92:7).

**This is the plague with which the LORD will strike all the nations that fought against Jerusalem (*14:12*).**  They had committed a most monstrous evil in opposing and acting against the LORD's people and city.  The vengeance taken on them will therefore be commensurate with their crime. 'Plague' is often the divine means of retribution against those who have opposed him (Ex. 9:14; 1 Sam. 6:4; Ps. 106:29; Rev. 15:1; 16:1-21).  **Their flesh will rot while they are still standing on their feet, their eyes will rot in their sockets, and their tongues will rot in their mouths.**  This describes their gruesome fate which will be a living death from a rapidly wasting sickness. 'Rot' is rendered 'fester' in Psalm 38:5.  It may be that the eyes and mouth are particularly mentioned because their eyes had gloated over the fate of Jerusalem and their mouths had spoken against her.  One is reminded of the way in which Isaiah's prophecy ends with the worshippers of the LORD going out and looking upon 'the dead bodies of those who rebelled against me; their worm will not die, nor will their fire be quenched, and they will be loathsome to all mankind' (Isa. 66:24). The New Testament does not hesitate to repeat this description of the fate of the wicked in hell (Mk. 9:48).

There is another divinely ordained calamity that afflicts the enemies of God. **On that day men will be stricken by the LORD with great panic (*14:13*).** It is symptomatic of the way that the LORD overthrows the human forces arrayed against him that he causes internal dissension and confusion so that they destroy themselves (Judg. 7:22; 1 Sam 14:20; 2 Chr. 20:23). This was what had been promised Israel when they entered the promised land, that God would throw their enemies 'into great confusion until they are destroyed' (Deut. 7:23). **Each man will seize the hand of another**, presumably in an attempt to prevent the other assaulting him as they grapple in close combat. But with their free hands **they will attack each other**.

The next statement is ambiguous. **Judah too will fight at Jerusalem (*14:14*)**, or 'Judah too will fight against Jerusalem'. But the latter does not fit the context (see on 12:2). There is no hint of tension between the capital and the surrounding territory. Rather it is a picture of a role being assigned the people of God in the work of defeating the enemy. While the ranks of their enemies are torn by internal confusion and mistrust, the whole covenant people unite to claim the victory that the LORD has granted them.

**The wealth of all the surrounding nations will be collected— great quantities of gold and silver and clothing.** The scene which had begun with the plunder from Jerusalem being distributed by those who attacked her ends with their possessions being gathered— but for what purpose? It could be that these are spoils of war to be enjoyed by Jerusalem, just as Jehoshaphat and his men gathered the plunder for three days (2 Chr. 20:25). However, the ban that was imposed on apostate Israelite cities required the destruction of all the plunder as a whole burnt offering (Deut. 13:16). At the fall of Jericho all the silver, gold and articles of bronze and iron were devoted to the LORD and went into his treasury (Josh. 6:19). Also in the case of Achan, being under the ban involved all that he had being destroyed (Josh. 7:24). Probably what is intended here is that the victorious people of God will devote the ill-gotten gains of the nations to the LORD, their wealth to the Lord of all the earth (Mic. 4:13).

But in pillaging the camp of an ancient army there was one other item that would ordinarily be included in the booty—the animals. Apart from the horses used as cavalry or with chariots, there were the many animals that transported the army's baggage and food supplies. Zechariah explains why they do not form part of the booty on this occasion. **A similar plague will strike the horses and mules, the camels and donkeys, and all the animals in those camps (*14:15*).** They have already been killed in the judgment on the hostile armies.

*A Remnant Saved (14:16-19).* It is with some surprise that we then read **then the survivors from all the nations that have attacked Jerusalem (*14:16*).** The description given of the plague would have led us to surmise that there were none. 'Then' is literally 'and it shall be <that>'. The NIV rendering is unnecessarily paradoxical in leaving open the possibility that after the LORD has come in final judgment there is still some last chance salvation. What is being described need not be subsequent to the infliction of the plague, but a description of the LORD's dealings with those nations that have shown persistent hostility to Jerusalem (there is the on-going attack of 12:3 as well as the culminating hostility of 14:1-2). They are not going to be totally swept away in his wrath. The LORD's purpose also includes those from the nations being incorporated into the people of God and participating in the worship of the LORD. They **will go up year after year to worship the King, the LORD Almighty.** This is a picture of regular devotion to the LORD. The conversion of the nations is not pictured in terms of their being circumcised, or obeying the Law of Moses, but of worshipping the LORD. It must be noted that 'go up' still thinks in terms of pilgrimage to Jerusalem. The language of the Old Covenant is being used to express the reality of the New (Isa. 66:23), and especially in its culmination when John sees 'a great multitude that no-one could count, from every nation, tribe, people and language, standing before the throne and in front of the Lamb' (Rev. 7:9).

John's great multitude also 'were holding palm branches in their hands' (Rev. 7:9), and while this may reflect on Christ's triumphal entry into Jerusalem (Jn. 12:13), it also fits in with what is said here **to celebrate the Feast of Tabernacles.** On the first of the seven days of this feast the Israelites were instructed to 'take choice fruit from the trees, and palm fronds, leafy branches and poplars, and rejoice before the LORD your God for seven days' (Lev. 23:40). But why is this festival singled out for mention? It came at the end of the religious calendar and so in measure summed up all the worship of Israel (note its position in Lev. 23 and Deut. 16.) It was also a festival in which the resident alien was permitted a role (Deut. 16:14). During this time the people lived in booths constructed out of branches to remind them of how they had lived during the period in the Wilderness and how the LORD had guided them at that time (Lev. 23:42-43). It was also a time when they remembered the LORD's on-going bounty to them in the harvest (Lev. 23:39; Deut. 16:13-15). The nations in coming to this feast were therefore making a double acknowledgment: that it was the LORD who had guided them to where they were, and that it was his bounty that they enjoyed in the harvest. In the light of the LORD's providential and saving goodness, the feast was one characterised by joy. 'Be joyful at your Feast. ... your joy will be complete' (Deut. 16:14, 15). This is why the redeemed of the nations celebrate it with joy.

The prophet then envisages circumstances in which there are those who are not prepared to render the LORD the worship that is his due. **If any of the peoples of the earth do not go up to Jerusalem to worship the King, the LORD Almighty, they will have no rain (14:17).** Not engaging in the worship of the king is an act of rebellion, which must be punished. 'Rain' here stands for all the blessings that the LORD bestows, particularly in the harvest (10:1). These will be withheld from those who persist in their rebellion. Such a consideration causes problems for those trying to fit this description into some eschatological scheme. If the LORD has come in his final power, how are there rebellious nations left? It seems best to view this in terms of the imperfection of the view given of the future in the Old Covenant. What is being stated by means of this hypothetical description is a complete assertion of the power and rule of God. 'No rain' does not point to some borderline existence, but to being deprived of all divine blessing, being 'punished with everlasting destruction and shut out from the presence of the Lord and from the majesty of his power' (2 Thess. 1:9). There will be no possibility of continued rebellion in the eschaton, and even the blessings of common grace will cease.

**If the Egyptian people do not go up and take part, they will have no rain (*14:18*).** The mention of 'no rain' in the previous verse seems to lead on to consideration of Egypt. It was the one land of the ancient world that did not so obviously depend on rain for its farming, but rather on the annual inundation of the Nile. Would this provide them with a means of escape from the rigour of the LORD's demands? Egypt was also a power that had often stood against and oppressed the LORD's people (10:10-11). If they too have to submit or perish, it will show the completeness of the LORD's rule in this new age.

The NIV footnote suggests the deletion of one word, the negative 'not' with the support of several Hebrew manuscripts and early versions, so that since 'rain' is a translator's supplement, the text would read, 'If the Egyptian people do not go up and take part, then the LORD will bring on them the plague he inflicts ...' This seems to make better sense in that Egypt has such minimal rain anyhow, but they will not escape the LORD's judgment, just as they did not escape it when they oppressed the Israelites (Ex. 12:30). **The LORD will bring on them the plague he inflicts on the nations that do not go up to celebrate the Feast of Tabernacles.** It is not of course the celebration of the Feast as such that is so crucial, but what such celebration indicates by way of submission to and true acknowledgment of the LORD.

**This will be the punishment of Egypt and the punishment of all the nations that do not go up to celebrate the Feast of Tabernacles (*14:19*).** 'Go up' is the customary usage for travel to Jerusalem (1 Kgs. 12:27; Ps. 122:4; Mt. 20:18; Jn. 2:13; Gal. 1:17-18), and is certainly not used because of the earlier mention of Jerusalem being raised up (14:10). It is not that Egypt is being singled out for special mention. What the LORD is requiring is total and universal respect and submission.

*The Holy City (14:20-21).* Zechariah then describes a scene in the new Jerusalem that brings out all that the LORD's deliverance means. Rather than attempt to present a full description of the glory that will exist, the prophet selects significant details. From the way in which these particular details are arranged, we may well imagine what prevails in all other aspects of the lives of the inhabitants of the Holy City.

**On that day** HOLY TO THE LORD **will be inscribed on the bells of the horses** (*14:20*). The horses are not military animals but those used for carriage in the city. Metal bells hang as ornaments on their harness, and on the bells are the same words of dedication to the LORD as were inscribed on the gold plate that was hung at the front of the high priest's headdress (Ex. 28:36). It was indicative not only of his own position but also of the status of all in Israel (Ex. 19:6; Jer. 2:3). They were all holy, that is, set apart to the service of the LORD. How fully that will be carried out in the New Jerusalem is seen in that it extends even to the bells tinkling on the horses' harness. Even the smallest and seemingly most trivial details of life are consecrated to the LORD. This, of course, would involve the cessation of the Levitical distinction between sacred and common.

**The cooking pots in the LORD's house will be like the sacred bowls in front of the altar.** This presents another picture of the consecration to the LORD that will permeate the sacred city. 'The sacred bowls' renders a word that is used almost exclusively for the containers found at the sanctuary, for instance, those in which blood from the sacrifices was taken to be sprinkled on the altar. Consequently they were holy and exclusively dedicated to divine service. This now extends to the cooking pots that were provided in the temple for the use of families when they ate part of the peace offering. Where there had formerly been different degrees of holiness in terms of the function of the utensils, all are now viewed as of equal holiness in the sanctuary.

Indeed it goes further than that. **Every pot in Jerusalem and Judah will be holy to the LORD Almighty** (*14:21*). Every pot throughout the land will be dedicated to the LORD's use. This envisages a time when the distinction between sacred and secular will be totally done away with, not by the abandonment of the sacred but by the obliteration of the secular. There will be nothing that is ordinary and outwith being used in the service of the LORD. It will therefore be perfectly permissible that **all who come to sacrifice will take some of the pots and cook in them.**

The final significant detail that Zechariah adduces regarding the holiness of Jerusalem is that **on that day there will no longer be a Canaanite in the house of the LORD Almighty.** Because the word

Canaanite also stood for a 'merchant', there are two possible ways of understanding this statement. Taking it as 'merchant' raises the possibility that what is envisaged is an absence of that sort of behaviour that the Lord found when he visited the Temple (Jn. 2:14-16). On the other hand, it may be argued that 'Canaanite' stands for those who are firmly committed to a depraved life style, and who have no place among the Lord's people (Lev. 18:24-30; Deut. 7:1-6). This seems more plausible. Zechariah is saying that the worship of the Temple will not be marred by the presence of any who are implacably opposed to the Lord. The purity and holiness that characterises the holy city is not just an outward matter of horses' harness and cooking pots. They are but indications of what is required: heart commitment to the Lord. The mention of the Canaanite is not to debar any on racial grounds, but on ethical and spiritual. 'Nothing impure will ever enter it, nor will anyone who does what is shameful or deceitful, but only those whose names are written in the Lamb's book of life' (Rev. 21:27).

In Hebrew the final clause is structured so that the last words of the prophecy are 'on that day', the day when the Lord will come in fulness of power and the tensions and problems of this life are resolved in favour of his standards and his way. As faith struggles with the perplexities of the here-and-now, it looks forward to that day, and seeing what will prevail then, seeks to pattern its behaviour after the standards that are then vindicated. This was what Peter advised his readers, 'You ought to live holy and godly lives as you look forward to the day of God and speed its coming' (2 Pet. 3:11-12).

## Study Questions

**14:14** On what is the true oneness of the church of God based? Jn. 13:34; 17:22-23; 1 Cor. 1:10; 12:12; Eph. 4:3-6; Col. 3:12-17.

**14:20-21** How should holiness dominate our thinking and living? Rom. 6:22; 2 Cor. 6:17–7:1; 1 Thess. 3:13; 4:7; Heb. 12:14; 1 Pet. 1:15.

# MALACHI

## OVERVIEW

Although Malachi is the last book of the Old Testament in English Bibles, this does not reflect the order in which Old Testament books were composed. The writing of Malachi predates that of Chronicles, Ezra, Nehemiah and Esther. He ministered about sixty to seventy years after the completion of the Temple, and was roughly contemporary with Ezra and Nehemiah.

It was an age of widespread religious disillusionment and discontentment. Although the people of Haggai's day had fallen short of what God expected of them, when they were challenged about it, they acknowledged that they were in the wrong. They admitted that the Temple ought to be rebuilt, and they came to accept that they should start immediately. By the time of Malachi, the nature of the people's disobedience had changed. They could see nothing wrong with the way they were living or with the way they approached God in worship. When challenged about their attitudes, there was no acknowledgment of wrong-doing on their part. Instead they were prepared to defend their behaviour. Indeed, they more than hinted that what had gone wrong was that the LORD had not lived up to his side of the covenant.

It was a time of religious cynicism. The Temple had been finished, but where were the crowds from all nations flocking to it, as they had been promised (Zech. 8:20-23)? Their land was an economic and political backwater; what had happened to the shaking of the nations and the promises to Zerubbabel (Hag. 2:6-9; 20-23)? What about the Jews who were to return from the dispersion (Zech. 8:7-8)? Very few of them had come back, and Jerusalem was still very largely an uninhabited ruin (Neh. 7:4). Instead of the position of renown and wealth they had expected, there was the burdensome status of being under Persian domination. They felt that they had done their part for God, but he had not responded as he had promised. Indeed they rather thought that the way to get on was to ignore the LORD and get what they could for themselves (3:15). That sort of attitude was affecting all their living, even the Temple worship of which they were so proud.

Many of the sins against which the prophet inveighs are the same as those listed in the books of Ezra and Nehemiah: corruption of the priesthood (Mal. 1:6-2:9; Neh. 13:7-9), reluctance to pay tithes to support the temple worship (Mal. 3:8-10; Neh. 10:32-39; 13:10-14), advantage taken of the poor (Mal. 3:5; Neh. 5:1-5), and intermarriage with the surrounding heathen peoples (Mal. 2:10-11; Ezr. 9:1-2; Neh. 13:1-3, 23). We cannot be certain precisely how Malachi's ministry fits in with that of Ezra who arrived in Jerusalem in 458 B.C. or that of Nehemiah who followed in 445 B.C. They were both active there for some time. Twelve years later (433 B.C.) Nehemiah returned to Persia, but came back to Jerusalem again (Neh. 13:6). It may be that Malachi shortly precedes Ezra's return, say around 460 B.C., or that they were contemporaries in the following decade. It is improbable that Malachi comes after Nehemiah. He was a civil official and able to enforce compliance with his reforms, whereas Malachi's critique of Judean society contains no hint of reform. Also, 1:8 talks of animals being presented to the governor, and Nehemiah explicitly tells us he did not follow the practice of earlier governors in receiving such tribute (Neh. 5:14-16). On this basis it is reasonable to conclude that Malachi's ministry falls in the period before Nehemiah's return.

Malachi is sent to expose and counter the scepticism and disobedience to be found in Jerusalem. After the introductory title to the prophecy (1:1), there are a number of dialogues in which the prevailing religious cynicism is exposed and refuted. The first matter to be dealt with is the reality of God's love for his people, as compared with his rejection of Edom (1:2-5). Then the prophet probes the way in which the worship of the Temple had become perfunctory—an insult to God (1:6-14). This is followed by a divine rebuke of the priests whose failure to live up to the standards set for them and to educate the people in the ways of the LORD will bring on them open shame (2:1-9). There is then an exposé of the way in which the social norms of the covenant had been abandoned. Malachi forthrightly presents the LORD's condemnation of the way in which the people were marrying foreigners and divorcing their own wives (2:10-16).

It was an era in which the people were questioning the justice of God and his ability or willingness to enforce his covenant laws. They are reminded of the Coming One and of God's justice which will prevail (2:17–3:5). God was already chastening them. Because they were not contributing the tithe to support the Temple and priests, there had been droughts and poor harvests. They are challenged to repent and see how bountifully God will deal with those who are obedient to his commands (3:6-12). Although there were many in the community who had abandoned true standards of moral judgment, there were some who feared the LORD and whom he would remember when he came (3:13-18). Then all who set themselves to oppose him would be punished and the righteous blessed (4:1-3). The people were therefore urged to give heed to the demands of the covenant with Moses. There would be an Elijah to warn them of impending doom. If they did not respond as God required, the curse of the broken covenant would come on the land (4:4-6).

## Malachi 1:1-5:   The LORD's Covenant Love

The style of Malachi is plain and straightforward.  There are no perplexing visions such as those found in Zechariah.  We are left in no doubt about the message the prophet has to deliver.  But it is not presented in a flat or unimaginative way.  One technique that is employed throughout is the use of dialogue in which the people are presented as questioning what the LORD has said (1:2, 6, 7, 13; 2:14, 17; 3:7, 8, 13, 14).  The shallowness of their objections and the mistaken notions on which they are based are then exposed, and they are urged to renewed loyalty to the LORD. It must not be treated as merely a rhetorical technique used to engage the people's attention. It was employed because it was appropriate to their attitude of quizzing the LORD's actions and disputing the rightness of their own ways.  After the title (1:1), this first dialogue focuses on God's love for his people.

*Introduction (1:1).*  The title to the book of Malachi poses a number of problems.  The first is the significance of the word rendered **an oracle (1:1)**.  This is a matter of ongoing scholarly discussion.  The noun comes from a Hebrew verb meaning 'to lift up' or 'to carry'.  It has wide applications and can be used of a load carried by an animal (Ex. 23:5) or of the inner burden of guilt borne by an individual (Ps. 38:4-5).  When it is used in connection with a message from God, it is generally followed by an indication of the party to whom the message was addressed, for instance Babylon (Isa. 13:1), Moab (Isa. 15:1), or Damascus (Isa. 17:1). These messages conveyed warnings of impending judgment and destruction, and so it is argued that the noun itself is ominous and means a 'burden' which should weigh heavily on those to whom it is addressed.

But the predominant view in modern scholarship notes the existence of a Hebrew idiom that uses the same verb in the phrase 'to lift up the voice' and so give public expression to something. For instance, 'Esau wept aloud' (Gen. 27:38) is literally 'Esau lifted up his voice and wept', and Jothan 'shouted' (Judg. 9:7) is 'lifted up his voice and called'.  The verb can be used in this sense even when the noun 'voice' is not expressed, as in 'cry out' (Isa. 3:7; 42:2) and 'raise their voices' (Isa. 42:11).  Therefore it is argued that the noun may convey the sense of public utterance or declaration, and ought to be translated 'oracle', or word from God. This would fit in with the way it is used for messages of the false prophets, who were not given to making ominous declarations (Lam. 2:14), and with its twice being used before series of proverbs (Prov. 30:1; 31:1).

However, there is still much to be said in favour of understanding the word as 'burden'. This fits in with the content of the prophetic messages that follow it, whereas 'word of the word of the LORD' seems unnecessarily repetitive. The messages of the false prophets which proved false and misleading in Lamentations 2:14 might have been burdens against the enemies of Jerusalem predicting their defeat, and the NIV footnotes in Proverbs 30:1 and 31:1 indicate the possibility of understanding the word there as a place-name. Also, the question 'What is the oracle of the LORD?' (Jer. 23:33) shows that the negative overtones of the word were apparent to the people of Jeremiah's day, even without adopting the footnote rendering of the following words, '"You are the burden. I will forsake you," declares the LORD.'

So, from the start Malachi's message is presented as one that rebukes his audience. It is also described as **the word of the LORD.** Throughout the Old Testament this denotes divine revelation. Only rarely is the expression 'word of God' found (Judg. 3:20; 1 Sam. 9:27; 2 Sam. 16:23; 1 Kgs. 12:22; 1 Chr. 17:3), because the message is that of the covenant LORD who reveals himself to his people through his prophets. In the heading of this book the claim is being made that what follows is not a message of merely human origin, but one that has been divinely disclosed as a means of directing and recalling God's people to himself.

**To Israel** indicates that the intended recipients are specifically the covenant people. This message originates from the post-exilic period when the distinction between the northern kingdom of Israel and the southern kingdom of Judah was no longer operative. Israel, the alternative name given to Jacob (Gen. 32:28; 35:10), reverts to being a term to describe all of his descendants from the twelve tribes, or at any rate those of them who have returned to the land of Palestine, and who have the responsibility of living in accordance with LORD's requirements as expressed in the covenant. Indeed in the post-exilic history of Chronicles the covenantal sense of Israel is so established that 'Israel' is used even when the reference is to the former southern kingdom of Judah (2 Chr. 11:3).

**Through Malachi** renders a compound expression 'by the hand of Malachi', which indicates that the prophet is the human instrument that the LORD has used to bring this message to his people (Hag. 1:1; 2:1). The prophet is represented as a mediatorial figure, a channel of communication, who accepts the message and passes it on, just as Moses had put words in Aaron's mouth so that Aaron had become his prophet (Ex. 4:14-16; 7:1-2). This description fits in well with the fact that so much of the prophecy consists of the LORD addressing the people.

Malachi is a Hebrew word meaning 'my messenger', and many have supposed it was taken from 3:1 to indicate the author of what is really an anonymous work. (This is often linked to the proposal that the Minor Prophets originally ended with three anonymous burdens [Zech. 9:1; 12:1; Mal. 1:1], of which the last was mistakenly attributed to 'my messenger' understood as a person Malachi, and the others to Zechariah.) The name Malachi appears nowhere else in the Old Testament, and also the personal details (his father's name or place of birth) which might have been expected are omitted. Further there is early evidence to suggest that the word was not treated as a name. The Greek version used the translation 'his messenger' and early Jewish sources identified him as Ezra the scribe.

Such objections are not without weight, but are hardly conclusive. Of the twelve minor prophets Obadiah, Habakkuk and Haggai as well as Malachi have given us no personal information in their titles, and while Amos, Micah and Nahum tell us where they come from, they do not include genealogical data. The others do all, however, give their names at the beginning of their books, and that certainly leads us to expect a proper name here, though not necessarily with any further details. Though the name Malachi is unattested elsewhere, in form it is a possible Hebrew name. It may be shortened from Malachiah, 'messenger of the LORD', if it is not a full name in its own right.

But of Malachi himself we know no more than his name. However, on the basis of the contents of the book, it is possible to come to some conclusions as to when he lived and ministered. He clearly lived in Judah after the exile. There is the reference in 1:8 to the 'governor' representing the Persians. The temple has been rebuilt. This was completed in 515 B.C., and sufficient time must be allowed to pass for circumstances to have changed and malpractices in temple worship to have arisen. Malachi does not speak of recent innovations, but of evils that had become commonplace through use and wont.

*Declaration (1:2a).* Although a 'burden' (see on 1:1), the prophecy does not begin with threats of impending judgment, but with a tender reminder to the Jews of the reality of their situation. They are Israel, the covenant people, and so they are what they are because of God's attitude towards them. The LORD confronts them with the reality of his love, which is the basis of their obligation towards him. **"I have loved you," says the LORD (1:2).** The Hebrew means something like 'I have loved you in the past and still do.' The LORD's love stretched right back to the start of their national history. 'It was because the LORD loved you and kept the oath he swore to your forefathers that he brought you out with a mighty hand and redeemed you from the land of slavery, from the power of Pharaoh king of Egypt' (Deut. 7:8). This sovereign love of God was based solely on what he desired and determined. It did not result from the size of the people (Deut. 7:7) or any attractive qualities that they would display. 'Love', however, points to more than divine choice. It points to the closeness and intensity of the relationship that has been divinely initiated. 'The LORD appeared to us in the past, saying: "I have loved you with an everlasting love; I have drawn you with loving-kindness"' (Jer. 31:3; see also Hos. 11:3-4). It was also a love that demanded the response of willing conformity to his will. 'If you pay attention to these laws and are careful to follow them, then the LORD your God will keep his covenant of love with you, as he swore to your forefathers. He will love you and bless you and increase your numbers' (Deut. 7:12-13).

*Counter-question (1:2b).* But the people are not willing to recognise that God loves them. **But you ask, 'How have you loved us?'** It need not be supposed that they actually said this. What is being done is verbalising their inner attitude, an attitude of which they themselves may not have been totally conscious. It is similar to that of the expert in the law who 'wanted to justify himself' (Lk. 10:29). He thought he knew it all, and the people of Malachi's day were certain they knew more about the reality of their situation than God did.

'How?' is more literally, 'In what?' or 'Wherein?'. It occurs again in 1:6, 7; 2:17; 3:7, 8 and in a different form in 3:13. It is the catch phrase of their litany of defiance. They were not asking for precise specification of how the LORD had shown his love in the distant past. It was their own situation that concerned them. 'If God still loves us, how come things are like this?' As the people of God who had been given such great promises by the prophets, they wanted to know why none of them had been realised. The Temple had been built, but the nations were not streaming to it (Zech. 8:20-22). 'The city was large and spacious, but there were few people in it' (Neh. 7:4): what had happened to the promise of it being 'without walls because of the great number of men and livestock in it' (Zech. 2:4)? There was a Persian governor ruling over them: where was the great victory the LORD was going to win for them (Zech. 9:14-15)?

The community was disillusioned, discouraged, doubting, and cynical. It is a measure of the extent of polarisation between them and God that this is the first of 27 questions that the NIV identifies in Malachi's 55 verses. That is an average of just over one question every two verses. The relationship between God and the people was confrontational, as he probed their loyalty and they questioned the value of serving him. If God loves us, where is the evidence to prove it? Perhaps all the promises and visions of the prophets were no more than religious talk, without substance. Where are the hard facts to back up the claim that God loves us?

There were two deep-seated factors influencing their attitude.

*(1)* They had lost any sense of wonder at what God had done for them. They had failed to obey the injunction, 'Only be careful, and watch yourselves closely so that you do not forget the things your eyes have seen or let them slip from your heart as long as you live. Teach them to your children and to their children after them' (Deut. 4:9; see also 1 John 3:1). It was not just a matter of remembering what had happened in the days of Moses. They had not grasped what had

been given them in the return from Babylon and the rebuilding of the Temple. They could not see what they already had. All they knew was they did not have all they wanted—and unfortunately what they wanted was defined in increasingly worldly terms.

(2) Their religion had become formal. As long as the outward rites and ceremonies were performed, they were satisfied and thought well of themselves. They offered sacrifices (1:7, 8, 13); they professed repentance (2:13; 3:14); and they came before the LORD with vows (1:14). But at no point in the prophecy is there any hint that their religion went any deeper than that, or that they engaged in self-criticism. If things were not as they expected, it had to be God's fault. The thought that their behaviour might have affected the situation never crossed their minds. They had forgotten the injunction of Moses: 'And now, O Israel, what does the LORD your God ask of you but to fear the LORD your God, to walk in all his ways, to love him, to serve the LORD your God with all your heart and with all your soul, and to observe the LORD's commands and decrees that I am giving you today for your own good?' (Deut. 10:12-13).

Despite their disrespectful and irreverent attitude, the LORD deals gently with them, so as to bring them to see the danger they were in. He reacts to their complaint that they had been forgotten by him, virtually abandoned by him, by giving a lesson from history to prove his love. **"Was not Esau Jacob's brother?" the LORD says.** The question implies a positive answer, 'Of course he was!' 'Brother' comes first in the Hebrew order to emphasise the close bond between the twin sons of Isaac and Rebekah (Gen. 25:25-26). Esau is named first because he was the firstborn and had the right to the inheritance. But God had determined otherwise. Before they were born, he had told Rebekah, 'Two nations are in your womb, and two peoples from within you will be separated; one people will be stronger than the other, and the older will serve the younger' (Gen. 25:23).

**Yet I have loved Jacob, but Esau I have hated (1:3).** This carefully structured expression is unfortunately split across the verse division. The order of the NIV reflects that of the Hebrew in placing Jacob and Esau together to emphasise the different attitude of God towards them. God did not treat them as custom would have dictated, giving preference to the elder. It was with Jacob, despite his opportunism and deceit, that the LORD renewed the covenant promises he had made to Abraham and Isaac (Gen. 28:13-15; 35:11-12). By sovereign choice the LORD chose Jacob and saved him. He also made him the one through whom his covenantal purposes for Abraham's descendants and for the world would be advanced. 'All peoples on earth will be blessed through you and your offspring' (Gen. 28:14).

But what of Esau? In particular, how are we to understand the word 'hate'? At first it seems incongruous to talk of God hating, because our ideas of hatred are contaminated by the malice and bitterness of its sinful human expression. But Scripture has no difficulty in affirming that God hates (Ps. 5:5; Prov. 8:13; Isa. 1:14; 61:8; Jer. 44:4; Hos. 9:15; Amos 5:10, 21; Zech. 8:17). In Psalm 11:5 the inwardness and intensity of this holy revulsion is expressed by saying 'the wicked and those who love violence *his soul* hates', and Proverbs 6:16-19 gives a catalogue of the behaviour that arouses the LORD's hatred.

Many, however, find difficulty in ascribing this hatred not to God's reaction against sinful actions, but to Esau as an individual. Instead they argue that here we have an instance of a Hebrew idiom in which a direct opposite is used to express a lesser degree of comparison. When God says, 'I desire mercy, not sacrifice' (Hos. 6:6), this is not to be taken as meaning that God does not desire sacrifice, and therefore dissociates himself from the Old Testament system of worship. The rest of the verse—'acknowledgment of God *rather than* burnt offerings'—makes it clear that this is a statement of priorities, and not the absolute exclusion of one thing in favour of another. The sentiment corresponds exactly to Samuel's 'to obey is better than sacrifice' (1 Sam. 15:22).

In the same way it is possible in Hebrew to use 'hate' to mean 'love less'. It is said concerning Jacob that of his two wives 'he loved Rachel more than Leah' (Gen. 29:30), but in further reflecting on the same situation Leah is said to be hated (Gen. 29:31, 33. NIV: 'not loved'). The same Hebrew idiom lies behind Luke 14:26, 'If anyone comes to me and does not *hate* his father and mother, his wife and children, his brothers and sisters—yes, even his own life—he cannot be my disciple'; yet in the parallel passage in Matthew 10:37 we find, 'Anyone who *loves* his father or mother *more* than me is not worthy of me; anyone who *loves* his son or daughter *more* than me is not worthy of me'.

But it is difficult to understand 'hate' as being used in a lesser, comparative sense here. It is directly contrasted with 'love'. The consequences that are spelled out in the punishment and devastation of verses 3 and 4 are not a matter of 'loving less'. Nor does Paul understand the matter in that way when he cites these words in Romans 9:13 to show how God sovereignly makes a difference in electing Jacob and passing by Esau. His mercy does not derive from any commendable qualities in the one loved. It is an absolute act of his sovereign choice. It cannot be talked of in terms of 'more' or 'less'. It either is or is not. It is not a matter of ranking or priority. It is a Yes/No, on/off matter. It is not something that we can explain, but rather we are to wonder at the riches of God's glory made known to the objects of his mercy (Rom. 9:23).

But the argument in Malachi moves beyond the fact of God's choice of Jacob and his passing by of Esau to the implications of that for their descendants. God's covenant dealings are not only with individuals but also corporately with their descendants. He had promised to Abraham 'to be your God and the God of your descendants after you' (Gen. 17:7). This promise is renewed through the covenant. It does not automatically confer eternal salvation on an individual in the covenant community, but it does bring them into a position of inestimable privilege whereby God shows 'love to a thousand generations of those who love me and keep my commandments' (Ex. 20:6), which if rightly improved on, leads to eternal life.

But it also has its darker side. God punishes 'the children for the sin of the fathers to the third and fourth generation of those who hate me' (Ex. 20:5). It does not mean that their children are necessarily eternally lost, but that they have a legacy of spiritual deprivation, not being brought up 'in the training and instruction of the Lord' (Eph. 6:4). Esau, left outside the realm of privilege, showed himself to be 'godless' since he 'for a single meal sold his inheritance rights as the oldest son' (Heb. 12:16). This godless heritage he passed on to his children, and it worked itself out in their wickedness and opposition to the LORD and his people.

Esau went to live in the land of Seir (Gen. 32:3; 36), located to the south of the Dead Sea. The Edomites, the descendants of Esau (for the name Edom see Genesis 25:30), settled in the rugged territory that stretched from there to the Gulf of Aqaba. At the time of the Exodus, they refused the Israelites permission to travel through their territory along the trade-route known as the king's highway (Num. 20:14-21). Despite this, Israel was forbidden to abhor an Edomite (Deut. 23:7-8). Edom was conquered by David (2 Sam. 8:11-14), but there was on-going strife from the time of Solomon (1 Kgs. 11:14-22). When Jerusalem was captured in 586 B.C., the Edomites rejoiced and joined in the destruction (Ps. 137:7; Ob. 11-14). The prophets foretold that judgment would come on Edom because of their enmity against Judah (Jer. 49:7-22; Lam. 4:21-22; Ezk. 25:12-14).

**And I have turned his mountains into a wasteland and left his inheritance to the desert jackals.** This was the result of the absence of God's sustaining love. The people are left to their own resources, and so as fallen human beings inevitably plunge into wickedness. Because of God's judgment against Edom for its wickedness, the territory that was theirs had been devastated. 'A desolate waste' was a major theme of Ezekiel's prophecy concerning Edom (Ezk. 35:9). The desert jackals are found elsewhere in scenes of divine judgment (Jer. 9:11; 10:22; 49:33; 51:37; Ps. 44:19).

When did this occur? Edom did not share Judah's fate in the events of 586 B.C. Rather Edom joined in those who rejoiced over Judah and Jerusalem. Although Nebuchadnezzar did later (582 B.C.) invade Ammon and Moab, there is no record of him then having invaded Edom. Invaders from the desert, Nabatean Arabs, ransacked Edomite territory and forced them to move. Small groups of survivors settled in the Negev, to the south of Judah, during the period between the fifth century B.C. and 315 B.C. when we know that the Nabateans were in full control of the territory. The mention of this here suggests it was of recent occurrence in Malachi's day.

**Edom may say, "Though we have been crushed, we will rebuild the ruins"** (*1:4*). In their self-confidence Edom may well express the desire to reverse the calamity that has overtaken it and restore its national fortunes despite the devastating blows of their enemies. But without God's help, the exercise was doomed to failure. It will meet with the direct opposition of God. **But this is**

**what the LORD Almighty says: "They may build, but I will demolish."** Let the Jews take note of the fact that God had restored them to their land, and had promised them future blessing in it, if only they would live faithfully. He who has control over everything (see on Zech. 1:3) will tear down whatever they may set up in their efforts to restore their fortunes (Ps. 127:1; Lam. 3:37).

**They will be called the Wicked Land, a people always under the wrath of the LORD.** Edom's fate and guilt are related. Sin had left its mark on them. It had been allowed to grow unchecked, and they came under the judgment of God for what they had done. God's attitude towards Jacob and Esau is not co-ordinate in every respect. Faith is not the meriting cause of election, but Edom's sin is the meriting cause of their punishment. 'Always' indicates that they are permanently designated God's enemies. As a wicked country they will be subject to God's judgment. There is a contrast between their land and the 'holy land' (Zech. 2:12). Judah should be thankful for God's love to her.

**You will see it with your own eyes and say, 'Great is the LORD—even beyond the borders of Israel!'** (*1:5*). If they had not been so self-centred in their thinking, Israel would already have been aware of what God was doing. Now they are told that they will become unquestionably aware of how he acts, and so will be in receipt of an answer to their own impertinent question. The proof is something they will experience themselves, and they will be brought to confess the greatness of the LORD, which may be seen even outwith Israel in what he does to their enemies. There is also a hint of the freedom of God to choose or reject, and what he has done in other lands is not without implications for the conduct of Israel! If Israel were more outward looking, she would be aware of the LORD's hand at work elsewhere, and be able to assess what was happening to her. This is one of a number of places in Malachi's prophecy which indicate that God's plan is wider than the Jews (1:11, 14; 3:12). If they recapture the spirit of true gratitude for what the LORD has done for them, then they will be in a position to praise the LORD (Ps. 35:27; 40:16; 58:10-11; 83:17).

God's love for his people was unquestionably evident in their history. But it is a love that demands a response. The problem in Malachi's day was that an appropriate reaction had not been forthcoming from the people. The Jews were treating the LORD's covenant favour towards them as something that should automatically shower blessings on them, but they failed to appreciate their own responsibility. They were taken up with themselves, and not with pleasing the God who had saved them. The same type of attitude often still affects God's people. There can be no doubt about God's love. He has irrefutably demonstrated it by sending his Son. We then wonder why when we have received the ultimate gift, the church is not vibrant, attracting crowds and being effective in its moral and spiritual impact on our country. Why is there not revival? We must be careful not to fall into the way of thinking that it is because of some deficiency in God's love. Rather we are to question our response to his love. The fortunes of the church are blighted by the lack of Christ-centredness in the thinking and acting of those who are in his church. We ought to examine ourselves and expose what warps our thinking and respond with that total self-dedication that flows from recognising what his love has given us (Eph. 5:8-20).

*Study Questions*

**1:2** What role should self-examination play in our lives? Lam. 3:40; Mt. 7:3-5; 1 Cor. 11:28; 2 Cor. 13:5; Gal. 6:4.

**1:3** The doctrine of God's election, and his passing by or reprobation, is taught in Scripture. How ought we to respond to it? Lk. 10:20; Acts 13:38; Rom. 9; 11:5; Eph. 1:4-5; 2 Thess. 2:13; 1 Pet. 2:8; 2 Pet. 1:3-11.

**1:5** In what ways may we be blind to the blessings God has given to us?

## Malachi 1:6-14:  Blemished Worship

In the second disputation Malachi exposes the flaws in the worship of the covenant community. It was their highest privilege to serve the LORD who had saved them, but because they had lost sight of his love and the blessings he had bestowed on them, they had no real desire to praise him, and their worship had become sterile and corrupt. Both people and priests were at fault in the matter (Hos. 4:7-9), but it is principally against the priests that charges are levelled, because they were responsible for the conduct of worship in the Temple.

*The Accusation (1:6a,b).*  First of all the prophet states on behalf of God the area of their living which is deficient. **A son honours his father, and a servant his master (*1:6*).**  We might have expected 'a son loves his father', but it was a generally accepted social norm throughout the ancient East that honour and respect were due to parents even before love and affection.  The requirement to show respect had been reinforced for Israel by the covenant commands of God (Ex. 20:12; Lev. 19:3).  'Servant' here may describe either a free-born indentured labourer (Ex. 21:2) or a slave who is his master's property (Ex. 21:20-21).  They too were expected to recognise the difference in social position between themselves and their masters, and show them appropriate respect.  So by expressing truths which no one would deny, an attempt is made to gain an initial hearing from people who refused to accept that there was anything wrong with their own behaviour.  At least there could be agreement about the standards of behaviour expected from others.

The LORD continues by presenting them with a choice as to how they viewed their relationship with him—as a father or as a master. In either case the same conclusion could be drawn. **"If I am a father, where is the honour due to me? If I am a master, where is the respect due to me?" says the LORD Almighty.**  The relationship between the LORD and his people had frequently been presented in terms of a father and son.  'Is he not your Father, your Creator, who made you and formed you?' (Deut. 32:6; see also Isa. 63:16; 64:8; Jer. 3:4, 19).  Similarly, the people were called his sons.  'Israel is my firstborn son. ... Let my son go' (Ex. 4:22-23; Isa. 1:2; Jer. 31:9; Hos. 11:1).  The master-servant relationship is not used so often in this connection, but see Psalm 123:2 and Isaiah 26:13 and 42:19. Whichever way they thought of him, on the analogy of the human relationship, the people ought to have accorded God proper respect.

The word 'honour' is frequently translated 'glory' when used in connection with God. His glory is the visible expression of his intrinsic attributes and can be seen in the created realm he has made. 'The heavens declare the glory of God; the skies proclaim the work of his hands' (Ps. 19:1). To honour or glorify the LORD is to acknowledge these attributes as his and his alone, and to accord him the reputation and praise that are rightfully his for being what he is. 'Ascribe to the LORD, O mighty ones, ascribe to the LORD glory and strength. Ascribe to the LORD the glory due to his name; worship the LORD in the splendour of his holiness' (Ps. 29:1-2). The word rendered 'respect' here is ordinarily used of being afraid or terror-stricken. 'He is *the one you are to fear*, he is the one you are to dread' (Isa. 8:13). But in Malachi (here and in 2:5) it is used in the sense of 'reverence', to refer to the godly regard and respect that characterises the faithful as they put their confidence in their covenant God (see 4:2). Such honour and respect were missing from the worship of Malachi's day because there was no true appreciation of what the God they professed to worship was really like.

It is difficult to be sure whether the priests alone have been addressed since the beginning of the verse, but now they are singled out for mention because it was their attitude that was setting the tone of worship in the Temple. **It is you, O priests, who show contempt for my name.** The 'name' of God (also found in 1:11 [three times], 14; 2:2, 5; 4:2) stands for the whole of his revelation of who he is (Ps. 22:22). That teaching, given through those sent by God in the past and through all that he had done for their nation, was now being spurned by the current generation of those whose privilege it was to be custodians of that truth (Rom. 3:1-2). This was a problem that had been encountered in the past (Jer. 23:11; Ezk. 22:26). Perhaps their familiarity with the truth of God led them to treat it (and him) as ordinary and of no great account. Contrary to the revelation God had given of himself, they were doubting if he was really able to make any great difference in their lives (Isa. 5:18-19; Zeph. 1:12).

*The Protestation of Innocence (1:6c).* The priests do not recognise themselves in the charge that is brought against them. **But you ask, 'How have we shown contempt for your name?'** That they were genuinely unaware of their shortcomings is obvious, but 'hidden faults' (Ps. 19:12) are, as David saw, none the less culpable for that. This is particularly so when these faults had arisen because they had allowed their consciences to become spiritually insensitive despite the revelation that had been entrusted to them. Greater privilege involves greater accountability (Lk. 12:48).

*The Evidence (1:7a).* **You place defiled food on my altar (*1:7*).** The stress is on something that is continually done. The word rendered 'place' conveys the idea of 'cause to approach', and is used in a wide variety of ways. In particular it can refer both to an individual bringing an offering to the priests ('presented' in Ex. 32:6 or Lev. 8:14) and to the priests' action in subsequently presenting the sacrifice before God ('present' in Lev. 2:8). In this verse it is obviously used of the priests. 'Food' may apply to animal or cereal offerings, but here it is mainly the former that are in view (2:8) as they are presented as offerings by fire on the altar (Lev. 21:6; Ezk. 44:7). What might properly be offered to the LORD was strictly controlled. 'Defiled food' does not refer to the many types of animal that were designated unclean and not to be eaten (Lev. 11:1-47; Deut. 14:3-20). It was not a prohibited type of animal that was being brought, but blemished beasts that contravened the regulation, 'Do not bring anything with a defect, because it will not be accepted on your behalf' (Lev. 22:20). It spoke volumes about the inner attitude of the people that they were prepared to bring such animals, and even more about how little regard the priests had for the sanctity of what they were doing that they pronounced them acceptable and offered them in sacrifice. But while the priests accepted them, the LORD did not.

*Renewed Protestation (1:7b).* Again the priests rebut the charges brought against them. **But you ask, 'How have we defiled you?'** It is significant that there is a recognition that defiled offerings would slight the LORD himself. Worship offered to the LORD had to be holy, but the priests were sure that the accusations against them were being exaggerated. To talk of defiling God was so utterly outrageous that it could not possibly be true of them.

*Counter-rebuttal (1:7c-8).* There is a rebuttal of their protestation. **By saying that the LORD's table is contemptible.** It is unlikely they actually uttered these words, but this was the only interpretation that could be offered for the carelessness with which they undertook their duties. Their actions spoke louder than words. Their attitude revealed that inwardly they scorned the worship of the LORD and thought of it as something of no great significance. As it is blood sacrifices that are being discussed, 'table' does not refer to the table of the bread of presence (Ex. 25:23-30) or to the incense altar (Ezk. 41:22). Ezekiel also mentions tables at the entrance to the inner court that were used for slaughtering animals (Ezk. 40:39-43), but it is simplest to take the reference here and in verse 12 to the altar of burnt offering (Ezk. 44:16).

This time there is no further querulous protestation, and the accusations are pressed home. **When you bring blind animals for sacrifice, is that not wrong?** *(1:8).* 'Bring' and 'sacrifice' in the next sentence are the same word as 'place' in 1:7. It is again being used of the priests, but because it was a non-technical word it did not exclude the laity who would also bring sacrificial victims. An animal blind in one or both eyes was definitely disallowed as a sacrifice (Lev. 22:22; Deut. 15:21). **When you sacrifice crippled or diseased animals, is that not wrong?** For 'sacrifice' see preceding comment. A lame or crippled animal was also specifically forbidden (Deut. 15:21). It could be eaten, but not sacrificed. The offering of an animal that was unwell or afflicted by some malady was ruled out by the general rubric that they be without blemish or defect (Lev. 22:25). 'Is that not wrong?' is a rhetorical question, which is asked to make a strong affirmation. There was no doubt that they were acting improperly in deliberately accepting blemished animals. They had such a low view of the LORD and what they were doing in worshipping him that they had no qualms about it. It is that insensitivity that is the more horrifying. Both priests and people were involved, but the priests had the greater blame because they were responsible for monitoring the situation.

To bring home to them the enormity of their behaviour, a comparison with a lesser relationship is employed. None of them ('you' is now singular) would behave in such a fashion to the local governor and expect to get off with it—why then are they trying it with God? **"Try offering them to your governor! Would he be pleased with you? Would he accept you?" says the LORD Almighty.** It is not a theological argument based on the rationale of sacrifice that is used, but an everyday example. This offering may have been a voluntary gift (gifts were used in the East not only to extend thanks, but also to secure future favours). But more probably it was part of the tribute demanded from them. The word 'governor' has an Assyrian origin, and is used of those appointed by foreign rulers. At this time he would have represented the Persians, but he might himself have been a Judean, like Zerubbabel (Hag. 1:1) and Nehemiah (Neh. 5:14). To ease the burden on the people Nehemiah refused the food allotted to the governor (Neh. 5:14-15), which indicates that Malachi was speaking before his arrival. 'Accept you' is literally 'lift up your face', an idiom that perhaps derives from a superior raising one prostrated in obeisance before him. But there is no doubt that the previous governors would have demanded nothing but the best from the people, and rejected the sub-standard as an insult. How much more absurd it was to bring such animals to God himself, and expect acceptance!

We must make sure that we do not give to God only what is left over and unwanted for other purposes. As with his judgment on the offerings of Cain and Abel, the LORD looks first at the person and then at what they offer (Gen. 4:4-6). What is required for true giving is first to give oneself to the Lord (2 Cor. 8:4). It is not the amount of the gift that matters but the spirit in which it is given. 'For if the willingness is there, the gift is acceptable according to what one has, not according to what he does not have' (2 Cor. 8:12; see also Mk. 12:41-44).

**Now (1:9)** draws an ironic inference from the state of affairs that prevailed in the Temple worship. The priests are urged to perform their duties on behalf of the people and **implore God to be gracious to us.** For the idiom 'implore', see comments on 'entreat' at Zechariah 7:2. Prayer to God would often be with a view to him extending mercy, but if they try that the result will not be what they expect. The word used for God here is *El*, which outside the book of Job is rarely applied to the true God without some accompanying epithet, as in *El-Shaddai* in Genesis 17:1 or *El Elohe Israel* in Genesis 33:20. It is probably used here to emphasise the supremacy and might of God in comparison to the power of the civil governor. If they would not get away with such behaviour towards the civil governor, how could they expect to do so with God? **"With such offerings from your hands, will he accept you?"— says the LORD Almighty.** 'Accept' is the same phrase as in verse 8. Arguing from the lesser to the greater shows that they could not expect favour while they were displaying such an outrageous attitude towards the ultimate authority, the LORD Almighty.

The LORD's revulsion at their behaviour is such that he views a closed temple as preferable to the perpetuation of worthless and insulting worship (Isa. 1:12; Jer. 6:20; Amos 5:21-24). **Oh, that one of you would shut the temple doors, so that you would not light useless fires on my altar!** (*1:10*). The doors are the double doors which granted access to the inner court where the altar of burnt offering was. If the doors were shut, sacrifice would be impossible. The fires are 'useless' because the offerings themselves are an insult. As they were not expressing true devotion to the LORD, but were rather a sham, they poisoned rather than furthered the relationship between the people and God.

**"I am not pleased with you," says the LORD Almighty, "and I will accept no offering from your hands".** 'Pleased' denotes that acceptance which comes from delight in an object. God is pleased with and desires inner truth (Ps. 51:6), mercy and acknowledgment of him himself (Hos. 6:6). He also does whatever he pleases (Ps. 115:3; 135:6). Because of their inner alienation, their offerings afforded him no satisfaction. The object of sacrifice was that 'it will be acceptable to the LORD' (Lev. 1:3). But just as the governor would not 'be pleased with' (1:8) them if they brought blemished gifts, so God would not judge what they presented as meeting the required standards (Hos. 8:13; Jer. 14:12; Ezk. 20:40-41; 43:27).

The connection between verses 10 and 11 may be understood in two ways. *(1)* Verse 11 begins with a word often rendered 'for', which would indicate that it expresses the reason for the LORD's rejection of their sacrifices. He is not dependent on Israel for whatever they are prepared to bring to him. He will receive proper worship from elsewhere. *(2)* Alternatively, the introductory particle may be used to emphasise what follows, 'yes, indeed!' It would then mark what follows as an unexpected truth which cuts across the expectation of the priests and people in Jerusalem.

**My name will be great among the nations (*1:11*).** 'Great' occurs four times in this chapter (twice here; 1:5, 14). In contrast to the small and demeaning ideas they entertained of the LORD and his worship, the LORD is great and most worthy of praise (Ps. 48:1; 96:4; 99:2). 'My name' points to the complete revelation that God has given of his character and purpose (1:6). If Israel cannot appreciate it, then there will be others who will display a right and proper attitude to him. 'Among the nations' need not imply that they are all going to be converted to the worship of the LORD. It may just envisage groups here and there magnifying his name. The point is that Jerusalem will no longer be the focus of true worship (Jn. 4:21-24; Acts 13:46). It will be universalised **from the rising to the setting of the sun** (Ps. 22:27; 67:2; 113:3; Isa. 45:6; 59:19). It is unlikely that Malachi is thinking of the Jews of the dispersion scattered throughout surrounding lands. The wall of partition is broken down between Israel and the nations, and the true worship of the LORD has become worldwide.

**In every place incense and pure offerings will be brought to my name.** Acceptable offerings will be brought as opposed to the unworthy sacrifices that Israel was hoping to get away with. 'Offering' is the most general word for gift of any sort. 'Pure' (morally and spiritually as well as physically, 'without blemish') is not used elsewhere in respect of offerings, and here indicates offerings from the accepted categories of animal, brought by persons who were ceremonially clean, and under the whole ritual set out in the law. This would have debarred sacrifice in heathen territory, which was polluted by their idolatry. But the picture is not that of the nations coming to Jerusalem to worship (Isa. 2:3; Zech. 8:20-22), but of their worship being 'in every place'. 'The nations on every shore will worship him, every one in its own land' (Zeph. 2:11; see also Isa. 19:19).

For this to occur, there must first have been a radical change in the conditions prevailing in other lands. **"Because my name will be great among the nations," says the LORD Almighty** looks forward to the conversion of the Gentiles. It certainly does not imply that pagan sacrifices become acceptable to the LORD. It is in acknowledgement of 'my name', as those who know his name and trust in him (Ps. 9:10) and rejoice in all that the LORD of the covenant has revealed himself to be, that their worship is acceptable. But, although the vision granted to Malachi breaks out of the narrow bounds of Jewish exclusiveness and looks forward to the conversion of the nations in accordance with the covenant blessing (Gen. 12:3; Acts 13:47), he is still seeing the worship to be offered in terms of what is prescribed in the law. There is great light in one respect but not in all.

This glimpse of future worship contrasts with the reality obtaining in Jerusalem. The accusation of verses 6-7 is repeated, and the contrast stressed. Perhaps the motive was like that of Paul to arouse his own people to envy in the light of the gospel being brought to the Gentiles (Rom. 11:13-14). **But you profane it by saying of the Lord's table, 'It is defiled', and of its food, 'It is contemptible.'** (*1:12*). The first 'it' refers to the name of the LORD. 'Profane' means the same as 'despise' and 'defile' (1:6-7). To 'profane' is to treat unworthily and so to pollute. To profane God's decrees was to treat them as of no consequence, to violate them and fail to keep his commands (Ps. 89:31). When Zephaniah prophesied shortly before the fall of Jerusalem, the priests were profaning the sanctuary and doing violence to God's law (Zeph. 3:4). Ezekiel spelled out more clearly what was involved in this. 'Her priests do violence to my law and profane my holy things; they do not distinguish between the holy and the common; they teach there is no difference between the unclean and the clean; and they shut their eyes to the keeping of my Sabbaths, so that I am profaned among them' (Ezk. 22:26). The LORD takes action to ensure that his holy name is no longer profaned (Ezk. 39:7). 'The Lord's table' is the altar, as in verse 7. The change from LORD (*Yahweh*) to Lord (*Adonai*) emphasises his sovereign control (see on 3:1) rather than the covenant relationship which the priests are making little of. The priests have no respect for the stipulations of the law, and therefore none for the God who stands behind and gave that law. 'Its food' renders two words 'its fruit, its food'.

There is something more that needs to be said. **"And you say, 'What a burden!' and you sniff at it contemptuously,"** says the LORD Almighty (*1:13*). 'Burden' is not the same word as discussed in 1:1. It indicates how wearisome they found worship (Amos 8:5; Mic. 6:3). The priests were bored with their duties. Having lost sight of the reality of the God they served, the duties allotted to them had become monotonous drudgery. What they were about was trivial and contemptible to them, they could take no interest in it, and just did it because it brought them a living. 'Sniff at it' is a gesture of contempt, perhaps blowing out (rather than in) at it as something so light that it can be removed with a puff of breath. Religion was a matter God took care of and no great effort was called for from them.

**"When you bring injured, crippled or diseased animals and offer them as sacrifices, should I accept them from your hands?"** says the LORD. The same categories of animal are mentioned as in verse 8, except that in place of 'blind' there is now mentioned 'injured'. The word denotes something that has been taken or snatched. It could be an animal mauled by another, or one that has been stolen. An offering of an animal would be meaningless if it did not belong to the offerer. Mauled animals could not be consumed by humans, and were to be thrown to the dogs (Ex. 22:31). The accusation and motivation of verse 8 are repeated. The mere mechanical act of sacrifice is in itself worthless and the LORD would not be impressed with offerings made in such an empty spirit (Mic. 6:6-8).

The next verse looks at the other aspect of the problem—that the people were prepared to bring such offerings, as well as the priests accept them! **Cursed is the cheat who has an acceptable male in his flock and vows to give it, but then sacrifices a blemished animal to the Lord (*1:14*).** A particular example is given of the way the people were behaving in the matter. 'The cheat' is one who acts with deliberate cunning, not inadvertent oversight ('plotted' Gen. 37:18; 'deceived' Num. 25:18; 'conspire' Ps. 105:25). When they made a voluntary vow to God (Num. 30:2), they were not fulfilling it even though they had the means to do so. 'To give it' is an NIV supplement. The vow was quite general, but it was a male that the law specified for such a sacrifice (Lev. 22:19). While there would always be a temptation to forget vows made in moments of stress—and hence the injunction 'Make vows and fulfil them' (Ps. 76:11)—what is envisaged here is fulfilment, but in an unworthy fashion. He could have done it properly, but instead brings a blemished animal, perhaps one that was mutilated or castrated (contrary to Lev. 22:23).

Such behaviour called down the curse of the covenant (see also 2:2 and 3:9) on the cheat. He had approached the LORD and pled for his help, while promising to make an offering as a token of his gratitude. Now he has reneged on the full terms of his commitment. God would not leave such an individual unpunished. In New Testament terms one is reminded of Ananias and Sapphira who pretended to give the whole of the proceeds from selling a plot of land, but in fact kept some back. They had been at liberty to do that. Their offering was voluntary, but they were not prepared to live up to the full extent of the commitment they entered into regarding it (Acts 5:1-11). We must always remember with whom we are dealing in sacred things. 'It is better not to vow than to make a vow and not fulfil it' (Eccl. 5:5).

**"For I am a great king," says the LORD Almighty, "and my name is to be feared among the nations".** 'Feared' echoes the same word translated as 'honour' in 1:6 by the NIV, and the repetition is a device to indicate that this section is coming to a conclusion. 'Jacob's King' (Isa. 41:21; see also Jer. 8:19; Zeph. 3:15), the ruler of Israel, is not only sovereign over the chosen people. He is a 'great king'—a term used by the conquerors of the East when they established mighty empires and had many lesser kings under their sway (2 Kgs. 18: 19, 28). For 'great', see on 1:11. The LORD is 'the great King over all the earth' (Ps. 47:2; 48:2) and 'the great King above all gods' (Ps. 95:3). There is no authority greater than his, and nowhere and no one in heaven or earth lies outwith his domain. Israel should therefore realise the folly and futility of trying to cheat him, and the impiety of worshipping him in a deficient manner. But equally, there is the wider vision renewed from 1:11 that this King does not depend on Israel for his worship. He ought to be feared among the nations of the earth (Ps. 102:15; Rev. 15:4), and the time would come when that would be realised.

We no longer sacrifice animals to God. The blood offerings of the Law prefigured that of Christ, and now that he has offered the final sacrifice, they are done away with (Heb. 10:9). But Scripture still uses the language of sacrifice for the New Testament church, which consists of 'a holy priesthood, offering spiritual sacrifices acceptable to God through Jesus Christ' (1 Pet. 2:5). 'Through Jesus, therefore, let us continually offer to God a sacrifice of praise—the fruit of lips that confess his name. And do not forget to do good and to share with others, for with such sacrifices God is pleased' (Heb. 13:15-16; see also Rom. 12:1; Phil. 4:18). We must take care that such sacrifices are acceptable to God, not being offered in any way that we think will suffice, but in the way God requires and is pleased with.

*Study Questions*

**1:6** How may we identify, and counteract, formalism in the worship of God? Ps. 51:16-17; Isa. 29:13-16; Mt. 9:13; 12:7; 15:8-9; Lk. 13:24-27; 1 Cor. 7:19; Phil. 3:4-7; 2 Tim. 3:1-5.

**1:9** What 'sacrifices' is the Christian expected to make? Mic. 6:7-8; Lk. 6:35-36; 9:57-61; 18:22; Gal. 6:10; Phil 4:18; 1 Thess. 5:15.
    How may such sacrifices be presented in a way that is acceptable to God? Hos. 14:2; Rom. 14:18; 2 Cor. 8:12; Col. 3:16-17; 1 Pet. 4:11.

**1:11** Are the righteous in every nation pleasing to the LORD? Acts 11:9, 18; 17:27; Rom. 2:9-15; 3:22-23. Is the worship of the heathen when offered sincerely acceptable to him? 1 Cor. 10:20; Eph. 4:17-19; 5:12.

### Malachi 2:1-9:  The LORD's Rebuke
In the previous section Malachi had exposed the corrupt motivation that had led to Israel's worship of the LORD becoming a mockery. Now he addresses the priesthood particularly. If the exposure of their (and the people's) behaviour does not cause them to amend their ways, then warnings will turn into judgment. The LORD cannot let the

situation that has arisen continue with impunity, and will act to vindicate the honour of his name. The priests should be in no doubt that their violation of their covenant obligations would be punished.

*The Solemn Warning (2:1-4).* **And now (2:1)** indicates that what follows is a consequence of the behaviour described in the preceding section. **This admonition is for you, O priests.** The word 'admonition' is ordinarily translated 'order' or 'command'. It may be that this command refers to the curse and rebuke mentioned in the following verses as having been already ordained for the priests. This is what the LORD has commanded is going to happen to them (Nah. 1:14). Alternatively, since the word is repeated in 2:4 and might there be understood as the command that the covenant of Levi continue, it could here refer prospectively to the maintenance of the regulations affecting the priests specified in 2:5-7. 'Command' is sometimes used in a similar way to refer to what is required of a king (1 Sam. 13:13) or of a prophet (1 Kgs. 13:21). But the NIV understands the command to be the general one that arises from the situation that is described and requires an appropriate response from the priests. If they do not take these warnings to heart and repent, then disaster will inevitably come upon them. Hence it is rendered 'admonition'.

The priesthood had been divinely ordained, and therefore they were required to be faithful to the duties God had prescribed for them. **"If you do not listen, and if you do not set your heart to honour my name," says the LORD Almighty (2:2)** exhibits the disobedience that will provoke judgment. 'Listen' refers to the teaching set out for the priests in the law and also to the warnings given about their present conduct. 'Set your heart' is a phrase reminiscent of Haggai's 'consider' (Hag. 1:5, 7; 2:18). The reformation required had to affect their inner being. It was not just a matter of technical details of the rituals they engaged in. For 'to honour my name', see on 1:6. They must desire in their hearts to be faithful to God's self-revelation and to promote his cause. The way in which the condition is stated and the conclusion come to indicate that the priests' behaviour currently fell short of what was satisfactory. However, they did still have an opportunity to remedy the situation. The expression reflects that of the covenant curse in Deuteronomy 28:15, 'However, if you do not

obey the LORD your God and do not carefully follow all his commands
and decrees I am giving you today, all these curses will come upon
you and overtake you.' **I will send a curse upon you** is almost an
exact quotation of Deuteronomy 28:20. 'Send' is an intensive form
of the verb and so may be translated 'hurl' or 'let loose'. A curse,
literally 'the curse' (all the devastation of God's righteous judgment)
is the inevitable counterpart of the covenant blessing. It comes into
force because the requirements of the covenant have been ignored.

**And I will curse your blessings** might refer to divine action to
negate the priestly blessing that they were authorised to pronounce
over the people in the name of the LORD (Num. 6:22-27), or to a loss
of the material advantages that accrued to the priests in the exercise
of their office (Num. 18:8-21; Deut. 18:1). The use of covenant
language in the passage suggests that 'blessings' is more comprehensive than either of those, and includes all that came to the priests
through the covenant with Levi—their office, its functions and its
rewards. These would all come under the blight of divine disapproval. Indeed it had already happened. **Yes, I have already cursed
them because you have not set your heart to honour me.** The
misfortunes they were already experiencing were not some random
adversity but the chastening of God to recall them to a proper attitude
to himself.

There are three aspects to the curse that is pronounced.

*(1)* It is difficult to be certain of the translation of **because of you
I will rebuke your descendants (2:3).** 'Descendants' are literally
'seed', and this is used both of physical offspring and of crops.
'Rebuke your seed' might well mean 'blight your corn' (NIV
footnote). 'Rebuke' as part of the covenant curse (Deut. 28:20) could
include agricultural disaster (Deut. 28:18, 22-24, 38). But the covenant curses also affected their children. 'The fruit of your womb will
be cursed' (Deut. 18:18). 'Your sons and daughters will be given to
another nation, and you will wear out your eyes watching for them
day after day, powerless to lift a hand' (Deut. 28:32). Perhaps the
implication here is that the rebuke of God is so effective that they will
not have descendants. There will be total destruction because of the
LORD's wrath against their conduct.

*(2)* **I will spread on your faces the offal from your festival**

sacrifices. 'Offal' is repeated in Hebrew for emphasis, and refers to the part of the animal that was to be burned outside the camp (Lev. 4:11-12). It would include the dung and the entrails. It would be a gross indignity to be smeared with that, and cause intense humiliation. But its main significance is that it would render the priests ceremonially unfit and unclean, so that they could not perform their duties.

*(3)* **And you will be carried off with it.** The Hebrew text here has an impersonal expression, 'one will lift you to it', probably indicating to the place where the offal was discarded. The idea seems to be that they will be degraded from the sanctuary to the dungheap. As they thought so little of being in God's presence, they will be judicially deprived of appearing in the Temple.

**And you will know** *(2:4)* indicates that when judgment falls on them, the priests will come to understand what it was that the LORD had done, and why—but it would be too late. **That I have sent you this admonition** implies that the warning being conveyed by Malachi was with the intention that the priests would accept the rebuke and repent. All Biblical warnings are similarly positive in their aim (Ezk. 18:31-32). **"So that my covenant with Levi may continue," says the LORD Almighty.** If they acted properly, then the covenant would continue in the sense that its blessings would be enjoyed. Disobedience would bring the curse and the abrogation of the covenant. All evil priests had to amend their way or be swept away so that God who is true to his covenant commitment would be able righteously to continue the covenant with Levi.

*The Covenant with Levi (2:5-7).* The Old Testament does not provide a formal description of the establishment of a covenant with Levi. In this connection Levi refers to the tribe rather than the son of Jacob, who is generally presented in an unfavourable light (Gen. 29:34; 34:25-26; 49:5-7). The tribe came to prominence in the days of Moses and Aaron, who belonged to it, when all the Levites rallied to Moses' side after the incident of the golden calf (Ex. 32:26-29). Moses told them they had been set apart (Ex. 32:29). In Deuteronomy 10:8-9 Israel was told how God had set the tribe of Levi apart, and they are commended for guarding the covenant (Deut. 33:9).

Jeremiah 33:20-21 mentions a covenant with Levi, presumably made at some point early in the history of the people, and Nehemiah talks of 'the covenant of the priesthood and of the Levites' (Neh. 13:29). Probably this is a way of referring to all the stipulations made regarding the tribe, such as Numbers 3:44-50. Numbers 18:19 refers to 'an everlasting covenant of salt' in connection with the offerings for priests and Levites. There is also a 'covenant of peace' mentioned in Numbers 25:11-13, made with Phinehas, Aaron's son, who was zealous for the honour of his God (Ps. 106:28-31). In Malachi's day the priests had sadly fallen away from the example he had shown.

Malachi (like Deuteronomy) does not distinguish between the priests and the Levites, nor does he mention the high priest. The priests had been at first the sons of Aaron (Lev. 8:1-4) and later more narrowly the sons of Zadok (Ezk. 44:15). The other members of the tribe of Levi served as temple attendants. Malachi addresses all who were engaged in the work of the Temple.

**My covenant was with him, a covenant of life and peace (2:5).** 'Him' is the tribe. 'A covenant of life and peace' is found only here, though 'covenant of peace' is found elsewhere (Num. 25:12; Isa. 54:10; Ezk. 34:25; 37:26). 'Life and peace' summarise the covenant blessings that would be bestowed by the LORD. 'Life' is not merely health or length of days, but the total fulfilment of all one's potential that comes from enjoying the favour of God (Deut. 30:15-20). With him is the fountain of life (Ps. 36:9), which stretches beyond this world to 'everlasting life' (Dan. 12:2). Though 'peace' is basically absence of strife and warfare, it is frequently a much wider concept than that, encompassing all aspects of one's welfare. The individual whom the LORD blesses, keeps and is gracious to, is the one who knows peace (Num. 6:24-26). 'You will keep in perfect peace him whose mind is steadfast, because he trusts in you' (Isa. 26:3). These are what the LORD as the covenant suzerain undertook to provide for his vassal. **And I gave them to him.** The LORD did in fact fulfil his covenant obligations towards the tribe of Levi.

But there was another side to the covenant. There were obligations that the vassal had to fulfil if he was to continue to enjoy the protection and blessing of his overlord. **This called for reverence** describes the attitude of respect and holy regard the priests ought to

have towards God (1:6). It would be evidenced by a careful performance of the duties he assigned them, and that had in fact happened in
the past. **And he revered me and stood in awe of my name.** This
contrast with the behaviour that was in evidence in Malachi's day
increased their guilt, and deprived them of the excuse that they were
doing as well as any ever had done in living up to the commands of God.

More detail is given about the way in which past generations of
priests had performed their duty.

*(1)* **True instruction was in his mouth** *(2:6).* The emphasis is
not on their cultic duties, but on their role as instructors of the people.
It was one of the primary functions of the priests and Levites to 'teach
the Israelites all the decrees the LORD has given them through Moses'
(Lev. 10:11). The people 'must act according to the decisions they
give you ... Be careful to do everything they direct you to do. Act
according to the law they teach you and the decisions they give you'
(Deut. 17:10-11). When in the past the priests had been faithful to
their divine remit, their teaching was 'true', that is, dependable and
reliable. That was because it was based on the revelation of 'the God
of truth' (Ps. 31:5), whose laws, commands and words are true (Ps.
119:142, 151, 160). When the people wanted to know how to live to
please God and sought guidance from the priests as the LORD's
appointed teachers (Ezk. 44:23-24), they were directed in accordance
with God's law. It was 'in their mouths', that is, the priests did not
only know, but were ready to communicate it. **And nothing false
was found on his lips.** Their teaching had nothing contrary to God's
will mixed in with it. 'False' relates to what was unrighteous or
wicked, what deviated from God's standards. There were no half-
truths or distortions of the law.

*(2)* The priests had been effective leaders in the community
because they themselves lived by God's law. They did not just teach
it. **He walked with me in peace and uprightness** continues the
description of what was true of the tribe of Levi as a whole at their
best, and what still constituted the norm for Malachi's day. In their
private living as well as their public ministry they lived as those in
communion with God. Walking is an idiom frequently found in
Hebrew, based on the idea that life is a journey. 'Walking with' God
is a rarely used description of living in close fellowship with him

(Gen. 5:22; 6:9). It is more intimate than 'walking before' him, with an awareness of his presence and scrutiny (Gen. 17:1), or 'walking after', 'following him', acknowledging his guidance and leadership (Deut. 8:19; 13:4; 2 Kgs. 23:3; Jer. 7:9; Hos. 11:10). 'Peace' refers to full harmony with the will of God. 'Uprightness' points to the integrity of their behaviour. There were no negative influences in their personal or official relationship with God.

*(3)* Their ministry was blessed. **And turned many from sin.** There was an inevitable impact from their personal piety and scrupulous fulfilment of their official duties on their effectiveness as moral and spiritual guardians of the people. 'Sin', or 'iniquity', is much broader than technical infringement of the ceremonial law. It was used in connection with all acts that were crooked or perverse in God's sight (see also on Zech. 3:4). 'Turned' refers both to 'turning away' from misbehaviour that was contemplated and to 'turning back' those who had sinned into the paths of covenant rectitude.

What they had done was in accordance with the standards expected of them. **For the lips of a priest ought to preserve knowledge (2:7).** The knowledge referred to is that of God's revealed will. Moses had said of the tribe of Levi, 'He teaches your precepts to Jacob and your law to Israel' (Deut. 33:10). Practical examples of this can be seen in the reign of the reforming king Jehoshaphat (873-848 B.C.) when he sent princes, priests and Levites with the Book of the Law of the LORD on an itinerant preaching programme throughout Judah (2 Chr. 17:7-9), and later in the way in which the Levites assisted Ezra by translating the message so that the ordinary people could understand it (Neh. 8:8-9). But Hosea's testimony was that in his day (late eighth century B.C.) in the northern kingdom the priests had rejected such knowledge of the LORD, and without sound teaching the people were being destroyed from lack of knowledge (Hos. 4:6). **And from his mouth men should seek instruction.** The people were obligated to do this in cases of difficulty (Deut. 17:10-11), and the implication is that it will not be in vain that they seek the LORD's guidance from a faithful and upright priest. Ezra who 'devoted himself to the study and observance of the Law of the LORD, and to teaching its decrees and laws in Israel' (Ezr. 7:10) illustrates what should have been the norm for the priests.

**Because he is the messenger of the LORD Almighty.** The priest's ability in this respect is grounded in the fact that he is the duly authorised and commissioned representative of God, who can pass on his message. The term 'messenger' is applied to Haggai (Hag. 1:13), and in the plural is frequently used of the prophets in general. Malachi will use the term 'angel' or 'messenger' to refer to the forerunner of Christ and to Christ himself in 3:1. Malachi is not suggesting that the priests replace the prophets. He is looking back to the best days of the priesthood, or to what they ideally ought to have been, and saying that in those circumstances they had a similar function. However, the prophet directly received a specific 'word' from God, whereas the priest is the interpreter and applier of what has already been revealed. Zechariah's fourth vision depicted the priest with access to God and so equipped to function as a messenger (Zech. 3:7).

*Indictment (2:8-9).* **But** 'as for you' **(2:8)** marks the turn from the ideal of what the priests should be doing to their contemporary failure. **You have turned from the way.** The 'way' was the course of conduct required by the LORD, with due observance of all his statutes and ordinances (Gen. 18:19; 1 Kgs. 2:3; Ps. 25:4; 27:11). It derives from the idiom of life as a journey or 'walk', and may refer to the course in fact taken (Hag. 1:5) or which ought to be taken (see 2:6, 8). Here it specifically refers to the conduct required by the covenant with Levi, and set out in 2:6-7. Unlike the psalmists, the priests had turned from the LORD and his laws (Ps. 18:21-22; 119:102). The idea that is conveyed is that they have deliberately done so.

Many aspects of the priests' behaviour after the Exile were creditable. They had played an important role in re-erecting and dedicating the temple (Ezr. 6:16). We see them installed according to their ranks and purifying themselves for their work (Ezr. 6:20-22). They were involved in the reforming activities of Ezra and Nehemiah, perhaps just after Malachi's time. But there were negative features: the reluctance of Levites to leave Babylon with Ezra (Ezr. 8:15), and mixed marriages (Ezr. 9:1; 10:18, 20-44; Neh. 13:4-5). Even the conduct of one of the sons of the high priest was detestable

(Neh. 13:29). Malachi points to their personal lack of loyalty to the LORD, their slipshod ways in the worship of the Temple, and their failure with respect to a teaching ministry.

**And by your teaching have caused many to stumble.** 'Many' parallels that of 2:6, but now it is 'stumble' rather than turning away from sin. The teaching of the priests was no longer true to God's prescriptions and could not provide reliable guidance for others. 'Stumble' usually refers to the result of being unsteady on one's feet, but the prevalent Hebrew conception of life as a journey ('walk' in 2:6 and 'way' earlier in this verse) led to the idea of failing to keep to, or progress along, the path of life. It was the aim of the wicked to 'make someone fall', literally, 'cause them to stumble' (Prov. 4:16), and the worthless idols of Jeremiah's day had made the people 'stumble in their ways' (Jer. 18:15). The idiom lies behind the expression 'cause to sin', literally, 'put an obstacle in someone's way so as to cause them to stumble and fall into sin', that is found in the New Testament (for instance Mt. 5:29-30). Jesus warns sternly about the dangers of leading others astray. 'But if anyone causes one of these little ones who believe in me to sin, it would be better for him to have a large millstone hung around his neck and to be drowned in the depths of the sea' (Mt. 18:6).

**"You have violated the covenant with Levi," says the LORD Almighty.** The word rendered 'violate' is found only here in reference to a covenant. It means to corrupt morally and hence to destroy (Mal. 3:11). Malachi is not saying the covenant no longer exists. Their perverse behaviour meant that they had forfeited their right to continue as God's intermediaries to the people.

The obligations of the covenant cannot be modified and must be maintained. But if one party does not live up to their obligations, then the other has the right to take appropriate steps. **So I have caused you to be despised and humiliated before all the people (2:9).** 'I' is emphatic, 'I on my part', and sets the LORD's action over against the priests' failure. He has already started to act and will continue. As they had not lived up to the responsibilities of their privileged position, God will publicly depose them before those they had led astray. **Because you have not followed my ways but have shown partiality in matters of the law.** It is hinted that their instruction and decisions on disputed matters were not always motivated by loyalty to divine standards but rather on what they could get for themselves out of the situation. The idiom for 'show partiality', literally 'lifting faces', is the same as in 'accept' in 1:8, but now with overtones of undue favour. This was forbidden to those who judged in Israel (Lev. 19:15; Deut. 1:17).

In the New Testament church the teaching ministry is liable to the same corruptions as affected the priests and Levites in the Old Testament. The teacher 'must hold firmly to the trustworthy message as it has been taught, so that he can encourage others by sound doctrine and refute those who oppose it' (Tit. 1:9). It is not enough to preach if one's conduct does not match the doctrine one sets forth. As Paul exhorted Timothy, 'Set an example for the believers in speech, in life, in love, in faith and in purity. ... Watch your life and doctrine closely. Persevere in them, because if you do, you will save both yourself and your hearers' (1 Tim. 4:12, 16). Of course, no human teacher is able to live out the Christian message perfectly. But any who openly or persistently set aside the moral standards of God's word are to be shunned as unreliable guides. Their conduct and teaching will fail to turn many from sin.

## Study Questions

**2:5-6** Consider how Scripture views our speech as an index of our inner character. Ps. 15:2-3; Prov. 12:17-19; 18:4; Mt. 12:33-37; Lk. 6:45; Jas. 1:26; 3:2-12.

**2:8** What problems do false teachers cause, and how may they be avoided? Mt. 7:15-16, 21-23; Acts 20:29-30; 2 Cor. 11:3-15; 1 Tim. 4:1-7; 6:3-5; 2 Tim. 2:14-18; 3:6-9; 2 Pet. 2:1-3; 1 Jn. 4:1-5; 2 Jn 7-11.

**2:9** Why is favouritism or partiality to be avoided? 1 Tim. 5:21; Jas. 2:1-10.

## Malachi 2:10-16:  Unfaithful Judah

When the religious leaders of the people fall short of what is required of them, a general moral decline takes place.  In the previous section of the prophecy, the priests had been charged with violating their covenant obligations.  Malachi now shows that the same spirit pervaded the community as a whole.  'Breaking faith' (2:10, 11, 14, 15, 16) is the key theme of this section.  It ought not to have occurred because of the unique privileges of Judah (2:10a), but the community could not be relied upon to be true to one another (2:10b).  This was particularly shown in their attitude to pagan marriages (2:11-12) and divorce (2:13-16).  The spiritual well-being of the land was undermined by the break-up of the family which was the fundamental unit in the structure of the nation.

*Israel's Unique Role (2:10a).*  Malachi uses the same technique as was employed in 1:6.  By means of rhetorical questions, he begins by asserting a general and uncontroversial principle without initially hinting at its devastating application to the situation of his day.  **Have we not all one Father?** (*2:10*) presupposes an affirmative answer, and points to the common origin of the nation.  But who was this father?  Because of the mention of 'the covenant of our fathers' later in the verse, many have thought it a reference to 'Abraham, your father' (Isa. 51:2), or at any rate Jacob whom Malachi mentions frequently (1:2; 2:12; 3:6)—and of course all twelve tribes of Israel were descendants of Jacob.  Such an approach is reflected in the NIV footnote 'father'.  On this understanding the following question **Did not one God create us?** is a heightening of the original question.

But it is more probable that 'Father' refers to God, who has already been likened to a father in 1:6.  Such a description of God is found frequently in the Old Testament (Ex. 4:22-23; Deut. 32:6; Isa. 63:16; 64:8; Jer. 2:27; 3:4, 19; 31:9).  It is God's covenant relation to Israel by which they were adopted as sons and daughters of the Lord Almighty (2 Cor. 6:18) that is being presented, and not some universal fatherhood of God.  'We' are the people of Malachi's own community.  Having been brought into being by one Father, brotherly loyalty should be a trait displayed by Israel.  The nation was meant to reflect the character of the Father who had taught them to walk in his ways (Hos. 11:1).

'Create' does not militate against this interpretation, because it is used in connection with the origin of the nation of Israel (Isa. 43:1, 7, 15; see also Deut. 32:6; Ps. 100:3; Isa. 43:21; 44:2, 21). It reminds Israel of their exceptional origin, by the direct action of God. They were therefore a unique nation. 'Who is like your people Israel—the one nation on earth that God went out to redeem as a people for himself?' (2 Sam. 7:23). Their unique origin in the action of *one* Father and *one* God should have provided the basis for national solidarity in the bond of the covenant.

*Breaking Faith (2:10b).* Malachi associates himself with the people and asks a perplexed question as to why the cohesion that this unique origin should have supplied is not being found in practice. **Why do we profane the covenant of our fathers by breaking faith with one another?** The NIV translation seems to reverse the emphasis of the original, which may be rendered, 'Why do we break faith a man with his brother in respect of profaning the covenant of our fathers?' The consonants of the word rendered 'break faith' are the same as those of a common Hebrew word for a garment, and it has often been suggested (but never really established) that the basic idea is that of putting a cloak over something, and so acting falsely and perfidiously. 'Break faith' is used of one who does not honour the terms of an existing agreement. When the citizens of Shechem rebelled against Abimelech, they 'acted treacherously' against him (Judg. 9:23). The 'unfaithful' display duplicity (Prov. 11:3), have a craving for violence (Prov. 13:2), and cannot be relied on in time of trouble (Prov. 25:19). The word is also used of treachery and unfaithfulness within the marriage relationship (Ex. 21:8; Jer. 3:20; 9:2). Inevitably it often has to be used in connection with breaches of God's requirements. The faithless do not obey God's word (Ps. 119:158).

Here 'breaking faith' does not just refer to the heathen marriages and divorces mentioned later. The Mosaic covenant, 'the covenant of our fathers' (Deut. 4:31; 5:3; 8:18), included many stipulations as to how the LORD required one Israelite to treat his fellow countryman, precisely because he was his brother in the covenant (Lev. 19:13-17; 25:25-28, 35-43; Deut. 15:1-18; 22:1-4; 23:19-20). The sacred pledge to maintain such standards was being disregarded in Judah.

Their untrustworthy and inconstant behaviour was rupturing the harmony that should have existed in the community, making light of the heritage they had received from their fathers and despising the ordinances of God. For 'profane' see on 1:12.

*Pagan Marriages (2:11-12).* Malachi now makes his charges more specific. The ideas of 'breaking faith' and 'profane' are repeated in 2:11, where the NIV translates the latter as 'desecrated'. **Judah has broken faith (*2:11*).** Judah (the country) stands for the inhabitants. They have not lived up to the standards of the covenant. **A detestable thing has been committed in Israel and in Jerusalem.** This refers to an act which is abominable in the sight of God, such as idolatry or impurity (Deut. 32:16; Isa. 44:16). Israel had been warned not to imitate the detestable ways of the nations who were already in Canaan (Deut. 18:9-13). This indicates a slipping away into the pagan practices of those around them. The change from Judah to Israel is not a reference to the former division of the people. Rather Israel here stands for the people who are in covenant bond with the LORD, and whose capital, Jerusalem, was the place where he had revealed himself. Their sin is against light and privilege. **Judah has desecrated the sanctuary the LORD loves.** This is presented as the substantiation of the charge. 'The sanctuary' is literally 'holiness of the LORD'. This may be understood of the Temple as the holy place. The sin of pagan marriages would thus be an affront to the presence of God in their midst, which was symbolised by the Temple. Alternatively, 'holiness of the LORD' may refer to the people themselves. As those set aside to the service of the LORD they are called 'holy' and 'holiness' (Ex. 19:6; 31:13; Lev. 20:26; Deut. 7:6; Jer. 2:3). 'Judah became God's sanctuary' (Ps. 114:2), the people he loves (1:2). So by their actions they had profaned their national dedication to the LORD and his service.

**By marrying the daughter of a foreign god** makes the matter more specific. It was not just a matter of contravening the prohibition regarding marrying Canaanite women (Ex. 34:16; Deut. 7:3). Nor is it a condemnation of inter-racial marriage in general. They had married gentile women, but what was most significant was that these women had retained their own religion. They had not become converts to the LORD, but had brought their pagan beliefs and practices with them. Being 'the daughter of a foreign god' meant having an ethos opposed to that of the LORD. That was the gravamen of the charge. The frontier between the covenant people and the heathen, between the church and the world, between those in fellowship with the LORD and those in rebellion against him, had been obliterated. A mixed multitude had left Egypt with Israel, but they had been circumcised and kept the Passover (Ex. 12:48; Num. 9:14). Ruth had come from Moab, but she had allied herself to Israel's God (Ruth 1:16). A great many pagan marriages were entered into at this period, and Ezra and Nehemiah had to grapple with the problem (Ezra 9–10; Neh. 9:2; 10:30; 13:1-3, 23-29). The LORD had warned that if the Israelites intermarried with the Canaanites, their foreign wives would 'turn your sons away from following me to serve other gods, and the LORD's anger will burn against you and will quickly destroy you' (Deut. 7:4). The example of Solomon's marriages to unconverted women presented a grave warning as to what was liable to happen (1 Kgs. 11:1-8; 16:31; Neh. 13:23-27), but the prevalence of the practice indicates the people did not see how potentially ruinous it was.

Malachi himself shows the abhorrence with which he responded to this serious situation. **As for the man who does this, whoever he may be, may the LORD cut him off from the tents of Jacob (*2:12*)**. It is not the community in general that is seen as being subjected to the LORD's chastisement, but the specific individuals involved. 'Whoever he may be' renders a Hebrew idiom, literally, 'one arousing and one responding'. Its purpose is to indicate the totality of those involved by naming two opposite categories, and so its thrust is clear, even though we are at a loss to explain the precise background of the idiom. It may have arisen from the way in which watch was kept around tents and cities at night.

The punishment envisaged is that of being 'cut off'. It is often difficult to decide whether this refers to death (Gen. 9:11), or to banishment from the people of God and the land of promise (Ex. 12:15, 19). 'From the tents of Jacob' (2 Sam. 20:1; 1 Kgs. 12:16) is from the midst of the covenant people. The introduction of such an alien and possibly dangerous element into the life of the covenant community requires divine action against the transgressor.

The NIV footnote records another understanding of the first part of the verse, 'May the LORD cut off from the tents of Jacob anyone who gives testimony on behalf of the man who does this.' 'Gives testimony' seems to arise out of a change in the consonantal text of the Hebrew. It is not the offender who is to be punished—that goes without saying—but so grave is the offence that those who ally themselves with him and say his behaviour is permissible must be dealt with similarly.

**Even though he brings offerings to the LORD Almighty** shows that such a serious and deliberate breach of the covenant regulations could not be atoned for. Offerings were allowed for unintentional sin and the offence would be forgiven (Num. 15:22-29), 'but anyone who sins defiantly, whether native-born or alien, blasphemes the LORD, and that person must be cut off from his people' (Num. 15:30). No extenuating circumstances are to be allowed. Since apostasy had been responsible for the Exile, it was unthinkable that the community should be put at risk again.

*Divorce (2:13-16).* **Another thing you do (*2:13*).** Malachi then draws attention to a second notorious abuse: divorce. Before identifying it, he comments on how their behaviour affects their religious activities. **You flood the LORD's altar with tears.** The people had no access to the altar, but this does not spoil the impact of this figurative statement. It was their sacrifices that were being offered amid general sorrow. (The subject has not changed, and it is unlikely to be the sorrow of the divorced wives.) But their grief, however great, and their sacrifices, however many, would not accomplish anything if there was an unresolved moral issue between them and God. **You weep and wail because he no longer pays attention to your offerings or accepts them with pleasure from your hands.** 'Pleasure' is from the same root as the word rendered 'accept' in 1:10. The people were perplexed and disturbed because it was evident that their worship and prayers had gone unanswered by God. But their sorrow was worldly, not godly. They were disturbed by the earthly blessings they did not have, but unaware of the true cause—their alienation from God.

**You ask, "Why?"** *(2:14)*. The people were surprised. They could not understand why God was displeased with them and their worship. So the prophet tells them. **It is because the LORD is acting as the witness between you and the wife of your youth.** We do not know how marriage ceremonies were conducted in ancient Israel, but this verse shows that there was some religious ceremony in which the LORD was invoked as a witness to the agreement. There are a few other texts in which marriage is called a covenant (Prov. 2:17; Ezk. 16:8; see also Gen. 31:50), and as such the divine witness would be called on to note and watch over the pledges given. It is not just to the fact that they have been entered into, but also to monitor that they were carried out. Now the LORD is indicating that the pledges given were not being fulfilled. 'Wife of your youth' is the first of three phrases used to make the violation of the marriage vows more poignant. In the ancient east marriage was contracted at an early age. A man would ordinarily be married by the age of twenty (Isa. 54:6; Prov. 2:17; 5:18; Joel 1:8). Broken marriage vows concern not only the human partners to the bond, but God as well.

**Because you have broken faith with her, though she is your partner, the wife of your marriage covenant.** The assumption is that the marriage has been dissolved and the wife divorced, as 2:16 makes clear. The second phrase to describe the divorced wife is 'partner' or 'companion'. This word is usually employed of a close friend with whom interests are shared (Ps. 119:63; Prov. 28:24; Isa. 1:23). It is only here that it is used of a wife, as one with whom there ought to be much held in common and jointly worked for. But this mutual interest and trust is lacking. The accusation is shaped in such a way as to stir their consciences to the hardheartedness of their action. The third phrase to denote the woman being abandoned 'the wife of your marriage covenant' emphasises the breach of trust that was involved in the dissolution of the arrangements so solemnly entered into.

But why was the wife being divorced? It is generally assumed that this had something to do with the marrying of foreign wives. Perhaps the custom of polygamy was not as common as it had once been, but more probably what was happening had something to do with the status of the new wife. It was the first wife who had the highest honour accorded to her, and the Jewish wife may have been divorced to give that place to the heathen wife, an arrangement perhaps forced on the Israelite by her father. It may have been for economic advantage or security that the new marriages were being contracted.

The next verse is one of the most difficult to understand in the Old Testament. Its general import is clear: husbands should remain true to their first wife. But the details of the argument are obscure, and have caused problems even from the earliest translations. There are perhaps four approaches which merit consideration. They are listed in decreasing order of probability.

*(1)* The first three elliptical words 'and not one he made' may be understood as a rhetorical question referring to the institution of marriage related in Genesis 2. This underlies the rendering in the NIV text, **Has not <the LORD> made them one?** *(2:15)*. 'One' in the context of marriage would remind a Jew of the words 'they will become one flesh' (Gen. 2:24). It was to this same text that Jesus appealed when he was in dispute with the Pharisees regarding the permissibility of divorce (Mt. 19:3-9). The strength of a similar reference here to the creation ordinance is that it suitably reinforces the argument in the context. They should not be divorcing the wife of their youth in that it is improper to sever the bond whereby God has united the two—the man and the woman—and made them one.

The problem for this interpretation arises in the following words, which literally are 'and remainder of spirit to him'. The NIV deals with this by changing one vowel of the text (there is no change in the consonants which were all that was originally written) to read 'flesh' instead of 'remainder', though the word for 'flesh' is different from that found in Genesis 2:24. 'Him' is understood of God, and the translation becomes, **In flesh and spirit they are his.** This makes good sense. As created by God, the man and woman are not independent of him in any aspect of their being, and so they are answerable to him for what they do in marriage. (Note an alternative without emendation suggested under the next interpretation.) **And why one?** Why is it the case that God has structured marriage in such a way that there is this exclusive bond between man and wife? **Because he** (that is, God) **was seeking godly offspring.** That aim would be threatened by a man having more than one wife at a time (polygamy), or by his divorcing his wife and breaking the marital bond to marry another (serial polygamy). Only when both partners remain true to the structure God has designed for marriage will it be the case that the children are provided with the environment of security and upbringing with a respect for God and his commands, which is what he wants.

(2) Another possibility is to understand the mention of 'one' as picking up the theme of 'one Father' and 'one God' in 2:10 with its implications for the oneness of the nation which should not be disrupted (see references at 2:10). 'And not one he made' would then assert by means of a question, 'Did not <the LORD> make <us> one <nation>?' 'And remainder of spirit to him' might then be understood of the Spirit as God's creative power. Having formed one nation, it was not lack of power that prevented him from forming others, but rather his intention to form a single people, separated to himself from the nations of the earth. (A similar proposal could be made for the phrase in terms of interpretation (1). It was not from lack of power that God did not create other partners for Adam, but because it ran contrary to his intention.) But 'why one?', literally, 'the one', that is the one nation being talked about. 'Because he was seeking godly offspring', and this was more likely to be achieved if marriages were formed within the covenant nation pledged to him. In this way the nation would not in succeeding generations be tempted to be disloyal to the covenant, and so would be fit to be the one from which the Messiah might come. Marrying pagan wives imperilled this divine mission.

(3) A third interpretation stems from the fact that 'and not one he made' is an unusual way to express a negative question in Hebrew. Understanding 'one' as the subject of the verb, and taking it to refer to a typical individual who was loyal to his covenant commitment, the passage may be rendered, 'But no one has done <this>, and (while) he had a remnant of the Spirit'. Those in who hearts the Spirit was active to any extent at all would not engage in such unworthy behaviour. 'And what does the one seek? An offspring from God.' Faithful to the covenant, he seeks the realisation of the covenant promise by raising up children in the way of covenant truth.

(4) The fourth interpretation is found in the NIV footnote. It too

understands the initial 'one' as the subject and not the object of 'make', and takes the reference to be to Abraham. 'But the one <who is our father> did not do this, not as long as life remained in him. And what was he seeking? An offspring from God.' A supposed objection is being countered. In the first sentence the people argue that divorce is permissible because of the precedent set by Abraham sending away Hagar (Gen. 21:8-21). To this the prophet counters with a question which shows that the parallel is not exact. That incident only happened after Isaac was born, and because Abraham did not want to compromise his covenant inheritance. The people of Malachi's day were not concerned about their heritage, but about indulging their passions. This explanation is least likely because the introduction of Abraham as 'one' requires explanation (though note the possible reference in 2:10 footnote), and the argument from what he did is not immediately convincing. Abraham did not send away the wife of his youth, but a concubine who was not a covenant wife but a pagan one.

But whatever interpretation of the preceding words is adopted, the conclusion Malachi was urging on his hearers is clear. **So guard yourself in your spirit, and do not break faith with the wife of your youth.** If 'spirit' picks up the earlier mention in the verse, then it favours understanding it there also as referring to the inner consciousness of man with which he has been divinely endowed. It is in the spirit that an individual longs for God (Isa. 26:9). The man in whose spirit there is no deceit is blessed (Ps. 32:2), and so it is necessary to watch our inner attitudes and desires. It is from within that sin and uncleanness come (Mt. 15:16-20). When there are so many influences seeking to divert from loyalty to God, we need to watch ourselves very carefully not to be drawn into impure practices, but rather keep ourselves in the love of God (Deut. 4:15; Josh. 23:11). For 'do not break faith' see on 2:10b, and for 'wife of your youth' on 2:14.

The next verse begins 'for' adducing the divine attitude that gives rise to the preceding advice. **"I hate divorce," says the LORD God of Israel (2:16).** The vowels added to the consonants in the text preserved by the Massoretes (the Jewish scholars who standardised the Hebrew text in the centuries after Christ) show that this was read as '<if> he hates, send <her> away'. This seems to be an early attempt at harmonising this passage with the permission for divorce granted in Deuteronomy 24:1-4. It is preferable to read the word with different vowels, 'I am hating'. This is God's set attitude. The Mosaic legislation was designed to curb, not encourage, divorce by regulating strictly how it could take place. As Jesus pointed out, 'Moses permitted you to divorce your wives because your hearts were hard. But it was not this way from the beginning' (Mt. 19:8). The God of Israel, who is concerned for the future of the nation, hates 'sending away', the term used for divorce in Deuteronomy 22:19 (Isa. 50:1), and also for the husband's action in Deuteronomy 24:1-4.

It is not at all clear if what follows speaks of the same or another sin. **"And I hate a man's covering himself with violence as well as with his garment," says the LORD Almighty.** Literally, it is 'violence covers over his garment' or 'he covers <with> violence over his garment'. The first might be a figurative expression for all kinds of wickedness and injustice (Gen. 6:11; Ps. 72:14; Hab. 1:2), which leave their mark for all to see. A similar idea is present in the second rendering, though with more emphasis on the involvement of the perpetrator, and perhaps a hint of his shamelessness. 'Himself' is a translator's supplement for which the NIV margin suggests the alternative 'his wife'. This would link the statement more closely to the first. 'To cover one's wife with a garment' may be taken as an expression for marrying her, which was sometimes done by covering her with one's garment (Ruth 3:9; Ezk. 16:8). Not only is that done, but there is also injustice perpetrated in breaking off the marriage relationship. **So guard yourself in your spirit, and do not break faith.** This repeats the exhortation at the end of the previous verse.

How contemporary Malachi's situation sounds! There are two ways of approaching marriage—that of the world, which views it as little more than a mutually convenient arrangement that may be terminated when it becomes inconvenient, and that of God. Increasingly the church has caved in to pressure to accept as valid grounds for divorce what the civil authorities deem permissible. It is too embarrassing to ask if a divorce was granted on Scriptural grounds. But marriage is a creation ordinance of God, and he still wishes it to be honoured both within and without the church. 'Marriage should be honoured by all, and the marriage bed kept pure' (Heb. 13:4). This is particularly true of those who have taken their marriage vows before God as the marriage witness (2:14). The teaching of Paul still stands that divorce is not right. 'A wife must not separate from her husband. ... And a husband must not divorce his wife' (1 Cor. 7:10, 11). There are exceptional circumstances mentioned, but they are just that—exceptional. They are not the basis for easy and unthinking breaches of the marriage bond. When that becomes prevalent in a country, the whole social and religious fabric of the land is corrupted. The marriage bond and the family are divine institutions which cannot be set aside without horrendous consequences.

*Study Questions*

**2:11** What does Scripture teach about the separation of God's people from the world? Ps. 119:115; Isa. 52:11; Jn. 15:19; 17:16; 1 Cor. 15:33; 2 Cor. 6:14; 7:1; Eph. 5:11; 2 Thess. 3:6; Jas. 4:4.

**2:13** How does hypocrisy undermine worship? Prov. 21:27; 28:9; Isa. 1:11-16; Jer. 6:20; Lk. 12:1-3; Tit. 1:16.

**2:16** How are current standards on marriage and divorce affecting the ordinary life of the community? of the church?

## Malachi 2:17–3:5: The Messenger of the Covenant

The people considered that the LORD had abandoned his care of them and left the world to work out its own destiny untrammelled (2:17). But Malachi shows that their irreverent attitude is not justified. The LORD has not reneged on his responsibilities. He would have due preparations made and come to his Temple (3:1). The seeming delay in his acting on their behalf was not caused by his indifference, but by theirs. His coming would result in the exposure and judgment of those who had rebelled against him. He would test and purify his people so that they could serve him acceptably (3:2-4). Those whose living was at variance with his requirements ought therefore to take due warning (3:5).

*The Accusation (2:17a).* Malachi again uses the schema of accusation, counter-question and citing of the evidence, followed by a longer comment on the situation. This incidentally shows that 2:17 is to be read along with what follows it rather than with the preceding verses in chapter 2. **You have wearied the LORD with your words (2:17).** 'You' refers to the community as a whole though, as 3:14-16 will reveal, not all displayed this critical attitude. The words they had uttered were presumably not those of prayer, pleading his promises and giving him no rest till he acted (Isa. 62:6-7). Rather they were words of querulous complaint that he had not lived up to his promises. They deserved better from him. 'Wearied' usually refers to the exhaustion that comes from hard work, but the Creator of the ends of the earth who does not grow tired or weary from all that he does (Isa. 40:28) is wearied by persistent unbelief and sin (Isa. 7:13; 43:24).

*The Counter-Question (2:17b).* **"How have we wearied him?" you ask.** They respond with amazement. So certain were they that the accusation could not possibly be true of such as they were, they request more specific information, confident that the charge cannot be maintained in detail.

*The Evidence (2:17c).* Two related complaints that the people have about God are brought out into the open. Firstly they claim he is unrighteous, **by saying, "All who do evil are good in the eyes of the LORD, and he is pleased with them".** The identity of the individuals who are perpetrating the evil is not clear.

  *(1)* It might be that there were some within the covenant community who were prospering through treachery and exploitation. Asaph too had seen the prosperity of the wicked. They had seemed to him always carefree and increasing in wealth (Ps. 73:12). But he had kept his own counsel (Ps. 73:15), and in the sanctuary had come to realise their final destiny (Ps. 73:17-20), how stupid his envy had been (Ps. 73:22) and how greatly blessed he was in having God as his portion for ever (Ps. 73:26). The people Malachi describes had also seen the prosperity of the wicked, but they had blasphemously concluded that this was what God approved of. (See also on 3:14-15.) For 'pleased',

see on 1:10. 'With them' is strongly emphasised in the Hebrew, being contrasted with an implicit 'with us'. They were, in effect, saying, 'God is not pleased with our offerings but with the evildoers. We have not been wearying him with our words; he has been wearying us with his ways. That's not what we expect.'

(2) There is, however, no indication in Malachi's prophecy of three groups in the community: the pious remnant whom he will introduce in 3:16, the vast majority of the people and a further group who were openly and notoriously wicked. Those condemned in 3:5 are to be found among the speakers here. It is more probable then that the people were comparing themselves to the heathen nations surrounding them, who at this time were enjoying far greater prosperity than Judah. They considered themselves to be doing their best to serve God and getting little thanks for it. The evident blessings enjoyed by their neighbours showed that God was acting unrighteously in the rewards that he gave.

Or **"Where is the God of justice?"** presents an alternative thought running through their minds: if God was not unrighteous, then he had given up acting altogether (Ezk. 8:12; 9:9; Zeph. 1:12; 2 Pet. 3:3-5). Although it is in the form of a question, it is tantamount to an assertion that God was no longer interested in what was happening. Their experience seemed to them to confirm the truth that the law of retribution was not functioning any more. God had failed to 'punish the world for its evil, the wicked for their sins' (Isa. 13:11). To threaten, 'Woe to the wicked! Disaster is upon them! They will be paid back for what their hands have done' (Isa. 3:11) is but empty words, if nothing happens. And, of course, if one argues that sinners can act with impunity, then it is easier to fall into line with their conduct oneself. 'When the sentence for a crime is not quickly carried out, the hearts of the people are filled with schemes to do wrong' (Eccl. 8:11). Notice also the underlying assumption they were making about themselves. They could approach the God of justice without hesitation. To demand his intervention was a threat to others, not them. They did not see anything wrong with their own living. They were right with God.

*His Coming (3:1-4)*. The LORD himself responds to these grave charges being voiced against him by revealing how he is going to come. What is to happen will occur in two stages.

*(1) See, I will send my messenger, who will prepare the way before me (3:1)*. 'See' or 'Behold me!' demands that attention be focused on the LORD. He alone is in control of what will happen, and will first of all send his 'messenger'. The word translated in this way occurs frequently in the Old Testament. About half of its occurrences are in reference to human messengers who are used to carry messages between individuals, such as Jacob and Esau (Gen. 32:3, 6). They also functioned as the channels of diplomatic communication between national leaders, such as Moses and the king of Edom (Num. 20:14). The term is sometimes used of God's prophets whom he sent as his representatives to his people to bring his word to them (2 Chr. 36:15-16; Jer. 25:4; Hag. 1:13). The term is once applied to the priests in 2:7. The other times the word is found, it is translated 'angel' because the messengers are superhuman. One-third of these 'angelic' occurrences refer to finite, created messengers whom the LORD employs (such as the interpreting angel, Zech. 1:9; Ps. 103:20), and two-thirds are to the individual known as the Angel of the LORD (see on Zech. 1:11).

In the light of the New Testament evidence, there can be little doubt about the identity of the messenger here. Jesus quotes this sentence and shows it is fulfilled in John the Baptist (Mt. 11:10; Luke 7:27; see also Luke 1:76). The passage is also cited in Mark 1:2-3 along with words from Isaiah 40:3 (for the conflated citation, see on Zech. 11:13), which also speak about preparations being made before the arrival of the LORD. The imagery is drawn from the practice of ancient kings, who would inform their subjects in a province of their empire that they were about to come on a state visit, so that adequate arrangements might be made. This would include 'preparing the way' for the royal procession, by removing from it anything that would impede progress. It would thus be straight, level and free of obstacles (Isa. 40:3-4; see also Isa. 57:14; 62:10). The preparations that had to be made before the coming of the LORD were, of course, spiritual rather than physical. This was achieved through John's ministry, which called for repentance because the kingdom of heaven was near (Mt. 3:2). He had a wide impact (Mk. 1:5), and provided the basis for Christ's ministry (Jn. 1:35-37; Acts 19:4). That such a forerunner was necessary was also a warning to the people of Malachi's day that whatever they might think, they were not ready for the arrival of their king. See also on 4:5-6.

*(2)* **Then suddenly**, not immediately, but in a manner which causes surprise by its unexpectedness, **the Lord you are seeking will come to his temple.** Once the forerunner has done his work, the king will follow. Note that the 'Lord' is not in small capitals, LORD, which represents *Yahweh*, the unique and personal name of the covenant God. The word used is *Adonai*, which picks up the imagery of a visiting king by pointing to God as the sovereign ruler, the one who had dominion, authority and ownership (1:6; Zech. 4:14; 6:5). There is no doubt that when the word is used with the article it refers to 'the Lord Yahweh' (Ex. 23:17; Isa. 1:24), and not some other royal figure. He is the one who says he will send 'my messenger' ahead of him, and it is to 'his temple' that he comes to rule as king (see on Hag. 2:15) and dispense the justice which it had been claimed was lacking (2:17).

There is probably another reason for the use of Adonai here, and that is to allow a reference to Christ. This had already been done by David in Psalm 110: 'The LORD (*Yahweh*) says to my Lord (*Adonai*)' (Ps. 110:1; Mt. 22:41-45). While it does not reveal the doctrine of the Trinity, it can only be satisfactorily understood in the light of that revelation. Here it is the LORD Almighty (the Father) who is speaking of his coming, and yet refers to one who is distinct from him and one with him (the Son). This is none other than the Messiah, who is both God and man.

Notice also that the people 'are seeking' the Lord's appearance. They associated his coming with the defeat of their enemies and their own advance. They were waiting for the fulfilment of prophecies such as Isaiah 2:2-4 and Haggai 2:6-9. But in their specious self-confidence they failed to see that they were not ready for the Lord's presence in his temple. They were rather like the people of Amos' day, who were awaiting the day of the LORD when he would intervene in power. They thought it would be for their blessing, but they had to be warned, 'Woe to you who long for the day of the LORD! Why do you long for the day of the LORD? That day will be darkness, not light' (Amos 5:18). They did not see how unacceptable their conduct was to God, no matter how many offerings they brought, if justice and righteousness did not prevail in their land (Amos 5:21-24). So too the people of Malachi's day had to learn that the smug contentment of their self-righteousness would not survive the scrutiny of the God of justice.

**"The messenger of the covenant, whom you desire, will come," says the Lord Almighty.** This is not the introduction of a third individual whose coming is to be anticipated, nor is it the same figure as the previously mentioned messenger, who is the forerunner and has to come first. But this messenger is to be identified with the Lord, of whom 'messenger' or 'angel of the covenant' is a further description. Although the phrase 'messenger of the covenant' is found only here, it has many similarities with the expression 'the angel of the LORD' (see above and Zech. 1:11). Whereas the previous description 'Lord' points to the kingship of Christ, 'messenger of the covenant' principally points to his prophetic role. In this he continued the proclamation of the former messenger (Mt. 4:17 as compared with Mt. 3:2), but his teaching was with an unparalleled authority (Mt. 7:28-29; 13:54; Jn. 7:46). Furthermore, as the Word, Christ not only presented the message; he was the message (Jn. 1:14). In this way the title goes beyond the strictly prophetic. The Angel of the covenant is the one who is the mediator of the new covenant, whose role is that of the Angel of God's presence to save his people (Isa. 63:9; Ex. 23:20-23). For 'desire', see 'pleased' 1:10. Its use here may be ironic. They claimed to be eager for the Messiah's coming, but they did not really know what would be involved in it. The divine speech ends emphatically, 'Behold, he is coming!' There ought to be no doubt about that. His coming refutes the allegations of 2:17, and is taken up again in 4:1, 3, 5.

Would the people be ready for the coming of the LORD? The prophet asks questions which make clear that this is no matter to be trifled with. It would be unexpected; it could also be unpleasant. **But who can endure the day of his coming? Who can stand when he appears?** *(3:2).* The rhetorical questions suggest the answer that no one will be able to do so. 'Endure' implies a searching ordeal that none will be able to cope with. 'The day of the LORD is great; it is dreadful. Who can endure it?' (Joel 2:11). 'Stand' does not mean appear before the investigating magistrate (Deut. 19:17)—in that sense all will stand before the Judge of all the earth—but is rather a military analogy (2 Kgs. 10:4; Amos 2:15). 'Who will stand his ground?' Before the searching scrutiny of this judge none will be able to maintain a successful defence. 'If you, O LORD, kept a record of sins, O Lord, who could stand?' (Ps. 130:3; see also Rev. 6:16-17).

The question is often raised as to which coming of the Lord this refers. It is well-known that the distinction between the first and second comings was not clearly revealed in the Old Testament, and that the prophets could merge events connected with them. It is sometimes supposed that this is what has happened here. Having in 3:1 described the first coming of Christ (as is shown clearly by the reference to John the Baptist), it is supposed that he is now drawn forward to describe the day of final judgment. But we must avoid too simple an approach whereby the first coming of Christ is equated with salvation and the second with judgment. Although we are told that 'God did not send his Son into the world to condemn the world, but to save the world through him' (Jn. 3:17), yet Jesus also said, 'For judgment I have come into this world, so that the blind will see and those who see will become blind' (Jn. 9:39; see also Mt. 3:10-12; Lk. 2:34). There was begun a process of judgment and sifting at the first coming, which is consummated at the second. Whenever truth is revealed, those who do not believe stand condemned already (Jn. 3:18). This is continued in the ministry of the Spirit who throughout this age is convicting the world in regard to sin and righteousness and judgment (Jn. 16:8-11).

It would be wrong to take the following description as fulfilled exclusively in the experience of Israel, the nation. Though foreseen in Old Testament terms, it comes true in terms of the true Israel of God, which encompasses all—Jew and Gentile—who belong to Christ (Gal. 3:26-29). Furthermore, what Malachi goes on to describe is not a process of final judgment, as if it was just the second coming he had in view. It is rather a process of purification and sanctification. **For he will be like a refiner's fire or a launderer's soap.** Refiners and launderers do not destroy, but purify. Note the difference from the questions, which implied none would be acceptable before the LORD. But now the LORD is presented as taking action to make his people acceptable. This is fulfilled in what Christ does. He 'loved the church and gave himself up for her to make her holy, cleansing her by the washing with water through the word, and to present her to himself as a radiant church, without stain or wrinkle or any other blemish, but holy and blameless' (Eph. 5:25-27; see also on Zech. 13:1). All ungodliness will be removed like stains washed from a garment (Isa. 4:4; Ezk. 22:18; Ps. 66:10; Lk. 3:16; 21:22).

'Soap' in a modern sense had not yet been invented, but an alkaline solution probably obtained by running water through vegetable ash provided a simple detergent. The cleansing envisaged here is spiritual. If the people themselves attempt to 'wash the evil from their hearts' (Jer. 4:14), they will not be successful. '"Although you wash yourself with soda and use an abundance of soap, the stain of your guilt is still before me," declares the Sovereign LORD' (Jer. 2:22). It required the provision made by Christ for there to be effective spiritual cleansing (Acts 22:16; Tit. 3:5; 1 Jn. 1:7).

The comparison with refining is found frequently in the prophets (Isa. 1:25; 48:10; Jer. 6:29-30; Ezk. 22:17-22; Zech. 13:9). It is developed in greater detail. **He will sit as a refiner and purifier of silver (3:3).** 'Sit' indicates that this was a process requiring considerable care. The silversmiths of the time sat looking into their small metal furnaces to determine from the colour of the metal if it was pure (Ps. 12:6; Prov. 17:3; 1 Pet. 1:7). It was more technically intricate than the process used for gold. When the silver ore is molten, it gives off oxygen. It was treated with charcoal to prevent it re-absorbing the oxygen from the air as it cooled. If it did, it would lose its lustre. The process of purifying was complete and the dross all burnt away when suddenly the silver became a liquid mirror in which the refiner could see his own reflection.

**He will purify the Levites and refine them like gold and silver.** Remarkably it is the Levites who are here presented as the objects of this purifying work. They are not distinguished from the priests who are engaged in the service of the LORD in his temple. This purification is realised by the work of Christ, who purifies 'for himself a people that are his very own, eager to do what is good' (Tit. 2:14). The Levites are symbolic of the cleansed and sanctified church, the 'holy priesthood' (1 Pet. 2:5), the 'royal priesthood' (1 Pet. 2:9), the 'priests of God and of Christ' (Rev. 20:6). This purification is effected through the trials the Lord's people now have to undergo (1 Pet. 1:6-7; 4:12-14).

The result of this purifying process is that **Then the LORD will have men who will bring offerings in righteousness.** For 'bring', see 'place' at 1:7. The action described is not one-off, but habitual. 'Righteousness' envisages more than offerings brought in complete accordance with the outward, technical criteria of the ceremonial law, though that in itself would have been a marked improvement on what then prevailed (1:8, 13). 'Offer right sacrifices (literally, sacrifices of righteousness) and trust in the LORD' (Ps. 4:5) shows the link with faith that was required. 'The sacrifices of God are a broken spirit; a broken and contrite heart, O God, you will not despise. ... Then there will be righteous sacrifices, whole burnt offerings to delight you' (Ps. 51:17, 19). This is now achieved by the church as the priesthood of Christ, offering their bodies as living sacrifices (Rom. 12:1), the unceasing sacrifice of praise, confessing his name (Heb. 13:15), and bringing 'spiritual sacrifices acceptable to God through Jesus Christ' (1 Pet. 2:5).

**And the offerings of Judah and Jerusalem will be acceptable to the LORD (3:4).** 'Acceptable' indicates what is sweet or satisfying (Prov. 3:24; Jer. 6:20; 31:26). For Judah and Jerusalem, see on 2:11. They represent the whole of the covenant community. Presumably they too have undergone a similar refining process, and therefore what they bring to the LORD is pleasing to him. **As in days gone by, as in former years.** This may look back to the brightest periods of Israel's existence, in the time of the Exodus (Isa. 63:9,11; Jer. 2:2-3; Hos. 2:14; Mic. 7:14-15) and David (Amos 9:11), though there were other periods also, associated with Samuel (1 Sam. 7:3-17), Hezekiah (2 Chr. 30-33), and Josiah (2 Chr. 34, 35). The spirit of faith and devotion to the LORD that was then shown will be recaptured in the worship of the renewed and purified Israel that is envisaged.

*Present Condemnation (3:5).* Malachi then turns from the blessing of future purification that awaits the LORD's people to the reality of God's anger with their present practices. They were calling for the

God of justice, but his covenant threatened judgment on the disobedient as well as promising blessings for the faithful. The prophet cites a divine saying, **So I will come near to you for judgment** *(3:5).* What is a refining process for some is a time of judgment for others. The base elements must be removed.

**I will be quick to testify against** rebuts their accusations that he was slow to act. 'Quick' implies expert through training ('well versed' in Ezra 7:6 is from the same root). 'Testify against' indicates that the LORD acts as witness for the prosecution as well as judge and prosecutor. No other witness is needed because no other is competent (2:14; Jer. 29:23; Mic. 1:2). As Psalm 50 reminded them, the summons of the LORD to gather his covenant people need not be to commend them. 'Hear, O my people, and I will speak, O Israel, and I will testify against you: I am God, your God. ... I will rebuke you and accuse you to your face' (Ps. 50:7, 21)

Several categories of offenders are identified. Participles are used in Hebrew to indicate that this was not a matter of once falling into these sins—serious though that is—but of habitual indulgence.

*(1)* **Sorcerers** practised witchcraft and were forbidden in Israel (Ex. 22:18; Lev. 20:27; Deut. 18:10). They perpetuated ancient superstitions of the land (see on Zech. 10:2).

*(2)* **Adulterers** were those who had intercourse with the wife or fiancée of another man. This was forbidden in Exodus 20:14 and Deuteronomy 5:18, and both parties had to be put to death (Lev. 20:10; Deut. 22:22).

*(3)* **Perjurers** were those who swore falsely in the name of God (Ex. 20:7, 16; Lev. 19:12; Jer. 5:2; 7:9; Zech. 5:3,4). This sin might on occasions be atoned for (Lev. 5:4-6; 6:1-7). Perhaps here it reflects on the extent to which they were untrue to their marriage vows (2:10-16).

*(4)* **Against those who defraud labourers of their wages** looks to the social conditions of the day. The ordinary workers may have been underpaid or kept waiting for their wages (Lev. 19:13; Deut. 24:14-15).

*(5)* **Who oppress the widows and the fatherless** describes how they acted towards two of the most vulnerable groups in society. Deprived of their protector and main provider, they had no one to

shield them, and were at the mercy of the unscrupulous (Zech. 7:10).
They were of special concern to the LORD (Ex. 22:22-24; Lev. 19:10;
Deut. 24:19-22). 'Oppress' refers to the abuse of power and author-
ity, ill-treating those of lower status.

(6) The other group liable to harsh treatment was the 'alien', and
they too are mentioned here: **and deprive aliens of justice.** 'Of
justice' is a supplement justified on the basis of Deuteronomy 24:17
and 27:19. The settler or the immigrant were accorded rights in the
ancient world, though these were not always respected.

**"But do not fear me,"** says the LORD **Almighty.** Their actions
being contrary to the requirements of the covenant indicate their
underlying attitude to the God of the covenant. When he draws near,
his justice will be seen as regards those who ignore him. If the fear
of God were present in their lives, then they would hate evil and
delight in God's commands (Gen. 22:12; Ps. 112:1; Prov. 8:13).

Underlying the Jews' thinking about the coming of God was the
assumption that it posed no threat to them. Like the Pharisees of later
centuries they thought they were 'not like other men—robbers,
evildoers, adulterers' (Lk. 18:11). But a true assessment of where we
stand in relation to God is not achieved by measuring ourselves by
ourselves, or comparing ourselves with ourselves (2 Cor. 10:12). The
standard to be achieved is that set out in God's word and lived out
perfectly by Jesus Christ. It is still a temptation that has to be avoided
to think that salvation comes by associating with God's people or
frequenting divine worship. Such things are good, but by themselves
they condemn rather than save. What is needed is that reverential fear
of God that shows a heart submissive before him, and trusting in him
and his provision for all our needs. Then we can stand before him at
his coming, not on the basis of our achievements but in what is ours
in Christ.

*Study Questions*

**2:17** With what is God pleased? Ps. 51:6; Isa. 56:4; Hos. 6:6; Mic.
6:8.

What problems are there in understanding God's justice? Ezk. 8:12-17; 9:2, 11; Jer. 12:1-6; Hab. 1:2-3, 11-14.

**3:1** How do the parables of Jesus in Mt. 21:33 and 25:14 relate to the promise of the Lord's coming?

Why will people be surprised at the Lord's coming? Mt. 7:22-23; 24:36-39, 42-44; Lk. 12:2-3; 1 Cor. 4:5; 1 Thess. 5:2-3; 2 Pet. 3:4, 10.

## Malachi 3:6-12:   Robbing God

A vivid apprehension of what God is like is vitally necessary for a true relationship with him. Malachi continues to deal with the spiritual malaise that affected the people by reminding them of God's constancy. Their preservation was due to the LORD's unwavering commitment to the covenant, not theirs (3:6). They had departed from its norms, but a call for repentance only provokes another self-righteous response (3:7-9). The LORD continues to plead with them, and challenges them to put him to the test. If they fulfil the obligations laid on them in the covenant, they will experience the blessings of their covenant LORD, and will realise their promised role as a beacon to the nations (3:10-12).

*An Unchanging God and a Rebellious People (3:6-7a).* There is a problem posed by the fact that verse 6 begins with a connecting particle usually translated 'for'. This seems to indicate that **I the LORD do not change** *(3:6)* is the reason why God will act in judgment, as expressed in 3:5. However, the rest of 3:6 supports the break introduced by the NIV, and the introductory particle may be taken in its emphatic usage, 'surely' or 'truly'. The verse is structured to balance what is said about 'I' and what is said about 'you'. Regarding God, it is his unchangeableness that is emphasised, as summed up in his covenant name, *Yahweh*, or the LORD. (Indeed, the first part of the verse may be translated, 'I am the LORD. I do not change.')

The significance of the name Yahweh was first revealed to Moses at Horeb (Ex. 3:13-15; 6:2). 'I AM WHO I AM' was not just a static presentation of God's inner self-existence and constancy. It also pointed to what these divine attributes meant for the on-going covenant relationship he had entered into with his people. He already was 'the LORD, the God of your fathers—the God of Abraham, Isaac and Jacob' (Ex. 3:16), and he had determined to deliver their descendants because he remembered his covenant with the patriarchs (Ex. 2:24; 6:5; Deut. 7:8). He remains the same, and the passage of time will not diminish his commitment (Ps. 102:27). It is not possible that he will wish to be released from his word which therefore can be relied on absolutely. 'I will not violate my covenant or alter what my lips have uttered' (Ps. 89:34; see also Ps. 110:4).

The character of the God of the covenant has important consequences for the people he has sovereignly chosen to enter into covenant engagement with him. The possibility is envisaged of them falling short of the obedience the covenant demands (Ex. 19:5; 24:3). But even in these circumstances the LORD pledges, 'I will not take my love from him, nor will I ever betray my faithfulness' (Ps. 89:33; 2 Sam. 7:14-15). **So you, O descendants of Jacob, are not destroyed.** Since 'are not destroyed' is literally 'have not ceased', it is possible to translate this as 'and you <on your part> have not ceased to be descendants of Jacob', that is, as deceitful as Jacob had been (Gen. 25:31-33; 27:18-29). They have continued to display the same nature, and so the contrast is between two ongoing character traits. But it is more likely that the word should be translated as in the NIV. The LORD remains true to his commitment in the covenant, 'for the LORD your God is a merciful God; he will not abandon or destroy you or forget the covenant with your forefathers, which he confirmed to them by oath' (Deut. 4:31; Ps. 106:45). If therefore the people are not enjoying the blessings of the covenant, the reason for this must be sought in something other than divine unfaithfulness or forgetfulness.

The reason for the problem in the relationship between Israel and the LORD was not hard to find, and it was not of recent origin. **Ever since the time of your forefathers you have turned away from my decrees and have not kept them (_3:7_).** The whole history of Israel's covenant relationship with the LORD is here brought under review. It is not specifically linked to the generations immediately preceding the Exile. Over the centuries the people had time and again turned away from God (Deut. 9:24; Judg. 2:10-23; Ps. 78:17; 106:43). 'Decrees' may originally have referred to regulations of general interest, engraved on stone for public display. Since they are what God has imposed on his people, they are to be obeyed. The word is virtually equivalent to 'commands', 'judgments' and 'laws' (Ex. 15:25; 18:16; Lev. 26:46; Deut. 4:45; 5:31). For 'decrees', see also on 4:4.

*Divine Plea (3:7b).* But it is essential that such a breach of the covenant relationship be rectified. Therefore the plea is issued. **"Return to me, and I will return to you," says the LORD Almighty.** The covenant had always made provision for the people sinning and then coming to their senses, returning to God in repentance and with endeavour after new obedience (Deut. 4:29-30; 30:1-10; 1 Kgs. 8:46-51). The call to repentance here is accompanied by the motivating promise of the LORD's return to them (Zech. 1:3; 2 Chr. 30:6; cf. Jer. 31:18; Lam. 5:21). The clause denotes a consequence, an intended result. As it was their offences that had led God to turn away from them in aversion to their sin, so their repentance would allow him to show he still loved them and would perpetuate the covenant bond.

*Counter-question (3:7c).* The people, however, do not see this. **But you ask, 'How are we to return?'** In their estimation there was nothing wrong with their conduct that they needed to repent of. They were not conscious of any guilt on their part. This in itself indicates the malaise from which they were suffering—they had no sense of sin.

*Accusation (3:8a).* Their question is not given an immediate response. First, one area of their behaviour is singled out, and the change that is needed in it is spelled out. Matters are not left vague and general, as God gives detailed directions to the people as to how to please him. **Will a man rob God? (3:8).** 'Rob' is not the usual word for 'steal' (Ex. 20:15). It is translated 'plunder' in its only other occurrence (Prov. 22:23), and in post-Biblical Hebrew it came to mean 'take forcibly'. The rhetorical question obviously expects a negative answer. Malachi again uses antithesis between divine and human (1:6, 8; 2:10, 17). A man (a mere human) cannot snatch booty away from God. **Yet you rob me.** The accusation is put personally and bluntly. It has not happened just once or twice; it is an on-going fact.

*Counter-question (3:8b).* This provokes a response from the self-righteous people. **But you ask, 'How do we rob you?'** It would be wrong to take this as merely a rhetorical device. This is the way the people actually thought and viewed themselves. The priests had not given proper instruction (2:6, 8) and therefore the people were destroyed from lack of knowledge of what a true approach to God required (Hos. 4:6). Their commitment to God was largely nominal. Insensitive to what their position required, they failed to live out their obligations to him in every aspect of their behaviour.

*The Evidence (3:8c).* **In tithes and offerings.** The answer is blunt and specific. A tithe was a 'tenth part'. In Scripture it first occurs in the history of Abraham (Gen. 14:20) and of Jacob (Gen. 28:22). It reflects an ancient custom of giving a tenth of one's income and/or possessions to a superior, whether the king or the god one worshipped. Under the Mosaic covenant it became a compulsory contribution for Israel. A tenth of all produce was 'holy to the LORD' (Lev. 27:30) and was dedicated to him as part of the praise Israel gave to the LORD their God for the good land he had given them (Deut. 8:10). The Levites received this tithe to support them in their service of the LORD (Num. 18:24), and in turn they gave a tenth to the priests (Num. 18:28). Deuteronomy 12:5-19 and 14:22-29 provide further information about the procedure, emphasising that it was to the central sanctuary that the tithe was to be brought, and that every third year the tithe was to be used to support not only the Levites, but also the less well-off in the community. We do not know the extent to which these arrangements were subsequently practised, though Amos 4:4 suggests that tithing persisted in the Northern Kingdom, but not for the right reasons. Under Hezekiah's reformation, there had been a generous response to the renewed maintenance of the priests and Levites (2 Chr. 31:2-12). Though tithing was again reinstituted in

Nehemiah's day (Neh. 10:36-39; 12:44), it soon lapsed and the Levites had to provide for themselves (Neh. 13:10)—an abuse Nehemiah rectified (Neh. 13:12). Malachi is speaking just before the time of Nehemiah, and we may assume that the tithe was not fully contributed then either.

'Offerings' does not represent the Hebrew word usually rendered in this way (1:9), but is one which could refer to contributions made for various purposes—the materials for constructing the tabernacle (Ex. 25:2-3) or the half shekel paid as atonement money (Ex. 30:13). It does, however, have a technical meaning, which seems relevant here. It is rendered 'that was waved' (presumably from the action that was employed in presenting it) to denote the portions of sacrifices set apart for the priests (Ex. 29:27-28; Lev. 7:34; 10:14-15; Num. 5:9). Along with tithes, such 'wave offerings' played an important role in the upkeep of the priests.

**You are under a curse (3:9)**, literally 'by the curse you are being cursed'. For 'curse', see on 2:2 and Zechariah 5:3. They had violated the terms of their covenant relation with the LORD and were under the sanctions of the broken covenant. It was not just that they were under threat of future punishment for their misbehaviour, but God had already acted in fatherly chastisement of them, to recall them to obedience (Heb. 12:7-13). The blessing that is promised in 3:10-11 suggests that this curse was seen in drought and crop pestilence. That accords with the threatened outcome of disobedience in Deuteronomy 28:15-24, where this relatively rare noun 'curse' occurs in verse 20. But the people failed to see the significance of what was happening to them. Perhaps they used the poor economic conditions as an excuse to reduce their givings even further. **Because you are robbing me** shows how they were continuing to behave. 'Me' is strongly stressed to bring out the gravity of their offence. It was not just a matter of reducing the income of the priests and Levites. God had required that they be maintained in this way, and the action was against him. **The whole nation of you** conveys the suggestion that they have become practically heathen. 'Nation' is used to refer to foreigners (as in 1:11, 14; 3:12) and when it, rather than 'people', is used to describe Israel, it is generally as a result of their acting contrary to God's way (Deut. 32:28; Isa. 1:4; 10:6; Judg. 2:20; Jer.

7:28; Ezk. 2:3). The corruption was widespread in the land: even the priests are included in the charge.

**Bring the whole tithe into the storehouse, that there may be food in my house (*3:10*).** This is not a matter to be decided as the people think fit. God's commands must be obeyed. 'Whole' suggests part was being kept back, or part of the people were not contributing at all. But the former is more likely as the whole nation (3:9) had been involved. 'Storehouse' may refer to rooms in the Temple complex or a special building there for storing the contributions before they were distributed (2 Chr. 31:11; Neh. 10:37; 12:44; 13:5, 12). Although the word for 'food' here was originally what was torn off as prey by an animal, it is also used more generally (Ps. 111:5; Prov. 31:15). Here it refers to provisions for the Levites rather than what would be offered in sacrifice (1:7, 12).

*The Blessing (3:10b-12).* The LORD then urges the people to put practical obedience to the test. **"Test me in this," says the LORD Almighty.** 'Test' indicates proving or trying. This is usually conducted by God as he scrutinises man inwardly, searching minds and hearts (Ps. 7:9; 11:4-5; 17:3; 66:10; 139:23; Jer. 11:20; 17:10; Zech. 13:9). It is abnormal and an affront to God when his people lack faith and seek to put him to the test (Ps. 95:9), though he is willing to respond to the requests of weak faith to make his power evident (Judg. 6:36-40). Perhaps the Biblical incident nearest to this challenge is that given to king Ahaz, 'Ask the LORD your God for a sign, whether in the deepest depths or in the highest heights' (Isa. 7:11). With seeming piety Ahaz declines to put the LORD to the test (a synonym of the word found in this verse)—but it is really because he has already decided to act differently (compare Isa. 7:1 with 2 Kgs. 16:5-7). Here the challenge before the people is to see if the LORD Almighty, who has all under his sway, will indeed reward obedience. The command to test God is as much a test of them, for the required response involves a willingness to act in faith.

**And see if I will not throw open the floodgates of heaven and pour out so much blessing that you will not have room enough for it.** 'The floodgates of heaven'—a comparison with a sluice holding back water—had been opened at the time of the flood (Gen. 7:11;

8:2), and this might well indicate that the blessing promised is rain. That would be in accord with the blessing promised for covenant obedience, 'The LORD will open the heavens, the storehouse of his bounty, to send rain on your land in season and to bless all the work of your hands' (Deut. 28:12). But the phrase is also used of more general provision of food at uninflated prices (2 Kgs. 7:2,19), and the possibility of a more general reference cannot be ruled out. Assured rainfall would, however, lead to general prosperity in the land.

The clause 'that you will not have room enough for it' renders a phrase that is more literally 'until failure of sufficiency'. A similar phrase occurs in Psalm 72:7, where it is rendered 'till the moon is no more.' On that basis the phrase here would mean 'till sufficiency is no more', that is until the divine provision runs out—never! Perpetual obedience will meet with perpetual blessing. Alternatively, the thought may be (as the NIV favours) that the blessing will be so great that there will no longer be sufficient room to hold what God will provide.

**I will prevent pests from devouring your crops (*3:11*).** 'Prevent' is literally 'rebuke' (see on 2:3). 'Pests' are literally 'the eater'. It may more specifically denote the locust (Joel 1:4) in reversal of the covenant curse of Deuteronomy 28:42. **"And the vines in your fields will not cast their fruit," says the LORD Almighty.** The vines represent fruit trees in general. They will not 'miscarry' or 'be childless'. If in ordinary affairs it is true that 'one man gives freely, yet gains even more; another withholds unduly, but comes to poverty' (Prov. 11:24), how much more is this the case when the giving is to the LORD in accordance with his covenant.

**Then all the nations will call you blessed (*3:12*).** Israel will once more take up the central and unique position assigned to it in God's covenant (Gen. 12:3; Isa. 61:9; Zech. 8:13). 'Blessed' is a term of congratulations, looking to all that Israel will enjoy. 'All the nations' who in the past had opposed and ridiculed Israel (Ezk. 36:15) will be forced by the divine blessing to recognise her status.

**"For yours will be a delightful land," says the LORD Almighty.** 'Yours' might well be rendered 'you and yours' as it points emphatically not only to the land but to the people also, literally 'you will be, you, a land of delight'. Though the blessings that are bestowed attract the attention and approval of the nations, the delight is primarily in the eyes of God. 'You will be called Hephzibah' that is, 'my delight is in her' (Isa. 62:4; see Jer. 3:19; Ezk. 20:6, 15; Dan. 8:9; 11:16, 41; Zech. 7:14).

Are these demands and promises as applicable today? It is possible to emphasise the Lord's material blessings to such an extent that the whole gospel message is distorted and faith in Christ is presented almost as a business plan for economic success. But there is the opposite danger of divorcing material prosperity entirely from God. The Scriptural requirement is to seek first the Father's kingdom and his righteousness (Mt. 6:33). Those who do so will know his provision, for he is the one who gives us our daily bread (Mt. 6:11).

God still requires that we steward all the resources committed to us, acknowledging that 'every good and perfect gift is from above, coming down from the Father of heavenly lights' (Jas. 1:17). While tithing has lost its significance as a mandatory obligation under the new covenant, it is still the case that our giving to the Lord should be in keeping with our income (1 Cor. 16:2). We should respond to Paul's injunction to 'excel in this grace of giving' (2 Cor. 8:7). But to view it as an ironclad formula for material success is to betray a spirit alien to the gospel. Equally, to disregard the obligation to give to the Lord's cause is to reveal a failure to understand all that has been given to us. We must remember that Jesus himself said, 'It is more blessed to give than to receive' (Acts 20:35). 'Give, and it will be given to you. A good measure, pressed down, shaken together and running over, will be poured into your lap. For with the measure you use, it will be measured to you' (Lk. 6:38). Small faith and small giving still involve small receiving (2 Cor. 9:6).

*Study Questions*

**3:6** What does the constancy of God involve for the church today? Rom. 11:29; Heb. 13:8; Jas. 1:17; Rev. 1:8, 11, 17-18.

**3:8** How should preachers and other Christian workers be maintained? Mt. 10:10; 1 Cor. 9:14; Gal. 6:6; Phil. 4:14; 1 Tim. 5:18.

**3:10**  Is it right to test God?  Judg. 6:36-40; Ps. 95:9; Isa. 7:10-12; 1 Cor. 10:9; Heb. 3:8.

What principles should underlie Christian giving?  Deut. 16:17; Mt. 6:3; 10:8; Rom. 12:8; 1 Cor. 16:2; 2 Cor. 8:12; 9:6-15.

### Malachi 3:13-18:  The Faithless and the Faithful

There was a blurring of what was right and what was wrong throughout the community in Malachi's day, and it is to this problem that the prophet returns in the final dialogue he records. The people were complaining that they did not see what good it did them to serve God (3:13-15), but they are reminded that the day will come when the difference between the righteous and the wicked will be made abundantly evident (3:18). Indeed, there already was a detectable difference. Malachi describes a group of 'those who feared the LORD' (3:16). Their conduct was quite distinct from that of the community at large, and they will be suitably rewarded (3:17).

*The Faithless (3:13-15).*  The people had previously 'wearied' the LORD with what they were thinking and saying about the prosperity of the wicked, and how this reflected unfavourably on God (2:17). What they are now charged with reveals a more advanced stage of religious cynicism and spirit of alienation from the covenant.

*Divine Accusation (3:13a).*  **"You have said harsh things against me," says the LORD (*3:13*).**  'Said harsh things', literally 'your words have been strong', is also found in the sense of 'overrule' (2 Sam. 24:4; 1 Chr. 21:4). It can extend to the thought of 'became hard' (Ex. 7:13, 22), and as such would indicate the perversity they were displaying. The people had adopted a more aggressive attitude against the LORD than at 2:17. This expressed itself in strong criticism of him.

*Counter-question (3:13b).*  The dialogue continues with the sort of rejoinder that has become standard as the people fail to appreciate how the criticism can possibly relate to them. **Yet you ask, 'What have we said against you?'** The form of the verb 'said' pictures them as speaking to one another (it is also found in 3:16). The same construction is rendered 'slander' in Psalm 119:23. It is reminiscent of the murmuring that took place in Israel against the LORD's dealings with them in the wilderness (Num. 21:5, 7; Ps. 78:19). Again the people were reacting to unfavourable circumstances, not by questioning what was wrong with themselves, but by complaining against God. They should rather 'heed the rod and the One who appointed it' (Mic. 6:9).

*The Evidence (3:14).* The charge is again made more specific. **You have said, 'It is futile to serve God'** (*3:14*). 'Serve' goes beyond worship (Ex. 4:23; 7:16) to entail a life of total obedience (Deut. 10:12; Josh. 24:14). It was intended to be a matter of a total commitment to God, done gladly and willingly (1 Chr. 28:9; Ps. 100:2). This was what the LORD would bless. In contrast, what was 'futile' lacked substance and was worthless (compare the 'dreams *that are false*', Zech. 10:2). Contrary to what they had been taught, they had concluded that serving God was the road to ruin and disaster because it was all a sham and brought them no benefit.

**What did we gain?** presents a revealing insight into their mentality. The dominant motive in their lives was personal, material advantage. This drove a wedge between them and God, when they should rather have been praying, 'Turn my heart towards your statutes and not towards selfish gain' (Ps. 119:36; see also Prov. 1:19; Isa. 33:14-16). Such an attitude towards life debarred from leadership in Israel (Ex. 18:21) and in the New Testament church (1 Tim. 3:3; 6:6-11). Those who were greedy for gain were strongly condemned by the prophets (Isa. 56:11; Jer. 8:10; Ezk. 22:27). Their question presupposes that only a negative answer can be given to it: serving God brought them no gain.

**By carrying out his requirements** or 'observing what is to be observed' was behaviour that had characterised Abraham (Gen. 26:5). It is also used of the work of those in the temple (Lev. 8:35; 22:9; Ezk. 44:8, 15-16; 48:11; Zech. 3:7), and of all the people carrying out the separate ordinances (Lev. 18:30; Num. 9:19, 23; Josh. 22:2-3; 2 Chr. 13:11). In rejecting this, they were defying God and saying that they were no longer prepared to live as the covenant people.

**And going about like mourners before the LORD Almighty** shows the dismal view they took of serving God. 'Like mourners' as a word occurs only here, but it is an adverb from a root meaning 'to be dark' and seems to denote the sort of clothes they wore. They had tried to please the LORD by behaving like those who were grief-stricken. Either this was because they were accusing God of not wanting them to enjoy themselves, or more possibly they had understood his dealings with them as calling for them to repent, and so they had acted like those who were penitent. But *acted* was all that it was—they had not been convinced that they had done anything wrong and that there was a need for repentance. But having gone through the outward motions of religion, they expected God to be pleased with them.

**But now** (*3:15*) introduces the conclusions they felt compelled to draw because of the lack of return for all their efforts to please God. They aligned themselves with the wicked person who 'blesses the greedy and reviles the LORD' (Ps. 10:3). They will no longer try to act piously and put a religious veneer on their attitude. Rather they will speak plainly: **We call the arrogant blessed.** It is a perversion of the true ascription of blessedness (3:12) because the arrogant are those who are self-important, assuming that everything focuses on them. From this it is but a short step to straying from God's commands (Ps. 119:21) and setting themselves by any means at all against those who are true to him (Ps. 119:51, 85, 122). As such they are 'cursed' by God (Ps. 119:21), but the people refuse to see it that way.

Discussion of the identity of the arrogant follows the same lines as that of the evil-doers in 2:17. It may be that this refers to a group within Judah and Jerusalem, whose motives were like those who oppressed the poor, as is described in Nehemiah 5:1-13. Alternatively, the people may be thinking of other nations around them. 'Arrogance of the haughty' is used of the attitude of Babylon in Isaiah 13:11. If this is the pattern they were applauding, then they were in effect saying, 'Let us become pagan.'

They adduce two pieces of evidence to justify their conclusions. *(1)* **Certainly the evildoers prosper.** Those in view are the same as those called 'the arrogant'. They are viewed as being 'built', or established (it would seem by God) in their course of behaviour and so enjoying success. *(2)* **And even those who challenge God escape.** 'Challenge' is the same word as 'test' in 3:10, but here it is used for a presumptuous abandonment of God's way to see if retribution will follow. But they have escaped, and in the light of this, the people feel justified in adopting the same lifestyle. They were perilously close to concluding that they might as well abandon the worship of the LORD and the requirements of his covenant. This stance is an index of how far their hearts were from the LORD (Isa. 29:13; Mt. 15:8).

*The Faithful (3:16-18).* But though such thinking had become commonplace in the restored community, it had not become universal. **Then *(3:16)*** points to an antithesis in what follows. No longer do we hear the voice of the community in general setting itself to follow the arrogant in their practical atheism, but rather **those who feared the LORD talked with each other.** 'Those who feared the LORD' are those who displayed true reverence towards him, putting their trust in him. Such fear is of the essence of the Old Testament presentation of true religion. 'And now, O Israel, what does the LORD your God ask of you but to fear the LORD your God, to walk in all his ways, to love him, to serve the LORD your God with all your heart and with all your soul, and to observe the LORD's commands and decrees that I am giving you today for your own good?' (Deut. 10:12-13). It was in this way that the Teacher sought to sum up his discourse: 'Now all has been heard; here is the conclusion of the matter: Fear God and keep his commandments, for this is the whole <duty> of man' (Eccl. 12:13). Therefore true fear of God evidenced itself in walking in his ways (Ps. 128:1) and delighting in his commands (Ps. 112:1). Such fear leads to true blessing. It is the beginning of wisdom (Prov. 1:7), and because the LORD delights in those who display it (Ps. 147:11), it would be accompanied by his compassion (Ps. 103:13) and abundant blessing (Ps. 31:19; 34:9).

The same verb is used to describe their behaviour as the community had employed in its question (3:13), though here 'each with his neighbour' is also stated. When evil is rampant, standing for the truth is more difficult (Amos 5:13), and so they are presented not as taking on their adversaries, but engaging in a ministry of mutual encouragement (Heb. 10:25).

We are not told what it is that they said, but far more significantly we are told God's reaction: **And the LORD listened and heard.** He was not an idle spectator of what was going on, but was attentively taking note in his capacity as the witness whose evidence would be taken into account in the coming day of judgment.

**A scroll of remembrance was written in his presence concerning those who feared the LORD and honoured his name.** Kings of the ancient world had such records made of important events in their reigns (Est. 6:1; Dan. 7:10; Acts 10:4). God too is thought of as having a special book (Ex. 32:32; Ps. 139:16; Isa. 4:3; 65:6; Ezk. 13:9; Rev. 20:12) in which the names of the pious are held (Ex. 32:32; Ps. 69:28; 87:6) and sometimes also the ungodly (Isa. 65:6). Here it is a matter of angelic recorders taking down what the faithful had to endure, how they lamented because of the attacks of the wicked (Ps. 56:8), and what their king's verdict on it all was. 'Concerning' might also be rendered 'on behalf of' or 'in the interests of'. God will not forget their work and the love they have shown him (Heb. 6:10).

The description of them as those 'who feared the LORD' repeats that found earlier in the verse. 'Honoured his name' is an unusual phrase. It does not focus on outward action, but inward respect. The basic idea behind the verb is that of the mind engaged in thought. Here it seems to be a matter of frequent thinking or meditation. It has a positive note to it ('respected' in Isa. 33:8; 'think of' in Ps. 144:3). Those who fear the LORD are habitually meditating on all that he has revealed about himself (for 'name', see on 1:6), and in this way are seen to be setting a high value on all that he is and does. So they are glorifying God, and deriving comfort and strength for themselves.

**"They will be mine," says the LORD Almighty (3:17).** The reference is of course to those who feared him. 'Mine' is emphatic. **In the day when I make up my treasured possession** refers to the time of the LORD's final judgment. The people are already his treasured possession, but then it will be made evident when he will gather them together into final glory. His 'treasured possession' uses a word which in a secular context denotes the personal property of the king as distinct from what is his as monarch ('personal treasures' in

1 Chr. 29:3; 'treasure of kings' in Eccl. 2:8). In the Sinai covenant it was used of Israel to indicate the LORD's particular interest in them and selection of them before all other nations. 'Out of all nations you will be my treasured possession' (Ex. 19:5). Israel already was God's possession (Deut. 7:6; 14:2; 26:18; Ps. 135:4), but what is envisaged is a coming time when God will gather his elect together and openly vindicate them. As such, the promise is fulfilled in the church, the true Israel of God and his eternal possession, which is openly acknowledged and provided for in the day of his coming (Eph. 1:14; 2 Thess. 2:14; Tit. 2:14; 1 Pet. 2:9).

**I will spare them, just as in compassion a man spares his son who serves him.** The same verb is used twice. It means both 'have compassion' and 'spare' and the NIV brings out the two meanings of the word by adding 'in compassion' in its rendering of the second clause (see on Zech. 11:5-6). The pious are spared from the ordeal of the day of the LORD's coming (Jer. 50:14; Ezk. 8:18; Joel 2:18). The comparison refers back to the relationship of 1:6. It also answers the assertion that it is futile to serve the LORD (3:14). The truly righteous ones will be made abundantly clear on the day of the LORD's appearing.

**And you will again see the distinction between the righteous and the wicked, between those who serve God and those who do not (3:18).** For 'serve', see on 3:14. 'You' addresses those who spoke in 3:13, and 'again' refers to the fact that God had tried to make apparent the distinction between those who are his and those who are not on various occasions in the past. 'Then you will know that the LORD makes a distinction between Egypt and Israel' (Ex. 11:7). There had been specific judgments against individuals such as Achan (Josh. 7:15), Nabal (1 Sam. 25:38) and Uzzah (2 Sam. 6:7) and against nations such as Assyria (2 Kgs. 19:35; Nah. 1:7-8). From these they could have learned of God's discriminating justice. But they had not. In the final judgment the matter will be clear beyond any doubt (Mt. 25:46; Rom. 2:7-8).

The righteous are those who serve God and whose conduct is consequently in accordance with the demands of the covenant. It is not a matter of salvation by works, as if their good standing with God were achieved by their own efforts at keeping the demands of the covenant. On the contrary, their conduct is the evidence that they understand and appreciate all that God has done for them. Their obedience is an index of their indebtedness to him for salvation, and their love for him reveals itself in serving him with all their heart and soul (Deut. 11:13). They view themselves as subjects of their covenant saviour and king, and conduct themselves accordingly. 'Don't you know that when you offer yourselves to someone to obey him as slaves, you are slaves to the one whom you obey—whether you are slaves to sin, which leads to death, or to obedience, which leads to righteousness?' (Rom. 6:16).

There is a tendency, arising out of a false conception of love and a desire not to give offence, to blur the difference between those who serve God and those who do not. But this is an unscriptural practice. Jesus never did so (Mt. 7:21-22), nor Paul (2 Cor. 13:5; 2 Tim. 1:5), nor Peter (2 Pet. 1:5-11). The destiny of the impenitent should not be presented harshly, but solemnly and with tears that any should be so blind as to continue recklessly on their way. To those about to plunge themselves into outer darkness for ever, banished from the presence of God, it is not love to keep silent and withhold the gospel message that may be blessed to their eternal salvation. Scripture warns us that in the ultimate analysis there is no middle ground, no grey area. There is only the right hand and the left hand of the king (Mt. 25:33), and once he has drawn the line there will be no crossing over from one side to the other (Lk. 16:26).

## Study Questions

**3:15** Arrogance and pride—how do they block out a true understanding of God? Ps. 10:11-13; 36:1; 86:14; Jer. 43:2; Dan. 5:20; 1 Tim. 6:17; 2 Pet. 2:10.

**3:16** What is the significance of the book of life? Ps. 69:28; Dan. 12:1; Lk. 10:20; Phil. 4:3; Rev. 13:8; 17:8; 20:12; 21:27.

What role does fellowship have in strengthening believers? Ps. 119:63; Lk. 22:32; Jn. 17:21; Acts 2:42; Eph. 4:3; 1 Thess. 5:11, 14; Jas. 5:16.

## Malachi 4:1-6: The Great and Dreadful Day

The people of Malachi's day were confused as to what was right and what was wrong. They were no longer sure that the LORD existed— at least in any way that mattered for their living. They no longer considered that they lived under his scrutiny. So Malachi ends his prophecy by warning them that no matter how they felt, there was the certain and impending reality of divine judgment. This is the 'burden' that he has to present to them (1:1). If they do not amend their ways, they will experience the full wrath of God (4:1). But his message is a plea. Can they not see the provision the LORD will make for all who are truly his (4:2-3)? There is a twofold piece of advice that has to be followed: remember the law that the LORD had given through Moses to regulate the living of his covenant people (4:5), and pay heed to the injunctions to repent that had been the characteristic plea of the prophets (Zech. 1:3-4). It would also be the message of the last of the prophets, who would come in the spirit and power of Elijah (4:5-6).

*The Fate of the Wicked (4:1).* In the Hebrew text there is no chapter division here, and 4:1-6 are counted as 3:19-24. In many respects this is preferable, because there is no break in thought between 3:18 and 4:1. The separation of the righteous and the wicked spoken of in 3:18 will be clearly evident because the day of the LORD will have come. **Surely (*4:1*)**, or 'for', expresses this link.

**The day is coming.** Malachi does not use the phrase 'the day of the LORD', but there is no doubt that he is referring to the same reality. The LORD calls on a generation that is confused and uncertain about the existence of ultimate moral standards—indeed, doubting the justice of God himself—to give careful consideration to what is going to happen. 'The day' points to the time when the LORD openly confronts the rebellion of this world, and judges it. Because of the pervasiveness of sin, it will be a time of anguish and inescapable despair, even for those who expect the LORD to intervene on their behalf (Amos 5:18-20). Divine scrutiny causes all human institutions to be convulsed—both those of Israel and those of heathen nations. It is compared to a great slaughter (Isa. 63:1-6), to the ravages of war (Zeph. 1:10-13), and to an earthquake (Isa. 13:13). It also introduces a time of divine restoration for the people of God.

The day 'is coming' (Joel 2:1). When it is presented as imminent, this is not just a device to underline the certainty of the future event. It depicts the coming day as one which is not arbitrarily imposed on the world, but which is rather an inevitable consequence of what already exists. This day is the culmination of events and conditions that are already to be found. The God of holiness and truth cannot endure rebellion against himself indefinitely. The Old Testament prophets were not always permitted to see that the LORD's action against the rebellious would be in two stages (see on 3:2). Here the focus of Malachi's vision is undoubtedly on God's final coming in universal judgment.

**It will burn like a furnace.** Only here is it said the day will burn. But 'burn' is connected with divine anger (Isa. 30:27; Jer. 4:4; 21:12; Ps. 2:12; 89:46), as is the comparison with a furnace (Isa. 31:9). Such furnaces, or ovens, were made of clay, were roughly cylindrical in shape (about three feet high and two feet in diameter), and were often sunk into the ground. They would be heated for baking by lighting a fire in them at their base. This heated the sides, and after the removal of the fire, the hot sides and stones at the base of the oven would be used to cook the food. The point was that in such ovens the heat was far more intense than with an open fire. This is the character of the day as regards the wicked. 'This is how it will be at the end of the age. The angels will come and separate the wicked from the righteous and throw them into the fiery furnace, where there will be weeping and gnashing of teeth' (Mt. 13:49-50; see also Mt. 13:42).

**All the arrogant and every evildoer** refers back to the twofold description of those who do not fear the LORD (3:15). This furnace has a fire that is not to purify (3:2), but to consume. So all those who have opposed God **"will be stubble, and that day that is coming will set them on fire," says the LORD Almighty.** When the LORD comes in judgment, his wrath will be like a conflagration which completely engulfs those who have rebelled against him. There will be no escape. The word translated 'stubble'—the remains of the crop left in the ground after harvest—may also refer to straw or chaff. But all three burn well, and that is the point (Ex. 15:7; Isa. 5:24; 47:14; Joel 2:5; Ob. 18; Nah. 1:10).

**Not a root or a branch will be left to them.** Another metaphor is being employed, but the intent is the same. They will be completely wiped out. A graphic sketch of what is meant is given by Bildad when he describes the place of one who knows not God (Job 18:16-21). In Amos the LORD describes his overthrow of the Amorites in similar terms: 'I destroyed his fruit above and his roots below' (Amos 2:9). A tree with roots and branches suggests life, growth and prosperity (Ps. 80:9, 10). One side to the day of the LORD is that this will be taken away from the evildoers in Israel. All the insolent questions will be finally silenced.

The two images found here are also central to John the Baptist's description of the ministry of Christ. 'The axe is already at the root of the trees, and every tree that does not produce good fruit will be cut down and thrown into the fire' (Mt. 3:10). 'His winnowing fork is in his hand, and he will clear his threshing-floor, gathering his wheat into the barn and burning up the chaff with unquenchable fire' (Mt. 3:12).

*The Sun of Righteousness (4:2-3).* **But for you who revere my name (4:2),** literally 'fear my name' (see on 3:16), introduces the other side to the day for those who are loyal to the LORD. For 'my name', see on 1:6. Those who are loyal to the LORD are promised that action will be taken on their behalf. **The sun of righteousness will rise.** There is as yet no consensus as to where the emphasis should be placed in the unusual phrase 'sun of righteousness'. Most modern translations read it as 'sun of *righteousness*', that is, righteousness will appear on that day as clearly as the sun shines at dawn. Such a comparison of righteousness with sunlight is found elsewhere in Scripture: 'He will make your righteousness shine like the dawn' (Ps. 37:6). There had been those who had doubted God's justice and righteousness (2:16; 3:14-15), but for those who feared God it would be demonstrated with the clarity of 'the light of morning at sunrise on a cloudless morning' (2 Sam. 23:4) that they are right with God. His justice will prevail, though in mercy he does not act immediately.

But it is also possible to read the phrase as '*sun* of righteousness', that is, the sun which is characterised by righteousness. Since, however, that is not an attribute easily associated with the physical sun, 'sun' is taken as a metaphorical reference to a person. To avoid being implicated with the sun worship of surrounding nations, the Old Testament rarely uses 'sun' of God. But it is found. 'For the LORD God is a sun and shield; the LORD bestows favour and honour; no good thing does he withhold from those whose walk is blameless' (Ps. 84:11), and the same verb is employed in 'the LORD *rises* upon you and his glory appears over you' (Isa. 60:2). It would then be a reference to the coming king and deliverer whose name was revealed to be: 'The LORD Our Righteousness' (Jer. 23:6). It is in this sense that it is taken up by Zechariah, the father of John the Baptist, when he talked of 'the tender mercy of our God, by which the rising sun will come to us from heaven to shine on those living in darkness and in the shadow of death, to guide our feet into the path of peace' (Lk. 1:78-79). The Messiah will comprehensively and gloriously display God's covenant gift, restoring justice and bringing salvation to all who are his people.

**With healing in its wings.** 'Healing' is the opposite of 'disaster' (Prov. 6:15) and 'trouble' (Prov. 13:17) as well as of disease. 'He sent forth his word and healed them; he rescued them from the grave' (Ps. 107:20). 'By his wounds we are healed' (Isa. 53:5). Their whole existence will be radically changed by the gracious provision of God. The sun was often depicted as a winged disc in Egyptian and Mesopotamian religion, but that was a symbol of dominion, assuring the king of divine protection and victory. Here the sun is presented as beneficent whose rays provide light, warmth and health.

**And you will go out and leap like calves released from the stall.** A picture of animals leaping about in delight at their freedom is used to convey the exuberant joy of the pious on the day of the LORD.

**Then you will trample down the wicked (4:3).** It is part of the prophetic perspective that on that day those who have been previously 'trampled down' (Josh. 10:24; Isa. 51:23; Ps. 110:1; Mic. 2:12-13) will be granted victory over their enemies (Amos 9:1; Isa. 11:14; Zeph. 2:9; 3:19-20; Ps. 149:7). There will be a reversal of roles, just as Abraham said to the rich man, 'Son, remember that in your lifetime you received your good things, while Lazarus received bad things, but now he is comforted here and you are in agony' (Lk. 16:25). **"They will be ashes under the soles of your feet on the day when I do these things," says the LORD Almighty.** This describes the victory parade of the triumphant king and his people who have put down all rebellion against him. 'Ashes' may be from the fire (Ezk. 28:18), or 'dust' from the road. On the day of the LORD nobody will be able to doubt who has won the victory.

*The Two Ministries (4:4-6).* The dialogues and disputes are over, and Malachi brings his message to a conclusion with a twofold piece of advice, centring round two figures from the past: Moses and Elijah. They represent the two great divisions of Old Testament teaching—the Law and the Prophets. In the first, the norms for God's people were clearly set before them, and by the other those standards were restated and consciences aroused to obey them. Together they show that whatever hampers covenant fidelity must be dealt with if the day of the LORD is to be a time of blessing, and not of covenant curse.

**Remember the law of my servant Moses (4:4).** The work of Moses had been foundational as the mediator of the Sinai covenant. There is no suggestion with him, as there will be with Elijah, that he needs to come and lay his foundation again. Instead the people are urged to 'remember'. That was never just a matter of intellectual recall. To remember is to prepare to act. Nor is the reference to 'law' urging upon them some legalistic self-righteousness. 'Law' is instruction, the teaching of the covenant king as to how he wished his people to respond to the redeeming love he had shown to them. It is on that basis alone that the people will be adequately prepared for his coming. This is how the people should now react in the light of that coming day.

It is difficult to take the scope of what is referred to as anything other than the whole Sinaitic legislation, **the decrees and laws I gave him at Horeb for all Israel.** Horeb is an alternative name for Sinai, found mainly but not exclusively in Deuteronomy (Ex. 3:1; 17:6; 33:6; Deut. 1:2, 6, 19 etc.). Possibly it refers to the range of hills, of which Sinai was the one on which Moses received the law (Ex. 19:20). The covenant was for the entire nation, and no group could say it did not refer to them. 'Decrees and ordinances' ('laws' renders a different word from 'law' at the beginning of the verse) are parallel terms. For 'decrees', see on 3:7. Strictly they refer to the categorical law ('You shall not ...') and the case law ('if something happens, then

...') respectively, but together they are a common expression for the law of God in general (Lev. 26:46; Deut. 4:1,5; Ps. 147:19). It is more than 'gave' as if there were some option in the matter. It is literally 'commanded', these are the laws of their covenant king and they were imposed on the people without any option on their part.

**See, I will send you the prophet Elijah (4:5).** This is patterned after 3:1, and refers to 'my messenger, who will prepare the way before me'. He will not only come to Israel, but will also act for their good. Elijah was the prophet who had come abruptly and unannounced into the public life of Israel (1 Kgs. 17:1). His departure from earth was shrouded in mystery (2 Kgs. 2:11-12). His mission was to call back to the standards of the covenant (1 Kgs. 18:36; 2 Chr. 21:12), and in accomplishing this he acted boldly and forthrightly (1 Kgs. 18:18) as also did John the Baptist to a wicked dynasty and apostate nation (Mt. 14:4).

Some interpreters try to distinguish between 'my messenger' of 3:1 whom they identify as John the Baptist, the forerunner of the first coming, and Elijah, who will return to herald the second coming of the Lord. But this results from failing to appreciate the foreshortened perspective that the Old Testament prophets frequently had of the future. They were not always permitted to distinguish clearly between the first and second coming of Christ.

Though the Jews at the time of Christ expected Elijah to return in person (Mt. 17:10-11), probably because of Elijah's ascension to heaven, this prophecy was not fulfilled literalistically by the reappearance of the Old Testament prophet before the first coming of Christ, any more than we are to suppose such a reappearance will occur before the second coming. The promise was realised in the ministry of John the Baptist, as the angel Gabriel authoritatively announced to Zechariah regarding the son who would be born to him, 'And he will go on before the Lord, in the spirit and power of Elijah, to turn the hearts of the fathers to their children and the disobedient to the wisdom of the righteous—to make ready a people prepared for the Lord' (Lk. 1:17). Jesus himself later confirmed this recognition of John's forceful preaching of repentance and judgment as the realisation of this prophecy. 'If you are willing to accept it, he is the Elijah who was to come' (Mt. 11:14). 'Jesus replied, "To be sure,

Elijah comes and will restore all things. But I tell you, Elijah has already come, and they did not recognise him, but have done to him everything they wished. In the same way the Son of Man is going to suffer at their hands.' Then the disciples understood that he was talking to them about John the Baptist' (Mt. 17:11-13).

When the Jews quizzed John the Baptist if he were the Christ, or Elijah, or the Prophet, John answered 'No' (Jn. 1:19-21). But he was answering their question in the spirit in which they asked it. The Jews were looking for the reappearance of the Old Testament Elijah. Such excessive literalism is, however, alien to the interpretation authoritatively given in Scripture.

**Before that great and dreadful day of the LORD comes** shows Elijah as paving the way for the LORD. 'Great and dreadful' is found in Joel 2:31, see also Joel 2:11.

**He will turn the hearts of the fathers to their children, and the hearts of the children to their fathers (4:6).** This is the purpose of Elijah's coming. Does this mean he will establish a new social order by pacifying family quarrels and bridging the generation gap? Some have taken 'fathers' in the sense of forefathers and have understood the prophet to refer to the patriarchs, who had previously not recognised their offspring (Isa. 63:16), but who now look down from heaven with approval as their descendants turn to the LORD as a result of John's ministry. The repentant offspring also come to a new appreciation of their forefathers' faith, and there is a harmony throughout the people of God of all generations.

It is more likely, however, that the reference is to the circumstances of Malachi's day where mixed marriages (2:11) and easy divorce (2:14) had disrupted and soured family life. It seems these were still prevalent practices in Christ's day (Mt. 5:32; 19:9). Family life is of the utmost importance for the spiritual and physical well-being of those in the family group, and also of the church and society in general. The ministry of the forerunner called for repentance in all aspects of life, including the family.

There is, however, the solemn possibility that Elijah might not succeed. **Or else I will come and strike the land with a curse.** It is not of course the LORD's coming that is prevented, but his striking. The 'curse' is the ban, the utter devotion to destruction (Isa. 43:28—

and NIV footnote; Jer. 25:9) of what is an abomination in the LORD's sight. The land includes the people (2:11; 3:11). In the synagogue reading of Malachi it was customary to read the next to last verse again after the last verse because its serious and solemn message seemed an inappropriate and harsh ending. The Septuagint, the early Greek translation of the Old Testament, seems to have known of a similar custom in that it puts verse 4 after verses 5 and 6.

But these are the basic alternatives of the covenant, and they form a fitting conclusion to the prophetic books. The prophet's words were not intended to stimulate idle curiosity, nor yet spiritual complacency. The blessings of the covenant are conditioned on obedience, and given the reality of the grip that sin has on human hearts and lives, the prophets confronted their generation and ours with the need for a repentant response to avoid the curse of disobedience.

The same message needs to be presented today. The foundation of the gospel message has been irrevocably laid. What is needed is not a new gospel, but a genuine response to what already exists. There are indeed those who think the master is taking a long time in coming (Lk. 12:45) and begin to behave as if he will never return at all. But how erroneous that conclusion is will be revealed when the master of that servant will come on a day when he does not expect him and at an hour he is not aware of, and punish him (Lk. 12:46). The lesson has to be learned before it is too late that we are all accountable to God, and that our account reveals a woeful shortfall. Our debt can be made good only if we apply to Christ now and receive by faith what he alone can provide. To spurn his offer now will lead to our being unable to meet the demands of divine scrutiny on the day that is surely coming.

*Study Questions*

**4:2** What part does 'fear' play in a Christian response to God? 2 Cor. 7:1; Eph. 5:21; Phil. 2:12; Col. 3:22; Heb. 5:7; 12:28; Rev. 14:7; 19:5.

**4:5**  Show how obedience to God's requirements is necessary for a correct response to him. Mt. 19:17; Jn. 13:17; 14:15, 21; 1 Cor. 9:21; Gal. 6:2; Eph. 6:6; Phil. 2:12; Jas. 2:8.

**4:6**  Family relationships play an important part in Christian living. What does the Bible tell us about them? Prov. 27:11; Isa. 38:19; Lk. 11:11-13; 2 Cor. 12:14; Eph. 6:4; Col. 3:21.

## Appendix: The Interpretation of Prophecy

In looking at these three post-exilic prophets we have frequently encountered the question of how prophecies relating to the future of Israel or Jerusalem or Zion should be interpreted. This is a matter about which there is considerable divergence of opinion, and so it may be helpful to bring together in this Appendix the arguments that have been presented at different points in the book. When assessed together, they make a substantive case for the particular type of interpretation adopted here.

The fundamental principle that has been employed is that *the church of God is one in all ages*. Ultimately this is based on the primary Scriptural perspectives that 'all have sinned and fall short of the glory of God' (Rom. 3:23) and 'salvation is found in no-one else, for there is no other name under heaven given to men by which we must be saved' (Acts 4:12). Humanity has a common problem in sin, and there is only one remedy, that provided by God in Jesus Christ. Therefore the church, consisting of all those who are saved, is united by a common faith in Christ. But the church is not only the whole number of those chosen to salvation by God, and ultimately known only to him. It is also a visible organisation on earth, consisting of those who profess faith in Christ and their children. This visible organisation has been differently structured by God at different periods.

In the Old Testament we find a narrowing of God's dealings from mankind in general, first to the line of Shem (Gen. 9:26), and then to the descendants of Abraham (Gen. 12:2-3). Thus in the period up to the coming of the Messiah the focus of divine revelation was on Israel, and it was there that almost exclusively the people of God were to be found. The LORD had chosen Abraham and his descendants out of all the nations of the earth for that special role—to preserve the light of his truth in a world of darkness until he who is the Light should arise from within their number.

During that period, God's revelation took a special form associated with the tabernacle and Temple, the sacrificial offerings made there, and the many duties enjoined on the nation-state of Israel by the Mosaic law. These were real religious requirements of the time, teaching the people vital spiritual truths. But they also looked forward for their ultimate significance to the Messiah who would come. During this period, the church consisted of those who 'were all commended for their faith, yet none of them received what had been promised. God had planned something better for us so that only together with us would they be made perfect' (Heb. 11:39-40).

When Christ came, the outworking of the divine purpose of salvation moved epochally forward. It had always been the case that the narrowing of the line of promise to Abraham was so that 'all peoples on earth will be blessed through you' (Gen. 12:3), and with the completion of Christ's mission on earth the time for going to all nations had arrived (Mt. 28:19; Lk. 24:47; Acts 1:8). The church emerged from its Old Testament chrysalis. There were many changes—principally that it was no longer tied to ethnic Israel—but at the same time it was organically linked to what had gone before. Behind its newness there was a fundamental sameness, so that in a very real and important sense it is the one church in all ages, consisting both of those from the church which awaited the Messiah's coming and of those from the church which rejoices in the risen Lord.

The basic oneness of the church, whether in its spiritual essence or in its outward visible form, can be seen in the way Jesus constituted the New Testament church round the twelve apostles. Twelve corresponded to the number of the tribes of Israel, and the apostles were the centre of a new Israel. Jesus said to them, 'I tell you the truth, at the renewal of all things, when the Son of Man sits on his glorious throne, you who have followed me will also sit on twelve thrones, judging the twelve tribes of Israel' (Mt. 19:28; Lk. 22:30). Note also the description given of the redeemed in Revelation 7:4-8, and of the gates of the New Jerusalem (Rev. 21:12). Concepts drawn from the Old Testament organisation of God's people are naturally employed to describe their New Testament counterparts and successors in the consummation of God's saving purpose. In the same way the Old Testament institutions of Passover and circumcision are organically linked with their New Testament equivalents of the Lord's Supper and baptism (Lk. 22:14-20; 1 Cor. 5:7; Col. 2:11-12). Remodelled to reflect the decisive change brought about by the coming of Christ, they express from a new perspective the same fundamental spiritual realities.

It was Christ himself who emphasised that he had 'other sheep that are not of this sheep pen' (Jn. 10:16). He would bring them also so that 'there shall be one flock and one shepherd' (Jn. 10:16). Paul delights in showing the oneness of the church (Rom. 12:4-5; 1 Cor. 10:17; 12:12, 20; Eph. 4:4-6; Col. 3:15), as embracing equally Jew and Gentile (Gal. 3:28). Christ 'has made the two one and has destroyed the barrier, the dividing wall of hostility' (Eph. 2:14) by which the ceremonial law separated Jew from Gentile.

But this breaking of the barrier did not just mean that Jew and Gentile were able to enter the church on the same conditions. It also meant that the people of God were one. Gentiles who had once been 'excluded from citizenship in Israel and foreigners to the covenants of promise' (Eph. 2:12) were 'no longer foreigners and aliens, but fellow-citizens with God's people and members of God's household' (Eph. 2:19). In this way the joint church of Jew and Gentile assumes the prerogatives and titles of the Old Testament church. 'If you belong to Christ, then you are Abraham's seed, and heirs according to the promise' (Gal. 3:29). The church can be called 'the Israel of God' (Gal. 6:16) as in it covenant promises of old come true. Paul uses the figure of the olive tree from which branches of Israelite stock have been broken off and into which Gentile branches have been grafted (Rom. 11:17-21). But the whole illustration hinges on the fact that it is the one olive tree throughout. Peter transfers the Old Testament titles 'a chosen people, a royal priesthood, a holy nation, a people belonging to God' (1 Pet. 2:9) to those who are the New Testament people of God.

This is of considerable significance when it comes to interpreting Old Testament prophecies regarding Israel, Jerusalem or Zion. If such terms are used in prophecies which are fulfilled prior to the coming of Christ or in the events of his life on earth, then it is clear that they refer to the Old Testament embodiment of God's people. However, if their fulfilment falls after the ascension of Christ, then the New Testament has no hesitation in finding their fulfilment in the New Testament embodiment of God's people. Jeremiah talked of a new covenant that the LORD would make with the house of Israel and with the house of Judah (Jer. 31:31-34). That new covenant was sealed by the shed blood of Christ as he indicated in the Upper Room: 'This cup is the new covenant in my blood, which is poured out for you' (Lk. 22:20). The writer to the Hebrews found no difficulty in seeing that covenant operative in the church (Heb. 8:7-13). Indeed, following the example of Paul who talked about 'the Jerusalem that is above' (Gal. 4:26), he could characterise

Christians as those who 'have come to Mount Zion, to the heavenly Jerusalem, the city of the living God' (Heb. 12:22). This was not a destination they aspired to reach in the future, but one they had already reached.

The Old Testament realities, divinely ordained and meaningful in their own age, pointed forward to what is realised in the New Testament. It is not that the terms of the prophecies are broken, but rather that they are fulfilled in an even more glorious way. These prophecies were not mere predictions formulated to be fulfilled in some mechanistic way. That would be to require that the Old Testament order be re-created and that burnt offerings be again offered (Ezk. 44:11; 45:13-25)—a viewpoint which is in fundamental conflict with the once-for-all offering of Christ (Heb. 10:12). The prophecies were promises couched in language that was meaningful to their first recipients in Old Testament times. As a sheer necessity for communication, terms had to be employed that they understood, and the continuity of God's purpose very readily enabled future reality to be pictured under the guise of what they then knew and were familiar with. But when it comes to the fulfilment of such promises in the New Testament age, there is no restriction to the entities that were previously employed to express them. The realisation is in terms of the heirs and successors of the Old Testament Zion, Jerusalem and Israel. This is not to rewrite the promise, but to satisfy it in its fullest and proper extent. The outcome superabounds above that which the Old Testament church had anticipated and in no way falls short of what had been revealed.

Paul calls it a mystery that Jew and Gentile should be found together in the church. 'This mystery is that through the gospel the Gentiles are heirs together with Israel, members together of one body, and sharers together in the promise in Christ Jesus' (Eph. 3:6). In Paul's language, a 'mystery' is something that could never have been discerned by human reason, but which had to be divinely revealed before it could be known. Some aspects of this truth had been made known before Christ's coming, but the administration of the mystery was only fully revealed to the apostles. The mystery of Christ 'was not made known to men in other generations as it has now been revealed by the Spirit to God's holy apostles and prophets' (Eph. 3:5). Note the 'as' of comparison. It is not 'no light' as compared to 'full light', but 'less light' as compared to 'more light'.

Romans 11 does, however, bring up another aspect of the situation. While there is clearly no special way of salvation for the Jews in the New

Testament, for all have to believe in Christ and acknowledge him as their Lord, may there not be a special future time of blessing for those of Jewish race? Paul talks of a mystery, that 'Israel has experienced a hardening in part until the full number of the Gentiles has come in. And so all Israel will be saved' (Rom. 11:25-26). There are various interpretations of this passage, but it is significant to note that in addressing God's future provision for ethnic Israel Paul does not talk of their restoration to the land, or of the establishment of a physical Jerusalem as a world capital of some sort. These Old Testament pictures have been taken up in the greater reality of the one church of all nations. Paul may indeed be talking of some future time of immense gospel blessing for the Jewish people, but I do not think this mystery is one that ought to be read back into Old Testament revelation. Those who do so ascribe some Old Testament passages that mention Israel, Jerusalem or Zion (in a context that was not fulfilled prior to the Cross) to the Jewish people, and other similar passages to the New Testament church. But the grounds on which they are allocated seem arbitrary. It is far sounder to consider all such prophecies as referring to 'the people of God' and determine the precise reference between the Old Testament and New Testament form of the people of God by their fulfilment. A special time of blessing for ethnic Israel—if indeed that is what Paul is writing about and not an age-long process of salvation of a remnant until the full complement of Israel is made up—is then a specifically New Testament revelation. It was not given until it was clear that the old forms of Jerusalem, the Temple and Israel had been superseded in the outworking of God's saving purpose. If this is so, then the question of a time of special blessing for ethnic Israel does not impinge on the interpretation of Old Testament prophecy.